China's Next Act

China's Next Act

*How Sustainability and Technology
are Reshaping China's Rise and
the World's Future*

SCOTT M. MOORE

OXFORD
UNIVERSITY PRESS

OXFORD
UNIVERSITY PRESS

Oxford University Press is a department of the University of Oxford. It furthers
the University's objective of excellence in research, scholarship, and education
by publishing worldwide. Oxford is a registered trade mark of Oxford University
Press in the UK and certain other countries.

Published in the United States of America by Oxford University Press
198 Madison Avenue, New York, NY 10016, United States of America.

Library of Congress Cataloging-in-Publication Data
Names: Moore, Scott, 1985– author.
Title: China's next act : how sustainability and technology are reshaping
China's rise and the world's future / Scott M. Moore.
Description: New York, NY : Oxford University Press, [2022] |
Includes bibliographical references and index.
Identifiers: LCCN 2022012696 (print) | LCCN 2022012697 (ebook) |
ISBN 9780197603994 (hardback) | ISBN 9780197604014 (epub)
Subjects: LCSH: China—Economic policy—2000- | Environmental policy—China. |
Technology and state—China. | China—Foreign economic relations. | China—Foreign relations. |
China—Politics and government—2002-
Classification: LCC HC427.95 .M66 2022 (print) | LCC HC427.95 (ebook) |
DDC 330.951—dc23/eng/20220505
LC record available at https://lccn.loc.gov/2022012696
LC ebook record available at https://lccn.loc.gov/2022012697

DOI: 10.1093/oso/9780197603994.001.0001

1 3 5 7 9 8 6 4 2

Printed by Integrated Books International, United States of America

To Isaac, the most important thing in the world

Contents

Contents

List of Figures and Tables

Figures

Tables

List of Figures and Tables

Figures

Tables

Preface

Soon after I finished graduate school, and thanks to a fellowship awarded by the Council on Foreign Relations, I was given an opportunity to serve at the US Department of State. The standard advice at the time was to aim for the Department's Policy Planning Staff, an office geared toward strategic planning traditionally seen as an academic paradise. Sitting serenely on the State Department's rarified seventh floor, Policy Planning is famed for its bird's-eye view of US foreign policy and for crafting grand strategy on the big geopolitical problems of the day. But one previous fellow had very different advice: find yourself a spot on the China Desk, he said, where you'll see how government really works.

That's how I ended up three floors below Policy Planning, in the Office of Chinese and Mongolian Affairs, with a portfolio known as Environment, Science, Technology, and Health (ESTH), covering everything from disease surveillance to satellite orbits to nuclear waste. It was, quite clearly, the catch-all category—things that didn't fit with or seemed less important than the matters occupying my colleagues with the more prestigious political and economic portfolios. My first thought, having come out of academia, was that it was somewhere between laughable and downright dangerous to expect a single person to keep track of so many highly varied and highly technical issues.

But in the years that followed, I began to see the wisdom of grouping together ESTH issues, at least when it comes to China. I started to notice similarities across these disparate matters: unlike in discussions on human rights and the South China Sea, US and Chinese representatives in dialogues on environmental and scientific issues usually looked genuinely pleased to see each other. Often scientists or other technical specialists, they seemed to share an altogether different bond than the professional diplomats who handled the more important, and contentious, geopolitical and economic issues. At the same time, the notion of existential risk, whether to the world's climate, public health, or biodiversity, cut across ESTH discussions. There was a shared sense that, whether anyone else knew it or not, these issues were every bit as important as, and deeply related to, the more traditional foreign policy concerns of war, peace, and trade.

For a time, ESTH even seemed to be getting more fashionable. During my time at State in 2015–2016, environmental and technology issues became a significantly more important area of the US–China relationship and expanded dramatically in scope and scale. A coordinated response to the 2014–2016 outbreak of Ebola in West Africa appeared to show that the United States and China could effectively work together on global challenges. Joint action on climate change, meanwhile, dominated high-level interactions, and new initiatives were launched on fisheries, seismological research, national parks, and everything in between. When the Paris Agreement on climate change was signed in December 2015, largely on the strength of Sino-American cooperation, it looked like ESTH issues would not only become a pillar of US–China relations, but one of the most constructive areas of an otherwise problematic relationship.

Soon afterward, though, ESTH devolved from being perhaps the most promising area of US–China relations to yet another arena of competition and contention. Technology that once seemed sure to link countries like the United States and China closer together became battlegrounds on which differences on censorship and other matters played out, while China's growing prowess in advanced technologies like artificial intelligence ignited foreign fears about being eclipsed in a new Chinese century. The failure of US, Chinese, and other national officials to do much at all to prevent the global spread of COVID-19 meanwhile signaled that cooperation on global challenges would be much harder than it once appeared.

The arc of this short history—from ESTH issues differentiating themselves from their more traditional diplomatic counterparts, then growing massively in importance, before becoming increasingly politicized—frames this book. I became convinced that to understand China's relationship with the world at large, and its implications for countries like the United States, it is essential to get a handle not just on a range of new, newer, and emerging issues like pandemic prevention and synthetic biology, but also how they fit together and relate to long-standing political and ideological tensions.

Speaking of differences, my aim in writing this book is to provide a nuanced take on the rise of China. But I do not claim to be impartial. I believe, and argue throughout the book, that liberal values and institutions promise a far brighter future for the world than any Beijing-backed alternative. Moreover, this book places special emphasis on the role of the United

States, which as an American I believe has a unique ability and responsibility to preserve and uplift liberal values. Even so, we must all think differently about how to do so in a world shaped by climate change, pandemics, and disruptive new technologies.

There is, I admit, a big risk in attempting to cover all this terrain. My initial graduate-student trepidation at trying to grasp so many different issues remains, and rightly so. In the pages that follow, there are quite likely errors both of commission and omission. I hope that the risk, and possibly the offense, is outweighed by the value of drawing connections between the public goods and emerging technologies, as well the much longer-standing political and ideological differences, that increasingly frame China's rise and its place in the world.

If I had to collapse this book into a sentence, it's this one from the Conclusion: in a future shaped by climate change, pandemics, and technology, all countries ultimately need China to succeed—and vice versa.

I hope, nonetheless, you'll read on.

Scott Moore
Bryn Mawr, Pennsylvania
Fall 2021

Acknowledgments

As is usually the case, this book owes much to many. I begin with gratitude to Professor John DiIulio of the University of Pennsylvania, who first encouraged me to write this book. Without the support of my other colleagues at Penn, especially the two to which I report, Amy Gadsden and Ezekiel Emanuel, it would not have been possible. I am also deeply indebted to David McBride of Oxford University Press, who believed in this book and was willing to take a chance on its author. Without the expert research assistance and graphics design wizardry of Julia Maenza and Chardonnay Needler, this book would have taken ages longer to complete, and perhaps never would have been. Speaking of support, I'm grateful to Israt Sonam and Riana Breedy for taking loving care of my son, Isaac, while I worked to finish this book.

As I note in the Preface, the risk of getting a few things wrong in covering so many different issues remains high. Nonetheless, without the expertise and feedback of a long list of friends and colleagues, the risk would be even higher. I'm sincerely grateful to all who provided encouragement, comments, and feedback on portions and aspects of the book: Thorsten Benner, Peter Dougherty, Myles Thompson, Rafe Sagalyn, Jay Mandel, Jill Marsal, John DiIulio, Ken Lieberthal, Joe Narus, Robert O'Brien, Daniel Alderman, Yingyi Ma, Tom Gold, Abigail Coplin, Joan Kaufman, Craig Allen, Benjamin Shobert, Richard Danzig, Christine Fox, Emily de la Bruyere, Susan Thornton, Elsa Kania, Kevin Rudd, H.R. McMaster, Rosie Levine, Steven Cook, Damien Ma, Judith Shapiro, Stephen Orlins, John Holden, Sophie Richardson, Avery Goldstein, Michael Rawding, Sara Plana, Andrew Mertha, Michael Franczak, Stan Katz, Brad Conger, Jamie Metzl, Aynne Kokas, and Kyle Haddad-Fonda.

My thinking on the issues addressed in this book was greatly enriched by my participation in the National Committee on US–China Relations' Public Intellectuals Program, and I'm grateful to the National Committee; the program's funder, the Carnegie Corporation; the speakers who spent time with us; and my fellow PIP VI'ers for shaping my thinking on how China shapes the future.

I am also grateful to the students in the spring 2020 and spring 2021 iterations of my "China and the World in the 21st Century: Science, Technology, and Environmental Politics" seminar at the University of Pennsylvania. Their views and research papers also helped inform my thinking about the issues addressed in this book.

Above all, I thank my family: Marisa, my biggest fan; Isaac, my greatest joy; and Disco, my closest and furriest companion.

A Note on Chinese Characters and Transliteration

Simplified characters are provided for most Chinese names, places, systems, and organizations referenced in the text upon first mention. In subsequent mentions, only the Romanized text is used. In general, accompanying *pinyin* Romanization for simplified characters is not provided. Characters are not provided for certain very common and well-known place names such as Beijing.

Introduction

A Shared Future Shaped by China

As visions of the future go, they do not get much brighter than the one US
President Bill Clinton laid out in a speech marking the hundredth anniversary of China's Peking University, commonly known as Beida (北大), on
June 29, 1998. Clinton began by pointing out the size of his accompanying
delegation, which included six members of Congress and three Cabinet
secretaries—proof, the president offered, of "the importance that the United
States places on our relationship with China."

In the half hour that followed, Clinton made clear he envisioned this relationship to be a very wide-ranging one. He devoted a surprising amount of
attention not just to long-standing issues like human rights, free trade, and
international security, but also to newer ones, especially education, the environment, healthcare, and even social security. The president made a point
of urging action on climate change, the need to prevent the spread of new
diseases, and China's crucial role in tackling each of these twenty-first-century challenges.

For an American president, Clinton seemed oddly upbeat about the
leading position he foresaw for China in the century ahead. It could, he told
the assembled Chinese students, be "your century." Perhaps anticipating
unease from his fellow Americans, Clinton expressed faith that technology
would ease any tensions that China's rise might cause. The internet and other
advances would, he predicted, enable "the freest possible flow of information, ideas, and opinions" and foster "greater respect for divergent political
and religious convictions."[1]

After his speech, Clinton was peppered with questions from Beida
students, many of them pointed critiques of American politics and policy.
But the president was seemingly energized by the exchange. Shunning the
carefully controlled confines of the gleaming new auditorium where he
spoke, Clinton carried his message outdoors. Amid the faded splendor of
the old imperial gardens, now the heart of the Beida campus, the president

China's Next Act. Scott M. Moore, Oxford University Press. © Oxford University Press 2022.
DOI: 10.1093/oso/9780197603994.003.0001

addressed a crowd of thousands, entirely off the cuff: "I believe a large part of the next chapter in America's history will be its partnership with the new China."[2]

What a difference a few decades can make.

The years following Clinton's speech at Beida were marked not by the wide-ranging partnership he envisioned, but by growing political, economic, and ideological tensions between both countries. Even as the costs of climate change, the COVID-19 pandemic, and other shared challenges mounted, they became new sources of hostility. Instead of forging closer cooperation, Washington and Beijing took turns blaming the other for failing to protect the planet. And instead of bringing the United States and China closer together, technology became an economic, geopolitical, and even ideological battleground. China itself, meanwhile, turned away from what looked in Clinton's time like cautious steps toward political, economic, and social liberalization toward a greater embrace of authoritarianism, protectionism, and nationalism.

In hindsight, it is tempting to treat Clinton's unrealized optimism as Exhibit A for wishful thinking when it comes to dealing with a rising China. But the truth is, he was on to something. Climate change, public health, and technology are reshaping China's relationship with the world in the twenty-first century, and they demand that we think differently about how to respond to China's rise. We must refocus our thinking about China in terms of global public goods, on one hand, and emerging technologies on the other. This reframing is needed not only because, as Clinton observed, none of these increasingly pressing challenges can be tackled without China; but also because ecological and technological issues are themselves becoming areas of intense economic, geopolitical, and ideological competition. Re-envisioning China's rise in terms of public goods and emerging technologies is just as essential for those who wish to counter Beijing as for those who desire more engagement with it.

Global public goods are things like climate protection, pandemic prevention, and knowledge production that benefit the citizens of all countries, yet typically cannot be provided by any one country alone. They are critical and indispensable for peace, prosperity, and even civilization itself.[3] Emerging technologies, meanwhile, are tools, systems, and processes that are not fully mature and whose economic, geopolitical, and ethical implications are not entirely clear—but are clearly profound. Emerging technologies include artificial intelligence, quantum computing, and genetic engineering. Many of these technologies promise to help provide public goods, but others threaten to create new hazards.

These ecological and technological challenges share a crucial common feature: they are highly disruptive both for China and the world at large. Public goods and emerging technologies pose political, economic, and ethical questions that are shared across countries, and existential risks that are as severe to the United States and Germany as they are to China and Brazil. Runaway climate change will render huge swaths of the planet uninhabitable. Future pandemics will likely be even deadlier than COVID-19.[4] Emerging technologies, meanwhile, are double-edged swords: they hold great promise to improve the human condition, but also to create new forms of destruction, including biologically engineered weapons and an increased risk of nuclear war. China is essential to avoiding all of these planetary catastrophes.

But instead of bringing China, the United States, and other countries closer together, the common challenges of the twenty-first century have only sharpened political, economic, and ideological differences. Even as the world faces increasingly shared challenges, and at the center of those challenges stands China, Beijing has grown more repressive at home, more belligerent abroad, and more willing to challenge liberal values everywhere. That dual reality demands that we think more deeply and deliberately about how to provide public goods and regulate emerging technologies by competing, as well as cooperating, with China.

The rest of this Introduction outlines a different way of looking at China's rise through the lens of sustainability and technology, and what the implications are for foreign countries, companies, and other organizations. An important message is that although climate change, pandemics, and technological disruption present challenges that are increasingly common to China as well as other countries, they have not made China's rise any less problematic from the perspective of democratic and liberal societies. Shared ecological and technological challenges do not always produce cooperation: they also present opportunities for countries, companies, and other organizations to compete more intensely for economic, geopolitical, and ideological advantage.

As this book details, newer ecological and technological issues have become, if anything, even more pitched battlegrounds over basic liberal values, including democracy, free enterprise, and cosmopolitanism; and their il-liberal alternatives, especially authoritarianism, protectionism, and nation-alism. The challenges of the twenty-first century, though shared, cannot be isolated from deep disagreement over these basic values between Beijing and more liberal-leaning societies. That means it will be essential for them to both cooperate and compete with China. The future will be fundamentally shared, but also fiercely contested.

The Need for New Thinking on China

The rise of China was one of the defining developments of the late twentieth and early twenty-first centuries. China's rapid growth after the late 1970s, the fastest ever for a major economy, made it once again the biggest and most important country in the world on a long list of metrics.[5] By the 2010s, China had become the largest consumer market; the biggest source of interna-tional tourists; the leading oil importer; and the chief trading partner for 40 countries—10 more than the United States.[6] While in 1980 the world's eco-nomic center of gravity was in the middle of the Atlantic Ocean—reflecting the overwhelming importance of Europe and North America—by 2050 it will be in western China.[7] And though China remained, by most meas-ures, the world's second largest economy into the 2020s, increasingly wealthy Chinese consumers accounted for no less than one-third of global spending on cars, fashion, and food, shaping these sectors more than any other single country.[8]

Moreover, throughout the early twenty-first century, Beijing busily trans-lated China's growing wealth into other forms of power. China amassed the world's second-largest military budget, which it used to curb the United States' ability to project military power, especially in the western Pacific.[9] Beijing built the world's largest diplomatic network, with more overseas posts than any other country.[10] China's role in the world even became something of a pop-culture phenomenon. In 2019, a Chinese sci-fi film, *The Wandering Earth* (流浪地球), became one of the highest-grossing non-English-lan-guage films of all time, and played in 22 cities across North America. Its theme? China saving the world.[11]

But perhaps the most outstanding impact of China's rise was that it made China's state, its firms, its universities, and its other institutions indispensable players in nearly every global issue of any significance, from environmental sustainability to advanced technology. In the four decades following its reform and opening, China steadily climbed the economic value chain from low-cost manufactured goods to high-value services like e-commerce. Just as important, Beijing mounted a major effort to develop and deploy advanced technologies. These efforts included programs to train and retain high-tech talent; to mobilize state, military, and private resources for scientific research and development; and to synchronize diplomacy, trade, and market access policy to preferentially advantage Chinese firms. Beijing also put forward ambitious policies to leapfrog ahead of other countries in a range of technology-intensive sectors, including the cyber and digital economies.

In combination, these efforts made China a key player in artificial intelligence and mobile payments as well as consumer electronics and textiles. And as a result, China became a leading producer of intangible assets like data and algorithms, as well as in the production of physical goods. Having put itself at the center of these crucial twenty-first-century issues, sectors, and technologies, Beijing became indispensable to tackling shared global challenges. Yet working with Beijing became more difficult for foreign countries, companies, and other organizations, not least because newer ecological and technological challenges proved hugely disruptive for China itself.

China's break-neck economic growth created and exacerbated challenges more common to wealthy nations than still-developing ones, including a rapidly aging population; unaffordable housing, education, and healthcare costs; and large-scale employment disruption due to automation.[12] Rapid growth also dramatically increased China's exposure to severe air, water, and soil pollution and imposed an escalating burden from non-communicable diseases, including cancer and heart disease.[13] As the economic gap between China and developed nations shrank, their challenges began to look more and more alike: protecting the environment, providing quality healthcare, and dealing with the consequences of disruptive new technologies.

Amidst these changes, twenty-first-century China came to resemble what the German sociologist Ulrich Beck called a "risk society": one where political, economic, and social systems struggle to respond to new, complex, and often intractable ecological and technological challenges. The risk society is a concept that ties together the issues examined in this book. Environmental sustainability, public health, and emerging technology poses existential risks; requires collective action to address; and underscores differences in basic values and agreed ways of doing things—often referred to as norms. As Beck observed, the challenges of the risk society are fundamentally disruptive, and difficult for existing institutions to tackle. Instead, they demand, as he put it, "a fundamental rethinking."[14]

Much as Beck predicted, throughout the early twenty-first century Beijing embarked on a fundamental rethinking of many of its policies and priorities in light of growing ecological and technological risks. Pollution, healthcare, and education became pressing concerns for newly affluent consumers, prodding Beijing to invest considerably more resources in environmental protection and social services.[15] Sweeping energy, environmental, and innovation policies promised to transform the Chinese economy from one centered on resource-intensive physical goods to one based on intellectual property and technology—much the same as richer nations.

Ecological and technological concerns also reframed China's foreign policy. Beijing invested considerable resources in becoming an important financier of global public health initiatives; an indispensable actor in climate change diplomacy; and an influential player in international organizations like the World Bank and the World Health Organization that help provide global public goods. China further became a prominent voice in the obscure but important international bodies that set technical standards for next-generation telecommunications and other critical technologies.

Yet China's growing involvement in tackling shared global challenges did not lead to greater cooperation with other countries. Instead, political and economic tensions grew more serious between China and other nations over a host of issues, including trade, cyber theft, and the South China Sea. The most glaring and gnawing divide was over basic values, especially human rights. These issues had long been a point of contention between the People's Republic and more liberal-minded countries. But throughout the first decade of the twenty-first century, Beijing devoted much of its expanding power and resources to repressing dissident groups and voices, to pursuing restrictive and protectionist economic policies, and to stoking nationalist sentiment.

Most alarmingly, Beijing embarked on a steadily more ruthless approach to governing the Muslim-majority region of Xinjiang (新疆).[16] In January 2021, US Secretary of State Mike Pompeo formally said Beijing had committed genocide in Xinjiang, a conclusion that his successor, Antony Blinken, pointedly upheld.[17] These intensifying human rights abuses created a moral cost to cooperation with Beijing that foreign governments, firms, and other organizations found harder to justify.

As this book explains, the fact that increasingly pressing, shared global challenges have been accompanied by greater contention between China and other countries is not a coincidence. Shared ecological and technological risks are highly disruptive to existing frameworks and institutions both in China and other countries. These growing risks highlight significant barriers to greater international cooperation between all countries, among them the inability of institutions at all levels to keep pace with technological change; the growing number of actors involved in areas like biodiversity protection and biosafety, which include nongovernmental organizations, universities, consumer groups, and individual researchers; and the dual-use nature of many emerging technologies, which have both peaceful and dangerous applications.[18] The case of China, though, highlights an even bigger and more fundamental barrier to greater cooperation on shared challenges: the lack of shared values.

Twenty-first-century China is a diverse society, including in its views and values. Some of Beijing's policies comply with international norms and standards, and parts of Chinese society both celebrate and practice liberal values. But unfortunately for the cause of global cooperation, Beijing's approach to public goods and emerging technologies has for the most part been shaped by three fundamentally illiberal influences: authoritarianism, protectionism, and an aggressive form of nationalism. Though hardly unique to China, these influences have played a prominent role in Chinese politics, economics, and social policy for decades.[19] And as this book explains, they have been revitalized and redeployed as the basis of Beijing's response to newer ecological and technological challenges.

Even more worrying, China's growing economic and geopolitical influence creates a risk that these illiberal influences will distort the world's response to a range of issues, including climate change, public health, and emerging technologies. If the United States and other liberal-minded countries fail to lead the response to shared ecological and technological challenges, the cost could be not only a more barren planet and a more dangerous future, but also one where liberal values are effectively out-competed by Beijing's illiberal alternatives.

Climate change, pandemics, and emerging technologies intensify the core dilemma posed by the rise of China: how to address shared challenges in the face of deep differences in basic values—or, put another way, how to work together in a few especially critical areas while contesting many others. This balancing act itself is not new: for big multinational companies and major-power diplomats, the challenge of cooperating with Chinese counterparts on some issues while competing on others is a familiar one.

But getting this balance right is both more important and more difficult than in the past. Protesting Beijing's human rights abuses is a moral imperative—and so is halting climate change. Moreover, juggling cooperation and competition is becoming harder for a growing number of actors. Beijing's steadily expanding economic and political power allows it to make life more difficult for a broader range of countries and companies than used to be the case. Amazon and Airbus, and Japan and India, may have the resources to simultaneously compete and cooperate with their Chinese counterparts. The smaller countries, companies, universities, and nonprofit groups that play an increasingly important role in China's relationship with the world, though, more likely do not.

Re-envisioning China's rise in terms of sustainability and technology means a greater focus on shared challenges. But it also means a greater focus on economic, geopolitical, and ideological competition. As this book explains, China's state and its firms view areas like data, education, and even environmental protection as arenas for economic, geopolitical, and ideological competition as well as cooperation.[20] Foreign countries, companies, and other organizations must do the same if they are to respond effectively to China's rise in the decades ahead—and protect principles like open markets, basic tolerance, and the rule of law.

Tackling shared challenges and competing effectively in the twenty-first century entails three major changes in thinking and practice when it comes to China.

First, addressing shared challenges cannot come at the cost of competing for economic, geopolitical, and ideological advantage: both are necessary to respond effectively to China's rise. As we will see throughout this book, China's growing role in global governance, from public health to telecommunications standard-setting, creates a risk that illiberal rather than liberal values will shape the world's response to critically important issues in the decades to come. Fortunately, there are some areas, such as clean energy development, where competition can be good for the planet.

Second, traditional measures of strength and influence, like market power and military might, still matter in competing with China, but intangible assets are equally important. A common feature of most emerging technologies is their reliance on large, diverse, and multidimensional data sets, while one of the most important factors in innovation is the ability to attract, retain, and deploy highly skilled individual talent. Staying ahead economically, militarily, and otherwise requires investing as much in people, information, and ideas as in fighter jets, aircraft carriers, and high-speed railways.

Third, competing for economic, geopolitical, and ideological advantage is a whole-of-society effort, not limited to national governments. A common thread across the issues explored in this book is that non-state and sub-state entities, including corporations, universities, and industry associations, have a growing role in working with Chinese counterparts to combat climate change, enhance scientific collaboration, and forge common technological standards. But they are also increasingly on the front lines of China-linked data theft, censorship, and other challenges to liberal values. Like it or not, they too are part of the competition between liberal and illiberal values when it comes to a host of emerging issues. It is in their interest to equip themselves to compete as well as cooperate.

A Shared but Contested Future

In the seven chapters that follow, this book explores several important aspects of how China shapes a future marked both by shared challenges in the fields of sustainability and technology and pervasive competition, including over basic values and ideology. Chapter 1 frames this discussion, examining how China's rise has been marked by authoritarianism, protectionism, and aggressive nationalism. It shows that contesting Beijing's growing repression at home, belligerence abroad, and challenge to liberal values everywhere means focusing on newer ecological and technological challenges alongside more traditional areas of friction. Though not the only country to display illiberal tendencies in the early twenty-first century, China's increasingly central role in global governance and economics makes Beijing's illiberal impulses especially dangerous. The test of the decades ahead lies in navigating a shared but contested future defined in large part by China's rise as an illiberal influence on everything from decarbonization to data privacy.

Each of the subsequent chapters highlight both the necessity of and the problems involved in working with China to address shared global challenges. A common theme is that the need for China and other countries to work together cannot be entirely isolated from economic, geopolitical, and ideological competition. These chapters also provide an important insight into how to compete effectively—and it has more to do with people, ideas, and values than with technology itself. Yet as important as it is for liberal-minded countries and companies to compete more effectively when it comes to China, this book also underscores why it is essential to engage Chinese counterparts, especially to help regulate disruptive and potentially dangerous new technologies.

Chapter 2 makes these points through the lens of public health. The need to prevent future pandemics is one of the most powerful reasons for China and other countries to work together to provide public goods. Unfortunately, the case of public health also shows that is difficult, if not impossible, to isolate public goods from political and geopolitical tensions. Chapter 2 also highlights the important role of non-state and sub-state actors in providing global public goods, and how they present an alternative to problematic, and politicized, intergovernmental cooperation.

Chapter 3 focuses on climate change and the environment. It stresses that while China's contributions to environmental protection have been considerable, they have fallen short of what is needed to protect the planet and have relied in part on problematic practices including the co-option of environmental activists and discriminatory trade practices. Moreover, while addressing climate change unquestionably requires China's participation, competition between countries and companies might help make clean technology cheaper and more efficient.

Chapter 4 covers knowledge production and cultural exchange—one of the most underappreciated ways in which China contributes to global public goods, and an essential part of responding to ecological and technological challenges. Chinese migrants and the Chinese diaspora have added immeasurably to economic growth, science and technology, and cultural flourishing across the globe. Yet as Chapter 4 stresses, human capital and mobility are also intensely political issues. Chapter 4 also highlights the fact that the geographic focus of economic, geopolitical, and ideological competition with China is shifting from the developed to the developing world.[21]

Chapter 5 discusses the role that technological development, deployment, and innovation plays in underpinning economic and geopolitical power. It emphasizes the fact that Beijing's massive investments in technology, though largely inefficient, create advantages for its firms in certain areas. At the same time, the assets that sustain the United States' innovation advantage are primarily intangible ones, especially talent recruitment, free and open information exchange, and a culture that tolerates and even venerates failure.

Chapter 6 centers on digital data and information. A central theme is that while intellectual property protections and data privacy provisions are being strengthened within China, foreign companies, universities, and individuals are increasingly at risk from China-linked digital information theft, censorship, and surveillance beyond China's borders. At the same time, the priority Beijing places on security, protectionism, and control in digital and cyber policy puts foreign firms at a distinct disadvantage. This approach also gives Beijing and other authoritarian governments more and better tools to repress their populations.

Chapter 7 covers standard- and norm-setting, especially in the emerging technologies of artificial intelligence, autonomous systems, and genetic engineering. It shows that although the United States, China, and other countries are far apart on common rules and regulations, only genuine cooperation, at both the nation-state and sub-state levels, can mitigate the risks and maximize the rewards of these disruptive new technologies.

The Conclusion, finally, more fully outlines how liberal-minded governments, businesses, and other organizations should respond to a shared but contested future defined by the challenge of providing global public goods and regulating emerging technologies, and doing so as much by competing with China as cooperating. The Conclusion also offers guidelines to help governments and non-state entities, including companies, universities, and industry associations, decide when and how to cooperate and when and how to compete with Chinese counterparts.

Before delving into how we can better understand and react to China's next act, I should clarify several key terms and concepts. The terms "liberal societies" and "liberal-minded countries, companies, and other organizations" are used throughout the book in contrast to contemporary China. These terms refer both to the developed democracies often referred to as "the West," as well as developing ones like India and Nigeria, which, as we will see, play an increasingly important role in shaping how the world responds to China's rise, especially in areas like data governance.[22] Though extremely diverse, these countries practice and feature common values and institutions, including pluralism, the rule of law, and, to a degree at least, free enterprise alongside representative democracy, mostly independent judicial systems, and a largely free press.

Admittedly, this distinction is imperfect: liberal societies, including India and the United States, score unevenly on measures like free expression and social inclusion. Moreover, many of these broadly liberal societies are prone to their own nationalist and nativist impulses and pursue some illiberal policies in trade, immigration, and other areas. But the contrast is still a meaningful one. Liberal societies, though varied and wracked by contradiction, share a general commitment to civil and human rights, multiparty political systems, and broadly open market economies.

It is also important to define what I mean by "competition," in contrast to "cooperation." Cooperation stems from the belief and expectation that interaction and exchange are inherently desirable and produce gains for all sides, for the most part equitably. Competition, in contrast, is driven by the belief that interaction and exchange are only sometimes desirable, and the aim is fundamentally to gain an edge or outsized benefit over a rival. When I refer to promising areas of cooperation, I mean areas where the interests and incentives of key players in both China and other countries converge so that they expect working together to produce benefits for all sides. When I say that an issue has become an arena of competition, I mean that these interests and incentives differ, so that while both sides can gain, the aim of interaction is to ensure that one side gains more than the other. Importantly, cooperation and competition can coexist, especially in different issue areas.[23]

"Conflict," finally, refers to interactions where the aim is to prevent the other side from gaining any benefits at all. On this understanding, cooperation is preferable because it implies the greatest benefit for the greatest number of parties and builds trust that strengthens relationships over time. Conflict, on the other hand, is the most destructive form of interaction. Competition is not ideal, but it is far better than conflict. In fact, part of the goal of competition is to avoid outright conflict.[24]

The core message of this book is that understanding how sustainability and technology, and cooperation and competition, intersect and relate is central to seeing how China shapes the future in the twenty-first century. But this does not mean that more traditional political, military, or economic issues can be ignored. Trade disputes, tensions over Taiwan, and human rights frame how both China and other countries approach global public goods and emerging technologies. Re-envisioning China's rise does not mean discounting these issues, but rather understanding how they relate to newer, less familiar, ecological and technological challenges. Runaway climate change could swamp the expeditionary bases the United States and its allies need to respond to a conflict in the Pacific, for instance, while censorship and surveillance have moved almost entirely to the digital domain. At the same time, China has not yet escaped long-standing challenges like extreme poverty. China's future may be shaped by sustainability and technology, but older ills frame and constrain how this process plays out.

Of course, this book cannot address every significant global public good or emerging technology. Its coverage is necessarily selective, and subjective. It focuses especially on areas like decarbonization and data privacy where global public goods and emerging technologies intersect. Given the range of topics it covers, this book does not presume to be the last word on any one of them. Rather than diving deeply into individual issue areas, this book draws lessons across them and identifies implications for specific actors. To do so, the chapters ahead integrate sources and concepts from a wide range of fields, including macroeconomics, sociology, and science and technology studies. The evidence it presents includes both quantitative data as well as narratives and anecdotes. It draws on peer-reviewed research, as well as the author's personal experience and interviews conducted with leading China specialists.[25]

In doing so, I hope to recast increasingly shrill debates on China's rise in the context of a shared but deeply contested future marked by profound ecological and technological risks—as well as opportunities. Indeed, re-envisioning China's rise presents tantalizing opportunities for greater global cooperation as well as vexing challenges. Especially promising areas include biodiversity conservation, addressed in Chapter 3; and biosafety and nuclear security, covered in Chapter 7. This book also calls attention to the many cases where the risks and threats posed by China's rise are overstated or misunderstood. For example, though Chinese firms are often alleged to be joined at the hip with the Chinese state and Communist Party, in fact their interests frequently differ.

Finally, it is important to acknowledge that this book is not the first or only one to call attention to sustainability and technology issues when it comes to China.[26] Its emphasis on the need for a mix of confrontational and cooperative measures when engaging with China echoes many others.[27] What I hope this book adds to the debate over China's rise is that re-envisioning it in terms of sustainability and technology sheds light not just on how to tackle shared challenges, but also how to compete more effectively for economic, geopolitical, and ideological advantage.

Along with creating a greater need for cooperation, the shared challenges of the twenty-first century have opened new arenas of contention and competition between China and other countries. That means understanding how sustainability and technology are reshaping China's rise and the world's future as it enters its next act in the decades to come.

1

The End of Growth and the Return of Ideology

The 40-year period after China began its economic reform and opening process in 1978 was an exceptionally peaceful and prosperous one, both for China and the developed democracies, including Japan, Germany, and the United States, which were among its leading trade partners. Commerce, communication, and cultural exchange between China and these nations boomed, thanks largely to Beijing's decision to dismantle much of its centrally planned economy and replace it with one at least partly responsive to market forces. But China's acceptance of market economics was always cautious, tentative, and partial. As growth rates slowed and development dilemmas became more acute in the years following the 2008 financial crisis, critics of capitalism became more vocal and influential, and long-standing ideological conflicts flared. The previously trade-centered economic relationship with other major powers, especially the United States, began to fray, and with it, a broadly shared belief in mutually beneficial cooperation. In its place emerged the conviction that China and the West were locked in a long-term economic, geopolitical, and ideological competition. Instead of convergence, China and other nations seemed set on entering values-laden contests between multiparty democracy and socialist authoritarianism, between market- and state-led capitalism, and between Chinese and foreign nationalisms. These ideological conflicts came to the fore even as China and the world faced increasingly globalized challenges like climate change and regulation of emerging technologies.

From Growing the Pie to Slicing It: Slowing Economic Growth and Rising Ideological Discord

The year 2012 was, in retrospect, one of the most pivotal years in the history of the People's Republic. As is so often the case in China, this significance

China's Next Act. Scott M. Moore, Oxford University Press. © Oxford University Press 2022.
DOI: 10.1093/oso/9780197603994.003.0002

stemmed in part from changes at the top. It was the year that the latest in China's long line of strongman leaders, Xi Jinping (习近平), took over from the more unassuming Hu Jintao (胡锦涛) as head of the Chinese Communist Party, and the year that the rising leftist mayor of Chongqing (重庆), Bo Xilai (薄熙来), was deposed and imprisoned—an earth-shattering moment in China's carefully scripted political theater. But it was a far more obscure figure who signaled that a great tension at the heart of twenty-first-century China, namely that a staunchly Communist regime had grown painfully reliant on a paradoxical form of market economics, had become unbearable.[1] And, just as important, that the prospect of greater convergence with Western norms, values, and institutions would be deeply contested and fiercely resisted.

Not long after Chinese New Year in 2012, the great and the good from China and the West gathered for a press conference to mark the release of a landmark report called "China 2030." A joint product of the influential Development Research Center of the State Council (国务院发展研究中心) and the World Bank, the report was a clarion call for China to embrace liberal economic policies, including dismantling its big, powerful state-owned enterprises. This, most every economist agreed, would be necessary for China to continue growing and, eventually, to assume developed-country status. But just as World Bank President Robert Zoellick began his remarks in praise of fundamental reform, a lone protestor named Du Jianguo (杜建国), whose first name translates as "build the nation," ambled to the front of the room and began shouting, "the World Bank report is poison!" The market-driven policies advocated by the Chinese elite and the World Bank, Du warned, would condemn China to suffer the same economic calamity the United States had experienced during its financial crisis just a few years before. Du was quickly removed from the room. Yet his actions were widely praised by China's influential netizens, and for a time, he became a featured guest on news programs.[2]

Though it quickly faded into obscurity, Du's protest showed even more poignantly than Bo's downfall that for all China's growing power and influence, its political and economic system rested on a fragile and contested ideological foundation. Nowhere were these ideological tensions clearer than in Xi's careful treatment of the legacy of Mao Zedong (毛泽东), whose portrait still gazes watchfully over Tiananmen Square. In December 2013, in one of his most high-profile acts after taking power, Xi led members of the Politburo Standing Committee, the highest rung of the Chinese Communist Party's leadership, on a visit to Mao's mausoleum in Beijing. "Mao is a great figure who changed the face of the nation and led the Chinese people to a new destiny," Xi later remarked, though he went on to stress the need to "allow people to point out and correct their errors."[3] But no amount of rhetorical nuance could hide the irony in the fact that, from his perch on the gate of the Forbidden City, Mao could almost spy a Starbucks.[4]

For all its carefully laid five-year plans, early twenty-first-century China was a profoundly unsettled place, torn between its socialist ideology, nationalist mythology, and largely state-led economy. Du's protest and Xi's struggle to address the legacy of Mao laid bare the fact that decades of break-neck growth had papered over gaping fault lines in, and lingering tensions over, the ideological shape of China's future. Like every regime, the Chinese Communist Party has always had its moderates and radicals, reformers and reactionaries, nationalists and cosmopolitans. These factions were frequently at odds, and their conflicts and controversies shaped the history of the People's Republic. But after 40 years of nearly unbroken economic expansion, China in the 2010s entered a new phase of slower, more uneven growth, and its ideological divides began to widen. As the Party navigated the rocky path toward high-income country status, a long-simmering struggle between market economics and Marxist ideology was reignited with a vengeance. Though Chinese politics had long been marked by ideological contradiction,[5] this struggle eroded a broadly pragmatic consensus that prevailed for most of the reform era, with worrying implications for China's role in the world.

China's Internal Ideological Struggles

Every society has its fundamental contradictions, but Du's protest highlighted what might be the world's single most glaring ideological paradox: the world's second-largest economy was officially socialist, but effectively capitalist. For the first few decades after 1978, when China began to reopen itself both politically and economically to the outside world following the Cultural Revolution, this contradiction grated on China's political thinkers, but failed to contain the rush to reform.[6] Chinese Communist economic thought was always less dogmatic than its Soviet counterpart,[7] and during the reform era economic pragmatism grew even more pronounced. Deng Xiaoping's (邓小平) famous aphorism that "it doesn't matter if the cat is black or white as long as it catches the mouse" for the most part defined the times: growth should come first, and ideological debates second.[8] Political ideology, Deng signaled, could be put to one side amidst the overwhelming, urgent task of modernizing and developing China after the chaos of the Cultural Revolution.

Officially, though, the Chinese Communist Party's seeming embrace of market economics was a partial and strictly temporary measure. When China began what became known as its "reform and opening" process (改革开放), it was portrayed by Party leaders as simply the first phase, the "primary stage of socialism," in a long-term transition to a fully socialist economy under which the means of production would become fully owned by the proletariat.[9] As time went on, China's leaders became more indefinite as to how long this transition might take. During a major speech to mark the 80th anniversary of the founding of the Chinese Communist Party in 2001, China's then-top leader, Jiang Zemin (江泽民), warned that the country "is still at the primary stage of socialism. . . . To release and develop our productive forces will remain our central task for a long period to come." In the same speech Jiang, ignoring the obvious irony, proposed that the Party become the vanguard of "private entrepreneurs" and "freelancers" as well as the working class.[10]

Many Chinese executives and entrepreneurs, and their counterparts abroad, read these statements as a sign that China's leaders intended to pay lip service to Marxist dogma, but were mostly covering their tracks in a full-on sprint toward Western-style capitalism and free-market ideology. Beneath the surface, though, these moves sparked intense controversy. Jiang's attempts to side-step the ideological contradictions inherent in China's embrace of market economics produced a furious counterattack from left-leaning intellectuals. One party elder wrote bluntly, "We must be clear that private entrepreneurs cannot join the Party," while another charged Jiang with "political misconduct unprecedented in the history of our Party" for having created "ideological confusions."[11] Such critiques fueled the rise of what became known as the New Left movement (新左派) in Chinese politics, which became an increasingly influential ideological current in the first decade of the twenty-first century.[12]

The contradictions embraced by Jiang also created an opening for Western-style democratic thought. Constitutional democracy on the American model held widespread, though not universal, appeal among Chinese liberals, many of whom had lived and studied in the West (more on this rich intellectual exchange in Chapter 4). In the eyes of Western-inspired reformers, China's economic development and modernization seemed sure to lead eventually to greater political pluralization, if not Western-style multiparty democracy. But Western liberalism quickly drew the ire of Party censors. The later years of the Hu Jintao era were marked by the suppression of Western-inspired political thought, most notably the Charter 08 (零八宪章) movement, which saw some 300 Chinese intellectuals sign a manifesto proclaiming that "freedom, equality, and human rights are universal values of humankind and that democracy and constitutional government are the fundamental framework for protecting these values." Thousands more subsequently signed the manifesto, but it was quickly wiped off the internet and many of its drafters, including Liu Xiaobo (刘晓波) who was later awarded the Nobel Peace Prize, were harassed and placed under surveillance.[13]

The Charter 08 movement eventually fizzled in the wake of this suppression, as did subsequent movements that threatened China's underlying political system. But the proliferation of critical ideologies and political movements in the early decades of the twenty-first century highlighted a growing tension between the fact that, as Kerry Brown observed, China "succeeded as no other country has in creating a notionally free market economy . . . but with no meaningful political reform"—at least, that is, with respect to the Party's effective monopoly on the legitimate exercise of political power.[14]

Like his predecessors, Xi Jinping attempted to manage rather than to resolve this basic contradiction, in Xi's case by adopting an ever-more-delicate ideological balancing act. On economic fundamentals, Xi still sounded like a committed free marketeer. In a 2017 speech before the World Economic Forum in Davos, he issued a list of laissez-faire policy promises that could have been made by Milton Friedman, including to "pursue supply-side structural reform as the general goal."[15] Yet when it came to political ideology, Xi was happy to wrap himself in older socialist influences. In March 2018, Xi pointedly cited Mao's famous dictum that "the Party leads everything: government, military, society, schools, north, south, east, west, and center."[16]

In response, old-fashioned instruments of Party control, like the "party cell" (党组), intended to ensure that every organization of any size serves the interests of the proletariat, promptly made a comeback. The proliferation of party cells in institutions like tech firms and China's elite universities that formed key bridges to the outside world seemed to signal Xi's determination to avoid ideological convergence with the West.[17] Indeed, another hallmark of the Xi Jinping era was the conviction that liberal values, and especially Western-style critical histories of the People's Republic, must be rejected.[18]

A document issued soon after Xi came to power, known as "Document No. 9," cast many Western-inspired ideas as inherent threats to the Party's continued rule, and antithetical to China's own ideals.[19]

Yet for all the effort expended under Xi to contain China's deep ideological tensions, searching debates over basic norms, values, and priorities became an increasingly prominent part of China's national life and discourse in the 2010s. Indigenous faith movements like Buddhism and Daoism grew markedly in the first years of the twenty-first century, as did imported ones, most notably evangelical Christianity.[20] As the journalist Ian Johnson observed, "Faith and values are returning to the center of a national discussion over how to organize Chinese life."[21] Ideological debate also became a more pointed concern of secular thinkers. The political philosopher Ci Jiwei (慈继伟) wrote, for instance, that "more than thirty years after the winds of change started sweeping across the moral and spiritual landscape of China, the dust is still swirling around. . . . All members of Chinese society, myself included, are part of this dust, this morass, and our understanding of our own situation is, for the most part, no less unsettled and confused."[22]

At the same time, after decades of break-neck growth, China became far more diverse in opinion, experience, and outlook, a reality memorably described by New Yorker correspondent Evan Osnos: "the national narrative, once an ensemble performance, is splintering into a billion stories."[23] Amidst these centrifugal forces, there were more questions than answers when it came to the shape of China's future. The authors of Charter 08 were not the only ones to ask, "Where is China headed in the twenty-first century?" The absence of clear answers became especially glaring as China's economic miracle turned 40 and began to show its age amidst a growing number of development dilemmas. The fraying of a pragmatic, centrist ideological consensus on how to resolve them weighed heavily as the twenty-first century deepened, both on China's domestic politics and its foreign relations.

China's Development Dilemmas

For all its scale and speed, China's macroeconomic transformation concealed a mixed track record that left many of its people behind. Despite its economic heft, China in the early twenty-first century remained relatively poor, not just compared with wealthy developed countries but with other developing ones as well. In 2017, China's per capita national income was less than

US$17,000—higher than India or Brazil, but lower than Mexico, Venezuela, or even Gabon (see Figure 1.1).[24] When accounting for the burdens associated with China's high pollution levels, some estimates suggested it was only about a third as wealthy as America.[25] And when measured in terms of how much its torrid growth translated into increased wealth per person, China's performance placed it below countries like Singapore, South Korea, and Botswana.[26] Despite impressive-sounding increases in total gross domestic product (GDP), meanwhile, China's increase in average income was only about one-half as much as that of Korea and one-third that of Japan at a comparable point in each country's postwar economic growth trajectory.[27] The comparison was even less flattering when it came to marginalized segments of the population, like China's farmers, whose income growth significantly lagged that enjoyed by their Asian Tiger counterparts.[28]

What growth there was in the first decades of the twenty-first century came at a cost, as Beijing spent heavily to steer the economy through economic downturns. In 2008, to counteract the effects of the global financial crisis, China's party-state instituted a US$550 billion stimulus, most of which was devoted to infrastructure construction via local governments.[29] As a result, total government debt ballooned from 16% of GDP in 2013 to almost 40% in 2017. Much of this was held by local governments, who invested in

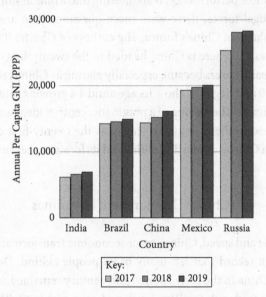

Figure 1.1. Per capita national income, selected countries, 2017–2019.
Source: World Bank 2019.

speculative activities like construction and property development—and, just as concerning, concealed much of the borrowing by shifting it off official balance sheets.[30] Fortunately for these over-stretched local authorities, the central government implicitly guaranteed local government debt, and continued growth absorbed much of the post-2008 spending binge.[31] Even so, in late 2018 ratings agency Standard & Poor's downgraded many local government credit ratings, citing "a debt iceberg with titanic credit risks."[32] China's fiscal war chest was sure to be barer in future decades than in the heady days of the first decade of the century.

An even more deeply rooted problem was China's hugely inefficient state-owned sector, which acted as a giant brake on long-term growth. In the decades following China's accession to the World Trade Organization in 2001, a gusher of cheap credit, much of it subsidized by state-controlled banks, flowed to state-owned enterprises (SOEs). Instead of being used to transform SOEs into lean, competitive enterprises, these funds went primarily to propping up their colossal losses and inefficiency. According to one estimate, money was lent to SOEs at rates equivalent to 500–1,000% of profits—a staggeringly wasteful use of capital that kept massively uncompetitive sectors afloat, at great cost to the public purse. The state-owned sector nonetheless consistently managed to skirt, slow, and water down reforms intended to level the financial playing field for China's far more efficient private firms.[33] As a result, the Chinese economy faced ever-fiercer competition with lower-cost overseas rivals with the equivalent of one hand tied behind its back.

In this context, other long-term challenges such as demography weighed ever more heavily on China's economic future. Because of its long-running one-child policy, China's population aged more rapidly than that of most other developing countries. Low birth rates meant that by 2040, the population was projected to decline by about 4 million people annually, leaving China with an ever-shrinking workforce to support an expanding elderly population. This was a problem for several countries in the early twenty-first century, but most others, such as Italy and Japan, enjoyed far higher levels of per capita income, providing more resources to deal with the challenge. Just as concerning, aging societies tend to act as a drag on economic growth, because younger workers tend to account for the majority of consumption and productivity enhancement.[34] According to one widely cited estimate, changing demographics were predicted to depress China's annual growth rate by about 0.5% per year.[35] At growth rates of 7% or more per year, this drag might be manageable, but with projected future rates well below that, it would likely become much more painful.

Gaps in China's human capital base also called future productivity growth into question. Average educational attainment remained comparatively low. Some 40 years after the introduction of economic reforms in South Korea, for example, the average citizen possessed over 11 years of schooling. In China, the comparable figure was just 8.5—raising significant concerns over future productivity.[36] Doubts grew that China's economy could provide meaningful employment for its millions of young university graduates, many of whom had invested in expensive degrees from Western institutions. If the Chinese economy failed to provide these increasingly well-educated youth with well-paying jobs to meet their expectations, social tensions might soon follow.[37] In rapidly growing fields like artificial intelligence, meanwhile, talent shortages grew acute.[38] To make matters worse, China's manufacturing-heavy economy was likely to be heavily impacted by automation. According to one study, 14 million Chinese manufacturing workers could expect to be displaced by robots by 2030.[39] The still-large numbers of unskilled rural farmers and laborers, meanwhile, were likely to become left even further behind by automation and workforce changes.[40]

Adding to the litany of long-term development challenges, corruption remained common, despite a high-profile anti-graft campaign launched under Xi, and economic inequality was estimated to be higher than in all but 30 other countries, most of them wracked by decades of conflict and political instability.[41] Not surprisingly, social capital was also much lower than in other major economies. As the journalist Ian Johnson wrote, "China's relentless drive to get ahead economically has created a spiritual vacuum, and sometimes justifies breaking rules and trampling civility. Many people do not trust one another."[42] In isolation, these challenges might have been manageable. But in combination, they made China's long-term future in the twenty-first century anything but a sure bet.

To buck these worrying trends, it became increasingly apparent that China's economic policymakers would have to completely transform the country's economy from one focused on investment—which in China's case mostly meant building things—to consumption, meaning spending. Much of China's economic success was based on its world-leading savings rate—at over 45% of GDP, it had long been one of the highest in the world.[43] These savings, most of which were controlled by state-owned or directed banks, allowed Beijing to strategically deploy investment to areas like infrastructure

that fueled continued growth. But high savings rates also depressed domestic consumption, which China needed to power growth into the future.[44] Throughout the post-reform period, China's consumption rate was so
low that its only analogs were periods of war and economic depression. In
2011, for example, consumption accounted for just over one-third of GDP
against a global average of 65%.[45] Replacing investment with consumption
was a daunting task for China's economic policymakers; as one observer
commented, "consumption growth is hard to engineer."[46]

Perhaps China's greatest developmental challenge, though, was navigating
the transition from middle- to high-income country status. Forty years of
growth catapulted China, once one of the world's poorest countries, into the
ranks of upper-middle-income countries, alongside Armenia and South
Africa. But in 2011, China's annual GDP growth entered what began to look
like a secular slowdown. Economists worried that China might be falling into
what became known as the "middle-income trap." This concept, in which
once fast-developing economies cease to meaningfully grow for prolonged
periods of time, stems from the observation that in the mid- to late twentieth
century, most developing countries experienced rapid growth followed by
extended stagnation due to rising labor costs, a failure to produce technological innovation, and other malaise-inducing factors.[47] Twenty-first-century
China was a larger and more diversified economy than most of those whose
growth had plateaued in the second half of the twentieth century, leading
some economists to discount the idea of stagnating Chinese growth. But dis-
turbingly, on measures like the ratio of corporate debt to GDP, China began
to look more like a developed country instead of a still-developing one—
suggesting it may have little room left to grow.[48]

Even if Beijing managed to avoid the dreaded middle-income trap, it still
faced another sobering reality: in the post-1945 era, very few countries managed to make the leap to high-income status without some significant degree
of political liberalization. In their journey to becoming wealthy industrialized societies, China's neighbors South Korea and Taiwan both adopted
representative democracy. And even the two major exceptions to the general rule that democratization and development go hand in hand in East
Asia—Singapore and, pre-2020, Hong Kong—are only partial ones: both
score far higher than China on measures of democratic accountability (see
Figure 1.2).[49] The question hanging over China's leaders by the turn of the
twenty-first century was: Could they break the rule that economic afflu-
ence and political liberalization appear to go together? Unfortunately, both

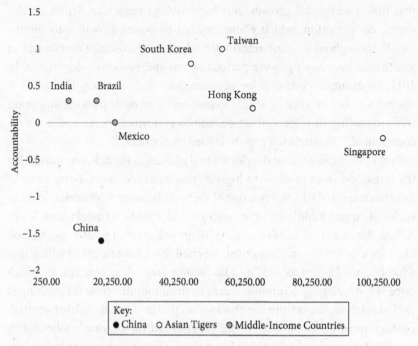

Figure 1.2. The relationship between income and democratic accountability, selected countries.
Source: World Bank 2021.

for China's citizens and prospects for cooperation with other nations on a host of global challenges, Beijing's response was to leave little to chance in clinging to power through a campaign of growing repression at home and belligerence abroad.

Beijing's Formula for the Future: Authoritarianism Plus Nationalism

You would be hard-pressed to find a grander monument to the global status quo than the annual meeting of the World Economic Forum in Davos, Switzerland. For decades, the international elite huddled in ritzy Swiss hotels to take stock of the planet's economic, political, and cultural direction. Throughout the years since the first gathering in 1971, most of the names and faces were familiar ones from the Western-dominated worlds of Washington and Whitehall, Airbus and, later, Amazon.

Yet by 2018, something had clearly changed. The star of Davos was no longer the leader of a Western country or company. In fact, he was not an executive at all, either national or corporate. Instead, he was Liu He (刘鹤), a previously little-known Chinese economic official. In the absence of China's highest-ranking leader, Xi Jinping, who had given his own marquee speech at Davos the year before, Liu was given top billing alongside heads of government including US President Donald Trump and British Prime Minister Theresa May.

The room was packed, and as the suave, Harvard-educated Liu took the stage, the crowd fell into a hushed silence. Though Liu spoke in Mandarin, his words, even before translation, had the gravity of a prime-time presidential address.

Liu's message, too, was the kind of thing that might once have come from an American president. "Together," he pledged, "we will stand for multilateralism, for the multilateral trading regime, and for common development and progress."[50] German Chancellor Angela Merkel gave a less-noticed address warning that the world risked repeating the mistakes, of allowing nationalism and protectionism to shape politics and economic policy, that had led to the First World War a century before.[51] Yet while the enthralled global elite seemed smitten by Liu's confident message of stability and progress, it was Merkel's address that proved the more prescient as Beijing leaned toward a combination of authoritarianism, protectionism, and nationalism.

Beijing's Resilient Authoritarianism

One of China's great paradoxes in the decades after 1978 was that even as it become more pluralistic, with more diverse values and interests, the effective political monopoly of the Chinese Communist Party grew more assured. Though its authority was far from absolute, China's party-state proved to be remarkably resilient in the post-reform period. In large part that was because, unlike that of other countries, Chinese authoritarianism proved to be notably flexible, adaptable, and even restrained. A key feature of authoritarian governance in China was devolution and decentralization: while decision-making was tightly controlled, in many ways it also operated like a free-agent system. For the most part, individual citizens, companies, and local officials were given plenty of leeway provided their actions broadly served goals set at the top. This fragmented, but coordinated, authority played a major role in helping the Chinese Communist Party stay in power despite the wrenching changes of the reform period.[52]

Central to this coordination was the target-setting process. Most of China's policies were set through numerical targets that were then passed down to officials at local levels. These officials were issued a kind of report card, known as the cadre evaluation system, or *kaohe* (考核), that showed how their jurisdictions performed against these targets.[53] How they achieved these targets, though, was largely left up to the officials themselves. This system, along with a gradual approach to policy reform that allowed for considerable local experimentation, was credited with helping drive economic growth—one of the key targets was GDP growth rate—as well as stability. But it was far from perfect, giving rise to many perverse incentives and outright scams.

One of the best examples is pollution. Rather than forcing local companies to install expensive wastewater treatment equipment, for example, many officials simply encouraged highly polluting factories to be built on waterways near boundaries with neighboring localities—once the polluted water flowed downstream, it became someone else's problem, and part of someone else's statistics.[54] As we'll see throughout the rest of this book, this free agent approach to governance produced a number of undesirable outcomes, including inadequate public health spending (Chapter 2), poor local pollution enforcement (Chapter 3), freewheeling talent recruitment programs (Chapter 4), and widespread intellectual property theft (Chapter 5). From a macro-economic and political point of view, though, China's perplexing combination of centralized policymaking and decentralized implementation proved remarkably successful, sustaining rapid growth while containing political discontent.

To be sure, the resilience of China's authoritarian system was not all thanks to its flexibility and adaptability. When it chose to concentrate its coercive resources, China's party-state could be brutally repressive. Human and civil rights were closely circumscribed throughout most of the reform period, and especially after 1989. With few exceptions, there was no free press; demonstrations were tightly controlled; and the regime ruthlessly suppressed groups that directly challenged the rule of the Chinese Communist Party or the supposed core interests of the Chinese state. For members of the Falun Gong (法伦杠) religious sect or the Uighur ethnic minority, this repression could be shockingly severe, including mass imprisonment, torture, and pervasive surveillance.[55]

Much of Chinese society, though, experienced a different form of author-itarianism. An approach known as "consultative authoritarianism" allowed China's leaders to accommodate society's growing pluralization without ceding meaningful political power. Under this approach, non-Party actors were permitted to voice concerns over issues like pollution or the quality of public services, as well as to advise Party leaders on how to address them. This gave China's party-state critical information on public opinion and allowed it to act proactively to nip potential sources of mass discontent in the bud.[56] But consultative authoritarianism stopped well short of tolerating any alternative to Chinese Communist Party rule. Instead, it bolstered authori-tarian resilience without necessarily enhancing the accountability of the state to its citizens, and certainly without challenging its hold on power.[57]

A related feature of Chinese authoritarianism was that, in most aspects of everyday life, the hand of the state could be surprisingly gentle. The Party was most concerned about being the sole legitimate political organization within China. As long as individuals did not appear to threaten this unique status, they could, to a significant extent, say and do what they wished. Throughout most of the 1990s and the first decade of the twenty-first century, China's party-state permitted critical voices online, provided they did not coalesce into a broader movement.[58] It was, however, a different story when anything resembling a popular movement took shape, either online or, more threat-ening still, in the real world. It was no coincidence that some of the most brutal crackdowns took place against religious groups, especially Muslims and Christians. Because these faiths were not indigenous to China, to the Party, they represented an insidious foreign influence that threatened its own.[59] And though some online criticism remained possible, restrictions on internet speech tightened considerably after Xi's accession to power.[60]

Perhaps the most important source of the Party's authoritarian resilience in the years after the 2008 financial crisis was a quasi-social contract to ad-vance bureaucratic and institutional reform, even as it resisted the political kind. Though the Party retained control of all significant decision-making and organizational management, it also expanded institutional capacity, pro-fessionalism, and a limited form of bureaucratic autonomy in most parts of the state apparatus, including the judiciary.[61] The quality of public services and those who ran them was widely perceived to improve after Xi took power, as did the state's responsiveness to citizen complaints. In a landmark 2017 speech, Xi committed to providing, among other things, "better education, better social protection, and better-quality housing," along with a "richer cultural spirit," seemingly in a nod to pervasive social mistrust.[62] His anti-corruption drive, though of dubious intent, was likewise widely credited with curbing the graft that was previously endemic throughout the economy.[63] Xi's "common prosperity" (共同富裕) agenda, meanwhile, aimed to tackle China's gaping inequalities by bolstering the philanthropic and charitable sectors.[64]

Another important element of China's authoritarian politics was its approach to maintaining the support of the commercial class. In most countries, authoritarianism tends to be accompanied by economic dysfunction. But China's leaders managed to grant just enough autonomy to its entrepreneurs and businesspeople to sustain their confidence, even while largely avoiding fundamental institutional reforms in areas like the rule of law. Key to this balance was what political economist Yasheng Huang termed "directional liberalism," meaning an implied commitment to property rights and the fundamentals of market economics that provided enough certainty for entrepreneurs and investors to place big bets on the Chinese market.[65] In combination, tactics like directional liberalism and consultative authoritarianism kept China's economic engines humming throughout the post-reform period—and its growing middle class generally content with Communist Party rule.

These tactics went a long way toward explaining why pluralization and ideological conflict did not shake the political foundations of China's party-state in the early decades of the twenty-first century. But from a foreign perspective, the continued resilience of China's authoritarian party-state was plenty problematic. As the following chapters explore, it positioned twenty-first-century China to shape the future with an unsettled sense of its own values and the capacity to export forms of social control that were fundamentally at odds with more liberal societies. Yet it was the second half of Beijing's formula for the future, an aggressive brand of nationalism, that threatened to make China an especially problematic and unappealing partner for solving the world's global challenges in the twenty-first century.

Nationalism and Its Consequences at Home and Abroad

Prospects for a broadly constructive and cooperative relationship between China and the world are deeply clouded by one popular political movement that China's party-state encouraged rather than repressed: an aggressive form of nationalism. Nationalism has always been a potent political force in modern China, including in the May 4th student movement in the early twentieth century. But nationalism played an especially important role in the political development of the People's Republic after 1949. The Chinese Communist Party's growth in the 1940s and its eventual overthrow of the Kuomintang government was due in no small part to its willingness to embrace a homespun version of Chinese nationalism alongside more universal aspects of Communist ideology like global working-class solidarity.[66] This combination proved hugely potent, so much so that in the twenty-first century it led to an ever-more-delicate balancing act for China's leaders of continuing to harness popular nationalism while preventing it from subverting Party control.[67]

Chinese nationalism and national identity are complex, and their relationship to politics and policy nuanced.[68] But what makes Chinese nationalism something special is the extent to which the CCP deliberately nurtured and constructed it. The Tiananmen Incident (六四事件) of 1989 marked a turning point, after which a more extreme version grew progressively more influential in Chinese politics. As we will see in the chapters that follow, this more aggressive and in some ways chauvinistic nationalism began to color everything from public health (Chapter 2) to climate change (Chapter 3) to cyber policy (Chapter 6) to biotechnology (Chapter 7). In part this shift was orchestrated by the Party itself, which in the aftermath of Tiananmen ramped up its propaganda efforts to prevent future youth-led challenges to its rule.[69] One such initiative is the patriotic education campaign, which has taught generations of Chinese schoolchildren that the Party rescued China from centuries of humiliation and oppression by foreign powers.[70]

Yet in attempting to gin up nationalist sentiment, China's leaders were also tapping into a concept with genuine appeal. A flood of celebrated books and TV series throughout the 1990s, much of it created by young intellectuals, fed a popular as well as propagandized narrative of the Party standing at the vanguard of not just China's working class, but the entire nation—one newly confident and determined never to repeat its recent history of victimization at the hands of foreign powers.[71] Representative was the account of one Beijinger who was born in a cave in China's dry northwest but rose to run an energy company: "Since the Opium Wars we went through the shame of being invaded by Western countries. For more than a hundred years we suffered, now we want our glory back."[72]

As this account attests, Chinese nationalism largely justified itself in opposition to foreign oppression of the kind China experienced in the nineteenth and twentieth centuries, popularly known as the period of "National
Humiliation" (国耻).[73] But in the post-1989 era, nationalist narratives acquired a more potent anti-foreign and anti-Western message that increasingly seeped into foreign policy. In the decades after 1989, China's leaders
frequently stoked the flames of nationalism when they wished to make a
point about foreign policy, such as after the 1999 US bombing of the Chinese
Embassy in Belgrade, or in 2005 in response to UN Secretary-General
Kofi Annan's proposal to give Japan a permanent seat on the UN Security
Council.[74] As time went on, though, the broad appeal of nationalistic
narratives threatened to outstrip the Party's ability to control them.[75]

In the twenty-first century, this struggle became apparent as Beijing
showed an increasingly uncompromising and bellicose face to the world.[76]
To be sure, this shift was prompted by several factors, including the perceived belligerence of the United States in both Iraq and Afghanistan and the
global financial system's near-death experience in 2007–2008, which shook
Beijing's faith in the Western-led economic system.[77] But it also reflected a
growing embrace of nationalist narratives following Xi's accession to power.
His vision for a "Great Rejuvenation" (伟大复兴), in which China becomes
too strong to be humiliated by any foreign power, combined elements of nationalist as well as Marxist and Maoist ideology.[78] The impact of this synthesis proved profound in China's relations with other countries. In many
of its external relationships, nationalism came to look less like the means of
Chinese policy than its end.

A striking trend in China's Xi-era foreign policy was the deterioration of
relations with a broad swath of countries, including European developed
democracies and developing nations in South, Southeast, and Central Asia.
This shift was reflected in a rise in tensions over long-simmering territorial
disputes with Japan, Vietnam, and India, as well as political-economic fights
with Australia, Canada, the Czech Republic, and Sweden, among others,
over a long list of grievances, including diplomatic recognition of Taiwan
and calls for an international investigation into the causes of the COVID-
19 pandemic.[79] Beijing's lengthening list of grievances increasingly found
expression in a sharply confrontational, belligerent approach to foreign
policy: China's ambassador to Sweden memorably responded to the award
of a literary prize to a dissident jailed by Beijing by warning a reporter, "For
our enemies, we got shotguns."[80] Such jingoistic language became such a

common feature of China's foreign policy that it gained a new name, "wolf warrior diplomacy" (战狼外交), after a popular nationalistic film.[81]

This belligerence, though seemingly thrilling to Beijing bureaucrats, played poorly abroad, not least because it increasingly clashed with foreign nationalisms and regional identities, especially in the developing world. Chinese overseas investment sparked a serious backlash in several countries that were centerpieces of the multi-trillion-dollar Belt and Road Initiative (一带一路). In Kazakhstan, one of the Initiative's linchpins, a 2019 spy scandal implicating a senior government official in selling secrets to Beijing laid bare growing tensions over its political influence, treatment of Uighurs in neighboring Xinjiang, and other differences. "China's presence in Kazakhstan," reported a leading Kazakh observer, has "become a divisive issue, and fears are growing that they're getting too powerful."[82] Though far from universal, this kind of pushback became increasingly common—countries typically welcomed cheap Chinese cash, but resented attempts to translate it into political or geopolitical influence.

Yet the risk that extreme Chinese nationalism could provoke a clash with other nations was greatest even closer to home, in China's restive outlying regions.[83] In the case of Hong Kong, matters were brought to a head by a growing sense of Cantonese identity in the early decades of the twenty-first century. The percentage of 18–29-year-old Hong Kongers who identified as Chinese began to fall around 2008 and by the late 2010s was well below 20%.[84] A series of high-profile demonstrations, including the 2014 "Umbrella Revolution" and the even larger-scale 2019 Hong Kong protests, signaled widespread opposition to mainland rule. These developments gravely threatened Beijing's long-standing prioritization of political stability in the territory and stoked nationalist fears of Hong Kong independence. Beijing's response, though, a fierce crackdown on civil liberties following passage of the 2020 National Security Law, provoked an equally strong reaction in the West, where it was viewed as proof positive of China's intentions to quash any Western-inspired political movements.[85]

The collision of Chinese nationalism, regional identity, and geopolitics was equally worrisome with respect to Taiwan. As in Hong Kong, the bonds of shared history, culture, and economic interdependence that tied older generations to the mainland began to fray as the twenty-first century advanced. The percentage of Taiwan's population identifying solely as Taiwanese, as opposed to Chinese or both Chinese and Taiwanese, consistently increased after the 2008 Beijing Olympics, and by 2020 had reached over two-thirds.[86] These trends provoked growing alarm among both Chinese officials and its nationalist netizens.[87] In the late 2010s, reports of Chinese intentions to take military action against Taiwan proliferated, and in March 2021 a senior US commander warned that Beijing might attempt an invasion before the year 2030.[88] In response, foreign powers signaled their own uncompromising stance on defense of the island. During one of the first high-level meetings of the Biden administration, Japan's defense chief pledged to "closely coordinate" with Washington in the event of a crisis over Taiwan—a veiled, but unmistakable, warning to Beijing.[89] Taiwan remained perhaps the single most worrying flashpoint in relations between China and other major powers.

Beijing's embrace of nationalism was aimed primarily at audiences at home and became part and parcel of the Party's governing philosophy. Its greatest impact, though, was arguably abroad, where it did much to undermine the idea that China could be counted upon as a constructive and equal partner in meeting global challenges. Even more tragically for the cause of global cooperation, Beijing's turn toward extreme nationalism coincided with structural economic shifts that fractured China's relationship with other major economies, in what came to resemble an economic and political great divorce. There was, increasingly, little love lost in the balance.

The Great Divorce: China and the West in the Twenty-First Century

Proof that commerce has long underpinned cordial ties between China and the West can be found in an ornate corner of the University of Pennsylvania campus, where a plaque marks the 1900 visit of China's then-Ambassador, Wu Tingfang (伍廷芳).[90] Officially, Wu was there, alongside Supreme Court Justices Oliver Holmes, John Marshall, and future US President William Taft, to help open the University's brand-new School of Law. But Wu was at least as enthused about Penn's recently announced intention to establish an entirely new type of professional school devoted to commerce—what would become the Wharton School, the first modern business school. It was, Wu proclaimed, a brilliant idea. "A special school of commercial and diplomatic training, intended to qualify students for business employment or for public service in the East," was, he gushed, exactly what China and the United States most needed.[91]

Wu's visit came at a fraught time in China's relationship with the West. The Chinese Exclusion Acts had been passed only 18 years before, and even as Wu spoke, the Boxer movement sought to drive all foreigners out of China.[92] Yet his focus on trade and commerce foreshadowed the privileged position they played in Sino-Western ties throughout much of the century that followed. Beginning in the 1980s, but accelerating sharply in the 1990s and early 2000s, China and the West enjoyed a boom in trade, with predominantly Western capital financing a vast industrialization that subsequently served Western consumer markets. It was also a period in which long-standing historical grievances, ideological differences, and diplomatic tensions were, for the most part, put to one side. In the 2010s, though, it became clear that China's economic relationship with the West was on the rocks, with the past half-century of mutual commercial interest beginning to fray.

Unfortunately, without the common logic of commercial interest to ballast ties between China and the West, and especially the United States, old conflicts over politics, geopolitics, and ideology returned to the fore. This even as global sustainability challenges like pandemics and climate change, and new technologies like quantum computing and synthetic biology, increasingly shaped the relationship. The irony that marked Trenton's civic slogan became painful, a source of grievance rather than nostalgia. China and the West both stood on the brink of a new, and deeply uncertain, phase of their long relationship with one another. Though trade and commerce remained an important part of this relationship, its foundations looked shakier than at any point in recent history. In place of the old trader's logic of mutually beneficial, if sometimes unequal, exchange, the notion of a broad-based, zero-sum competition increasingly took hold.

China's Climb Up the Global Value Chain

Following China's reform and opening to the world in the late 1970s, the big story was of its increasing economic integration with the West. The late twentieth-century Chinese economy was built on exports, especially to developed democracies like the United States, Germany, and Japan. In 1960, China's exports accounted for less than US$3 billion. By 2014 this figure had jumped a thousand-fold to US$2.5 trillion (see Figure 1.3).[93] During the first decades of the twenty-first century, China was by far the world's largest exporter, producing everything from iron stovetops to integrated

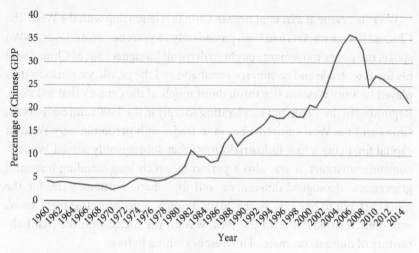

Figure 1.3. Chinese exports, 1960–2015.
Source: World Bank 2019.

circuits.[94] This made China an essential link in the world's global economic food chain—essentially the largest single motor of the global trade in goods. China played a central role not just in making products sold in other countries, but also in making the inputs, like machine parts, that other countries use to manufacture their own goods for export to third countries. In a 2016 study, China outranked all other countries as a contributor to other countries' exports.[95] In electronics, for example, China became a key node in all parts of global trade, from upstream manufacturing to downstream sales. This nodal role was one that only a few other major economies, mostly wealthy ones like the United States and Germany, enjoyed. And what set China apart even from these competitors was its dominant position at each stage of the global goods trade, from basic manufacturing to reprocessing and re-exporting.[96]

This growing role at the center of global trade certainly made China far richer than it once was, though in relative terms, not as much as one might expect. For the first few decades after 1978, China's exports were mostly low-value-added products like textiles, but over time they became steadily more sophisticated. In 1992, less than half of China's exports were considered to be in the "mid- to high-skill" category. But by 2005, this had increased to over two-thirds.[97] At the same time, China became less reliant on foreign technology. The "foreign content" of China's exports decreased from over 26% in 2005 to less than 17% in 2016, below the average for G-20 countries.[98]

Yet while China's export economy rapidly became more sophisticated, the West still reaped most of the benefits. Only in a few industries like electrical equipment did Chinese firms capture a significant share of global value chains. Though most iPhone manufacturing took place in China, for example, only about 4% of the value added went to Chinese corporate coffers.[99] Of the roughly US$238 expended to make an iPhone in 2016, US and Japanese firms each got about US$68, Taiwan about US$48, South Korea US$17, and China less than US$9.[100] Despite the disparity, this unequal distribution of gains seemed for years to suit governments and companies in both China and the West just fine. But in the first few decades of the twenty-first century, things began to change quickly, as both China and the West decided, for different reasons, that their marriage of global trading convenience was not what it used to be.

The discontent began, as it often does, with money. Throughout the 1990s and early 2000s, China's growing exports produced an enormous flow of cash, largely denominated in US dollars. By 2015, these foreign currency reserves exceeded US$3.8 trillion.[101] China's policymakers, keen to protect these hard-earned foreign currency earnings, plowed most of the proceeds into US Treasury bonds, generally considered one of the world's safest and most dependable investments because of their consistent returns. By the late 2010s, about 40% of China's vast foreign currency reserves was invested in US Treasuries, which effectively subsidized borrowing by the US government—one of the more striking examples of the two economies' growing interlinkages.[102] But though safe investments, Treasury bonds were also low-yield. As China's foreign currency reserves piled up, pressure mounted to seek out higher-return investments.[103]

At the same time, China became a victim of its own success as an exporter. The sheer scale of China's manufacturing sector meant it could not continue to grow simply by exporting more low-value-added products. Some existing foreign markets became saturated, and Chinese firms became less competitive as wages rose. Chinese policymakers began an effort to coax the massive Chinese economy away from low-cost, export-led-manufacturing toward higher-value-added manufacturing, services, and consumer spending.[104] In many respects, it worked. According to official statistics, in 2018 the value added by China's high-tech manufacturing industries increased by nearly 12%, with sectors like information technology growing by nearly 40%.[105] By 2017, the service sector accounted for more than half of China's GDP.[106] The share of domestic consumption in the economy grew more slowly, and was only two percentage points higher in 2019 than in 2007, when then-Premier Li Keqiang (李克强) first pledged to increase it.[107] But even with relatively low rates of annual increase, China was poised for significant long-term growth in consumer spending. In 2017, for example, Morgan Stanley forecast it to rise from roughly US$4 trillion to almost US$10 trillion by 2030.[108]

The increasing importance of domestic consumption to China's economy altered some of the basic terms of its trading relationship with the West. First, Chinese firms became less wholly reliant on large, developed export markets like the United States and the European Union. Strikingly, exports accounted for only 18% of China's GDP in 2018—down from 35% in 2006.[109] Second, Chinese firms became bigger players in higher-value-added industries and sectors that rich-country companies had grown accustomed to dominating. Beginning in the late 1990s, Beijing began to encourage some of its more efficient SOEs to invest outside of China, a strategy known as "going out" (走出去). At first, Chinese foreign direct investment was heavily concentrated in natural resources in developing countries, which the Chinese economy needed to sustain its own booming industrial sector. After the 2008 financial crisis, though, Beijing encouraged its banks and companies to look for underpriced Western companies in which to invest.[110] Foreign investment by Chinese firms boomed and began to sway sectors like finance and biotechnology (more on the latter in Chapter 7).[111]

In the first decades of the twenty-first century, Chinese firms, especially SOEs, went on a corporate shopping spree, acquiring everything from Volvo to Pirelli tires to New York's iconic Waldorf-Astoria Hotel. Overseas acquisitions by Chinese firms grew from US$49 billion in 2010 to US$227 billion in 2016.[112] This blitz made Chinese firms and investors a much more important part of the commercial landscape in foreign countries, and stirred fears of an economic juggernaut. But these were generally overblown: despite headline-grabbing purchases like that of the Waldorf, most Chinese-backed acquisitions were relatively small, averaging only about US$30 million. Moreover, many of these deals were financed not with cash from Chinese companies themselves, but rather foreign financiers. The 2016 acquisition of Swiss chemical firm Syngenta by ChemChina for US$46 billion involved loans totaling some US$33 billion, with much of it fronted by Western banks. Nonetheless, the perception that iconic Western firms and brands were increasingly threatened by competition from China grew.[113]

In truth, despite these fears, Chinese investment may have produced too little change rather than too much. Unlike many Western firms, Chinese acquirers tended to prioritize business stability, and did not insist on rapid business integration.[114] Partly as a result, returns on these investments proved to be mixed, to the detriment of both acquired Western firms and Chinese firms' confidence in Western markets. In June 2019, for example, China's ambassador to Switzerland commented in an interview that "if Switzerland wants to have Syngenta back, I will convince ChemChina to sell the company. . . . It wasn't a good deal for the Chinese side."[115] Indeed, for a growing number of Chinese executives, investing in the West proved to be not quite as good a business deal as they had hoped. It also became considerably less politically appealing as China and the United States entered an era of trade warfare in the late 2010s.

From Customer to Competitor and Partner to Rival

The years leading up to the COVID-19 pandemic witnessed a decisive change in China's trade relationship with many developed economies. Major foreign firms, especially those based in the United States, moved from China-centric to "China-plus" supply chains. Following the onset of the US–China trade war in 2018, many foreign firms adopted a "China + 1" strategy, splitting production between China and other developing economies.[116] A 2019 survey of foreign firms operating in China conducted by the American Chambers of Commerce in Shanghai and Beijing (AmCham) found that over 40% had either already shifted manufacturing operations outside of China, primarily to Mexico or Southeast Asia, or were considering doing so.[117] The same year, Apple asked its principal suppliers to assess the feasibility of shifting up to 30% of production from China, where nearly all of its supply chain had previously been concentrated, to Southeast Asia.[118] Google, meanwhile, announced it would expand its operations in Taiwan, especially for critical, high-demand items like motherboards.[119]

Much of this sudden shift was triggered by US-imposed tariffs, which began in 2018 under the Trump administration in response to alleged unfair Chinese trade practices. The effect of tariffs on US investment in China was so dramatic that the United States fell from being the third-largest foreign investor in China in March 2019 to the sixth largest in April of the same year.[120] But the tariffs also accelerated preexisting trends. According to an executive with knowledge of Apple's proposed pullback from China, the decision was motivated as least as much by factors like "a lower birth rate, higher labor costs, and the risk of overly centralizing . . . production in one country."[121] Foreign firms had also long felt unfairly treated by Beijing. AmCham members reported that some 39% had experienced potential discriminatory actions like increased inspections and slower customs clearance—both tactics that China's party-state employed to signal its displeasure.[122]

Breaking up is always hard to do, and even as political and commercial tensions rose, it was clear neither side could entirely free itself from the other. Despite a growing footprint in emerging markets, China remained heavily invested in the developed world, and looked set to remain so for the foreseeable future. Total Chinese investment in the United States during 2005–2017, for example, was over US$170 billion, compared with less than US$12 billion in the Democratic Republic of Congo, the largest single destination for Chinese investment in Africa.[123] Partly because large-scale investment opportunities in emerging markets remained limited, China seemed likely to remain a major player in rich-country markets. Nor were major trading relationships entirely beyond repair. The "Phase 1" trade deal negotiated by the US and Chinese governments in early 2020 removed barriers to foreign investment in some areas, as did a major bilateral investment treaty with the European Union reached later the same year. Trade in sectors like financial services saw rapid growth following these agreements, especially as the COVID-19 pandemic ebbed.[124]

Yet it also became clear that China's pre–trade war economic relationships had changed for good, replaced by generally lower-volume investments exposed to greater political risk. The surge in tensions between China and Western countries, especially the United States, after the election of Donald Trump in 2016, dramatically slowed Chinese investment abroad. The value of overseas deals involving Chinese firms fell from US$222 billion in 2016 to just US$78 billion in 2018.[125] China's foreign reserves fell from a peak of nearly $4 trillion in 2015 to US$3 trillion just a few years later, primarily due to increased investment in non–US Treasury instruments.[126] The deadly spread of the COVID-19 pandemic in early 2020, meanwhile, masked an equally shocking shift in global trade: thanks to plunging exports, in the first quarter of the year the Association of Southeast Asian Nations overtook the two largest developed economies, the United States and the European Union, as China's largest trading partner.[127] The speed with which the world's largest developed and developing economies moved apart was nothing short of stunning.

These economic shifts had a decisive impact on China's relationship with other major economies. The ambitious goals set in the US-China Phase 1 agreement looked unlikely to ever be met, especially with post-pandemic shifts in both countries' economies.[128] The steady expansion of political- and security-related restrictions on Chinese investment in major developed economies, from Australia to Germany, in the late 2010s and early 2020s, moreover, dimmed the appeal of overseas markets. The COVID-19 pandemic, meanwhile, lent new impetus to Xi Jinping's strategy of "dual circulation" (双循环), which called for boosting domestic sources of growth in order to balance the economy's reliance on exports and foreign investment. As political tensions between China and developed economies increased, this strategy began to look less like a deliberate choice than an acknowledgment of geopolitical necessity.[129] The upshot of these trends was that the Chinese and Western economies, as well as their polities, began to modestly but decisively part ways in the late 2010s.

As these bilateral trade relationships changed, competition between Chinese and foreign firms took on a geopolitical dimension as both increasingly sought growth in third-country emerging markets. Chinese firms became increasingly formidable competitors for foreign rivals both at home and abroad. As Jason Ding of Bain & Company noted, "Chinese companies that used to be business partners and suppliers are becoming rivals."[130] At the same time, political and economic tensions with several major Western economies led many Chinese firms to focus with increasing determination on other developing economies. Chinese investment giant Fosun Group (复星), for example, began busily expanding investment teams in places like Sao Paulo and New Delhi. According to executive Kevin Xie, "We think these emerging economies will have a growth profile similar to what China underwent in the past 15 years, and this will boost demand for everything from hospitals and clinics to insurance and labs."[131] Western firms, especially large consumer brands such as Pepsi and Marriott, also began looking for growth in these same emerging markets—setting the stage for a serious economic, political, and even ideological competition.[132] As Ben Harburg, managing partner at MSA Capital, observed, emerging markets are where "the real battleground lies" between China and the West, and it's an open question whether Western or "Chinese-built, backed, or inspired business models" will win out.[133]

Meanwhile, even as China and the West drifted further apart economically, political anxieties seemed set to keep them from reconciling. A combination of growing economic dislocation in many major economies, allegations of intellectual property theft and discrimination by Beijing, and a growing sense of geopolitical rivalry caused politicians from Washington to Warsaw to sour on large-scale trade and economic interdependence with China. Steve Bannon, a former top advisor to President Trump and an influential conservative intellectual, wrote in a 2019 op-ed that China "has emerged as the greatest economic and national security threat the United States has ever faced" and warned that America had joined "a years-long economic and strategic war with China."[134] Bannon was often regarded as a fringe voice—yet the normally cautious European Union sounded only slightly less strident in a March 2019 policy paper in which it named China a "strategic" competitor for the EU that had "fail[ed] to reciprocate market access and maintain a level playing field."[135]

No divorce, economic or marital, is easy, but the split between China and the West showed signs of being harder to reconcile than most. This was most dramatically illustrated in a seismic shift in public opinion toward China across most of the developed world in the 2010s. Throughout most of Europe, views of China had historically been slightly more unfavorable than favorable, though not by much.[136] Meanwhile, in the United States, the opposite was true, with more people expressing a favorable than unfavorable opinion.[137] Throughout most of the early twenty-first century, for example, a greater percentage of Americans described China as "friendly, but not an ally" than either as "unfriendly" or as an "enemy."[138]

Amidst economic and social tension and the pandemic, though, this relatively moderate attitude changed decisively across the West. During his successful 2016 US presidential campaign, Donald Trump proclaimed, "We can't continue to allow China to rape our country."[139] While 2018 polling data still showed more Americans held favorable than unfavorable views of China, in 2019, ratings flipped by a 16-point margin.[140] And in 2020, a Pew Research Center survey recorded unprecedentedly negative opinions toward China. In every one of the 14 industrialized countries surveyed, majorities voiced an unfavorable opinion. In half of these, including Britain, Germany, the United States, and South Korea, negative views reached their highest level in the 12 years the Pew survey had been conducted.[141] The survey revealed several surprises—it also recorded greater confidence in Chinese leader Xi Jinping than US President Donald Trump—but in sum showed a growing divide between China and more liberal societies.

Shorn of its long-standing commercial foundations, by the 2020s the Sino-Western relationship faced a set of daunting shared challenges without many of its reform-era moorings. In place of the physical goods that once made up much of China's economic relationship with the developed world, public goods like climate protection, pandemic prevention, and knowledge production steadily gained in importance. In this shift from physical to public goods, there was no alternative to seeking constructive partnership in at least a few areas. Yet these fundamental economic changes and shared challenges unfolded just as long-brewing ideological conflicts between China and the West flared anew. And despite that growing divergence, the new virus that was first detected in January 2020 showed that the fates of China and the West remained very deeply intertwined.

2

Doctor's Orders

China and the Politics of Public Health Cooperation

The signal event of the first two decades of the twenty-first century was the COVID-19 pandemic, which killed millions of people and turned life upside down across the globe. Like virtually everything else about the twenty-first century, it was closely tied to China. The coronavirus that causes COVID-19, known as SARS-CoV-2, was first detected in the city of Wuhan in early 2020 before spreading around the world. Yet SARS-CoV-2 was not the first new coronavirus to emerge in China in the twenty-first century. In 2003, its close cousin, SARS-CoV-1, spread the illness known as Severe Acute Respiratory Syndrome (SARS) in what was, until COVID-19, one of the world's most dire public health emergencies. These twin outbreaks show that despite the many ways that China's rise has changed the world, its single most significant global impact is in public health. This importance had long been foreseen. Some of the earliest ties between China and the West in the post-1978 period involved medicine and healthcare, and efforts to identify and stop the spread of new diseases had been ongoing for decades. But tragically, governments on both sides consistently put politics before public health, producing a series of missed opportunities to prevent new outbreaks. The result—untold death and economic damage—shows more poignantly than any other issue that public goods cooperation between China and other countries is essential, but also that it cannot be divorced from politics and geopolitical competition. Preventing the next pandemic means confronting and correcting old prejudices while better integrating China into the global health landscape.

A Tale of Two Pandemics: From SARS to COVID-19

The streets were still littered with leftover firecrackers marking the start of the Year of the Goat when, in early 2003, a 64-year-old doctor named Liu Jianlun (刘剑伦) checked into the aptly named Metropole Hotel in the crowded

China's Next Act. Scott M. Moore, Oxford University Press. © Oxford University Press 2022.
DOI: 10.1093/oso/9780197603994.003.0003

heart of Hong Kong. Like business hotels the world over, the Metropole caters to people on the move. The plentiful flowers look real only from a distance, the Chinese landscape paintings serene unless you pause for a second look—and realize they are cheap, formless knockoffs. Everything about the Metropole seems to discourage close examination. Including, that is, Dr. Liu himself.

Supposedly in Hong Kong to attend a wedding, the middle-aged, mundane-seeming Liu turned out to be a walking medical mystery. A respiratory disease specialist at the famous Sun Yatsen Memorial Hospital in Guangzhou (广州), the main city of Guangdong Province which borders Hong Kong, Liu had for weeks been seeing patients with what doctors referred to simply as an as yet undiagnosed "atypical pneumonia."[1] No one knew what caused it—but they did know it could spread, and kill, with terrifying speed. The clerk at the Metropole may have seen Dr. Liu cough, or noticed that he seemed a little pale. But if he did, there was no sign he sensed just what an eerie harbinger it was to hand Dr. Liu a key to Room 911. As it turned out, Dr. Liu was about to create one of the biggest public health panics in modern times.[2]

Dr. Liu never made it to the wedding. Instead, a day after checking in to the Metropole, he trudged down the street to a hospital just a seven-minute walk away. Whether this was a fortunate coincidence or part of a pre-planned attempt to get better medical care than was available on the Chinese mainland, by the time he entered the emergency room Dr. Liu clearly knew he was a threat to millions.

"Don't touch me," Liu warned perplexed fellow physicians at the Kwong Wah Hospital. "I have contracted a very virulent disease."[3]

But it was too late. Within hours, Dr. Liu was dead. And within days, his fellow guests at the centrally located Metropole Hotel had spread a previously unknown disease that would later be dubbed Severe Acute Respiratory Syndrome (SARS) across Asia, Europe, and North America. By the time the outbreak was over, this new disease had infected thousands of people around the globe, including 250 in Canada, 75 in the United States, and 10 in Germany. Hundreds died—making SARS one of the most widespread public health emergencies in recent times.[4]

While the SARS outbreak's most serious impact was loss of life, it also put a big dent in livelihoods around the world. Within a few weeks of Liu's arrival at the Metropole, SARS had caused a sharp slowdown in global tourism and travel. The panic soon spread from hospitals in Hong Kong to transit systems in Toronto and boardrooms in Britain. In a bizarre press conference, Toronto's clearly rattled mayor defended the safety of riding the subway and begged citizens to help make up for lost tourist revenue by watching more Blue Jays baseball.[5] Rod Eddington, then chief executive of British Airways, confided to a reporter in a moment of remarkable candor that SARS constituted "the worst crisis the aviation industry has seen."[6]

Yet as bad as SARS was, it could easily have been much worse. At a press conference announcing the end of the outbreak, Gro-Harlem Brundtland, then director-general of the World Health Organization (WHO), did not pause to celebrate. Instead, she called SARS "a warning" that "pushed even the most advanced health systems to the breaking point. Those protections held, but just barely. Next time," she cautioned, "we may not be so lucky."[7]

Unfortunately, she was right. Almost exactly 17 years after the first reports of the SARS virus emerged, a new coronavirus, so closely related to the first that it was named SARS-CoV-2, was identified in southern China. It proved to be far more dangerous, spreading much more efficiently between humans and producing a series of mind-boggling statistics: millions of people killed and billions forced to quarantine, at a cost of many trillions of dollars. Strikingly, this new coronavirus was first detected in the city of Wuhan, just a few hundred kilometers north of where SARS is suspected to have first emerged in Guangdong. It is one of China's wealthiest, most developed regions, and the center of much of its export industry. Which raises the question: How did two new coronaviruses join the long list of southern China's exports to the rest of the world?[8]

China as a Pandemic Hotspot

Before COVID-19, the most notorious pandemic in modern history was the 1918–1919 influenza, which killed as many as 100 million people and became commonly known as the Spanish flu. That name, though, is highly misleading; it is unclear where the pandemic first began, but it almost certainly was not Spain. The pandemic became associated with the country only because, thanks to wartime censorship, most other countries suppressed news of viral outbreaks—a pattern of secrecy and politicization that would subsequently be repeated many times, including by Beijing during both the SARS and COVID-19 pandemics.

Proposed sites of origin for the 1918–1919 pandemic include India and a British Army camp in France. But other evidence points to the last place one might expect: a sparsely populated patch of prairie known as Haskell County, Kansas, where a local doctor provided the first known report of an apparently new, unusually deadly strain of flu in early 1918. Whether or not the 1918 influenza really originated in Kansas or not, it shows that the invisible threat of disease can come from just about anywhere. As the leading proponent of this Kansan origin theory observed, "The fact that the 1918 pandemic likely began in the United States matters because it tells investigators where to look for a new virus. They must look everywhere."[9]

This insight, that highly infectious diseases can arise from anywhere but harm people everywhere, lies at the core of why public health is a global public good—something that benefits the people of all countries, but cannot be provided by any one country alone. But while all countries bear more or less equal responsibility for detecting and preventing the spread of infectious disease, China plays an especially important role in global public health and pandemic prevention. That is because, while in principle a pandemic can begin anywhere, in practice, they tend to arise disproportionately in areas known as pandemic hotspots. And by the early twenty-first century, thanks to its growing wealth and relationships with the outside world, southern China had become perhaps the best-connected pandemic hotspot on the planet.

Pandemic hotspots share several features that can—though do not automatically—make them more likely to incubate and spread new infectious diseases. These features include large, densely clustered numbers of humans and domesticated animals; extensive biodiversity; and culinary or nutritional preferences and practices that encourage the consumption of exotic or wild animals. The risk is especially high where, as was customary in southern China until recently, backyard farming is commonplace and people and animals live in close proximity.[10] All these conditions can facilitate host switching, the process whereby a virus previously hosted by animals adapts to spread among humans. The risk of viral outbreaks also appears to be linked to land-use changes like deforestation. As humans push deeper into previously isolated ecosystems like tropical forests, they create more opportunities for new viruses to jump from one species to another. Many regions across the globe fit this description, including much of South Asia and parts of equatorial Africa.[11]

Like several of these areas, southern China in the twenty-first century was densely populated, biodiverse, and rapidly urbanizing. But it also stood out for one big reason: it grew exceptionally well connected with the rest of the world. As the heart of China's manufacturing base, the region centered on Guangdong Province became closely integrated with other economic centers across the globe. By the late 2010s, the region's major cities, which include Hong Kong, Guangzhou, and Shenzhen (深圳), hosted four of the world's 20 largest seaports and two of its 20 busiest airports (see Figure 2.1).[12] South China also acted as the hub of some of the world's most important diaspora networks and the ancestral homeland of many Chinese emigrant communities abroad. These networks supported extensive familial and commercial ties between south China and other countries, playing a crucial role in trade and investment.[13] Unfortunately, this extensive integration with the rest of the world also carried a significant drawback: under some circumstances, it made it quicker and easier for viruses to spread from south China abroad, and vice versa. The N5N1 strain of avian influenza, one of the most virulent in recent times, was first isolated in southern China in 2003.[14] And the same year, just a few days after Dr. Liu checked into the Metropole Hotel in

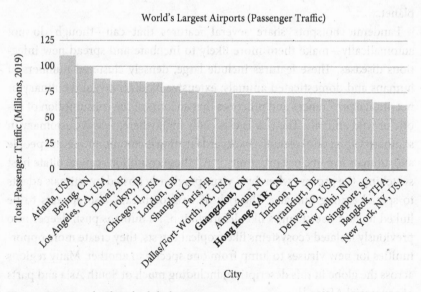

Figure 2.1. South China's global integration.
Source: World Economic Forum 2019 and Airports Council International 2020.

Hong Kong, SARS spread from the region across the world, via Hong Kong International Airport.

It is important to separate these economic and geographic factors that made south China the world's best-connected pandemic hotspot from the politics and prejudice that often surrounds discussion of China and infectious disease. In the late nineteenth century, Western newspapers began describing the Ottoman Empire as the "sick man of Europe" in reference to its political and economic weakness. Soon the phrase was adopted by both Chinese intellectuals and European journalists to describe Qing-era China, beset by similar woes and largely dominated by foreign powers. The term "sick man of Asia" subsequently became a synonym for anti-Chinese prejudice in the early twentieth century.[15]

Over time, a dark stereotype emerged of China and Chinese people as being prone to spread disease. This led to many instances of anti-Asian behavior during the COVID-19 pandemic, and shamefully framed some of the Western media's initial coverage of it. An article published in *The Wall Street Journal* in early February 2020 under the unfortunate headline "China is the real sick man of Asia" produced understandable outrage among Chinese.[16] China was no more prone to spread disease than any other country. But because of its dense integration and growing wealth, it did have an especially important role in preventing it.

Increasingly, China's impact on public health extended beyond its own borders. While hard numbers were tough to come by, China was generally estimated to be among the top 10 bilateral global health donors, with African countries among the largest recipients.[17] Beijing also became an enthusiastic participant in global health diplomacy, hosting several high-level meetings and playing a growing role in the WHO, the main international health body. Its donations to the organization in 2016–2017 totaled almost US$70 million, making it one of the largest single contributors, though relative to the size of its economy a considerably smaller one than countries like Canada or the United Kingdom.[18] But Beijing's motives for such investment were hardly selfless, and have as much to do with politics as public health. That makes it a problematic, but indispensable, partner in preventing future pandemics, both in China and abroad. The need to think differently about how to work with China is powerfully illustrated by the history of Sino-American health cooperation—one of the world's most ambitious efforts to cooperate on public goods, but one that ultimately became defined more by politicization and geopolitical competition than public health.

The Saga of Sino-American Health Cooperation

Every country has its unique, awe-inspiring public spaces. It is difficult not to feel a twinge of trepidation when you walk into the US Capitol, or soak in the size of St. Peter's. But few places are quite as overpowering as the Great Hall of the People (人民大会堂), the home of China's National People's Congress. One of Mao Zedong's pet projects, the Great Hall was designed to inspire the same sense of grandeur and gravitas as the Forbidden City which it faces. But while the Forbidden City stands as a monument to the artisans of ancient China, the Great Hall is spartan and spotless—resembling nothing so much as an overgrown hospital hallway.

It was fitting, then, that the Great Hall played host to the signing of one of the earliest Sino-American agreements following the restoration of diplomatic ties, the 1979 Protocol in Cooperation on Medicine and Public Health. Over the next 40 years, the United States and China forged a deep partnership in these areas, yet one that failed its most significant test, control of the COVID-19 pandemic, thanks to a persistent tendency on both sides to put politics before public health.

The United States was not the only foreign country to cultivate a strong relationship with China in the public health and healthcare arenas. Exchanges of physicians and healthcare workers with Communist and non-aligned nations were active throughout the Cold War, and in the 1980s and 1990s, health partnerships were forged with several European nations, as well as multilateral bodies like the WHO, the World Bank, and others.[19] But by far, China's most substantial public health partnership was with the United States. Throughout the early twentieth century, American nongovernmental organizations (NGOs) played a critical role in shaping China's modern healthcare system and medical community. The Rockefeller Foundation and the missionary-affiliated China Medical Board provided fellowships to Chinese physicians to study in the United States, including seven of the 10 presidents of China's National Medical Association in the first decades of the twentieth century.[20] Peking University Medical College, China's preeminent teaching hospital, was founded by a group of foreign missionary associations, and in the early twentieth century was purchased and substantially enhanced by the Rockefeller Foundation. Yet, well-intentioned though they were, these early efforts at Sino-American medical philanthropy also proved to be, as historian Mary Bullock put it, both "a tribute to the durability of Chinese culture and as monument to an American effort to change it."[21]

These dense, long-standing, and primarily nongovernmental ties between the Chinese and American medical communities faded after 1949. But they laid the foundation for health to once again become an important dimension of Sino-American relations following the resumption of diplomatic relations. As early as 1974, US officials expressed a belief in "the need for Chinese participation in international bodies discussing major health problems of the world."[22] Unfortunately, just as Bullock observed in the early twentieth century, Sino-American health cooperation remained laden with false hopes, romantic notions, and political motives that often conflicted with the goals of saving lives and curing disease.

From the start, America's post–Cultural Revolution engagement with China on public health was tinged with political motives, especially the idea that it might prod Beijing to adopt more liberal, open, and modern practices. The report of a 1979 delegation led by the US secretary of Health, Education and Welfare exclaimed, for example, "The team was impressed by the willingness of the Chinese to share information . . . and by the forthright reference to the suppression which occurred during the Cultural Revolution. There is clearly now in China a spirit of intellectual movement and a commitment to enter the ranks of modern day science."[23]

In the 1990s, China seemingly obliged American aspirations by deciding to transform its public health system from a Soviet-inspired model to one closely and consciously based on the US Centers for Disease Control and Prevention (CDC). The US model was judged by China's health experts to be the world's best, and in imitating the CDC, they hoped to lend credibility and professionalism to what eventually became known simply as the China Centers for Disease Control, which were established both at national and provincial levels. Before its creation, China's local public health establishments were known rather blandly as "stations." As a public health worker later told an American researcher, the change in nomenclature was significant and deliberate: "we changed the name to the American name—center. This sounds like something big and important, something that does something."[24] China's move to adopt the CDC model was strongly encouraged by US health officials, who among other things helped their Chinese counterpart agency develop a fully computerized data-collection system that, at the time, was more advanced than the partially fax-based system utilized by the United States itself.[25]

Sino-American health cooperation was ride-ranging and included important research on the role of folic acid in preventing birth defects, much of it sponsored by American foundations and nonprofit organizations.[26] The focus of intergovernmental cooperation in the decades leading up to SARS, though, was in countering China's HIV/AIDS epidemic. US officials provided considerable technical assistance and funding, including US$7 million annually from the Global HIV/AIDS Program budget, to help China tackle the disease.[27] In 2002, the US National Institutes of Health (NIH) awarded another US$15 million grant to China CDC for HIV/AIDS prevention research, treatment, and vaccine development. Perhaps of greater long-term significance, NIH also trained dozens of Chinese scientists through a program known as the AIDS International Training and Research Program.[28] A separate program run by the CDC, known as the Field Epidemiology Training Program, taught Chinese public health workers how to follow American-style disease surveillance and detection practices.[29] These programs had a critical impact in creating a cadre of highly capable Chinese public health professionals who could communicate almost seamlessly with their US counterparts. Unfortunately, politics often prevented them from doing so.

The political motivations of US health assistance were made clear during the HIV/AIDS epidemic. In testimony before a congressional commission, a US health official expressed support for "going beyond . . . bilateral government-to-government arrangements," specifically citing a program funded by the Kaiser Family Foundation to educate Chinese journalists about HIV and broadcasts by Voice of America and Radio Free Asia that attempted to draw attention to the scale of China's HIV/AIDS pandemic. Elsewhere, the same official was even more forthright about his belief that "in the process of helping them, I am hoping also that we can transmit some basic values that are fundamental to our own system here, such as transparency and accuracy in reporting."[30]

This effort to use public health cooperation as an entry point to promote political and institutional reform was well intentioned, but it also made Chinese officials deeply suspicious of working with foreign powers and reluctant to share information when it mattered most to the outside world. As the SARS outbreak raged in spring 2003, an American scholar remarked, "There are numerous international healthcare related programs in China, but most of them are run on a very small scale at a pilot level. And one of the problems of scaling them up again on local levels is precisely the political one. . . . The central authorities or even provincial authorities are more reluctant to see those programs expanded to a larger scale for political reasons." Another researcher warned a US congressional commission that attempts to leverage public health cooperation with China for political ends would ultimately prove counterproductive: "The use of public health challenges as shorthand political critiques is a real danger as we move forward to combat this newest global threat, SARS. . . . Statistics on disease and death rates are often used like Rorschach tests to measure the legitimacy of the government."[31]

In the initial aftermath of SARS, it seemed that a shared interest in public health and pandemic prevention would trump any such political considerations. In 2005, China and the United States signed a Memorandum of Understanding known as the China-US Collaboration on Emerging and Reemerging Infectious Diseases, which established a bi-annual high-level meeting between the US secretary of Health and Human Services and China's minister of Health, the frequency of which was later increased to annual meetings.[32] Lower-level exchanges between US and Chinese public health officials multiplied, and by the end of the Obama administration, the CDC's Beijing office alone employed some 50 staff. When the Trump administration took office in 2017 and political priorities shifted, however, most of these staff were transferred or left without replacement. As a former US diplomat recounted, this had the effect of "signaling to the Chinese government significantly less U.S. interest and support for health cooperation and leaving U.S. CDC with few eyes and ears on the ground to assess and prepare for the COVID-19 pandemic."[33]

Just as unfortunately, the temptation to treat pandemics as political Rorschach tests proved irresistible when the COVID-19 outbreak emerged in early 2020. Western newspapers became awash in stories critical of China's response, with many blaming its authoritarian political system for suppressing news of the outbreak. To be sure, Chinese officials initially repeated many of the mistakes of SARS, with local officials underplaying the extent of the outbreak until forced to admit it by a whistleblower, Dr. Li Wenliang (李文亮). But after COVID-19 began a nearly uncontrolled spread in the United States, and despite the Chinese Foreign Ministry offering to make epidemic response a "platform for Sino-American cooperation,"[34] American officials and politicians quickly began casting Beijing as a villain. The US Secretary of State announced that Washington would withdraw from the WHO, alleging it to be in thrall to Chinese interests, and endorsed an unproven claim that the SARS-CoV-2 virus had been intentionally created and accidentally released from a Chinese laboratory.[35]

That intergovernmental cooperation on public health might be colored by politics is itself unsurprising. But by the time even the US president began channeling the worst stereotypes of China and disease, referring to COVID-19 as "the China virus," it was clear that not only had Sino-American health cooperation failed to prevent the COVID-19 pandemic, it had also become deeply and perhaps irredeemably politicized. Far from anchoring cooperation between the United States and China, public health became one of the biggest sources of acrimony between Washington, Beijing, and the people of both countries.[36] The question became, could public health cooperation be resuscitated?

Politicization, Decentralization, and Obfuscation: China's Public Health Pathologies

When I moved to Hong Kong in August 2002, the former British colony was just five years into a profound transformation. While Public Queuing Campaigns, double-decker buses, and street names like Queen's Road provided ready reminders of the city's colonial past, Hong Kong had long since begun looking more to Beijing than Britain for its future. In fact, soon after I arrived, the government announced that all humanities classes would be taught in the official mainland dialect of Mandarin instead of the local Cantonese, and ATMs began dispensing mainland Chinese currency alongside Hong Kong dollars. Giant billboards proclaimed Hong Kong to be "Asia's World City," the world's gateway to the riches of the mainland's burgeoning middle class.

Yet as I soon discovered, there was a dark side to this seeming economic bonanza. Along with profits and productivity, China's economic rise and political integration with Hong Kong brought with it a public health disaster. Within a few months of arriving in Hong Kong, Dr. Liu had spread SARS across the border, and I was soon wearing a government-mandated face mask in school. Like everyone else in Hong Kong, I wondered if every cough or sneeze on the subway was simply a winter cold or something far more deadly. And as it turned out, the panic had a lot to do with the paranoia of the Chinese Communist Party.

Beijing was first alerted to the existence of a strange new respiratory disease more than a month before Liu's fatal trip to Hong Kong—but the report was marked "Top Secret," meaning that only the most senior health officials could read it. Even so, word filtered out: by early February, just days before Liu checked into the Metropole Hotel, text messages were ricocheting around Guangzhou warning of a "deadly flu." Days later, on February 10, the local government even published a notice in newspapers advising citizens of how to protect themselves against the new disease.[37]

But this transparency proved short-lived. Soon after the notice was published, officials in Guangdong Province instituted a news blackout that continued until well after SARS had spread around the globe. The decision, like many others made by Chinese officials during the outbreak, was more about politics than public health. SARS occurred at a notably inconvenient time: in the run-up to the annual March meeting of China's National People's Congress. "To publicly acknowledge the outbreak at this critical juncture," an official later recalled, "might have risked not only causing socioeconomic instability but sullying the Party's image among the people."[38]

It says a lot about China and its role in the twenty-first century that People's Congress public relations concerns helped spark one of the deadliest disease outbreaks in modern history. Had officials in Guangdong Province not been so concerned with political pageantry, the world might have been spared hundreds of disease-related deaths. But that is also a bit like saying if only the United States didn't have a federal system, or Britain a monarchy, things would be so much more efficient. From the earliest years of the People's Republic, public health was shaped by the interests of the Chinese Communist Party and the political system it created—which meant that, as in other countries, political considerations usually trumped public health ones.

Politics, Propaganda, and Public Health in the People's Republic

In the 1930s and 1940s, the West's view of China, and of the growing Communist movement led by Mao Zedong, was framed in large part through the lens of health. Healthcare was an important part of the work of the many Western missionary and philanthropic organizations operating in China during this period, many of which employed, in the words of one historian, "piteous narratives of the plight of epidemic-stricken Chinese peasants" and images of "a vulnerable population in need of charitable medical aid and intervention."[39] Determined to counter this narrative of weakness and dependency on foreign powers, the post-1949 Communist state placed considerable emphasis on highlighting the health and vitality of the People's Republic to audiences both foreign and domestic.

In many respects, Mao's China had much to showcase to the world. After 1949, infant mortality was reduced by 75%; life expectancy was doubled; and the debilitating, once-common parasitic disease schistosomiasis was effectively eliminated.[40] Drug addiction, a significant social ill since the time of the Opium Wars, was curbed, albeit by crude methods. And against all odds, smallpox was eliminated within little more than a decade, with the last verified Chinese case recorded in 1960. Over the following decades, the People's Republic succeeded in vaccinating some 500 million people.[41] The success of this mass immunization campaign played a key role in the Chinese Communist Party's efforts to portray China as a capable, modern, and scientifically literate society.[42]

Much of the success of these efforts was due to the Party's prioritization of healthcare in rural rather than urban areas—something that, in the words of one medical historian, "almost no government has ever been able to do."[43] The backbone of this system was the "barefoot doctor" (赤脚医生) corps, a group of semi-professional medical workers who were trained to provide basic but accessible care throughout the countryside. Some 1.3 million of these barefoot doctors worked across China by the mid-1970s.[44] The system's focus on rural areas proved to be good public health policy, but it was also intensely political. In 1965, Mao issued an "Instruction on Health Work" which charged that "the broad masses of the peasants do not get medical treatment. . . . The Ministry of Public Health is not that of the people and it is better to rename it as the Ministry of Urban Health or the Lords Health Ministry or the Health Ministry of the Urban Lords."[45] The message was clear: China's public health system was to follow the political line established by Mao's Cultural Revolution.

Somewhat surprisingly given its high political profile, China's healthcare system was both highly decentralized and largely independent of state support. Rural healthcare was self-financed through a mutual insurance scheme which was capitalized by both individual and communal contributions. In Guangdong, for example, peasant farmers paid 0.3 RMB per month in insurance premiums, in addition to co-pays and funds provided by the commune, which accounted for roughly 10% of its total welfare budget. Only in cities, where healthcare was provided largely through facilities operated by work units, or *danweis* (单位), was the system largely state-funded.[46]

Despite this highly decentralized structure, China's rural health focus became a key part of its international image and influence-building campaign throughout the Cold War. In the 1970s, China's often-stylized portrayals of its rural healthcare system helped inform a "horizontal" model of global public health that was focused on the needs of local communities. This model was championed by the WHO and led to a diplomatic triumph for Beijing in 1978, when a landmark conference was held in Alma Ata, Kazakhstan. The conference, first proposed by China, produced a highly influential document, known as the Alma Ata Declaration, that called for a holistic and equitable approach to public health, and endorsed the emphasis placed by Beijing on primary care.[47]

Public health also proved useful as a means of securing diplomatic support at the expense of the rival Republic of China government based in Taipei. Throughout the Cold War, the People's Republic vied with Taiwan in using medical diplomacy as a means of projecting its influence abroad, especially in Africa. In 1964, for example, every Chinese province dispatched medical teams to Tanzania, where they established a rural health program modeled on the barefoot doctors and encouraged free mass vaccination.[48] These efforts often paid rich geopolitical dividends. In 1973, just a few months after Beijing dispatched hundreds of thousands of vaccine doses to Burkina Faso, then in the midst of a devastating famine, its government recognized the People's Republic instead of Taiwan.[49]

In another instance of healthcare being deployed in the service of geopolitics, in the late 1960s reports emerged that Indian exiles had contracted smallpox in Tibet, contradicting Beijing's prior claims to have eliminated it in 1960. Of greater concern to Beijing, these reports undermined China's claim to Tibetan territory. To counter them, Chinese leaders mounted a major campaign to deny the existence of smallpox in Tibet, concocting a far-fetched astrological explanation to discredit the Tibetan exiles' claim. Despite its implausibility, in the end the WHO accepted Beijing's explanation. "The PRC," historian Mary Brazelton observed, "asked the WHO to accept its eradication of smallpox on faith, and it did."[50] While there is no hard evidence to support the exiles' claims, questions over the accuracy and politicization of critical health data would remain a persistent theme in China's approach to public health in the post-reform era, including in response to the SARS and COVID-19 outbreaks.

The Unraveling of the Healthcare System
in Post-Reform China

China's Mao-era public health policy gave rise to several distinctive features of its healthcare system that continued to shape its response both to SARS and COVID-19. The first of these was a decentralized, often patchwork financing structure for public health. This structure proved highly vulnerable to disruption in the post-Mao reform era as economic growth took precedence over public health. According to one estimate, in 1978, about 20% of the national health budget was devoted to rural care, but by the mid-1990s, this had plummeted to 4%.[51] Funding for local public health centers was slashed by two-thirds.[52] The mentality during the reform period was that "if the top priority is on health, economic issues will be moved down a notch, which may lead to more unemployment and more social and political instability."[53] As another observer put it, "China, like many developing and developed countries, puts emphasis on ministries that generate revenue, not ministries that lose revenue. Health loses revenue."[54]

This inattention left China's public health system woefully unprepared to deal with infectious disease outbreaks. The overwhelming focus of most healthcare providers was on providing curative, rather than preventative or diagnostic, care.[55] Even after the China Centers for Disease Control and Prevention were set up in 2002, they were allocated, by one account, the shockingly small sum of US$10,000 for the resource-intensive activities of disease surveillance and detection.[56]

Even as it constrained resources, decentralization also made it difficult for central authorities to obtain accurate information and coordinate action with local officials—both critical points of failure in responding to infectious disease outbreaks. In the mid-1970s, a visiting US physician expressed surprise at how "little emphasis was placed on the collection of aggregate data. . . . Our impression was that the national Ministry [of Health] was relatively unimportant" in comparison to local authorities.[57] The marginalization of central health authorities only intensified during the reform era as the pace of urbanization skyrocketed and society became increasingly diverse. As a local public health official recounted, Mao-era vaccination campaigns succeeded because "you could go to a village and they would round everyone up and do it. . . . Not like now when people don't listen, and the population is too mobile."[58]

The challenges of mobilizing this decentralized, diffuse healthcare system were widely viewed as contributing to China's initial failure to control the SARS outbreak. A US government report, for example, concluded that "the universe of what effectively can be controlled by the core central elite today is ... shrinking, while the capacity of non-central actors to manage, influence, and interfere in day-to-day activities is seen to be expanding. The struggle of dealing with SARS highlighted these strains and contradictions in the PRC political system."[59] In explaining patterns of interaction with Chinese health officials up to and during the SARS crisis, a US public health official likewise emphasized to a congressional commission that "China, functionally, is a federal system in the sense that the provinces operate pretty independently of the center."[60] Though such systems have many advantages, they could also prove difficult to coordinate amid pandemics, as SARS and COVID-19 would later show in both the United States and China.

The most profound and significant feature shaping China's response to pandemics, though, was a fundamentally authoritarian one, namely an obsessive desire to avoid scrutiny of the weaknesses of the post-reform healthcare system. The first major test of this system came during the HIV/AIDS epidemic of the 1990s, which for years officials largely pretended did not exist. As in the case of SARS (described below), it was largely thanks to the efforts of a single fearless physician, Gao Yaojie (高耀洁), that the public became aware of the scale of the outbreak.[61] Even as it became clear that the system was not equipped to handle outbreaks among highly mobile, marginalized populations like sex workers, officials initially resisted attempts by China's growing NGO sector to help fill the void. While NGOs were eventually given a significant role in responding to the HIV/AIDS epidemic, local officials kept a close watch, fearing their involvement would draw attention to the deficiencies of China's state-run system.[62]

This defensive response to HIV/AIDS also meant that many important lessons on preventing disease outbreaks were not institutionalized within the bureaucracy, and by the time of the SARS outbreak had largely been forgotten. As an American scholar later observed, the lessons of HIV/AIDS were largely ignored because it was more politically convenient for officials to "tuck it into Xinjiang, tuck it into Yunnan, blame the drug users and so on, and not really confront the weaknesses in the system."[63]

A similar fear contributed to a secretive stance on public health information, particularly among local officials. Added to this was the still-common practice of distorting data on healthcare outcomes and the incidence of disease in order to meet performance targets (more on this practice in Chapters 1 and 3). As one expert noted, this practice meant that local officials "routinely inflate data that reflect well on the regime's performance while underreporting or suppressing bad news such as plagues and diseases." Meanwhile, infectious disease outbreaks were by law effectively treated as state secrets. Though it obliged the central government to "publicly announce the true epidemic situation," China's 1988 Infectious Disease Law required lower-level authorities to obtain authorization from the Ministry of Health before releasing information on disease outbreaks.[64]

Unsurprisingly, these incentives made it difficult for high-level officials to obtain accurate information when disease outbreaks did occur. During SARS, these practices "not only obstructed the information flow within the system but also distorted the information itself . . . the country's refusal to enfranchise the general public in overseeing the activities of government agencies makes it easy for upper-level government agencies to be fooled by their subordinates."[65]

These distinctive features of China's approach to public health undermined public trust and confidence in the healthcare system, indirectly aiding the spread of deadly diseases. By the 2010s, health insurance coverage rates had grown to over 95%, and made many forms of routine healthcare much more affordable.[66] But care was often poorly coordinated between primary and specialist providers, and inadequate fiscal support for healthcare by local governments in China's decentralized system meant that many providers generated revenue from prescribing unnecessary tests and procedures.[67] Hospitals remained outside the jurisdiction of the Health Ministry, inhibiting coordination for disease control purposes, and were set up primarily for income generation rather than public health.[68] Though partly ameliorated by increased oversight and policy reforms in the latter part of the first decade of the twenty-first century, these perverse economic incentives continued to undermine trust in China's healthcare system. Trust in physicians, healthcare providers, and medical researchers remained considerably lower among Chinese citizens than those of most other countries.[69]

In addition to undermining domestic trust in the healthcare system, these lingering weaknesses in the wake of SARS and the COVID-19 pandemic also dented the international community's confidence in Beijing's commitment to the cause of global public health and pandemic prevention. Yet it would be a mistake to draw the conclusion that future engagement would be futile. As a US public health expert commented in the aftermath of SARS, "it is shortsighted to come down too hard on the way the Chinese have dealt with this crisis. I am not sure how our country would have dealt with this crisis."[70] Nearly two decades later, COVID-19 provided a dispiriting answer—and a reminder that efforts to protect public health would have to move forward against a backdrop of rising global tensions and geopolitical competition.

Geopolitical Competition and Public Health Cooperation

Few academic research reports draw a crowd. But on April 12, 1955, you could barely get in the door at the University of Michigan's Rackham Auditorium to hear Thomas Francis release the official report of something called the Poliomyelitis Vaccine Evaluation Center. Reporters and press photographers mobbed the waiting area, as a hapless crew of assistants wheeled by a cart filled with copies of the first scientific study of the recently developed polio vaccine. A few enterprising newsmen literally snatched the report off the shelf and were already filing breathless press reports detailing the impending demise of one of the planet's most feared diseases.

Francis then stepped up to the microphone. "The vaccine works," he said with a smile, pausing for a few seconds to enjoy the moment. "It is safe, effective, and potent."

Francis had good reason to smile. So did the polio vaccine's inventor, Jonas Salk, who sat in the audience, beaming throughout the press conference.[71] Few discoveries in the history of the world gave greater cause for joy than the cure for polio. Before the vaccine became widely available in the late 1950s, parents from Ann Arbor to Singapore lived in fear that their children might develop the debilitating disease that paralyzed hundreds of thousands around the world. People wept as they heard news of the vaccine; car horns blared and church bells tolled.[72] Within a few decades of the vaccine's introduction, polio had disappeared from America and most of the developed world. By the early twenty-first century, it stood on the verge of total eradication.

Salk remains widely remembered today, and development of the polio vaccine is still celebrated as one of America's great medical achievements. But virtually no one remembers that without the United States' great Cold War rival, the Soviet Union, the eradication of polio would have been impossible.

Salk's polio vaccine, though highly effective, had a major drawback: it was injected with a syringe, making it costly, time-consuming, and dangerous to administer to millions of children. Another American medical researcher, Albert Sabin, had an answer to this problem: an oral polio vaccine that could be inserted into a sugar cube, which kids around the world were more than happy to swallow. But because the Salk vaccine was so widely used in the United States, Sabin needed to look abroad to conduct clinical trials. And in the process, he helped show that while public health often comes second to politics and geopolitics, the two can still coexist—a critical lesson as relations worsened between China and the West in the twenty-first century.

Geopolitics: Global Public Health's Persistent Companion

Despite sky-high tensions between the United States and the Soviet Union following the launch of Sputnik in 1957, Soviet officials quietly offered to host large-scale clinical trials of Sabin's oral vaccine.[73] After all, polio was just as big a problem in Moscow as in Michigan. A Soviet scientist, Mikhail Chumakov, first put the oral vaccine into mass production, and a Soviet bloc country, Hungary, was the first to initiate large-scale vaccinations— four years ahead of the United States. And it was the Soviet, rather than the American, model for mass vaccination campaigns that the WHO used in its successful effort to eradicate polio in subsequent decades.[74]

This low-profile partnership proved so effective that in his 1958 State of the Union address, President Eisenhower proposed that the United States and the Soviet Union, though in the midst of a bitter Cold War rivalry, launch a major effort to cure other diseases like malaria.[75] As a historian later remarked, "An American was able to conduct an extensive polio vaccine trial in the Soviet Union at the height of the Cold War because the fear of polio was stronger than political differences."[76]

Even more significant than government-to-government health cooperation during the Cold War, though, were individual collaborations between scientists. These thrived across the Iron Curtain in spite of political tensions. In 1964, the then Communist government of Czechoslovakia reluctantly allowed an ebullient biochemist named Antonin Holy to take up a postdoctoral fellowship in what was then capitalist West Germany. Still-fresh memories of the Second World War, combined with anti-capitalist propaganda, conditioned the Czechs to view Germany as an enemy; yet they recognized the value of international scientific exchanges to boost their blossoming biochemical industry. Czech authorities, a historian of the period wrote, "disdained the way that West Germany would attract Czechoslovak scientists with money and research possibilities but they also realized that the knowledge gained in these exchanges was invaluable for their country's progress."[77] So scientists like Holy were allowed to cross the Iron Curtain—and in the process, saved a great many lives (more on the value of these international collaborations in Chapter 4).

While in the West, Holy developed several contacts with scientists in both Germany and Belgium. His work focused on phosphonates, a class of chemical compounds that, thanks to his Western connections, led to the creation of a whole new type of antiviral drugs. In a landmark 1986 paper in the journal *Nature*, Holy and his Belgian colleague, Erik De Clercq, described research showing that one type of phosphonates, known as acyclic nucleoside phosphonates, Holy's specialty, could help prevent viruses from reproducing. This quickly caught the attention of Western pharmaceutical companies, including Bristol-Meyers. Holy and De Clercq's collaboration led to the development of tenofovir, an antiviral drug that can be taken by mouth and has proven to be one of medicine's most important weapons in the fight against HIV/AIDS and other viral diseases. But this inspired partnership took place against a backdrop of high geopolitical drama. Bristol-Meyers executives had to persuade the FBI that Holy was not an espionage threat during his periodic visits to the company's headquarters in Connecticut.[78]

The world changed quite a bit in the decades after Holy crossed the border into West Germany in the mid-1960s. In the twenty-first century, China played much the same role that the Soviet Union once did in medicine and public health: an often reluctant, but still indispensable, partner to the West. Thanks to rapidly growing investment and the influence of Western methods and training, important medical discoveries were increasingly made by Chinese researchers. Despite Eisenhower's plea, the United States and the Soviet Union never managed to cure malaria. But a Chinese physician came much closer to doing so.

In 2015, the Nobel Prize in Medicine was for the first time awarded to a Chinese doctor, Tu Youyou (屠呦呦), for developing a highly effective anti-malaria drug that saved tens of thousands of lives.[79] Tu is nowhere near as famous outside China as Salk or Sabin—but her discovery underscores the importance of working with China's scientists and public health experts despite persistent political tensions. And while Sino-American health cooperation became increasingly prone to politicization, it had one noteworthy success that bears mention as an example of what can be accomplished when public health is put ahead of politics.

By 2015, the same year Tu won the Nobel, SARS had become a distant memory, but a new disease seized the headlines: Ebola. Officials in Washington, Beijing, and other capitals were reeling from the worst-ever outbreak of the mysterious, deadly Ebola virus, which began in late 2013 in Guinea before eventually spreading throughout West Africa. By late the following year, news reports were warning that it was only a matter of time before Ebola spread to Europe and America.

As with most previous medical outbreaks, the global response to Ebola was largely led by the US government's premier public health agency, the CDC. Since the mid-twentieth century, the CDC has served as a kind of real-life Dr. House for the planet as a whole. When physicians the world over think they have detected a new or emerging disease, one of their first calls is almost always to the CDC's headquarters in Atlanta. But this time, when the 2015 outbreak emerged, the CDC had an unlikely source of backup: China.[80]

Over the course of the Ebola outbreak, some two dozen CDC-trained Chinese epidemiologists were deployed to West Africa, greatly easing communication between Chinese and Western health experts. They spoke the same language, both literally—most communication was in English—and figuratively, following near-identical processes and protocols. Even more striking was the sight of elite People's Liberation Army units building clinics that were quickly occupied by US Army medics, and the use of US Air Force equipment to unload medical supplies sent by China to Liberia.[81] In all, according to Chinese sources, Beijing provided over $112 million in aid to West African countries and trained some 10,000 local medical workers.[82] Though significantly smaller in scale than the aid provided by the United States, it nonetheless represented an important contribution to containing the Ebola outbreak.

Sadly, though, the fight against Ebola looked to be the high-water mark for Sino-American public health cooperation. Increasingly, geopolitical rivalry between the two countries sharply limited the scope of collaboration. One particular stumbling block was US support for Taiwan. Democratic Taiwan was often regarded to have one of the world's best healthcare systems, and it had long sought to bring its expertise to bear in multilateral health bodies like the WHO. Washington encouraged Taiwan's health diplomacy efforts, but always over Beijing's strenuous objections. Taiwanese engagement in public health, or any other major international issue, was perceived to undermine the legitimacy of Beijing's claim to sovereignty over the island. In 2004, then US Health and Human Services Secretary Tommy Thompson shook hands with his Taiwanese counterpart, creating a diplomatic firestorm that halted bilateral health cooperation for half a year.[83] Sixteen years later, China's National Health Commission pouted that a 2020 visit to Taiwan by Thompson's successor Alex Azar, the highest-level visit to the island by an American official in decades, had "severely harmed Sino-American public health cooperation."[84]

Growing Sino-American geopolitical competition also spilled over into multilateral health cooperation initiatives. In 2016, shortly after the West African Ebola outbreak was successfully curbed, Washington and Beijing signed an agreement to jointly support the development of an Africa Centers for Disease Control, intended in part to prevent future epidemics and pandemics on the continent. In its first year of operation, the United States gave $14 million to the new organization. But when Beijing offered to build it a new, $80 million headquarters several years later, the Trump administration balked. "Out of nowhere the Chinese swoop in and want to build the Africa CDC headquarters," a US official complained to *The Financial Times* in early January 2020. "If the Chinese build the headquarters, the US will have nothing to do with Africa CDC."[85]

That Washington was concerned by the geopolitical implications of China's gift to the Africa CDC is hardly shocking. But tragically for public health, instead of competing with Beijing by upping its own contributions, the Trump administration largely abandoned US leadership in public health. Though the US CDC continued to support its African counterpart during the COVID-19 pandemic by seconding personnel, Beijing's efforts were considerably larger in scale, and much more visible. At the groundbreaking ceremony held in the midst of the pandemic for the Beijing-funded Africa CDC's headquarters building, a Chinese official proudly called it a "flagship project in China-Africa practical cooperation." The United States, meanwhile, continued its retreat from global public health engagement by moving in May 2020 to cut all funding for the WHO, despite its critical role in responding to the still-unfolding pandemic.[86]

The history of global public health cooperation shows that while it has always, and almost inevitably, been colored by geopolitics, it can still be effective when countries agree to work together on certain issues, like pandemic prevention, even while competing for influence in other realms. No matter how much Washington and Beijing disagree on manufacturing tariffs or military expansion, preventing the next major disease outbreak simply cannot be accomplished by one country alone.

The lingering lessons of SARS and COVID-19 show that a certain degree of public health cooperation is essential, not optional. In particular, no country can be allowed to suppress information on infectious disease outbreaks, or to withhold vaccines for the use of their own populations. But while the world must find new ways to hold nations responsible for meeting their global public health responsibilities, networks of nongovernmental researchers and public health workers are more important than ever.

The Threat of Public Health Protectionism and Vaccine Nationalism

The outside world first learned of the existence of SARS in early March 2003, when Chinese officials contacted the WHO to request help in identifying the still-mysterious disease. By then, though, it had been spreading within China for more than two months. Just two days after Beijing's message, the WHO reported SARS outbreaks in Vietnam and Hong Kong. Three days after that, on March 15, the WHO issued an unprecedented "emergency travel advisory" calling the new disease a "global health threat." China's Health Minister, Zhang Wenkang (张文康), publicly complained that the advisory was unnecessary because the disease was "under control."[87]

Several weeks later, however, a retired army surgeon, Jiang Yanyong (蒋彦永), emailed Chinese news outlets to warn that the state was deliberately understating the number of people infected in Beijing, far from the initial outbreak site in southern China. Finally, on April 16, the WHO announced that SARS was caused by a previously unknown coronavirus, a highly infectious family of viruses that can also cause the common cold.[88]

Following this initial period of confusion and concealment, Chinese and international authorities swung into action. Beijing, caught off-guard both by the initial outbreak and the international community's panicked response, sensed it would be judged harshly if it did not change course. Yanzhong Huang, one of the foremost scholars of China's health sector, told a US congressional commission that in the midst of SARS, "the Chinese leadership is facing the most severe social-political crisis since the 1989 Tiananmen crackdown."[89]

The Party's actions suggest Huang was right. Both Zhang and the mayor of Beijing were stripped from their positions in the Chinese Communist Party—the first time in modern Chinese history that senior officials had been removed for cause. Beijing soon lifted controls on media reporting of SARS and began sending daily updates to the WHO, an unprecedented burst of transparency for China's notoriously opaque health sector. US president George W. Bush, meanwhile, pledged aid to Chinese leader Hu Jintao, and dozens of US health officials were detailed to the WHO, many directly advising their Chinese counterparts on controlling the SARS outbreak.[90]

The first lesson of SARS was that attempts to suppress information on disease outbreaks cost time, money, and lives. Speaking a few months after the SARS outbreak receded, a US public health official confidently predicted that "China's leaders have realized that they have neglected basic public health and disease surveillance . . . I also believe that they were stung by the global condemnation they received for allowing this to happen and are eager to show the world that they won't let this happen again."[91]

Certainly, that was how it looked like for a while. As a major study later concluded, "Stung by the loss of face that this bad publicity produced, then-President Hu Jintao declared that the improvement of health systems would be a top priority for his government," and subsequently invested nearly $3 billion in public health and healthcare reforms, including a major expansion of health insurance coverage.[92]

But old habits die hard. Just six months after the SARS outbreak ended, Chinese officials were once again forced to admit they had concealed an outbreak of avian flu, again in southern China.[93] And 16 years after that, the mayor of Wuhan, where the COVID-19 outbreak was initially detected, was forced to apologize for minimizing the scale of the crisis—just as his counterparts had during SARS years before. To be sure, Beijing was considerably faster to share information on the COVID-19 pandemic than on SARS: it released the full SARS-CoV-2 genome in early January 2020, very shortly after the new virus was first identified.[94] Yet when, a full year later and as the pandemic continued to rage, a WHO team arrived in early 2021 to probe the origins of COVID-19, Chinese authorities imposed onerous restrictions on their movements, prompting the WHO's head to issue a rare rebuke of Beijing.[95]

One way to shortcut this persistent penchant for secrecy is to fund scientific efforts to detect and track the spread of viruses even before they enter human populations. And that is something that scientists are better equipped to do than health ministries. A successful Sino-American effort to find out exactly how SARS spread provides a good example. After years of diligent searching, a group of Chinese scientists, partially funded by grants from the US government, finally found a group of horseshoe bats living in an isolated cave in southwestern China with viral strains that matched the one that causes SARS. The work was excruciating, involving collection of tons of bat dung. Even then, no single bat was found to have the SARS virus. Instead, the researchers found 15 separate viral strains that in combination provided all the genetic material needed to produce the SARS virus. It was not certain exactly how these strains mixed and then jumped to infect human populations some 1,000 kilometers away.[96] But what the research did show is that it is critical to catalog viruses in known pandemic hotspots and create a library of potential pandemic threats. If scientific collaborations can accomplish this on a global scale, they might lessen the global public health community's reliance on states and governments to identify new diseases.

Supporting scientific networks can help spread critical public health data in other ways. During the initial spread of COVID-19, some Chinese physicians reached out directly to their colleagues in the West, providing some of the first reports of the outbreak.[97] In China, the phenomenon of "internet hospitals" (联网医院), which typically pair traditional brick-and-mortar facilities with dedicated online platforms for treatment and diagnosis, offered new opportunities to collaborate directly with physicians and public health practitioners overseas.[98] While Beijing is likely to remain skeptical of nongovernmental, and especially foreign, involvement in its health sector (more on the constraints on and opportunities for civil society in Chapter 3), and privacy concerns were likely to limit the exchange of specific data, direct virtual connections nonetheless promise to cut out the middle man when it comes to sharing medical observations and best practices.[99]

Detecting and preventing new pandemics is one global public health good; distributing vaccines to all nations is another. As a 2018 study concluded, "Preparation for new vaccines depends not only on domestic [research and development] investment but also on international collaboration,"[100] especially to test potential vaccines in different climactic and socioeconomic conditions. Unfortunately, this looks like yet another lesson from past pandemics the world has yet to fully absorb.

As China began developing what appeared to be an effective COVID-19 vaccine in mid-2020, it began to offer first dibs on its distribution to countries like Pakistan and the Philippines that had proven willing to follow Beijing's lead on political and foreign policy issues. The US Trump administration appeared to be even more patently self-serving, saying that it would share a vaccine with other countries only once its "own needs have been met."[101] Yet fundamental features of US- and Chinese-developed vaccines were in many ways complementary, with China's approach likely better suited to distribution in developing regions with sparse refrigeration and other infrastructure.[102] And, most critically, future pandemics simply cannot be averted if vaccines are distributed on geopolitical, rather than public health, grounds. Unvaccinated populations anywhere mean viruses remain a threat to people everywhere.

The greatest lesson of recent pandemics is that while public health will always be shaped by politics, it is both possible and essential for countries to compete and cooperate at the same time. In the aftermath of SARS, it was obvious to many that the outbreak was a sign of China's growing global integration and would not be the last to spread to the outside world. In May 2003, a US expert observed to a congressional commission that SARS was "a direct if unintended consequence of economic reform and integration into the global community." At the same hearing, a prominent US China-watcher echoed the belief that "the progression of the epidemic from Guangdong to Beijing, into the Chinese countryside, and across the world, clearly demonstrates the mainland's increasing economic and social openness, its mobility internally, and interdependence within the country itself, interdependence within the East Asia region, and across the planet. . . . We can hope that this will spark a greater degree of openness and accountability within the Chinese leadership."[103]

Such hopes went largely unrealized—even as public health cooperation has become more critical to the world at large. Openness and accountability are indeed essential, but using public health to push political and institutional reform in China proved to be a misguided strategy. Not only did it fail to meaningfully advance transparency, it also failed to prevent the spread of the COVID-19 pandemic. Going forward, public health cooperation must be focused relentlessly on the two essential public goods of disease surveillance and detection on one hand, and vaccination on the other. The first step toward the former is to strengthen multilateral bodies like the WHO and use them to build irresistible pressure on countries like China to share public health data more freely. To do, the United States and other Western countries must redouble their support of and engagement with the WHO.

They must also commit to strengthening vaccine access following the pandemic. There are several successful models to build on. The US-funded President's Emergency Plan for AIDS Relief, which provides support for research, prevention, and treatment in the poorest countries, is widely regarded as one of the most successful single healthcare interventions in history and offered a promising model for expanding access to vaccines, including to prevent future pandemics. The former Global Alliance for Vaccines and Immunizations, now known by its acronym, Gavi, offers a similarly successful model that buys drugs in bulk and uses the economies of scale to distribute them cheaply throughout the developing world. Its Covax initiative, a partnership with the WHO, became the most prominent international COVID-19 vaccine distribution initiative. Just as important, Gavi is a public-private partnership—and given the politics that are inherent to public health, such nongovernmental channels offer some of the best hope for expanding health cooperation in the years ahead.[104] It is also notable that even as the Trump administration largely abandoned US support to the Africa CDC, the nongovernmental, US-based Rockefeller Foundation awarded the Africa CDC a $12 million grant to expand COVID-19 testing and contract tracing across the African continent.[105] Even when intergovernmental health cooperation is constrained by geopolitical competition, it can still thrive below the nation-state level.

Public health in general, and pandemic prevention in particular, might be the single best example of how closely China and the rest of the world are bound together when it comes to global public goods. But it is not the only one. Environmental challenges, especially climate and biodiversity protection, involve even greater difficult political and geopolitical issues than in public health—yet are just as dependent on Beijing to fully tackle.

3

The Unlikely Environmentalist

China and the Race to Save the Planet

As the world's largest emitter, China became essential to any effort to tackle global climate change in the twenty-first century. China's massive consumer market for animal products, seafood, and other natural resources meanwhile meant that Chinese consumer preferences became a decisive influence on the fate of the world's biodiversity. Moreover, China's emergence as the largest financier of infrastructure projects worldwide meant that dams, roads, and ports designed in Beijing and Guangzhou began shaping local environments from Sri Lanka to the Argentine pampas. China's leaders, aware of the implications, adopted a range of environmental policies that were, in some ways, the most ambitious in the world. But reality did not always match these sky-high sustainable ambitions, and authoritarian and protectionist motives drove much of Beijing's rush to go green. China's approach to environmental protection shows that competition between countries might play just as big a role in saving the planet as cooperation.

The Eco-Veto Player: China as the World's Most Important Environmental Actor

For a few days in late 2009, it looked like Denmark might save the world. By the time I and other delegates to the annual United Nations–sponsored climate change conferences gathered in the frigid Danish capital of Copenhagen in December of that year, hope appeared to be on the horizon for limiting the impact of global warming. Barack Obama had recently been elected president of the United States, based in part on a promise to finally tackle climate change. The European Union, meanwhile, was more committed than ever to reach a deal to replace the Kyoto Protocol, the first phase of which was due to expire in 2012. In an earlier era, that meeting of the minds probably would have made negotiations a breeze.

China's Next Act. Scott M. Moore, Oxford University Press. © Oxford University Press 2022.
DOI: 10.1093/oso/9780197603994.003.0004

But by the early 2000s, it had become clear there was no way out of the climate crisis without a newer key player: China. In 2006, it overtook the United States as the world's largest emitter of carbon dioxide. China had been an active participant in international climate negotiations since the early 1990s, but its record was not entirely encouraging. Although Beijing took climate change seriously, it consistently opposed legally binding climate commitments, even for developed countries, and resisted any attempt to impose emissions cuts on developing economies. In 2007, though, China became the first developing country to put forward a comprehensive climate and energy policy, the National Climate Change Program, which included efforts to promote non-fossil energy and afforestation.[1] These developments left one big unanswered question as the international community convened in Copenhagen: What would China do?

As it turned out, by the time China's leaders gathered inside the cavern-like Copenhagen conference center, they were in little mood for compromise. A year before, the New York– and London-led world financial system had come within a hair's breadth of collapsing, and Chinese leaders were even more loath than usual to be lectured by their Western counterparts, especially since rich countries remained averse to paying developing countries like China to adopt cleaner technologies. Within days, the entire Copenhagen conference came to a standstill. And while there were several differences between China and the industrialized countries led by the European Union and the United States, a major reason for the breakdown was a simple point of national pride: China's leaders saw a US demand that its emissions reductions be subject to external monitoring and verification as insulting.[2] So insulting, in fact, that in the end not only did Beijing refuse to support an agreement to reduce emissions; it also refused to endorse developed countries announcing their *own* climate commitments.[3]

China's leaders, in short, had chosen the Copenhagen conference to throw their weight around. The result was a massive disappointment for the world's attempts to prevent dangerous climate change. China did agree to take concrete steps to reduce its contribution to climate change even in the absence of foreign funding, something it had previously refused to do. But without Beijing's full buy-in, the best the West could manage was the timid Copenhagen Accord, which avoided the concrete emissions reductions target many environmentalists had expected and spoke instead only of peaking global emissions "as soon as possible."

At first, the United States appeared to take most of the blame for the Copenhagen conference's collapse. But it did not take long for China's central role to become clear, and extensively criticized. In a widely cited article in Britain's *Guardian* newspaper, a conference delegate wrote that "I am certain that had the Chinese not been in the room, we would have left Copenhagen with a deal that had environmentalists popping champagne corks in every corner of the world."[4] Whether or not he was right, Copenhagen showed the world something important: in the twenty-first century, there are no global deals on public goods without China. Copenhagen made clear that China had become the world's environmental veto player—a phrase political scientists use to describe an actor whose agreement or action is needed for something to happen, and therefore can stop it.[5]

In the years after Copenhagen, China only became more central to solving global climate change. Unfortunately, by the 2020s it was still not clear that Beijing was willing to do so on terms the rest of the world could fully endorse. China displayed a disconcerting tendency to use environmental policy to bolster its authoritarianism and geopolitical influence, and a determination to crack down on environmentally destructive activity at home while exporting more of it abroad. At the same time, China became the world's most important country when it came to combating wildlife trafficking, overfishing, air pollution, and even plastic waste. And while climate change was understandably the focus when it came to China and the environment, these other areas held generally better prospects for true cooperation between China and other countries.

China's Growing Global Eco-Footprint

What distinguishes China as the world's eco-veto player is that by the early 2000s it had become both the single biggest source of many environmental pollutants within its borders, as well as the biggest influence on natural resource use worldwide. This unique dual role stemmed from two features of China's rise: the size of its consumer market, which in 2019 surpassed that of the United States to become the world's largest; and its concentration of resource- and pollution-intensive manufacturing industries. According to United Nations figures, manufacturing accounted for almost one-third of China's total economic output in 2015, one of the highest percentages in the world and more than double that of the United States.[6]

China's economy, moreover, featured a large concentration of heavy industries like metallurgy, chemicals, and steel manufacturing, generating high demand for energy and other resource inputs. China became by a large margin the biggest producer of highly polluting coal- and carbon-intensive industrial goods like concrete and steel.[7] Unsurprisingly, given this concentration of heavy industry, China regularly topped world rankings not only for carbon dioxide emissions but also other pollutants like nitrous oxide and wastewater.[8] Though it steadily grew more efficient, China's heavy industrial sector was marked by high resource consumption, low productivity, and high pollutant emissions in comparison to its counterparts elsewhere.[9] These pollutant volumes were so large that, thanks to prevailing winds, China contributed up to 25% of some air pollution in areas as far away as California.[10]

Given its status as the world's largest exporter, a substantial portion of China's emissions and resource use was embedded in the production of goods destined for other countries. By one estimate, for example, the carbon emissions associated with China's exports accounted for about 15% of its 2017 total of 9.84 billion tons.[11] Similarly, exports accounted for about 10% of China's total water footprint, the largest in the world, placing serious stress on China's own water resources.[12]

Despite its regional and global environmental impact, though, China's people bore the brunt of the resulting environmental health crisis.[13] Heavy metal pollutants from industry were estimated to have contaminated up to one-fifth of China's farmland, and scores of towns and villages across China became effectively poisoned by toxic electronic waste, much of it imported from the developed world.[14]

The scale of this environmental devastation was reflected in China's poor performance on cross-national measures of environmental quality and protection. In the 2020 Yale Environmental Performance Index (EPI), China ranked 120th in the world and 12th in the Asia-Pacific region with scores that trailed the world average on most metrics, though it performed relatively well in areas like carbon intensity and sulfur dioxide emissions (see Table 3.1). Notably, China's EPI ranking also trailed that of countries like Malawi, Ethiopia, and Jordan, despite China's far larger gross domestic product (GDP), typically the strongest predictor of environmental performance.[15]

Not surprisingly, Beijing's most ambitious environmental efforts in response to these challenges focused more at home than abroad. It adopted some of the most stringent air and water pollution regulations in the world,

Table 3.1 China's Environmental Performance in Regional and Global Context (2020 Data)

Metric	RRank	EEPI Score	10-Year Change	Regional Rank	Regional Average
Air quality	137	27.1	6.7	21	39
Sanitation and drinking water	54	59.4	4.6	6	46.2
Heavy metals	129	37.6	6.5	18	55.4
Waste management	66	51.8	—	5	32.7
Biodiversity and habitat	172	19	−0.8	22	44.9
Ecosystem services	90	34.3	−0.2	9	33.8
Fisheries	31	18	1.1	12	28.6
Climate change	103	46.3	24.5	10	42.1
Pollution emissions	91	58.6	12.3	10	56.1
Agriculture	55	49.5	2.7	10	35.9
Water resources	67	9.4	—	5	11.9

Source: Yale Center for Environmental Law and Policy 2020.

and in 2012, China instituted a cap on total national water use, something no other country of its size has tried.[16] In combination, these policies gave early twenty-first-century China a credible claim to have done more to protect the planet than any other developing country at a comparable stage of development.[17] But even as Beijing began tackling its domestic environmental crises, China's ecological footprint expanded dramatically abroad, shifting much of the burden of China's pollution and resource use onto other countries.

The decidedly unsexy issue of plastic waste provided a good example of how China's efforts to clean up its act at home had unintended, and sometimes unfortunate, environmental impacts abroad. By the mid-2010s, China imported 70% of all the world's recycled plastic waste. Unfortunately, China lacked the necessary facilities to actually give old plastic a new lease on life, and less than 10% was actually recycled, with most of the rest simply dumped, creating a major environmental hazard of its own.[18] China accounted for about one-third of "mismanaged" plastic waste worldwide, meaning it was handled in a way that makes it likely it could end up washing into the ocean and contaminating marine food chains.[19] In an attempt to clean up its waste management sector, China in 2018 dramatically tightened restrictions on the import of plastic waste. But these restrictions had a perverse effect abroad, causing other countries to divert much of the waste previously exported to

China to poorer developing countries, where waste management practices were typically even worse.[20]

The sheer size of the Chinese economy by the early 2000s meant it not only tilted global pollution totals, but also became the single most important driver in natural resource extraction worldwide. The aggregate impact was staggering. Global demand for timber, for example, almost doubled from 250 to 450 million cubic meters over just 10 years, from 2006 to 2016, chiefly because of growth in demand from China. This rapacious demand placed severe strains on local environments. According to a 2013 estimate, almost one-sixth of China's timber imports were estimated to be illegal, meaning they were most likely derived from unsustainable forestry practices, fragile ecosystems, or both.[21] Because of its voracious demand for crops like wheat and soybeans for human and animal consumption, meanwhile, exports to China also accounted for a substantial portion of total water use in countries like Brazil.[22] In many places, meanwhile, China's overseas development projects exacerbated pressure on already scarce local resources. During a December 2018 conference, for example, a Chinese diplomat in the Pakistani city of Karachi complained that the country's chronic water shortages were holding up the massive Gwadar port project, a poster child for the entire Belt and Road Initiative (BRI; 一带一路).[23]

China's impact on the planet, though, was at least as great on living natural resources. The highways, hydropower dams, and other large infrastructure projects planned under the BRI were decidedly bad for biodiversity. A 2020 study, for example, estimated that BRI projects might impact up to 370,000 square kilometers of critical habitat.[24] China also became the world's largest market for animal products, including ivory from elephant tusks, shark fins, and tiger parts.[25] In large part, Chinese consumers' fondness for animal products stemmed from their use in traditional Chinese medicine (TCM), which has been widely practiced for centuries—so much so, in fact, that the World Health Organization estimated it to be a $60 billion industry.[26] TCM's popularity proved to be bad news for the planet's biodiversity, because many TCM remedies call for exotic animal-based ingredients. TCM was behind the industrial-scale harvesting of endangered animals like the pangolin, whose scales are used in medicines. The scale of this illegal trade could be staggering: 14,000 pangolins were seized by Hong Kong authorities in the first quarter of 2019 alone.[27]

Growing incomes also meant that China became the world's most enthusiastic customer for aquatic products of all kinds, as consumer demand for wild-caught fish and other ocean-dwelling creatures increased rapidly. Unfortunately, many of these products came from species that are either threatened, endangered, or unsustainably fished, including sharks and reef fish.[28] In addition to being the world's largest seafood consumer, China also became the biggest seafood exporter, packaging and reprocessing most of the frozen seafood that ends up in Western consumer markets. This makes it a key player in efforts to trace and label seafood to crack down on illegal, unreported, and unregulated fishing.[29]

China's importance to marine conservation increased further as its massive fishing fleet of over 700,000 vessels began to spend more and more time overseas, accounting for over half of all industrial fishing in international waters.[30] And while China adopted more stringent domestic fishing regulations in the late 2010s, its distant-water fleet also began fishing poorly regulated foreign waters with greater intensity. Data from the Fujian provincial fisheries bureau, where a good portion of China's distant-water fishing fleet is based, indicated for example that while the catch from domestic waters fell by over 5% in the first half of 2020, in part because of stricter fishing regulations, total output rose by over 25%, suggesting that the difference was made up by fishing abroad.[31] Unfortunately, even as attention shifted back to global environmental challenges like climate change after the COVID-19 pandemic, the pattern of adopting more stringent domestic environmental policies while exporting more environmental harm abroad looked set to continue.

China and the World's Continuing Climate Crisis

The growing discrepancy between China's efforts to protect its environment at home while its footprint grew abroad was even starker with respect to climate change. After Copenhagen, China's leaders changed their tune, publicly supporting climate negotiations and expanding discussions with other major emitters, most notably the United States.[32] Strikingly, this change in tone occurred even as relations with Washington deteriorated. In the 2010s, even as the diplomatic temperature rose over issues like the South China Sea and cybertheft, China and the United States dramatically expanded diplomatic and technical cooperation on climate change. The contrast between climate change and other issues was so great that US officials began referring to it as the "bright spot" in Sino-American relations. Both sides were eager to keep it shining. In 2014, China's president,

Xi Jinping, marked a visit to the United States by pledging to stop increasing carbon emissions before the year 2030. In exchange, US President Barack Obama committed the United States to decreasing its emissions by almost one-fifth within a few years.[33]

This joint announcement helped break the logjam that had long prevented progress on reducing emissions: China would not commit to reducing its emissions unless rich countries bore most of the burden, while US politicians balked at taking steps to slash emissions while China's continued to grow. Most notable of all, though, this climate cooperation unfolded not just despite geopolitical competition in other areas, but arguably because of it. Both sides, having grown reliant on climate change to show their constituents they could work together on at least one major issue, embraced the image of a tandem, leading the world's response to the climate crisis.

This breakthrough appeared to set the stage for major progress when world leaders gathered in 2015 for yet another global climate conference, this time in Paris, which I attended as part of the US delegation. In a contrast to Copenhagen's cavern-like conference hall, the Paris sessions were held in high, light-filled rooms, most of them named after European rivers—Seine, Loire, Rhine. But despite the Eurocentric names, the really important meetings were the near-daily dialogues between the US climate envoy, Todd Stern, and his Chinese counterpart, Xie Zhenhua (谢振华), whose first name, fittingly enough, roughly translates as "rouse the nation." Xie's rapport with his US counterpart was genuine: at one point, Xie joked that his wife was growing jealous because he was spending so much time with Stern. Their sessions lasted so long that I ran out of notebook pages and took to hauling in my heavy, government-issued laptop to every meeting. By the time the Paris conference ended on December 12, it looked like China had given up its eco-veto and had decided instead to give the planet a giant Christmas present in the form of the first truly meaningful global climate agreement. "We have a deal," I excitedly emailed my counterparts back in Washington, "And it's a good one!"

Over the next few years, though, my confidence was only partly borne out. Beijing ceased being a spoiler in multilateral climate negotiations and lived up to its Paris pledges to slow the growth of its emissions and dramatically expand renewable energy. In less than two decades, it built nearly three times as much wind, solar, and hydropower generation capacity as the United States.[34] But the world's emissions kept growing, implying a degree of warming that far exceeded the goals set in Paris.[35] The United States and European countries remained responsible for most of all human-related emissions since the start of the Industrial Revolution, but China accounted for over a quarter of all the carbon cast into the atmosphere in the first two decades of the twenty-first century.[36] In short, it became clear that China's contributions to fighting climate change, while critical, would not be enough to save the planet from overheating.

Beijing's efforts to reduce its emissions in the early twenty-first century were based primarily on meeting the growing power demand through building additional nuclear, hydropower, wind, and solar energy generation capacity. The fruits of this investment were substantial, but far less than what was required to avert climate disaster. In 2016, the switch to cleaner-than-coal alternatives helped China avoid, by one estimate, about 1.5 million metric tons of additional carbon emissions—a significant quantity, but not enough to make a dent in total global emissions. Moreover, the lion's share of China's avoided emissions came from low-carbon but ecologically destructive hydropower, rather than clean, green wind and solar.[37] China's renewable power revolution itself came with plenty of caveats: much of the wind and solar that was built was either not fully connected to the energy grid or lacked the storage capacity to replace fossil fuels for baseload power generation.[38] Worst of all, after falling for several years, China's coal consumption started growing again in 2017, dashing hopes for an early shift to phasing out the largest source of fossil fuel emissions.[39]

Against this dark background, President and General Secretary Xi Jinping (习近平) set environmentalists' hearts aflutter at the 2020 UN General Assembly, where he pledged to make China carbon-neutral by 2060. Doing so would require phasing out most fossil fuels in favor of renewables and deploying carbon capture technology at large scales—and, if realized, would probably sharply reduce the cost of clean technology.[40] Unfortunately, it was far from clear that this goal could be achieved, and in the aftermath of the COVID-19 pandemic, China showed serious difficulty meeting far more modest goals. Just a few months before Xi's eye-catching pledge, Beijing admitted that China would fall short of meeting its target of increasing energy efficiency by 3%, a key climate goal. Meanwhile, Premier Li Keqiang (李克强) soberly announced that the government would prioritize jobs growth over the coming year and would not set a specific energy efficiency improvement target for the first time since 2014. Worryingly, Beijing approved construction of more coal-fired power plants than in the previous two years combined as part of its post-pandemic recovery efforts.[41] And while China pledged to decrease its reliance on coal in the 2020s, the difficulties were daunting. A senior Chinese climate official confided that "for the moment we don't have another choice" but to rely on coal for electricity.[42]

Nor was China's lingering dependence on fossil energy confined within its own borders. No less than one-quarter of all coal plants under construction outside China were financed at least in part by Chinese entities.[43] Fossil fuel–based projects accounted for a large portion of investments made under Beijing's sprawling, trillion-dollar BRI (see Figure 3.1). Approximately one-third of total Chinese financing for overseas energy projects, or some US$44 billion, was devoted to coal-based projects, followed by some US$31 billion in oil, US$27 billion in gas, and US$13 billion in hydropower. By comparison, investment in wind and solar power projects accounted for less than US$2 billion each.[44] China's leaders began promising to make the Belt and Road more sustainable as criticism mounted in the late 2010s. In September 2021, a year after issuing his landmark decarbonization pledge, Xi announced that China would no longer build new coal-fired power plants abroad—a hugely important step toward reducing China's contribution to climate change at home as well as abroad. Nonetheless, China's overseas energy investments remained heavily concentrated on fossil fuels and looked set to continue to do so for the foreseeable future.[45]

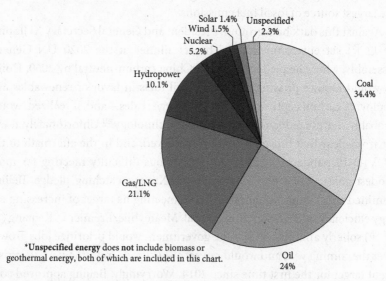

*Unspecified energy does not include biomass or geothermal energy, both of which are included in this chart.

Figure 3.1. Belt and Road energy projects by energy source, 2018.
Source: Mangi and Murtaugh 2018.

At the same time, in the late 2010s, cooperation on climate change and environmental issues, the onetime bright spot in Sino-American relations, was largely replaced by growing geopolitical competition. The Trump administration withdrew from the Paris Agreement and let wither the many cooperative programs that had sustained bilateral relations on climate. As part of a broader campaign to counter growing Chinese influence abroad, Washington began also calling out Beijing's dubious green credentials. As a State Department fact sheet undiplomatically declared, "The PRC's environmental record is abysmal. . . . Beijing threatens the world's economy and public health by unsustainably exploiting natural resources and exporting its reckless disregard for the environment via BRI."[46] Though unconstructive, such statements reflect an inconvenient truth. While China has arguably attempted more than any other country at a comparable stage of development to protect the environment, its efforts have so far fallen short of what is needed to avert environmental damage, especially beyond its borders. Just as concerning, China's motives for going green differ sharply from those of most Western countries, making it more likely than ever that tackling the world's environmental crises will have to depend less on cooperation with China than on competition.

Authoritarian Environmentalism: Protecting the Planet on China's Terms

The opening ceremony of the 2008 Olympic Games in Beijing was one of the defining scenes of the twenty-first century. Two billion people—one-third of the world's population—tuned in to see thousands of perfectly synchronized drummers deafen the vast, hyper-modern Bird's Nest stadium, sited due north of the Forbidden City.[47] The clamor heralded far more than just another pageant of record-setting sprints and jaw-dropping gymnastics. It also announced that, after two centuries of comparative marginalization, China had returned to center stage.

But while the 2008 Olympics were designed to send a message to the world at large, the lesser-known Shanghai World Expo that occurred two years later sent an even clearer message to the Chinese people about the future envisioned for them by the Chinese Communist Party. Intended to give Shanghai, China's second city, a consolation prize for having missed out on hosting the Olympics, the Expo sprawled across a former factory site crammed with futuristic, wildly impractical buildings known as pavilions, each sponsored by a different country. Most were little more than glorified advertisements for their respective country's wares, from Brazilian soybeans to German machine parts. But the hulking Chinese pavilion—by far the largest, it resembled a kind of upside-down Great Pyramid—did not sell any goods at all. Instead, it sold a story to the Chinese people and a handful of curious foreigners, myself included. In Shanghai to attend a conference, I decided to see what all the fuss was about.

After snaking through lines that put Disneyworld to shame, visitors— nearly all of them Chinese—were treated to a stirring, propaganda-laced tour through Chinese history. The Communist Party, full-screen videos proclaimed, had rescued a proud civilization from centuries of disunity and humiliation at the hands of foreign powers. I must admit, it was gripping, if grossly distorted. But it was the final exhibit, representing China's future, that really caught my eye. The Chinese people, giant screens proclaimed, could look forward not only to a prosperous and peaceful future, but a green one as well. The Chinese Communist Party, the screens promised, was building a "clean and low-carbon society."[48]

One could be forgiven for being surprised that China's leaders chose to focus more on carbon than consumer goods at its exuberant World Expo. But this seeming contradiction goes to the heart of one of the most important things to understand about China in the twenty-first century: going green is a critical part of the Party's strategy both to sustain its rule and to power economic growth in the decades ahead. And as a result, Beijing has concocted a distinctly authoritarian approach to environmental protection, driven in part by fear of developments in places like the sleepy southern Chinese town of Wukan.

Environmental Protest and the Pressure to Protect the Planet

Before 2011, few people had any reason to hear of Wukan (乌坎), an obscure fishing village in Guangdong Province, some 120 kilometers east of Hong Kong. But that December, Wukan witnessed something close to a revolution—so momentous, in fact, that under slightly different circumstances it might have become a Chinese version of Lexington, Massachusetts, the scene of a shot heard round the world.

Like many other villages across China, Wukan fell victim to a scam whereby corrupt officials would seize farmland to build houses and factories, offering the equivalent of pennies in return while lining their pockets with massive profits. But unlike most victims of such land-grabbing, Wukan's villagers fought back in what became known as the Wukan Incident (乌坎 事件). The revolt began with villagers ransacking the local Communist Party office; afterward, they strung banners around town demanding that officials "Return our land; return our livelihood."[49] Provincial Party officials, desperate to contain the chaos, agreed to meet with a delegation of elected village representatives. But soon afterward, one of the representatives died in police custody, allegedly from torture-related injuries. The people of Wukan responded by setting up roadblocks on main roads and hurling homemade weapons against police who tried to approach the town.[50]

For several days, it looked like the Communist Party's authority in Guangdong Province might be seriously called into question. The underlying source of the Wukan villagers' grievance, the seizure of farmland by corrupt officials, afflicted many towns and villages in Guangdong Province and the country as a whole. The situation was defused only when the provincial Party Secretary, Wang Yang (汪洋), who went on to become one of China's highest-ranking officials, offered villagers an exceedingly rare deal: they could choose their own leaders in a local election. The locals responded, in time-worn democratic fashion, by tossing out the incumbent village chief, who had been appointed by the local Communist Party, in favor of one of the protest leaders.[51]

This emergency experiment in democracy underscored the potential for spontaneous protests to challenge Party rule. The Wukan Incident also revealed to China's leaders the potential for an even more widespread source of local grievance, pollution, to produce mass discontent. A few months after the Wukan protests, citizens of another Guangdong town, citing the "good model" demonstrated by Wukan, gathered to protest construction of a coal-fired power plant, which they feared would pollute the skies and soil.[52] The following year, in 2012, thousands of people, many of them middle-class, gathered in the small Sichuan city of Shifang (什邡) to protest a proposed copper plant, carrying banners with slogans like, "Protect Shifang's environment and give back my beautiful home." The protests were violently dispersed by police, injuring dozens.[53] Similar protests wracked China consistently in the years that followed. In the summer of 2019, for example, thousands of residents of the central city of Yangluo (阳逻) rallied to demand that officials stop construction of a planned waste incineration plant and "Return us the green mountains and clear waters"—repeating a phrase that Xi Jinping had used to signal his commitment to protecting the environment.[54]

For any authoritarian regime, such scenes are disconcerting. But to the Chinese Communist Party, they are downright terrifying, because large-scale protests against environmental pollution played a key role in toppling dictatorships in neighboring South Korea and Taiwan. Environmentally related incidents accounted for about one-quarter of all protest activity in South Korea in the two decades before the fall of the country's authoritarian government, and more than half of all protest activity in Taiwan leading to the fall of its military dictatorship over roughly the same time frame.[55] Given this history, it surely raised the hair on Beijing officials' heads to discover that, according to a Chinese Academy of Social Sciences study (中国社会科学院), approximately half of all "mass incidents" involving 10,000 or more people from 2003 to 2013 across China were stoked by environmental pollution.[56] The number of environmentally related complaints and petitions received by the central government, meanwhile, increased from 1.05 million to 1.77 million in just the four-year period from 2011 to 2015.[57]

This fear that environmental protest might unfold in China as it did in South Korea and Taiwan persuaded China's top leaders that if they wished to stay in power, they would be well-advised to provide environmental goods like clean air and water along with economic growth.[58] Opinion research, though dubious in authoritarian China, suggested that the Chinese people increasingly expected the state to enhance social as well as economic well-being,[59] and in many cases the Party looked to be bending over backward to convince the populace of its commitment to continued improvement in quality of life.[60] This fear often found its way into the statements of Chinese officials. In late 2020, for example, the vice minister of Ecology and Environment confided that "the quality of the ecological environment remains far from people's expectations for a better life."[61] Many ordinary Chinese appeared to agree. As Mr. Duan, cited in Chapter 1 as representative of China's growing middle classes, said, "The Chinese economy has been a big achievement but now we have to focus on Chinese culture and a better education and better environment."[62]

That belief underpins a distinctive approach to environmental issues, known as authoritarian environmentalism, that differs sharply from a more liberal idea of what it means to be green in places like the United States and Europe. The story of environmentalism in the West is one of people power, grassroots activism, and subversive ideas. While causes like preserving wilderness and controlling water pollution were long-standing and often elite concerns in countries like Britain, Germany, and the United States from the late nineteenth century on, modern environmental policy frameworks, with their emphasis on strict pollution regulations, environmental impact assessments, and the notion that the natural environment itself possesses certain legal rights, are principally an outgrowth of the popular environmentalism of the postwar period. Think Rachel Carson, Greenpeace, and Earth Day. Their activism put pressure on political leaders to pass stringent environmental laws, like the US Clean Air and Endangered Species Acts, giving rise to the cleaner skies, streams, and preserved spaces that citizens of most developed countries came to enjoy. But along with these environmental goods, Western environmentalism emphasized democratic public participation and, frequently, common cause with related movements like feminism and racial justice.[63]

This model of environmentalism is not one that China's leaders are eager to copy. Sociologists often refer to environmentalism as a leading example of what are known as "new social movements." These are distinguished from older causes like labor rights by their appeal to the middle as well as working classes; their demand for radical, systemic changes to political, economic, and social systems; and, perhaps most importantly, their lack of an explicit relationship with economic or class interests in favor of "postmaterialist" values.[64]

For China's ruling Communist Party, this is effectively a toxic brew. Not only does popular environmentalism often demand radical change and threaten to mobilize large numbers of people, but its very existence conflicts with a key tenet of the Party's official ideology. In Marxism, *everything* is supposed to be class-based. Strictly speaking, mass, popular grassroots movements without reference to class struggle should not exist.[65] Given this conceptual as well as practical challenge to their rule, it is no surprise that China's leaders take a dim view of Western-style popular environmentalism.

Instead, Beijing developed its own approach to environmental issues that relies primarily on state regulation, control, and co-option rather than popular pressure. In the best tradition of central planning, this approach emphasizes an elaborate target-setting process that makes local officials responsible for meeting certain environmental quality metrics in their individual jurisdictions. China's "Three Red Lines" (三条红线) water policy, for example, sets supposedly uncompromising limits on total water withdrawals, pollutant levels, and water use efficiency at the provincial, municipal, county, and sometimes even more local levels.[66] Compliance with these targets is enforced in several ways, most effectively by the *kaohe* (考核) cadre evaluation system, essentially a report card issued to local officials showing how well they perform against predetermined targets.[67] Those who stack up well are promoted, while those who fail to do so languish in a kind of local-official limbo. This hierarchical, top-down process of environmental regulation is in many ways the opposite of the grassroots, popular environmentalism of the West.[68]

Far from being an outgrowth of popular, subversive social movements, environmental policy in China became part of a broader strategy to bolster the legitimacy of the Communist Party, especially for the benefit of the urban middle classes. One example was the increasing use of eco-friendly amenities like parks, running trails, and bike paths as sites for Party propaganda. On a visit to Kunshan, one of China's wealthiest small cities, my morning run through a local park unexpectedly produced a Party history lesson—the running trail was marked by stations describing the evolution of the Party and its political philosophy. A few months later, I went looking for a famous statue of Deng sited in a park in the heart of Shenzhen, only to find a billboard outlining the "12 principles of socialism."

More insidiously, sustainability became a veneer for repressive policies against China's minorities, such as the nomadic herders who were forced into sedentary (and more easily surveilled) lifestyles in the name of creating new national parks.[69] In Tibet, the need to respond to climate change was cited during a high-profile 2020 conference as a reason to redouble efforts to replace indigenous culture with a Han-dominated one.[70] Such broad subordination of environmental to state goals suppresses civil and political rights more broadly—a reason that the political scientists Yifei Li and Judith Shapiro preferred the term "environmental authoritarianism" to authoritarian environmentalism when it comes to China.[71]

This pernicious relationship is further illustrated by the extent to which China's authoritarian environmentalism limits the participation of civil society and nongovernmental organizations (NGOs). China's environmental civil society sector was large and vibrant in the early decades of the twenty-first century, with at least 7,000 organizations registered in 2013.[72] Unlike in the West, however, the sector included large "government-organized" NGOs like the China Environmental Protection Federation (中华环境保护基金会) that are directly affiliated with and funded by the state.[73]

Moreover, while Western environmental NGOs like Greenpeace or the Natural Resources Defense Council often seek policy change by publicly differing with existing policy, Chinese-style authoritarian environmentalism instead co-opts civil society and environmental NGOs, employing them to fill in gaps in environmental enforcement capacity, raise awareness among the public, and serve as a source of policy advice.[74] International environmental NGOs play an important role in providing input on China's air pollution, climate, and energy policies—but have little choice but to avoid direct challenges to state policy.[75]

Yet while Beijing does its best to co-opt Chinese environmentalism and excise it of the subversive qualities that distinguish its Western equivalent, the nongovernmental sector still plays an important role in China's environmental policy. Informal, but widely understood, limits on "permissible" NGO activity prevent meaningful opposition to the central state. Nonetheless, resourceful NGOs can and do find ways of circumventing official control, and opposition to *local* officials is often tolerated as a means of diffusing public discontent. When neighbors of a nearby chemical plant formed a group to complain about heavy air pollution in the east China city of Hangzhou (杭州), for example, local officials initiated a dialogue with the plant operators, encouraging the residents to make demands and the operators to respond.[76] Such examples highlight a fundamental tension in twenty-first-century China's environmental policy: it is firmly controlled by the state, yet still responsive to some popular demands.

Profits and Propaganda: China's Environmental Policy in Practice

The Hangzhou example serves to illustrate another aspect of China's authoritarian environmentalism: for all its problematic features, it is not entirely without its attractions. In the face of complex, seemingly intractable environmental challenges like climate change, it proved tempting, both among Chinese and foreign observers, to imagine that authoritarian regimes might be able to enact large-scale, transformational eco-reforms without regard to the special-interest opposition that has impeded change in countries like the United States or India. China's authoritarian model, which relies not only on political centralization but also broad state control of the economy, seemed to many commentators especially conducive to marshaling resources and compelling the cooperation of the public and private sector in the service of environmental protection.

Seemingly bolstering this theory, in the early twenty-first century Beijing embarked on a vast industrial restructuring, replacing outdated and inefficient, energy-intensive industrial equipment with cleaner, more modern technology. Small-scale coal and industrial plants were replaced with larger, more efficient ones—a dramatic illustration of the state's ability to quickly transform the economy through top-down policy action.[77] Beijing also deployed the hand of the state to create environmental markets at unparalleled scale, establishing the world's biggest markets for carbon and water rights trading. Where environmental issues were made a top priority, as with air pollution, the concentration of the state's coercive resources produced remarkable results. After Beijing declared a "war on pollution" in 2014, for example, air quality in major cities improved by between 21% and 42%.[78]

But despite these successes, China's top-down, target-driven system produced uneven results for its environment overall. The "campaign" approach to environmental protection frequently produced short-term gains built on extreme, unsustainable measures like the forced shuttering of highly polluting factories.[79] Local officials, responsible for meeting targets not only for environmental quality but also economic performance, social stability, and a host of other matters, frequently found ways to cook the numbers, pass the buck, or otherwise subordinate environmental policy to other priorities.[80]

At the end of the day, officials' top priority usually proved to be economic growth. China's post-reform development model relied heavily on close relationships between local officials, entrepreneurs, and industrialists. These networks helped build powerful, export-oriented industrial clusters, but they also discouraged strict enforcement of environmental regulations.[81] This contradiction began to ease in the 2010s as local economies grew richer, more diversified, and more demanding of cleaner air, water, and soil. In 2013, meanwhile, Beijing declared that GDP growth would no longer be the most important factor in evaluating local officials.[82] But old habits die hard, and the push to boost profits and power growth remained a central influence on China's environmental policy in the third decade of the twenty-first century, often to its detriment.

At the same time, and as the "low carbon society" vision laid out at the 2010 Shanghai Expo shows, China's leaders view clean technology as an opportunity to combine environmental protection with profit.[83] Beginning in the middle of the first decade of the twenty-first century, senior officials became convinced that technologies like solar power and electric vehicles would be in high demand in the future—and if Chinese firms could supply them, would help China transition from workshop of the world to a higher-value-added, higher-income economic model. One senior official, for example, declared himself "fairly confident that climate change and environmental protection will become a powerful new driver of the economy."[84] Accordingly, the 17th Party Congress held in 2007 put forward the concept of "ecological civilization"[85] (生态文明), a sort of Marxism-compliant synonym for sustainable development, and the 19th Party Congress in 2017 was replete with references to "low carbon development" (低碳发展).[86]

This conviction that clean technology could power the future led Beijing to bet big on renewable energy. China became such a firm believer in its future that its state and firms invested over twice as much in the sector as the United States, creating a booming export industry. The value of Chinese solar technology exports increased 26-fold, from virtually nothing to US$32 billion in just five years, accounting for 3% of the value of China's total exports by the year 2020.[87] These "new industries" conveniently dovetailed with Beijing's ambitions, more fully described in Chapter 1, to transform its economy toward less resource-intensive, higher-value-added goods and services.

Electric vehicles (EVs) became an even bigger success story. From 2010 to 2012, the Chinese government subsidized 40%–60% of the cost of buying EVs, and many local governments dangled additional benefits like tax breaks and special license plates that exempted drivers from local traffic restrictions. Thanks to this support, EV sales skyrocketed in China from fewer than 10,000 to over 330,000 units in just four years, making China by far the world's largest EV market.[88] As a result, though they still faced significant barriers to growth overseas, Chinese EV manufacturers gained a strong position in what became a booming domestic market.[89]

China's largely successful bet on EV production illustrates one of the major themes of this book: despite their benefits for the planet, clean technologies became arenas of geopolitical and ideological as well as economic competition. In March 2021, Beijing barred military personnel and state employees from using American-made Tesla electric cars, reportedly over fears their sophisticated electronics could be used to gather sensitive data.[90] Going green also proved to be good fodder for the Party's propaganda apparatus, often at the expense of the United States. In the years after signing the Paris Agreement, Beijing aggressively seized on climate change to portray itself to both its people and the international community as a responsible and influential world power. An official announcement marking the 75th anniversary of China's victory over Japan in the Second World War, a momentous event in the eyes of the Chinese Communist Party, boasted for example that "from Moscow to Jakarta, from the Yanqi Lake to the West Lake, from the United Nations Headquarters to the Palais des Nations in Geneva, Chinese leaders' vision of a shared future for humanity always resonates" thanks to China's "active participation in addressing global challenges such as climate change."[91] China's diplomats, meanwhile, wasted no opportunity to trumpet Beijing's leadership on issues like climate change while Washington retreated from the world stage under the Trump administration.[92]

China's attempts to bolster its soft power by going green were most evident—and most glaringly at odds with reality—with respect to the BRI. A giant, trillion-dollar infrastructure investment plan, the BRI came to be seen as the centerpiece of China's foreign policy and was widely perceived as a means of projecting Chinese economic and political influence across the globe. Beijing, though, sold the BRI as a win-win for the world at large. Chinese state media articles crowed that "China is building a green 'Belt and Road' to protect the green mountains throughout the countries along the line" and that "through the 'Belt and Road,' China and its partners share the clean dream of 'blue water and blue sky.' "[93]

In official policy statements, meanwhile, Beijing was careful to cast the Belt and Road as an apolitical development strategy calculated to deliver "mutual benefit" and "global partnership."[94] China's diplomats abroad began turning on the charm to emphasize the BRI's sustainability bona fides. Beijing's ambassador to Sri Lanka bragged that China "expect[s] our companies to help the Sri Lankan people with donations and corporate social responsibility work."[95] The reality was often more complicated: in Gwadar, Pakistan, site of one of the highest-profile BRI projects, protests broke out over claims that water, power, and other critical resources were being diverted to serve the interests of Chinese expatriates rather than local residents.[96]

Even as Beijing attempted to burnish its influence abroad under the guise of going green, the extreme nationalism that features prominently in Chapter 1 began to influence environmental policy debates within China, especially regarding climate change. As Yanzhong Huang observed, "Many Chinese nationalists view international pressures for emission control as just another Western plot to contain China's rise."[97] What Huang termed "environmental nationalism" looked to weigh more heavily on Beijing's environmental policy.[98] Soon after the Biden administration took office in January

2021 with a promise to act aggressively on climate change, a Chinese Foreign Ministry Spokesperson tweeted that "China is willing to work with the US on climate change. But such cooperation cannot stand unaffected by . . . overall China-US relations. It is impossible to ask for China's support in global affairs while interfering in its domestic affairs and undermining its interests."[99] Though Beijing and Washington did manage to produce a joint declaration during the 2021 Glasgow climate conference, the rise of environmental nationalism augured poorly for a common global vision of sustainable development and decarbonization in the remainder of the twenty-first century.

Unfortunately, in the early twenty-first century China's vision for green growth collided with the geopolitical interests and, increasingly, the values of other major powers like the United States. Though there is nothing wrong with Beijing justifying environmental action on economic or political grounds—most countries would do the same—when combined with the growing belief among Western political elites that their nations are engaged in a long-term competition with China it produced a zero-sum mentality even in areas like clean energy development. At the same time, Beijing's use of environmental and climate change policy as an instrument of geopolitical influence raised alarms in foreign capitals. To be sure, there remained promising areas to pursue cooperation on environmental goals. Under the circumstances, though, embracing economic, geopolitical, and ideological competition might offer a better chance of saving the planet from environmental destruction than counting on cooperation.

Green Geopolitics: How Competition, Not Cooperation, Might Save the Planet

Matthias Engelsberger may be the most important person you have (almost certainly) never heard of. An obscure German politician, Engelsberger represented the state of Bavaria for over 20 years before deciding to retire in 1990. In contemplating the end of his political career, Engelsberger began looking for a legacy. It was certainly a time when history was being made almost by the minute: the Berlin Wall had fallen barely a year earlier, and East and West Germany were soon to reunify, finally breaching the Iron Curtain that had torn Europe asunder for the past 40 years.

Unlike most of his contemporaries, though, Engelsberger felt the future lay less in the formerly Communist East, and more across the partisan aisle. The deeply conservative Christian Democrat unexpectedly called upon Wolfgang Daniels, then a young representative of the radical pro-environmentalist Green Party, with an unusual proposal: to work together to pass a bill that would require energy utilities to buy electricity, at a guaranteed, subsidized rate, from households and businesses producing renewable energy, including hydropower, wind, and solar.[100]

Engelsberger's vision wasn't especially grand or inspiring; he was hoping mainly to support small Bavarian hydropower plants.[101] But from his somewhat eccentric proposal arose one of the biggest and fastest technological transformations in the history of the world: the explosive growth of solar power.[102] And in the process, Engelsberger and Daniels unexpectedly demonstrated that countries, as well as companies, can compete to go green.

Thanks to Engelsberger and Daniels's unlikely partnership, the German Parliament passed an Electricity Feed-In Law in 1990. Initially, it had virtually no effect, and the cost of renewable energy remained stubbornly high. But thanks to the political power of the Green Party, interest in renewable energy remained strong, and the Greens won significant public support for clean technology research and development.[103] Eventually, their advocacy paid off. In 2000, a new, liberal-leaning German government passed another law, the Renewable Energy Source Act, that modified the Feed in Tariff (FiT) to pay anyone who produced power from renewable sources a preferential rate, guaranteed for 20 years.

Suddenly, Germany's households and businesses couldn't afford not to go green, and the country's fields and rooftops quickly became crowded with wind turbines and solar panels. Along the way, Germany created something that had not previously existed: a strong market signal that favored renewables over other sources of electricity.[104] With so much demand for solar and wind power, companies quickly figured out how to produce renewable power at lower cost, helping renewables climb what technology scholars call the "learning curve."[105] Thanks to Germany's FiT, the world learned how to build renewable power at scale, paving the way for the rapid growth of solar and wind energy around the world.

The planet's debt to Germany for leading the renewables revolution was financial as well as technological. Even its proponents agreed that the aggressive FiT established via the Renewable Energy Source Act was a very expensive way to promote clean energy, creating costs borne mostly by Germany's energy consumers. The FiT accounted for as much as 25% of the rate German consumers paid for electricity in 2019, already one of the highest in the world.[106] Germany's FiT survived and thrived not because it made imme-diate economic sense—few clean technologies do in their initial stages—but because it served broader political and geopolitical objectives. And therein lies a critical lesson for the world's attempts to slash its greenhouse gas emis-sions: under the right circumstances, geopolitical competition can help cata-lyze support for the long-term investments needed to bring clean technology to scale.

Germany's renewable revolution was not just a story of good intentions and inspired, if eccentric, ideas. It was also one of horse-trade politics and international competition. Germany's FiT almost didn't survive because of opposition from utilities, industries, and consumers who felt gouged by their comparatively high energy prices relative to the rest of Europe. But the renewable energy industry successfully argued that it could provide a still-green alternative to nuclear power, which had long been unpopular in Germany. At the same time, amidst rising regional tensions, Berlin grew des-perate for a way to reduce its dependence on Russian natural gas. Finally, but no less importantly, there was strong support from the Green Party and their allies for Germany to become the world leader in tackling climate change. A dramatic expansion of renewables offered a way to solve each of these po-litical and geopolitical problems.[107]

But becoming the world leader in renewable energy meant taking on other countries who were, prior to the FiT, well ahead of Germany.[108] In 1980, Japan passed an innovative Alternative Energy Act that poured money into renewable energy research and development. In the decades that followed, Japan led the world in both solar panel manufacturing and installed ca-pacity. During the 1990s, Japan installed roughly seven times more solar energy capacity than Germany. After Germany adopted its higher feed-in-tariff, though, Japan began to fall behind. By the 2020s, Japan remained among the world's leaders in solar technology research but was well behind Germany and other countries when it comes to installed renewable ca-pacity.[109] Clean energy development and deployment became an interna-tional competition—and Germany began to pull ahead.

These contrasting cases of Japan and Germany point to an important lesson when it comes to China, clean energy, and the fight against climate change: sometimes, virtuous competition can be good for the planet. That is a good thing, because by the early 2020s geopolitical and economic com-petition between China, the United States, and other powers increasingly colored international cooperation on fighting climate change, especially in clean energy development and deployment. Indeed, as major economies, including Japan and the European Union as well as the United States and China, announced ambitious mid-century emissions targets ahead of the 2021 Glasgow climate conference, diplomatic cooperation began to look less important than launching a race to develop and deploy a new generation of clean technology.

A Race to the Top for the Planet: How Competition Can Catalyze a Clean Tech Revolution

In principle, cooperation on clean technology and other environmental goods is certainly preferable to competition. This was especially true of China in the first few decades of the twenty-first century. The sheer size of the Chinese market offered foreign clean tech companies something incredibly valuable: a massive, low-cost, and favorably regulated market in which to pilot, test, and refine green technologies. These features of the Chinese market were particularly promising with respect to critical, but still immature, technologies like carbon capture, utilization, and storage (CCUS).[110] CCUS essentially offers a way to prevent carbon dioxide from entering the atmosphere by burying it deep underground, and several studies indicate it might be the most practical way to cut fossil fuel emissions.[111]

But despite considerable investment, CCUS proved slow to spread because of high capital costs and complex planning, zoning, and permitting requirements. In China, though, studies suggested CCUS plants could be built at half the cost of comparable facilities in the United States, promising to make China a valuable testing-ground for one of the world's most promising clean technologies.[112] China's manufacturing economies of scale, meanwhile, meant that in theory its factories should be able to churn out solar panels and other clean technologies at much lower cost than other countries.[113] If they were to do so using intellectual property owned by foreign firms, global free trade in clean technology could, in theory, be good for everyone.[114]

There was a big problem with this rosy scenario, however. Beijing, like Berlin, came to see clean tech as an arena of economic competition. Unlike Germany and Japan, though, China proved willing to play exceptionally fast and loose with the rules of global trade to get ahead in the renewable energy race. In the second decade of the twenty-first century, Chinese firms unleashed a flood of cheap solar panel exports on the world, decimating foreign producers, including Germany. In response, the United States threat-ened a trade enforcement case before the World Trade Organization, while the European Union imposed a modest level of tariffs. Instead of backing down, however, Beijing upped the ante, threatening action against European wine imports. In the end, a negotiated deal was struck—but not before Beijing showed unmistakably that it viewed clean technology as an arena for commercial competition, and that it intended to fight to win.[115]

While China was not the only country to compete aggressively on renew-able power—the European Union itself waged a long-running battle against Germany's FiT on competition grounds—its efforts to give its own firms and industries a leg up in the first decade of the twenty-first century were in a league of their own. In its zeal to seize the economic promise of clean tech-nology, Beijing doled out heavy subsidies for the development of wind and solar power.[116] These subsidies included local-content rules that pushed do-mestic firms to start manufacturing their own equipment rather than relying on foreign imports.[117] Moreover, foreign firms complained that weak intel-lectual property protections and biased regulations forced them to transfer technology to Chinese competitors.[118]

Just as worrying to Washington, Beijing's willingness to restrict exports of rare earth minerals, reportedly to harm US defense contractors who supplied weapons to Taiwan, threatened to disrupt supplies of a critical component in wind turbine manufacture, underscoring the danger of relying on China-centric renewable technology supply chains.[119] The fact that production of almost half of the world's supply of polysilicon, a critical component of solar panels, was concentrated in Xinjiang, where Beijing-backed human rights abuses were rife, fed opposition to reliance on Chinese solar technology.[120] All of this contributed to a growing consensus in foreign capitals by the late 2010s that clean technology development was a zero-sum, rather than win-win, situation.

These beliefs increasingly drove the policy of Western governments when it came to China and clean technology, even when the situation seemed to generate more benefits than costs. When US solar panel manufacturers complained of unfair trade practices that benefited their Chinese competitors in the mid-2010s, for example, Washington did not hesitate to impose high tariffs on Chinese solar panel imports, causing imports to decline by almost one-third and costing, by some estimates, tens of thousands of American jobs. This case shows a crucial lesson about clean tech competition: it typ-ically imposes higher costs than cooperation but can still be effective in meeting climate goals. Despite the increased cost of the tariffs, for example, the cost of solar panels fell so fast that the tariffs barely dented the growth of solar in the United States.[121]

Just as important, the idea of clean technology competition became politically more appealing than cooperation. In a 2019 *New York Times* op-ed, former Secretary of State and top climate negotiator in the Biden Administration John Kerry warned that "China may become the OPEC of the 21st century energy industry" and the world might become "dependent on Chinese technology" as a result. To prevent this dark future from coming to pass, Kerry proposed a "national strategy to lead the world in clean technology" through massive investment in clean tech research and development.[122] In Europe, too, climate change became an arena for geopolitical competition as well as cooperation. A 2020 report from the European Council on Foreign Relations, for example, lamented, "The broad notion of 'partnership' no longer reflects the true complexity of the EU's interactions with China in tackling the most important global challenge."[123]

As an economic competition, clean energy technology looked like a fair fight between Chinese and foreign firms. A 2020 World Bank report, for example, found that only 15% of solar-related patents filed by Chinese firms were cited in patent applications abroad, against 60% for German, Japanese, and American counterparts.[124] But, in a trend that features prominently in Chapter 5, Chinese firms also began quickly scaling the learning curve when it came to applied research and clean technology deployment, making the competition to scale up clean and green power a heated one. China became the world leader in building ultra-high-voltage transmission power lines, which allowed power generated from renewable sources like wind or solar to be transmitted over long distances—say, wind power generated in the mountains of Georgia for use in the cities of Germany—thereby overcoming local shortages and variations in supply.[125] And at the end of 2018, Chinese solar firms achieved what was once thought to be nearly impossible: construction of a large-scale solar power plant in southern China that pledged to sell power for considerably less than the cost of coal-fired alternatives—just five US cents per kilowatt hour, making it some of the cheapest, as well as greenest, power available anywhere in the world at the time.[126]

The real value of competition, though, lies in prompting countries and companies to invest in even more ambitious clean technologies. Despite the rapid expansion of wind and solar energy capacity, key parts of the clean energy ecosystem, notably advanced batteries and smart grids, remain underdeveloped, calling for a big boost in spending not just on technology research and development, but deployment and diffusion too.[127] Evidence that emerged in late 2020 that the massive West Antarctic Ice Sheet might be close to collapse, meanwhile, makes it increasingly likely that more radical geo-engineering and negative emissions technologies may be needed to avert catastrophic climate change in the later decades of the twenty-first century.[128] Competition between countries and companies might be the best way of quickly developing and deploying these more radical clean energy technologies.

At the same time, other competitive strategies show promise in holding Beijing to its more ambitious climate commitments, like becoming carbon neutral by 2060, and pushing it to adopt new ones, such as eliminating investment in fossil fuel infrastructure overseas. One such approach is to use trade measures such as a carbon border tax adjustment (carbon BTA), which would impose tariffs on goods imported from China or other countries that fail to meet certain climate criteria. Carbon BTAs are blunt instruments that threaten to impose significant costs on consumers but have the advantage of directly targeting the emissions embedded in imported goods. In the run-up to the 2021 UN climate conference, both US and European policymakers expressed a willingness to employ carbon BTAs to pressure China on climate change.[129]

A certain degree of competition, both technological and political, could benefit the planet in other ways, with infrastructure investments being a chief example. In 2020, a US research institute released a report showing evidence that Chinese dams had cut off a large portion of the flow of the Mekong River during a drought, creating a firestorm of controversy in downstream countries.[130] Such eco-backlash created an opportunity for the United States and like-minded countries to pressure China to make its overseas investments more sustainable—and, by extension, less geopolitically threatening. By engaging in a broad-based public diplomacy campaign, the United States and partner nations could highlight the potential social and environmental costs of BRI projects and offer more sustainable alternatives. Such a campaign might help persuade Beijing to adopt measures to make its overseas projects more sustainable, like banning financing for fossil fuel infrastructure and requiring all Chinese-funded overseas projects to incorporate biodiversity impact mitigation measures, such as building tunnels or bridges to allow wildlife to safely cross roads and railways.[131]

Competition and Environmental Cooperation:
Not Mutually Exclusive

Even as competition seems to offer better political prospects than cooperation to boost clean technology development and deployment, it should also be clear that the two are not mutually exclusive. The United States, the European Union, and China took pains to ensure that diplomatic engagement on climate change remained a top priority despite growing geopolitical tensions in most other areas into the early 2020s.[132] Even clean technology cooperation between China and foreign powers did not appear to be entirely off the table. Chinese firms became the undisputed world leaders in some unsung green technologies, like solar water heaters, that are decidedly unsexy but nonetheless important. Solar water heaters provide a cheap, clean way for households to get hot water, and are especially important for parts of the world that lack access to reliable electricity. Just as importantly, unlike wind and solar power, China's solar water heater sector developed almost entirely without public support.[133] Even amidst the tension that increasingly defined China's relationship with the United States and other major powers, it is hard to see why anyone would object to a joint project to speed diffusion of Chinese-made solar water heaters around the globe, just as the United States, China, and other countries previously worked together to promote cookstoves that were both cleaner and healthier than old-fashioned alternatives.[134]

Another promising area of cooperation is protecting the world's biodiversity. Soon after the COVID-19 pandemic began its deadly spread, suspicion turned to a live-animal market in the city of Wuhan as the site of the initial outbreak. This suspicion led Beijing to ban the sale and consumption of most wild animals, a monumental shift in the government's long-standing tolerance of the valuable wildlife trade. The ban promises to significantly reduce demand for endangered species like rhinoceroses and pangolins, relieving these highly trafficked species of a leading threat to their continued existence.[135] Given China's dominant role in the global wildlife market, teaming up with other major economies and NGOs to cut off entirely the wildlife trade promised to give struggling species a fighting chance at survival.

New regulations on distant-water fishing issued in 2020 similarly promised to make it more difficult, and legally risky, for Chinese-flagged vessels to engage in unsustainable fishing practices, especially illegal, unreported, and unregulated (IUU) fishing. Key provisions in these regulations included mandates to record the origin and quantity of all fish brought back to Chinese ports and to broadcast frequent location updates, allowing each vessel to be tracked. These measures paved the way for China to join multilateral fisheries sustainability agreements like the Port States Measures Agreement, widely regarded as the gold standard for preventing IUU fishing.[136]

While these measures offer promising opportunities to pursue intergovernmental environmental cooperation, direct appeals to China's increasingly values-conscious consumers may be an even more effective way to green China's economy. Environmentalists both in China and abroad have long recognized the fact that Chinese consumer preferences can make or break global environmental goals and began mounting aggressive campaigns to sway them in more sustainable directions. In the early years of the twenty-first century, a visitor to Beijing's international airport or a subway commuter to Wudaokou (五道口), home to the famous Peking and Tsinghua Universities, could expect to see NGO-sponsored posters featuring celebrities like Yao Ming and Jackie Chan urging consumers to "Never buy rhino horn."[137]

These campaigns appeared to have an impact. A 2016 study of 300 urban Chinese consumers found, for example, that 90% had seen these advertisements, and that on a 9-point scale, respondents agreed with them, on average, at a level of 8.29 points. On the other hand, those surveyed reported low awareness of endangered species issues, and overwhelmingly viewed their protection as a responsibility for governments rather than consumers. In contrast, food safety was reported as a significantly greater concern than sustainability. As education levels improved, however, awareness increased markedly, suggesting that Chinese consumers might change their behavior in response to continued awareness campaigns.[138] Other studies demonstrated a clear, though modest, willingness among Chinese consumers to pay more for food that minimizes greenhouse gas emissions and protects biodiversity.[139]

Even small changes in Chinese consumer behavior could have a huge impact. Further studies indicated that if China's consumers could be persuaded to eat less meat, for example, the water footprint of its food consumption could be slashed by over 40%, with corresponding benefits for greenhouse gas emissions reductions.[140]

Another promising approach to working with China on climate change is through the private sector, rather than government-to-government negotiations. China's state-led economic model means that the public and private sectors are more intertwined than elsewhere, and in the first two decades of the twenty-first century Chinese firms were not especially active participants in industry-led climate mitigation initiatives. However, China's green finance market grew rapidly during this period, and became a promising area for efforts to cut carbon by both Chinese and foreign firms. Because emissions mitigation is generally cheaper in China than in developed markets, China's green bond market, already among the world's largest, holds considerable appeal for foreign companies looking to offset their emissions. Nonetheless, considerable challenges remain, especially surrounding emissions reduction verification protocols.[141]

When it comes to the environment, it is tempting to think that countries should simply put aside their differences and work together to confront shared existential threats like climate change. In reality, it is not so simple—a truth most poignantly illustrated by the case of China. Despite its many laudable contributions to protecting the environment, Beijing's efforts in the first two decades of the twenty-first century still leave the world well short of what it needs to ensure a sustainable future. At the same time, deep normative differences between China and the West in terms of what it means to protect the planet—and why—makes it hard to conjure a truly common vision of sustainable development, and unwise to bank on wide-ranging cooperation to solve the world's climate crisis.

Fortunately, cooperation is not the only way to protect the planet: competition in clean technology development and deployment can produce real gains for the global environment. Meanwhile, avoiding governments entirely by relying on consumer influence campaigns offers great potential to point the world in a more sustainable direction. The growing importance of non-state actors in China's relationship with the world is even more significant with regard to another public good: knowledge production and cultural exchange.

4

The Global Talent Show

Knowledge Production, Human Capital, and Mobility Amid China's Rise

The flow of people and ideas between China and other countries, especially the United States from the late nineteenth century on, has been one of the largest and most productive exchanges of human capital and knowledge in history. In many ways, this sort of transnational knowledge production and cultural exchange are public goods. But as Chinese diaspora communities increased in size in the early decades of the twenty-first century, human capital and migration became yet another arena of contention. In the United States, home to the single largest such community, growing geopolitical rivalry with Beijing and the COVID-19 pandemic coincided with a resurgence in anti-Chinese xenophobia, racism, and suspicion of ethnically Chinese students and researchers. At the same time, economic growth in China reduced out-migration to the developed world while increasing the flow of expatriate workers to other developing nations, contributing to a sense of economic dislocation and social tension in Africa and elsewhere. Meanwhile, Beijing began an aggressive effort to retain homegrown talent while attracting more highly skilled foreigners, intensifying a growing global competition for talent. Knowledge production and cultural exchange may be a public good, but they are hardly immune to the geopolitical tensions that cloud so many other aspects of China's relationship with the world at large.

The Politics of People Movements

History is full of ironies, but the contributions that America's sometime adversaries made to some of its greatest achievements might just top them all. Landing on the moon, for instance, would almost certainly have been impossible without the aid of an ex-Nazi rocket engineer named Wernher von Braun, who was quickly spirited out of Germany at the end of the Second

China's Next Act. Scott M. Moore, Oxford University Press. © Oxford University Press 2022.
DOI: 10.1093/oso/9780197603994.003.0005

World War and put to work building America's space program.[1] But even von Braun's contribution to American industry pales beside that of a Chinese-born scientist named Qian Xuesen (钱学森). It is hard to overstate how significant an effect Qian had on the development of America's aerospace industry. So much so, in fact, that after von Braun was captured, no native-born American had the proper expertise to question him, so he was debriefed by Qian, who had been made a lieutenant-colonel in the US Army specifically for the task.[2]

Born in Hangzhou (杭州), near Shanghai, Qian came to the United States in 1935, eventually settling at the California Institute of Technology for further study. While there he attracted the attention of Theodore von Karman, then one of America's leading aerospace engineers. In 1943, Qian helped found the Jet Propulsion Laboratory, where America's first jet and rocket engines were designed and built. He was, von Karman later said, "an undisputed genius whose work was providing an enormous impetus to advances in high-speed aerodynamics and jet propulsion."[3]

Qian's time in the United States coincided with a strong belief that the presence of Chinese students served American interests. Support for Chinese students studying in the United States was so widespread amid the two nations' wartime alliance that in the late 1940s, when the Chinese civil war interrupted many students' source of funds, Congress appropriated nearly $4.5 million to cover their tuition and living expenses. Legislators made it clear they viewed this as an "investment for the broader aim of strengthening and encouraging democracy in China." Following the establishment of the People's Republic in 1949, US officials saw Chinese students as a potential source of American influence in the struggle against Communism. State Department officials even urged university administrators to help prevent "anxiety and frustration" among Chinese students and "treat them well and . . . keep them favorably disposed to the United States."[4]

The outbreak of the Korean War, though, ended this benevolent orientation. The war stoked fears that Chinese students, having accumulated advanced technical training at American universities, might seek to return home to support their Communist motherland. Instead of encouraging Chinese students to return to China to help contain Communism, US policy suddenly shifted to prevent them from leaving. Many Chinese students and scholars came under suspicion of having Communist sympathies and were frequently tailed by FBI agents. Some who attempted to return to China were arbitrarily detained out of a fear that their expertise would aid China's new Communist government. An eminent physicist named Zhao Zhongyao (赵忠尧) was detained for two months when attempting to board a China-bound ship in California, only to be arrested yet again during a stop in Japan, apparently at the behest of US authorities.[5]

Such tactics stoked widespread outrage. Chinese researchers subjected to harassment and detention appealed to President Eisenhower. "We would respectfully point out," they wrote, "that the technical training we have received here involved no codes of secrecy, indeed the spreading of scientific knowledge and technical know-how has been the very spirit of a great tradition of this country ever since its establishment."[6] A group of Americans who had resided in China before 1949 agreed, writing in *The New York Times*, "We are convinced that the technical knowledge they may take back to China will do America less harm than the ill-will created, here and abroad, by keeping them in this country against their wishes."[7] Indeed, in China the issue generated profound anger, and was a popular subject of anti-American propaganda.[8]

The greatest tragedy of the backlash to Chinese students studying in America, though, involved Qian himself. In 1950, despite having been named to a chaired professorship at Caltech, Qian was arrested and accused of secretly maintaining membership in the Communist Party. He was ordered to be deported to China but, because his knowledge was deemed too valuable, he also was forbidden to leave. For the next five years, Qian lived in a strange sort of legal limbo.[9] At the same time, Qian became the subject of high-level negotiations between Washington and Beijing. Because of his unique technical abilities, Qian was reportedly the Communist government's single highest-priority expatriate, and it spared no effort in an attempt to secure his return to China.[10] Finally, in August 1955, Qian was deported to China—where he promptly began building ballistic missiles for Beijing. A US official later remarked that returning Qian to China was "the stupidest thing this country ever did. He was no more a Communist than I was, and we forced him to go."[11]

In the decades that followed, Qian and several other Chinese deported by the United States after being accused of being Communist sympathizers provided crucial contributions to Beijing's fledgling space and nuclear weapons programs. As one scholar later wrote of the period, "in fact, the Chinese government decided to launch its missile program in large part due to the return of Qian. Both individually and as a group, it is difficult to overestimate the importance of these returned students and scientists to the Chinese nuclear weapons and space programs."[12] The case of Qian and his contemporaries shows both the promise and the peril of knowledge production and human capital when it comes to China: both a public good and a source of political tension and, often, prejudice.

A half-century later, history seemed to repeat itself. Beginning roughly in the first decade of the twenty-first century, what had been a steady flow in the number of Chinese studying and working abroad turned into a flood. Throughout urban China, a mania arose for studying abroad, especially in the United States. Banners in cities like Guangzhou (广州) appeared advertising English classes with slogans like "From Hello to Harvard."[13] The numbers of highly educated Chinese studying at foreign universities, especially in the West, continued to climb. These movements of people and ideas proved, for the most part, an enormous boon for host countries and regions. But in some cases, they also produced economic dislocation and political tensions; and, in the United States, they coincided with a renewed suspicion of Chinese students and scholars, threatening to turn the largely public good of knowledge and cultural exchange into a much darker exercise.

Geopolitics and China's Growing Contribution to Global Human Capital

US President Theodore Roosevelt is perhaps best remembered for his adage that it pays to "speak softly and carry a big stick." But Roosevelt also had a softer side when it came to foreign relations. In the early 1900s, China's government was forced to pay millions of dollars in war reparations to the United States and other countries in the aftermath of the Boxer uprising, which had seen an explosion of anti-foreign sentiment across China. The terms of the reparation agreement, though, resulted in the US government receiving more money than it had originally demanded. In response to pressure both from Chinese diplomats and American missionaries serving in China, Roosevelt agreed to use the excess amount to establish a scholarship program for Chinese students to study in the United States. "This Nation," Roosevelt told Congress in his 1907 State of the Union Address, "should help in every practicable way in the education of the Chinese people, so that the vast and populous Empire of China may gradually adapt itself to modern conditions. One way of doing this is by promoting the coming of Chinese students to this country and making it attractive to them to take courses at our universities."[14]

Thanks in large part to Roosevelt's leadership, other countries, including the United Kingdom and the Netherlands, also agreed to use portions of the Boxer indemnities for scholarships and the creation of Chinese studies programs. So began one of the largest and most consequential human capital exchanges in the history of the world: the presence of large numbers of Chinese students in foreign universities, especially in the West.[15] Of the roughly 1,200 Chinese students who studied in the United States under the Boxer Indemnity Scholarship in the early twentieth century, about three-quarters eventually returned to China, where most became university professors and helped establish its first departments of geology, biology, business, and aeronautical engineering.

Those who remained in America were equally as successful, playing critical roles in establishing new fields like electrical engineering.[16] One, the linguist Fang-Kuei Li (李方桂), became a leading expert on American Indian languages, and produced the only record of a now-extinct Athabaskan language.[17] The sheer scale of this exchange contributed enormously to knowledge production and cultural exchange in virtually every field throughout the twentieth century. But this public good was also influenced by more mundane realities, ebbing and flowing in response to China's economic fortunes and geopolitical place in the world.

The flow of students from mainland China to Western universities dipped markedly during the Cold War, though students from Taiwan continued to make up a substantial fraction of international students, especially in the United States. Numbers of mainland students studying abroad began to climb after the Cultural Revolution, and by 2018, over 5.2 million Chinese citizens had traveled overseas to study, almost certainly the largest contingent from any one country in the history of the world.[18]

Prior to the pandemic, nearly 1.5 million Chinese students could be found studying abroad in any given year. Though most went to large, developed countries, a small but steadily increasing number went to less conventional destinations. As China's relations with the developing world expanded throughout the 1990s and the following decade, so too did the number of Chinese students studying in less wealthy nations. According to China's Ministry of Education, in 2017 some 66,000 Chinese students were studying in 37 Belt and Road countries, most of which were in Asia and Africa. But the vast majority of Chinese students were still clustered in a few Western countries, especially the United States, Canada, the United Kingdom, and Australia.[19]

In the United States, large concentrations of Chinese students developed in several college towns, particularly in the Midwest, where they had a significant impact on local communities. At the University of Illinois, whose president helped lobby for creation of the Boxer Indemnity Scholarship Program in the early twentieth century, football games were broadcast in Mandarin. In Bloomington, Indiana, the home of Indiana University, city officials printed municipal notices in Chinese for the benefit of its Chinese student population.[20] The economic, social, and cultural impact of these populations was considerable: a letter written by two members of Congress in 2020 called Chinese students "essential to U.S. academic, economic, and foreign policy leadership" and cited an estimated direct annual economic impact of US$12 billion on host communities.[21]

A similarly beneficial impact was evident in migration. At some 35 million, China's diaspora population was by the first decade of the twenty-first century the largest in the world. Significant Chinese diaspora communities existed in Japan, Canada, South Korea, Australia, Singapore, and elsewhere, but the largest single community was in the United States, which boasted nearly 2.5 million Chinese-born residents in 2010.[22] Migration to the United States increased sharply in the 1990s, with nearly half a million Chinese crossing the Pacific, doubling the previous number of Chinese migrants living in the United States. This boom continued into the following decade, with another 350,000 Chinese settling in the United States, one of the largest single-country migration flows in American history.[23] Chinese migrants to the United States were always comparatively well-educated, but these waves featured even higher levels of educational attainment and wealth than in previous decades.[24]

Yet as China's booming economy generated more domestic economic opportunity, these flows of well-educated migrants slowed in relative terms in the second decade of the twenty-first century, replaced instead by growing numbers of expatriate workers. Chinese state media reported that in just the first nine months of 2019, Chinese firms dispatched almost 160,000 employees abroad on "foreign contracted projects," while an additional 200,000 Chinese traveled abroad for other types of employment. In total, over 1 million Chinese were working abroad by the end of 2019.[25] In proportional terms, the increase in overseas Chinese populations was largest in Africa, especially in southern African nations like South Africa and Zambia.

While these workers were often assumed to work for large state-owned firms involved in the Belt and Road Initiative and other overseas infrastructure projects, many of these migrants in fact went on to open small businesses. According to one estimate, in 2019 Africa played host to upwards of 10,000 Chinese-owned enterprises, 90% of which were small or family-owned concerns.[26]

For the most part, these flows of people proved hugely positive. Migration embodies human capital in the form of knowledge, skills, and expertise. International migrants moreover tend to exhibit particular skills, including adaptability and entrepreneurship, that benefit their host countries. Their economic success abroad also often contributes to their homelands in the form of remittances sent home. But the biggest benefit of people movements is the transfer of knowledge and ideas across national borders because in its pure form, knowledge production and exchange are a global public good.[27] This is most obvious in the form of highly specialized, scientific, or technical knowledge—like the Turkish immigrant couple who developed one of the first successful COVID-19 vaccines.[28] But it can also take the form of cultural and social knowledge, which enriches both host and source countries by creating shared understanding and direct, people-to-people communications networks that facilitate knowledge transfer.[29] Tragically, though, while the economic and social effects of migration and people movements are broadly positive, neither host country populations nor migrants themselves always see things in such a positive light.

The Globalization of Chinese Migration, Social Tensions, and Sinophobia

During the height of foreign influence in China in the nineteenth century, one of the most visible forms of colonial oppression was the presence of European-controlled police forces like the Shanghai Municipal Police, who answered to foreign rather than local authorities, and who, unsurprisingly, came to be focal points of anti-foreign sentiment.[30] So it was with more than a little historical irony when, in December 2017, the Zambian Police Service announced a plan to hire eight Chinese citizens to help police the sub-Saharan country's growing population of Chinese expatriates. To the Zambian government at the time, the plan seemed sensible enough: there would be no language barrier with the Mandarin-speaking Chinese cops.

Just a day after the plan was announced, however, overwhelming public opposition forced the government to change course. As a leading political figure exclaimed to the foreign press, "How would we be feeling to see a police officer and be saluting a Chinese in our own country?"[31]

Such sentiments, clearly tinged with Sinophobia, signaled another facet of China's growing contribution to global human capital: increasing numbers of students and workers spread out across the globe, often accompanied by social, political, and economic tensions. Anti-Chinese sentiment has a long history in many parts of the world, including the United States, where it was manifest in the Chinese Exclusion Acts of the nineteenth century, and in Southeast Asia, where it led to horrific violence, most notoriously in Indonesia in the 1960s.[32] While the highly educated, relatively affluent Chinese who increasingly populated Western universities differed in important respects from their counterparts who made up most expatriate worker communities in the developing world, social tensions and Sinophobia became a tragically common experience for both groups.

China's impact on the developing world is often viewed through the lens of infrastructure projects like the Belt and Road Initiative (also discussed in Chapters 1, 3, and 6). But Chinese migrants and expatriates had at least as great an effect on the economies of places like Sao Vicente, the second-largest municipality in the West African country of Cape Verde. Sao Vicente, settled by the Portuguese in the 1700s, might seem about as far away as one can get from China. But starting in the mid-1990s, Chinese businessmen began to open shops known as *baihuos* (百货), after a word meaning "a hundred items." The shops quickly expanded by taking advantage of Chinese entrepreneurs' ability to purchase goods cheaply at wholesale markets in China and then resell them at a still comparatively low price in Cape Verde. Within a decade, *baihuos* came to dominate Sao Vicente's commercial landscape, and Chinese merchants became one of Cape Verde's most important business communities almost overnight.[33]

The speed of this transformation, even in a place seemingly so physically and culturally distant from China as Cape Verde, underscores the far-reaching economic impact of China's rise. But as with so much about the phenomenon, its effects proved complicated. For one thing, it created new sets of economic winners and losers in developing-country communities like Sao Vicente. The *baihuos* benefited poorer Cape Verdeans by offering consumer goods much more cheaply than native-owned shops. But at the same time, they forced some native Cape Verdean merchants out of business, creating political pressure to limit Chinese immigration.[34]

In other regions, Chinese migrants were accused of creating insular "ethnic economies" that shut out locals and suppressed wages.[35] These allegations, often tinged with anti-Chinese sentiment, became a significant issue for Chinese firms operating abroad, both in Africa and beyond. According to an executive of a Chinese firm making shoes for major international brands, for example, "Enterprises like ours have all experienced anti-Chinese sentiment in Vietnam. . . . We are also very afraid that Vietnamese society is opposed to Chinese manufacturers moving to their country."[36] As China's economic and human capital footprint increased across the globe, tensions like these threatened to become an increasingly common reaction to its rise.

Yet while expatriate worker communities in developing nations became a growing source of hostility, longer-standing populations of Chinese international students also became a source of debate in countries like the United States. This debate had less to do with economics than allegations of espionage and other forms of insidious influence, especially among Chinese students and researchers studying at American universities. Though these concerns went back at least a decade before the Trump administration took office in 2017, tension flared in the late 2010s.[37] In early 2018, the Trump administration considered banning all Chinese students from studying in the United States, in part over fears they would contribute to theft of US intellectual property. "No Chinese student who comes here," a senior official proclaimed, "is untethered from the state."[38] A related but distinct set of concerns pertained to allegations of nefarious influence on the part of Chinese students and scholars, especially over politically sensitive issues like human rights and academic freedom. In the United States, these concerns focused on Chinese government-funded Confucius Institutes, which promote Chinese language and cultural study. In early 2019, a bipartisan group of US senators issued a report calling for the closure of all Confucius Institutes in the United States on the grounds that they compromised academic freedom by discouraging discussion of sensitive topics. The Trump administration later took steps to seek their closure.[39]

Despite these aggressive actions, the evidence behind allegations concerning both Chinese students and organizations like the Confucius Institutes proved to be remarkably thin, and in some cases thoroughly mischaracterized. Research showed that far from being tethered to the state, most Chinese students in places like the United States were independent-minded, privately funded, and sought to study abroad to escape the strictures of a grinding, regimented educational system.[40] A report from the independent US Government Accountability Office, moreover, concluded that most US institutions had "full control" over content and programming at Confucius Institutes, and many had contracts with the Chinese government that specifically protected academic freedom.[41] In many other cases, allegations of covert Chinese influence relied on unsubstantiated or anecdotal evidence, and worst of all carried disturbing echoes of anti-Chinese racist tropes.[42]

To be sure, concerns over the activities of Chinese students and scholars in American universities were not all specious. US government investigations uncovered substantial evidence of "non-traditional intelligence collection" on the part of a few Chinese students and researchers at American universities (more on this in Chapter 6). Credible reports indicated that a small number of Chinese students were enlisted by shadowy Beijing-based entities to monitor fellow classmates and academics working on politically sensitive topics.[43] Most alarming were cases of thought suppression and intimidation on the part of some Chinese students against their classmates, seemingly rooted in the extreme nationalism described in Chapter 1. In 2017, a commencement speech delivered by a Chinese student at the University of Maryland praising the "democracy and free speech" she experienced while studying in the United States prompted the university's Chinese Student and Scholars Association to issue a statement denouncing her, and she and her family were subjected to intense harassment by China's netizens.[44] In another well-publicized incident at Canada's McMaster University, Chinese students attempted to block a talk by a Uighur activist whom they labeled a "separatist."[45]

Such behavior is clearly at odds with the academic freedom and open debate fundamental to Western universities. But these incidents also belie a bigger, and certainly more widespread, concern: a profound sense of alienation and disillusionment among Chinese students, for most universities and communities the largest single population of international students. For Chinese students, at least, the simple act of studying abroad does not seem to automatically enhance cultural understanding or tolerance of other societies. In a widely cited study conducted in the mid-2010s, a slightly higher percentage of Chinese students studying at large American research universities, 29%, reported that their feelings about the United States had become more negative since arriving to study, against 26% who reported feeling more positive. Conversely, 44% reported that their attitudes toward China had become more positive, as compared to only 17% who reported that their feelings had become more negative.[46]

In large part, these mixed opinions on the experience of studying abroad seem to reflect a disturbing prevalence of racism and xenophobia in Western societies. Focus groups suggested that many Chinese students abroad felt isolated from Western societies, in part because of perceived anti-China prejudice.[47] At the same time, about 15% of Chinese students reported experiencing some form of racial discrimination during their time in the United States, an alarmingly high figure that anecdotal reports suggested may have increased further still following the onset of the COVID-19 pandemic.[48] These realities, coupled with the temptation to center social life in large Chinese expatriate populations, created considerable self-segregation among Chinese students in the West.[49] This isolation could prove costly to host countries: a large 2020 study found that Chinese undergraduates were much more likely to want to stay and work in the United States if they had more than three close American friends.[50]

The sense of alienation among significant numbers of Chinese students and scholars in the West, coupled with a shockingly high incidence of anti-Asian racism, represents a major moral and soft power failure for host countries, especially the United States. In particular, the widespread experience of nativism and discrimination unsurprisingly had deeply deleterious effects on Chinese student and scholar perceptions of host country values and institutions. A 2020 study found that while Chinese students who study in the United States were more likely than their peers who choose not to study abroad to have a positive view of liberal democracy, its favorability could be severely affected by experiences of discrimination. When Chinese students encounter discrimination, their support for liberal democracy sharply decreases, as does their belief that political reform in China would be desirable. Moreover, these effects are largest among those students who were initially most likely to reject Chinese nationalist sentiments.[51]

The prejudice experienced by so many Chinese students in the West is ethically unacceptable and plays directly into Beijing's propaganda—but it also prevents countries like the United States from fully benefiting from one of the world's richest flows of human capital. Amidst efforts by the Trump administration to further restrict Chinese student visas in 2020, former Google CEO Eric Schmidt warned that "this current trend to restrict Chinese student access to universities is against our own self-interest." Referring to his role as then-chair of the National Security Commission on Artificial Intelligence, Schmidt went on to explain that "the really, really smart Chinese researchers would prefer to be here. They love America! And they love the freedoms . . . they want academic freedom."[52] Seemingly bolstering Schmidt's conclusion, Chinese undergraduates who study technical subjects are more likely than their peers studying social sciences or the humanities to express a desire to stay in the United States after graduation.[53]

As such findings suggest, there are ways to address legitimate concerns over espionage, malicious influence, and the appropriation of research from Western universities and research institutes without harming the flow of talent and ideas from China and elsewhere that is essential to maintaining technological competitiveness. A bill introduced in 2019 in the United States called the Securing American Science and Technology Act, for example, aimed to create a special committee under the National Academies of Sciences, Engineering, and Medicine, a body representing federal research funding agencies, to review foreign sources of research funding.[54] At the end of the day, the biggest problem caused by America's failure to fully integrate Chinese students and scholars is that it risks losing more Qian Xuesens at a time when, thanks to increasingly fierce global competition for talent, it needs them more than ever.

The Global Market for Highly Skilled Talent

Ray Davis is the kind of person who made America the world's leading scientific and economic power. A chemistry professor, Davis led the development of techniques to understand how proteins, the building blocks of biology, work, unlocking new approaches to the development of drugs and medical treatments. The recipient of a long list of scientific awards, Davis also helped start several biotech companies—exactly the kind of translational research that powers economic growth and innovation (more on this in Chapter 5). But in 2011, Davis made a decision that would have been unthinkable for American scientists of his stature in a previous generation: he moved to China. "One of the big attractions was the energy and excitement the students had for science," Davis later told a reporter. "It won me over."[55]

Soon afterward, Davis joined one of several Chinese government-sponsored programs that shower overseas researchers with financial support and other benefits in exchange for relocating to China part-time. Davis also earned an appointment at Shanghai Tech, an elite new research-focused university itself supported by the Shanghai municipal government and began splitting his time between Shanghai and southern California—a living ex-ample both of growing human capital exchange between the United States and China, and the increasing global competition for highly skilled and educated researchers.[56]

In the twenty-first century, economic growth depends ever more on the Ray Davises of the world who possess both highly technical skills and entrepreneurial talent. But scientists like Davis depend in turn on international collaboration more than ever before. Science has always been international; even in pre-modern times, nearly every important idea and invention was circulated between major scientific centers across Eurasia and the Middle East.[57] But in the twenty-first century, two factors, cost and connectivity, make international collaboration even more essential, especially at the frontiers of scientific knowledge. In fields like high-energy physics and astronomy, the basic equipment needed for cutting-edge research is so complex and expensive that even rich countries can afford it only by pooling resources. On the other hand, technologies like cloud-based data-sharing and telepresence software make it easier than ever before to conduct complex research across borders and time zones.[58]

Aided by these factors, international scientific collaboration grew at an accelerating rate as the twentieth century turned into the twenty-first. International co-authorship of scientific articles grew from 10% of all papers published in 2000 to 20% by 2015.[59] Freer travel and communication, especially between the United States and China, greatly aided the creation of scientific knowledge, with benefits that accrued to all nations, and especially to America. But in the 2010s, a sharp rise in geopolitical tension between Washington and Beijing began to chip away at the free flow of people and ideas across the Pacific. Like its public health and environmental counterparts, knowledge production too became a realm of increasing economic and geopolitical competition.

The Inherently International Business of Scientific Research

The dual nature of knowledge production as both a public good in its pure form as well as an arena of growing contention and competition between major powers is especially evident in the inherently international business of scientific research. Despite massive growth in research capacity throughout the first decade of the twenty-first century (more on this in Chapter 5), cutting-edge research remained concentrated in the developed world rather than in developing countries like China, meaning that for the most part, data flowed one way.[60] But when it comes to the public good aspects of knowledge production, that asymmetry is largely beside the point. That is because there is something near-magical about scientific and technical cooperation across borders that makes even the best scientists, in China, the United States, and elsewhere, even better.[61]

A wide range of studies conducted throughout the first two decades of the twenty-first century found that international scientific publications have higher-than-average citation rates, meaning they are viewed as more influential than articles authored by researchers from a single country.[62] Strikingly, international collaboration also appears to improve the quality of research conducted within countries: research groups with international members produce both more journal articles and publish in higher-quality outlets than their single-country-group peers.[63] Most impressive of all, research published by foreign-born researchers is significantly more influential than that of native-born scientists—even accounting for the fact that more talented and ambitious researchers are more likely to move between countries.[64] Migration and mobility, these studies suggest, almost always go hand in hand with cutting-edge science.

International collaboration appears to carry benefits for researchers in all fields.[65] It exposes researchers to fresh ideas much different than those that percolate in smaller, regional, or national networks,[66] and helps researchers tap into sources of comparative advantage in research that exists in different countries.[67] Collaboration also facilitates knowledge transfer by allowing researchers based in one country to tap into other countries' talent pools.[68] In contrast, countries that are isolated from international scientific networks tend to have less productive research enterprises.[69] International collaboration is, in short, a secret sauce for doing cutting-edge science.

But the benefits of international collaboration are not limited to universities: it also makes companies more innovative as well. A major study of research and development in multinational firms found that cross-national collaboration not only improved the impact factor of inventions, but also made researchers with international experience more productive over time.

Teams with at least one member engaged in international collaboration produced 11% more citations than those with purely national networks.[70] A 2015 study similarly found that "innovative firms, in particular radically innovative firms, tend to be more involved in international personal and formal networks," and that "international networks tend to be more closely associated to innovation than regional/national ones."[71]

Though a thoroughly global enterprise, collaboration between researchers based in the United States and China became an especially important element of knowledge production in the first decades of the twenty-first century. In 1998, Chinese researchers and institutions were the 13th most popular international collaborator for their US counterparts—but by 2008 they ranked fourth.[72] Over roughly the same period, China's share of US publications involving international collaboration increased from 35% to nearly half.[73] The scale of US–China collaboration was even greater in emerging fields like nanotechnology, where over 50% of China's international research papers were coauthored with US researchers, far ahead of those of any other country.[74]

Yet while all countries benefit from collaboration with China-based researchers, the United States appears to benefit most of all.[75] Intriguingly, at least one study concluded that US research publications would have declined over the 2015–2020 period were it not for those that included at least one Chinese coauthor, while China's publication rate would have risen without publications coauthored with American researchers. Throughout the pandemic period, meanwhile, publications involving both US and Chinese coauthors ranked first among internationally coauthored articles, and the collaboration rate between US and Chinese researchers in fact increased following the onset of the pandemic, due primarily to publication of COVID-19-related research—yet another illustration of how knowledge production and exchange can be a public good.[76]

The public good aspects of knowledge production and exchange are in turn largely a function of researcher mobility. Because the benefits of international scientific collaboration arise from network effects, collaboration itself is dependent on the ability of certain highly skilled individuals to move and communicate freely across borders.[77] This mobility is important to all researchers, but some even more than others. Much of the research on how scientific and technological networks form and function points to the role of specific individuals. When leading researchers initiate partnerships with their counterparts abroad, the development of international networks tends to follow.[78] Most of the value of mobility seems to lie in sheer proximity: researchers who spend time with one another, even casually, share ideas that can inform scientific breakthroughs.[79] This effect is so strong that a group of microbiologists wrote that "governmental programs stimulating mobility are of unquestionable value."[80]

Science, perhaps the world's leading scientific publication, devoted an entire 2017 issue to the subject of mobility in research, and roundly concluded that the free flow of researchers is critical to scientific progress. One study featured in the issue found, for example, that "cross-border mobility comes with a boost in research quality that would have been absent without mobility" and that research teams performed significantly better when led by a foreign national.[81] These beneficial effects are especially marked for the United States and China: "Ties between U.S. and Chinese researchers," another *Science* article stated, "exemplify how migration advances knowledge and benefits [both] source and destination country."[82]

Throughout the twentieth century, the benefits of researcher mobility accrued primarily to the United States, whose companies, universities, and research institutes attracted the majority of highly skilled scientific migrants. The sheer scale of its scientific enterprise made it practically the only country capable of conducting truly independent research and development across nearly every field.[83] As a result, it captured the majority of the most talented researchers both among its own citizens, who most often sought positions within the United States, and from other countries, who are attracted by the breadth and depth of its research and tech communities.[84] As the economists Richard Freeman and Wei Huang observed, the United States was in many ways the biggest beneficiary of the investments that China and other large developing nations made in science and technology throughout the twentieth century, as many of their most talented graduates migrated to the United States for advanced study.[85]

The scale of this migration meant that in fields like computer science, international students made up close to 80% of total enrollments by the late 2010s.[86] But researchers hailing from China are especially important to US science. Freeman and Huang's 2015 research found that 14% of all US scientific papers were authored by Chinese-born researchers, and US-authored papers with a Chinese-born first author were more highly cited than those with a native-born lead researcher.[87] Without Chinese students and researchers, Freeman and Huang warned, many US laboratories and research centers would have to "close or shrink massively."[88] Former Google CEO Eric Schmidt was even blunter, telling audiences that "to tell you the truth . . . many of the top graduate students are foreign-born and typically Chinese."[89]

Yet despite the evidence that scientific collaboration and researcher mobility between the United States and China benefit both nations (but especially America), geopolitical tensions in the late 2010s threatened to curb one of history's greatest exchanges of knowledge and human capital. And while the United States had long attracted the lion's share of highly skilled talent from China and other nations, its appeal dimmed considerably amid a turn toward protectionism and skepticism of Chinese students and scholars, on one hand, and determined investment in talent retention and attraction by China, on the other.

Protectionism, Nativism, and the Reality of Growing Talent Competition

For most of the twentieth and early twenty-first centuries, Western countries, and especially the United States, were by far the most favored overseas destinations for work and study for ambitious, highly educated Chinese. But by the 2010s, signs had emerged that the United States in particular could not take for granted that it could continue to attract the most talented students and researchers from China and other countries. While several factors seemed to be behind this eroding edge in talent competition, rising geopolitical tensions between the United States and China played a significant role.

As China's economy boomed and economic opportunities at home expanded in the first decade of the twenty-first century, the percentage of Chinese students staying in the United States after finishing their degrees, a metric known as the "stay rate," began to decline.[90] In the second decade of the twenty-first century, evidence emerged to suggest that the appeal of US universities was waning among Chinese students not just because of economics, but also because of worsening relations between Washington and Beijing. A 2019 survey suggested that the number of Chinese students choosing other English-speaking countries over the United States for further study increased during the 2017–2020 US–China trade war. The percentage of students who named the United Kingdom as their country of choice of further study topped 20%, against 17% who named the United

States.[91] Similarly, undergraduate applications from Chinese students at San Francisco State University declined by a third from 2017 to 2019, roughly corresponding to the period of increased bilateral tensions under the Trump administration.[92]

At least part of this decline appeared to be a direct response to Trump administration policies targeting Chinese students and scholars. These policies included limitations on the length of visas issued to the many Chinese students studying in technical fields, ostensibly for national security reasons.[93] While reliable data on the effect of these changes is hard to come by, past evidence is disconcerting. When comparable changes to US immigration policy in 2004 resulted in new visa restrictions for international students from certain countries, undergraduate enrollment from affected countries fell by 14%, and SAT scores fell by an average of 20 points, suggesting that the changes persuaded the best students to look elsewhere for study abroad.[94] Anecdotal reports, meanwhile, suggest that visa restrictions do not necessarily deter Chinese students from studying in the United States, but rather discourage them from staying in the United States after graduation[95]—a potentially catastrophic loss of highly skilled talent.

Just as concerning was the potential impact of Trump administration restrictions on Chinese visiting scholars and researchers. As discussed further in Chapter 6, China-linked economic espionage and intellectual property theft from US universities and research institutions had clearly become a problem by the mid-2010s. Still, the damage done by overzealous policy responses was considerable. Following a crackdown by US federal research funding agencies on foreign research collaborations, again ostensibly for national security reasons, several Chinese researchers reported wanting to return to China because of what they perceived to be ethnic discrimination.[96] As the previous section indicated, even the loss of a few highly talented individuals could be devastating for individual American research institutions. As University of California–Berkeley Chancellor Carol Christ remarked, "I realize there are legitimate concerns about China's practices. But nonetheless, I think the world has so much more to profit by the sharing of research than putting up walls."[97]

An April 2019 move to revoke visas issued to Chinese scholars with alleged but often dubious links to security services meanwhile delivered a considerable blow to America's soft power and image as a prime destination for Chinese students and scholars. Zhu Feng (朱锋), a leading Chinese expert on the United States, was forced to miss his son's graduation from an American college because his visa was revoked. Unsurprisingly, he was unsparing in his criticism of what seemed like a pointlessly cruel policy. "The U.S.," he lamented in an interview, "is not helpful, is more unfriendly, and is getting more hateful."[98]

At the same time that protectionist and nativist policies discouraged the migration of highly skilled Chinese to the United States, Beijing began ramping up efforts to lure its most talented students and researchers back home.[99] As the Trump administration began tightening visa requirements for Chinese students, the Ministry of Education (教育部) began urging universities to offer spots to graduate students who were not granted visas to study in the United States.[100] At the same time, Beijing backed programs intended to draw overseas Chinese closer to their ancestral homeland, including a heavily subsidized two-week tour of China targeted at Chinese youth living abroad.[101]

Most concerning from a talent competition standpoint, Beijing also began offering long-stay visas to "high-end foreigners" like Nobel Prize winners, and recruiting ethnic Chinese living abroad to return to China through its "Thousand Talents" (千人计划) and related programs.[102] According to a leading expert on China's science and technology policies, "The Chinese government has been the most assertive government in the world in introducing policies targeted at triggering a reverse brain drain."[103] A widely cited report likewise found that Beijing backed a sophisticated infrastructure to poach foreign talent through a network of some 600 "talent recruitment stations" around the globe. These stations, according to the report, were usually run by local business, professional, or scholarly associations, and paid a commission of up to $29,000 for recruiting target individuals, as well as several tens of thousands of dollars a year for operating expenses. In an illustration of the decentralized approach to policy implementation described in Chapter 1, many of the recruitment programs that such stations serve were run not by China's central state, but by provincial and municipal governments. Of the 600 stations identified in the report, for example, some 580 were linked to municipal or provincial rather than national organizations.[104]

In their initial phases of operation, these talent programs failed to persuade many top researchers to permanently leave developed nations like the United States. But they nonetheless posed several challenges for developed democracies, especially the United States.[105] Several professors at US universities were found to have improperly transferred resources, including intellectual property, to Chinese institutions where they maintained concurrent appointments. China's talent programs also reportedly enlisted at least a few US government scientists, raising security concerns that Washington tried to address by barring government employees from participating.[106] But the biggest challenge posed by talent retention and recruitment policies like the Thousand Talents was less to national security per se than to increasingly outdated and misguided immigration policies common among developed democracies.

Competing for Talent in the Post-Pandemic World

One Sunday in September 2018, readers of Iowa's largest newspaper, the *Des Moines Register*, opened their morning paper to find an unfamiliar sight. Amidst the more typical high school sports rundowns and commodity price updates lay a four-page insert from *The China Daily*, Beijing's state-run English-language paper. An article captioned "Fruit of a president's folly" warned that "Trump's trade war may force China to look for alternative partners" and that "U.S. farmers may find it hard to regain their market share."[107] If the article's intention was to persuade Americans to oppose the Trump administration's tough trade policy, though, it seemed not to work. A few days later, an opinion article published in the same paper blasted the insert, saying "American voters should know such blatant propaganda when they see it."[108]

At almost exactly the same moment that Sino-American geopolitical rivalry was playing out in the *Register*'s opinion pages, in the tiny town of Clinton, Iowa, a Chinese high school student named Tiffany Yang was having her school ID photo taken next to a US Army National Guard recruiting poster proclaiming, "United We Stand." Yang was one of 15 Chinese high school students recruited to live in the dorms of a shut-down former college while attending the local public high school, Clinton High. Beset by hard economic times and a dwindling population in the first decade of the twenty-first century, Clinton's residents looked to Yang and her classmates to keep their town afloat. To do so, a group of civic leaders persuaded a private Chinese education company to buy the former Ashford University and pay Clinton High to enroll up to 72 Chinese students a year. "My goal," proclaimed a state representative who helped broker the deal, "was to keep the plywood off the windows." But others saw an educational as well as economic opportunity. "The opportunity for our kids to be exposed to someone from a different culture," recalled the local school board head, "was really exciting to us."[109]

These two tales of China in Iowa, unfolding at almost the exact same moment, spoke to the contradictions of China's role in human capital and mobility in the twenty-first century, and how it pulls countries, communities, economies, and societies in different directions. On the one hand, a growing sense of economic and geopolitical competition between China and other nations has stoked continued tension over the flow of people as well as goods, both in Iowa and Cape Verde. But on the other hand, even communities like Clinton benefit both economically and culturally from tapping into the rich flow of human capital from China and other nations. The challenge for communities across the globe is how to balance tensions and concerns stemming from China's rise while maintaining the open societies that draw Tiffany Yang to rural Iowa.

Unfortunately, maintaining this balance became more difficult as economic changes within China bore more directly on the livelihoods of people far beyond its borders—including in Iowa. The sheer size of China's workforce meant that labor prices in China began to affect wages around the world, often negatively, especially after China's accession to the World Trade Organization in 2001. According to one expert, over the following two decades, "Chinese disruption in American labor markets was at least on par with Amazon's disruption of traditional retail."[110] The biggest effect was on workers who perform "routine tasks," like most manufacturing jobs, who saw real wage declines because of offshoring and outsourcing.[111] Pressures like these reduced the political appeal of immigration and talent mobility in countries like the United States, even for highly skilled workers.[112]

These political pressures threatened to prevent the United States in particular from maintaining what had long been a considerable advantage over countries like China in attracting and retaining highly skilled talent. At a 2019 summit for young entrepreneurs in Shanghai, James Liang, CEO of Ctrip (携程旅行), a widely used Chinese travel website, observed that half of US tech companies have been built by immigrants. For China to replicate this success, Liang warned, it would "require significant reform by putting in place policies to . . . relax immigration and visa laws, and reform the education system."[113] These were all areas where countries like the United States still hold a considerable advantage—but one that requires significant reform and investment to maintain.

Reforming Immigration Policy and
Promoting Inclusive Societies

In the 2010s, what had long been a broadly liberal approach to immigration policy in the United States began to change under the Trump administration. In many respects, this change was part of a global trend. Following the 2008 financial crisis and growing migration from regions like the Middle East and Central America, several Western countries took steps to reduce immigration. These measures had a profound effect on the flow of people and ideas from China. Beyond instituting new restrictions on Chinese students and scholars, news reports indicated that the US government significantly reduced the number of Chinese nationals permitted to be hired for advanced engineering jobs at high-tech companies like Intel and Qualcomm. Such policies were justified based on preserving job opportunities for American citizens, but the evidence suggested that these reforms went in exactly the wrong direction.[114]

Instead, protectionist immigration policies flew in the face of compelling evidence that high-skilled immigration, both from China and elsewhere, plays an essential role in developed economies, and especially in entrepreneurship and innovation. A study of US patent-holders found that native US citizens were half as likely to hold patents, and that immigrants who come to the United States to study are most likely to apply for patents. According to the same study, immigration of college-educated foreign citizens is likely to have increased GDP per capita by up to 2.4%.[115] As a result, the study concluded, "The United States . . . is successful in choosing skilled immigrants who boost economic growth per capita and should consider expanding the number of such immigrants admitted."[116]

As this conclusion suggests, liberal immigration policy is critical to sustaining these economic benefits. For the United States, that means making it easier and more attractive for highly skilled students and researchers from China and elsewhere to work in the United States and eventually become citizens. One approach is to make it easier for foreign students and researchers to work, and eventually to seek citizenship. Visa policies can be ludicrously complicated—a flow chart created by Chinese students to help each other understand the process for obtaining and maintaining visas in light of US policy changes instituted during the pandemic proves the point (see Figure 4.1).[117] Outdated laws also tie work permits primarily to individual

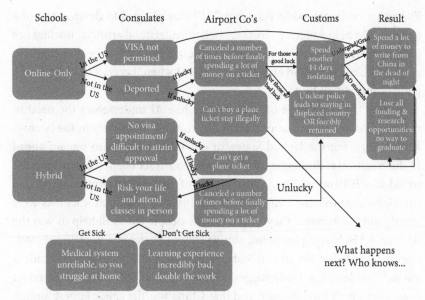

Figure 4.1. The complexities of US student visa procedures.
Source: Schneider 2020.

employers, which studies suggest channel highly skilled immigrants to-ward larger firms and discourage them from working in start-ups, where their skills might be put to best use.[118] Making allowances for Chinese and other foreign researchers to work in start-ups would help to tap this latent talent pool.

At the same time, policies in other, seemingly far-removed areas, such as taxation, could be tweaked to better retain highly skilled talent. At least one major study indicated that the single biggest reason for the concentra-tion of high-skilled migration to the United States during the late twentieth and early twenty-first centuries was the large skill premium reflected in wages for professional workers, coupled with its relatively low marginal tax rate.[119] Maintaining these favorable economic incentives is a critical part of attracting and retaining foreign talent to the United States.

To be sure, competing more effectively for foreign talent, whether from China or elsewhere, is only part of the answer to maintaining an economic edge in the twenty-first century. For countries like the United States, it is also essential to make better use of homegrown talent, including by improving education systems and training opportunities. A good example is a US

Executive Order issued in February 2019 that pledged to develop training programs to help American workers better understand artificial intelligence (AI) systems.[120] But these measures alone are unlikely to be sufficient for countries like the United States to stay ahead when it comes to the growing global competition for talent.

Indeed, the emergence of technologies like AI underscores the need to reform outdated immigration policies to compete effectively in the twenty-first century. For the United States, or any other country, to remain ahead in these critical technologies, it is essential to attract talent from around the world. In a 2019 op-ed, Oren Etzioni, head of the Allen Institute for Artificial Intelligence, noted that two-thirds of the Institute's research scientists were immigrants and argued they would be "the people who will help us win the AI race."[121] Bolstering his point, almost 60% of all degrees in artificial intelligence awarded in the United States in the late 2010s were to non-resident aliens.[122] At least one study suggested that over half of the top US-based AI researchers were foreign-born and that China was the single largest foreign source country.[123]

These realities point to the value of creating skill-specific talent recruitment initiatives. Etzioni, for instance, suggested dedicating at least 10,000 immigrant visas for AI specialists to help keep the United States competitive in attracting AI talent.[124] The US National Security Commission on Artificial Intelligence proposed a similar AI-specific work authorization program in its landmark 2021 report.[125] An alternative, but possibly complementary approach is Canada's 2017 Pan-Canadian Artificial Intelligence Strategy, which provided the infrastructure to recruit dozens of well-known AI researchers to Canadian universities and research institutes.[126]

A further promising approach is to leverage foreign talent through building stronger partnerships with foreign AI researchers and research institutes. The US Department of Defense, for example, has proposed to expand personnel exchanges in the AI field to do just that.[127] The Partnership for AI, a nonprofit group devoted to spreading awareness and understanding of AI, likewise has recommended creating a special visa category for AI researchers to aid in the free flow of people and ideas.[128] Given economic competitiveness and national security concerns in fields like AI, these exchanges could be structured in such a way as to link countries with shared democratic values and institutions. Notably, collaboration in advanced fields like AI tends to be especially strong between the United States and developed-country democracies in Europe, Japan, and elsewhere—suggesting that there is considerable potential to strengthen scientific networks among like-minded democracies (more on this in Chapter 6 with respect to a shared 5G telecommunications network).[129] Forging these networks should be made a priority for governmental science-funding agencies and science diplomacy.[130]

A final and more immediate priority is to better promote inclusion and integration between international students and surrounding communities, especially Chinese student populations. Studies show that while international students from all backgrounds faced considerable challenges in adapting to life at overseas universities, they are particularly marked for students from China.[131] In part, this is a function of sheer numbers. At almost any given institution, Chinese students can surround themselves with friends and classmates from similar cultural backgrounds. As a result, surveys of international students demonstrate that Chinese students often feel less well-integrated into the wider life of campus communities than students from other countries.[132]

One answer to this problem is to integrate Chinese and other international students more intentionally into host communities. Universities are the most obvious focal point for these efforts, and some major US universities have established entire offices devoted to communicating regularly with international students, organizing social and cultural education events, and providing support resources.[133] Nongovernmental organizations, including faith groups, also play an important role in outreach to Chinese students and scholars. But integration initiatives are highly variable across universities, and governments could help promote them by offering financial incentives and other policy support. And as this intersection of public and private actors suggests, non-state and subnational actors play just as important a role as national governments in addressing the human capital dimension of China's rise.

Thinking beyond the State and Preparing for the Future of Work

As the previous sections have highlighted, changes to immigration policy are important elements of effectively competing for highly skilled talent in the twenty-first century. But productive steps can also be taken by companies, cities, and institutions to better attract and retain talent from China and elsewhere, even in the absence of national policy reform. While much of the research on talent flows and scientific networks focuses on countries, cities also play an important role in capturing and mobilizing talent from around the world through industry-specific networks. Researchers in capital cities like Tokyo, Seoul, and Budapest develop strong international collaborations thanks to regional integration, even while their parent countries remain comparatively isolated within global scientific networks.[134] This effect is especially evident in fields like public health, where cities like Auckland and Mexico City form key nodes in international research collaborations.[135] These networks, centered on cities rather than countries, can be used to tap human capital beyond national boundaries, especially using virtual platforms.

Research also reveals several important lessons for how multinational companies can better mobilize talent across time zones. International collaboration is most important in generating innovative ideas within companies, meaning that it is more important for companies to have a presence in multiple countries than to have formal ties with research institutes or universities abroad. For companies, the takeaway lesson is that partnerships are no substitute for on-the-ground presence in China.[136] Other studies show that to benefit from a global talent base, companies need to have what researchers call "absorptive capacity," meaning they must be structured so as to leverage new ideas. Absorptive capacity includes executives and managers willing to back new ideas, a culture that encourages experimentation, and nimble research and development teams that can quickly try out product and process innovations.[137]

While businesses are important to the global talent competition, education systems and the subnational governments that typically run them are even more so. The realities of post-pandemic virtual work mean that many labor markets have become even more integrated, putting knowledge workers in China and other developing countries in more direct competition with those of developed economies.[138] This increased competition puts more onus on formal and informal education, especially early in life. The shortcomings of America's education system in fields like science, technology, and engineering underscore the stakes of this competition in fields like AI.[139] But studies on the future of work suggest that rather than traditional technical skills and knowledge, the workforce of the future will most highly value high-level thinking skills like creativity and complex information processing, and soft skills, like communication and emotional intelligence.[140]

These trends appear to favor a liberal arts approach to education over the more structured variety common in Chinese schools. Though easily caricatured, most accounts of China's education system emphasize its highly regimented, inflexible character. Studies find that reforms intended to encourage creativity and bolster the knowledge economy have been mostly cosmetic, and the system remains heavily focused on the university entrance exams known as *gaokao* (高考). "The central importance of exams," according to one such study, "impedes both interactive group learning and cross-subject learning, as well as it leaves little room for individual active engagement with learning content that goes beyond the content provided by the text books."[141] Chinese students studying abroad, moreover, seem to agree: one study of dozens of Chinese students studying in the United States found that "there was a consensus . . . that their previous Chinese education stifled their creativity, while American education fostered it by encouraging multiple interpretations when approaching a question."[142]

Yet it is equally clear that countries like the United States cannot be complacent when it comes to education. In the 2010s, a new generation of schools emerged in China specifically aimed at teaching creativity and critical thinking.[143] At the same time, research indicates that American educational systems need to foster new skills in order to equip students for the future of work. Some studies estimate that up to 40% of an organization's future work would be outsourced to freelancers, allowing more people to be their own bosses, but also requiring them to be more flexible, resilient, and adaptable.[144] Open societies have advantages in adapting to this future, but retaining a competitive edge is far from assured without concerted policy reform and investment. For countries like the United States, the key to competing effectively with China in the decades ahead may well run through the schoolhouse door.

In the popular imagination, the rise of China in the twenty-first century was often portrayed through the lens of physical goods or large-scale infrastructure projects, but it has always been very much about the flow of people and ideas. Moreover, when it comes to knowledge production, human capital, and mobility, China's rise has transformed economies and societies across the globe. These changes are broadly positive, but can also be deeply contentious. The tensions that pull places like Iowa in two directions—when it comes to supporting a tougher trade stance against China in the late 2010s even while bringing dozens of Chinese students to countryside towns like Clinton—are increasingly typical of communities across the globe. Most concerning, these tensions risk blinding liberal societies like the United States to the many benefits of their open immigration policies and liberal educational systems, a risk we return to in the Conclusion. More immediately, the central role that flows of people and ideas play in China's rise prove especially important with respect to emerging technologies, a subject to which we next turn.

5

The Fight for the Future

Technological Development, Deployment, and Competition

One of the biggest changes in China's relationship with the world in the early twenty-first century was its emergence as a source of advanced technology, from telecommunications to spacecraft. In many ways, this should not have been surprising. Successful economic development usually produces leadership in at least a few technological fields. In the process of its industrialization, tiny Finland gave rise to mobile-phone giant Nokia, which started out making boots, while Japan quickly moved from producing low-cost consumer goods to high-end electronics. But China's scale, and especially its investment in reaching parity with the United States and other developed economies in emerging technologies like artificial intelligence (AI), created a level of alarm and insecurity not seen since the days of Sputnik. The truth, though, is that China's growing prominence in science, technology, and innovation does not necessarily imply it will surpass other countries in technological prowess. While Chinese firms, developers, and the state itself will surely play an ever-greater role in global technology development and policy, China's science and technology ecosystem also faces major challenges that will not be easy to address without wholesale institutional reform. Even so, reforms and investment are necessary if developed economies like the United States are to maintain a technological edge.

Dreams and Delusions: The Realities of Technological Competition between Countries

It is difficult to imagine a more powerful symbol of technological leadership than the famous photo of US astronaut Buzz Aldrin saluting the American flag on the surface of the moon, which he planted there as part of the first manned mission to Earth's closest celestial neighbor. As is often the case,

China's Next Act. Scott M. Moore, Oxford University Press. © Oxford University Press 2022.
DOI: 10.1093/oso/9780197603994.003.0006

though, the photo captured only one aspect of a more complicated reality. Years later, Aldrin recounted how, lifting off to return to Earth, he saw the flag, originally purchased by NASA for $5.50 from a New Jersey vendor, knocked over by the rocket blast, probably causing it to disintegrate in the soft lunar soil.[1]

The flag planted by Aldrin may be the single most potent symbol of what it means for a country to lead the world in technological achievement. But it also signals the fragility of that leadership, and the difficulty of maintaining it in the face of constant change, evolution, and challenge.

Just over 50 years later, an unmanned Chinese lander called Chang'e 5 (嫦娥五号), named for the goddess of the Moon, touched down on a part of the lunar surface called Oceanus Procellerum, the Ocean of Storms. Oceanus Procellerum is the moon's largest visible feature, far larger than the Sea of Tranquility where the Apollo 11 astronauts landed. There, using a robotic arm, Chang'e 5 planted a Chinese flag—much smaller than the one Aldrin raised decades before, but much more durable. Chinese scientists, who spent over a year testing dozens of materials, promised the flag would fly proudly for years to come, even in the harshness of space. "The flag has been unfurled on the Moon," state media proclaimed, "and its five stars shimmer."[2]

Unlike the American Apollo missions, the Chang'e spacecraft were all unmanned. They were, however, clearly meant to challenge the technological dominance displayed in the Aldrin photo. That determination had been demonstrated 18 months earlier, in early 2019, when Chang'e 4 landed on the dark side of the moon, a region previously seen as a bridge too far for the United States, or any other space-faring country. Because the moon's dark side faces permanently away from earth, any spacecraft landing there lacks a direct line of sight for radio communications back home. China's Chang'e 4 probe, though, used a relay satellite called Queqiao (鹊桥), or "Magpie Bridge," named after a celestial span on which two lovers meet in a Chinese folktale, to finally open the far side of the moon to exploration.

China's National Space Administration struck a measured tone in announcing the landing, calling it "a new chapter in humanity's exploration of the moon." But a more revealing response came from a Chinese space scientist, who exulted, "We Chinese people have done something that the Americans have dared not try."[3]

In the weeks following the Chang'e 4 landing, American intelligence officials went before Congress to warn that America faces a "race for technological and military superiority" with China and other adversaries, and that leaders like Xi Jinping "view strong indigenous science and technology capabilities as key to their countries' sovereignty, economic outlook, and national power."[4] While techno-tensions between China and the United States had been building for some time, a line appeared to have been crossed. To its policymakers, the United States' technological superiority seemed as fragile as the five remaining American flags still standing on the lunar surface, fading in the harsh solar wind.

Of course, this was not the first time that America had experienced a crisis of technological confidence: the launch of Sputnik unleashed a wave of panic and anxiety that the world's leading socialist power was out-innovating the free world.[5] But over the decades that followed, technological superiority became a more central part of America's national identity, and the foundation of its national power.[6] In the twenty-first century, Beijing's stated intention to dominate emerging fields like AI shook American confidence to the point that leading commentators warned that China would soon outstrip the United States.[7] As we will see, though, it wasn't so much that the United States began to fall behind, as that China began to catch up. Though no cause for complacency, there are in fact few signs that China will challenge developed countries' technological leadership in the near future. Still, like so many other things about China, the scope and scale of its investment in science, technology, and innovation (STI) are so great that their implications cannot easily be dismissed.

China as a Science, Technology, and Innovation Superpower

China is famous for its well-laid central plans. Since the 1950s, five-year plans have been the basic organizing principle for state policy and economic planning, guiding allocations of funding and resources and, at least in theory, the work of millions of bureaucrats and employees across the country. Abroad, though, few plans have attracted as much attention, or concern, as the one known as "Made in China 2025." First put forward in 2015, the plan aimed to combat a "two-way squeeze" of automation, on one hand, and growing competition from low-cost manufacturing rivals like Bangladesh and Vietnam, on the other. In true centrally planned fashion, Made in China 2025 set out several key indicators for the nation to achieve by 2025, including increases in the number of patents filed and internal firm expenditure on research and development.

By meeting these targets, the plan proposed, China could not only fend off competition from lower-cost rivals, but also dominate new economic sectors like robotics, AI, and biotechnology that would drive growth well into the future (see Table 5.1).[8] By the mid-2010s, searching for "Made in China 2025" in English revealed a torrent of articles, many warning of the threat of a China-dominated future shaped by this ominous master plan. Strangely, though, searching by its Chinese name, 中国制造2025, yielded far fewer recent results. The reason for this surprising disconnect was that in the summer of 2018, China's leaders decided to censor the term, judging that it had become too sensitive—a byword for growing technological competition with the West.[9] It was a sure sign that science and technology, too, had become an arena of growing geopolitical and economic competition.

Even so, China's reliance on science, technology, and innovation (STI) to power growth into the future only mounted in importance. As detailed in Chapter 1, China faced a defining political-economic challenge in the 2010s and 2020s, namely to increase its economic productivity to keep climbing the income ladder toward rich-country status while avoiding common pitfalls to growth—the much-feared "middle-income trap." Meeting this challenge required transforming the Chinese economy from one deriving wealth primarily from inputs derived elsewhere, including foreign direct investment and raw materials, to one driven largely by indigenous innovation. The stakes of the middle-income trap challenge were especially marked for China given the extent to which the Chinese Communist Party staked its legitimacy on meeting certain benchmarks of prosperity.[10]

China's top leaders repeatedly stressed the importance of innovation in driving the country's development strategy. Apart from the Made in China 2025 plan itself, in a 2015 speech Premier Li Keqiang termed innovation the "golden key" to China's future prosperity.[11] In November 2020, meanwhile, Xi Jinping cited "innovation-driven development" as the core of the proposed 14th Five Year Plan (2021–2025), which charted a path for China to reach high-income country status.[12]

The problem, of course, was that many of the technologies and industries tipped in these plans to power future growth were the same ones that the United States and other developed countries expected to drive their own economies in the decades ahead. The perception of an eroding technological edge in the face of Beijing's ambitions stoked something close to panic in several Western capitals, especially Washington. Responses included a 2018 report from the Information Technology Industry Foundation, which warned,

Table 5.1 Key Indicators from the Made in China 2025 Plan

Category	Indicator	2013	2015	2020	2025
Creativity	Internal expenditure on R&D expenditure of manufacturing enterprises above designated size accounts for the proportion of main business income (%)	0.88	0.95	1.26	1.68
	Number of valid invention patents per 100 million yuan of main business income of above-scale manufacturing enterprises (pieces)	0.36	0.44	0.70	1.10
Quality benefit	Manufacturing Quality Competitiveness Index	83.1	83.5	84.5	85.5
	Increase in manufacturing value added	—	—	2 percentage points higher than 2015	4 percentage points higher than 2015
	Manufacturing labor productivity growth rate (%)	—	—	7.5 or so (annual growth rate during the 13th Five-Year Plan period)	Around 6.5 (annual average growth rate during the "14th Five-Year Plan" period)
Two-in-one fusion	Broadband penetration rate (%)	37	50	70	82
	Digital R&D design tool penetration rate (%)	52	58	72	84
	The numerical control rate of key processes (%)	27	33	50	64
Ecological development	Decrease in energy consumption of industrial added value of units above designated size	—	—	18% lower than 2015	34% lower than 2015
	Decrease in CO_2 emissions per unit of industrial added value	—	—	22% lower than 2015	40% lower than 2015
	Decrease in water consumption per unit of industrial added value	—	—	23% lower than 2015	41% lower than 2015
	Comprehensive utilization rate of industrial solid waste (%)	62	65	73	79

Source: Guowuyuan [State Council] 2015.

"Given China's Made in 2025 plan, coupled with unfair mercantilist policies, it is no exaggeration to suggest that, without aggressive action, leading economies such as . . . the United States will, within two decades, likely face a world wherein their industry firms face much stiffer competition and have fewer jobs."[13] In its report justifying the imposition of tariffs against Chinese goods in 2018, the Office of the US Trade Representative specifically cited the Made in China 2025 industrial policy and its threat to leapfrog the United States in advanced technologies.[14] In 2019, the European Union likewise branded Beijing an "economic competitor in pursuit of technological leadership and a systemic rival promoting alternative forms of governance."[15]

To be sure, the growth of China's scientific research and development apparatus after the late 1970s was astonishing. Beijing made high-technology sectors a high-level priority, and scientific research and development enjoyed lavish investment to boost both economic growth and Chinese military power.[16] In the twenty-first century, Beijing began to place special emphasis on breakthrough technologies it believed would be integral to the economy of the future. The 13th Five-Year Plan (2016–2020) pledged to "move faster to make breakthroughs in core technologies" like energy, materials, and biomedical research.[17] Just as important, these plans were backed by massive infusions of state funding. Total research and development expenditure increased approximately 30-fold from 1991 to 2016, to some US$410 billion, accounting for roughly 20% of the world total.[18]

By some estimates, the Chinese government pledged some US$350 billion to support strategic scientific research and technological development initiatives through 2025.[19] China's research and development (R&D) spending accounted for some 2.1% of gross domestic product (GDP) in the late 2010s—not far behind the United States, which as the world leader spent approximately 2.7% of its GDP on scientific research and technological development.[20] Perhaps most meaningfully, China's R&D spending as a percentage of GDP was higher than would be expected given its level of per capita income, suggesting that Chinese firms as well as the state viewed it as an unusually high priority relative to their counterparts in other developing countries (see Figure 5.1).[21] Meanwhile, university research spending in China increased at an average rate of some 15%—a pace equaled in history only in the United States after the launch of Sputnik in the 1950s.[22]

Just as in the Sputnik era, the scale of this investment created a seemingly serious challenge to America's leadership in science and technology. In 1980, the United States accounted for 37% of the entire world's science and

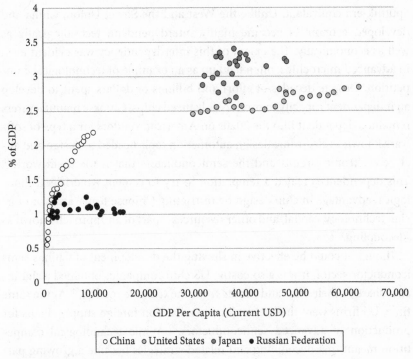

Figure 5.1. Research and Development spending as a share of gross domestic product, selected economies, 1996–2018.
Source: World Bank 2021.

engineering publications, but by 2011, it produced only about one-quarter, a relative decrease due mostly to a boom in Chinese research activity.[23] A landmark shift occurred in 2016, when for the first time, China surpassed the United States as the source of the single largest number of science and engineering publications, producing some 19% of the world's total, compared with 18% for the United States.[24] Over roughly the same period, China became the first developing country to form a manned space program, acquire the ability to design and build supercomputers, and give rise to world-class technology firms like Alibaba (阿里巴巴) and Huawei (华为) (more on Huawei in Chapter 5). It also became one of the few developing countries to feature multiple startup ecosystems, centered on Beijing, Hangzhou, Shanghai, and Shenzhen.[25]

This last feature, a partial embrace of market economics and American-style entrepreneurial capitalism, made technological competition between China and developed democracies decidedly different from its

Sputnik-era equivalent. Unlike the West and the Soviet Union, China and developed economies became highly interdependent, technologically as well as economically. The extent of this interdependency was evident even in advanced microchips, often held up as an example of technological competition. Despite decades of effort and billions of dollars spent to develop an independent capacity to produce advanced chips, Chinese manufacturers remained dependent into the 2020s on American vendors for a type of software known as electronic design automation tools needed to design and analyze electronic circuits and the semiconductors that made them work.[26] This dependence created a temptation to try to cement America's technological advantage in chip design by restricting Chinese firms' access to foreign technology, capital, and other resources—part of an approach known as "decoupling."[27]

Though it could be effective in slowing the development of China's semiconductor sector, it was also costly: US chip companies obtained a significant share of their sales and profits from the Chinese market.[28] At the same time, US firms were themselves largely reliant on foreign supply chains for production of advanced semiconductors.[29] While technological competition meant that decoupling and related strategies became a growing part of Sino-American ties, the reality of technological interdependence meant they would inevitably be limited in scope. As Richard Danzig and Lorand Laski wrote, "Rather than eliminating interdependencies, Chinese and American leaders appear to be trimming and policing them."[30] In early 2021, the Chinese Semiconductor Industry Association announced it would create a joint working group with its American counterpart to discuss intellectual property protection, trade policy, and other contentious issues—a sure sign that Chinese firms, at least, were keen to avoid decoupling.[31] It also reflected China's decidedly mixed track record on the development of other technologies—so much so, in fact, that it remained unclear whether it would ever be able to declare true technological independence.

Quantity over Quality: China's Mixed Record on Science, Technology, and Innovation

By the 2010s, China's STI capacity looked impressive on just about any metric. But quantity does not necessarily equal quality. In fact, the single most striking thing about the rapid rise of China's STI investments and outputs in the first part of the twenty-first century was that it favored volume over value. Even the Made in China plan began by acknowledging China's weaknesses in STI. The State Council's official notice on the plan described China's industrial base as "large but not strong," with weak innovative capacity, low product quality, and a lack of "world-famous brands."[32] This underwhelming performance proved remarkably consistent across a range of cross-national measures, including basic research and development, commercialization, and economy-wide innovation.

In most fields, the average citation impact index of China-based researchers, an indication of how significantly the research is viewed by their peers, remained well below that of developed economies, and below the level that would be expected based on China's share of all scientific publications.[33] In the mid-2010s, the average citation rate for China-authored papers, another indicator of quality, was 9.4, compared to 17.5 for the United States and a global average of 11.8.[34] The conclusion of a study on biomedical innovation that "the average academic impact of Chinese research does not match its exceptional growth in scientific investment and output" held across most fields.[35] Citations were also heavily clustered in certain fields, largely to the exclusion of humanities and social sciences. This amounted to a serious shortcoming, given that fundamental progress often relies on cross-fertilization from seemingly unrelated fields of study and research.[36] Perhaps most tellingly of all, surveys indicated that Chinese researchers in fields like nanoscience almost universally agreed they were in a position of weakness with respect to their colleagues abroad.[37]

Similar gaps were evident in AI, where following massive state investment in the 2010s Chinese researchers began to surpass their American counterparts in the quantity of research produced, but not necessarily quality. China produced 24% of all papers published on AI from 2013 to 2017, compared to 17% for the United States.[38] But a 2019 study found that the average citation impact of Chinese AI publications was less than 1, well behind the average US citation impact of 1.49.[39] Most top AI researchers and developers remained located in the United States.[40] China's AI development ecosystem, moreover, was considerably less well-integrated with industry than its counterparts elsewhere. Only about 2% of Chinese AI publications involved collaborations between the academic and private sectors, for example, compared to 9% in the United States and a global average of 3%.[41]

As these figures suggest, Chinese AI firms remained behind their American competitors as the AI race intensified in the late 2010s. In the early decades of the twenty-first century, most major machine learning frameworks, like Google's TensorFlow and Facebook's PyTorch, were built by American companies, giving the United States a significant advantage in AI software and platform development.[42] The gap appeared poised to persist. John Everett, a top AI official at the US Defense Advanced Research Projects Agency, one of the world's foremost new-technology funding agencies, predicted that China's investments in AI would allow its firms "to do incrementally better . . . by spending an enormous amount of money on it. But there's a declining return to incremental expenditures."[43]

On other measures of innovation, China consistently rose through the ranks in the early decades of the twenty-first century—but remained well behind most developed countries. In the 2019 Global Innovation Index produced by the World Intellectual Property Organization (WIPO), for example, China ranked 14th—up from 17th in the previous rankings, but not even placing first in its own region. Mainland China, in fact, was roundly out-innovated on the WIPO rankings by countries like Singapore (#8) and South Korea (#11). And notably, India's rise through the rankings left China in the dust: its 29-place jump since 2015 represented the fastest improvement in innovation rankings by any major economy on record.[44] A 2020 World Bank report, meanwhile, found that "China falls short of leading economies across a range of . . . important inputs" in STI, including "high-quality human capital, internet access and use, and the overall business and regulatory environment."[45]

Perhaps most damning given the emphasis China's leaders placed on innovation, the ability of Chinese firms to make use of new technology to become more productive appeared to be mediocre at best.[46] Total factor productivity—the most commonly used measure of how productive an economy is—declined from 3.5% in the period 1998–2008 to 1.5% during 2009–2019.[47] In part, this decline reflected a notably low rate of technological assimilation, a key measure of innovation capacity that reflects the extent to which firms can make use of new technologies. The ratio of spending by Chinese firms on assimilating versus importing new technology was about 0.56:1 in 2012; in contrast, the equivalent figure for South Korea in the 1980s was 2:1, suggesting that Chinese firms were far more dependent on foreign technology, and less effective in using it, than their competitors elsewhere.[48]

The extent to which China's STI policies promoted quantity over quality was most dramatically illustrated in patent data, often regarded as an important, if imperfect, measure of innovation.[49] The habitual tendency, described in Chapter 1, for Beijing to translate high-level goals into unrealistic targets for lower-level officials led to the inclusion of patent application numbers into the metrics used to evaluate performance of local officials. As a result, these officials leaned on would-be innovators located in their jurisdictions to submit large numbers of patent applications, many of them frivolous.[50] Thanks in large part to this push, in 2011 the number of patent filings to China's State Intellectual Property Office exceeded the number submitted to the US Patent and Trademark Office for the first time ever (see Figure 5.2).[51]

But the data suggested that, rather than reflecting an actual innovation surge, many of these new applications represented "junk" applications that promised only minor improvements on existing technologies and processes. This interpretation is strengthened by the fact that most of the new Chinese patent applications were from firms that had only infrequently applied in the past—not by firms that had previously shown themselves to be highly innovative, which would be expected had the Chinese economy actually become more innovative overall. In fact, the same study concluded that the majority of these new patent applications were likely a consequence of political pressure rather than innovation.[52]

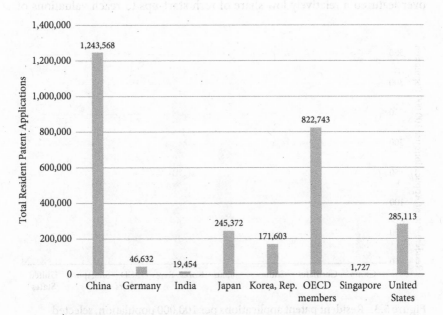

Figure 5.2. Total resident patent applications, selected economies.
Source: World Bank 2021.

A 2020 World Bank study, meanwhile, found that most Chinese firms appeared to have produced few innovations worth patenting. Only 9% of firms held any patents at all, and a small fraction of those accounted for over 90% of the total—a stunningly dense concentration, and one that implied very little collaboration either between firms or between firms and other partners like universities, a key feature of STI in developed democracies like the United States.[53] Comparatively low rates of patent renewal, which would be expected if innovations were considered useful, bolstered the conclusion that there was less than met the eye in China's patenting surge.[54] Moreover, while Chinese patent application figures looked impressive in absolute terms, when adjusted for population they placed China well behind more developed economies, including Japan and Korea (see Figure 5.3).[55]

The relative weakness of China's STI infrastructure was also reflected in the commercial sphere. Attempts to boost commercialization, including by adopting Western-style university technology transfer centers, produced disappointing results in the early decades of the twenty-first century.[56] While the number of patent applications showed no sign of decreasing, licensing rates for commercial and pre-commercial technologies increased at a far slower rate, suggesting a dearth of real-world applications.[57] China moreover featured a relatively low share of tech start-ups to reach valuations of

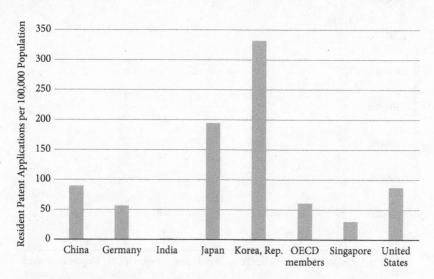

Figure 5.3. Resident patent applications per 100,000 population, selected economies.

Source: World Bank 2021.

over $1 billion, also known as "unicorns." According to a 2019 Credit Suisse report, China's share of unicorns in cutting-edge fields like robotics and bio-tech stood at just 14%, compared with America's 40%.[58]

Despite this patchy track record on STI in the first decades of the twenty-first century, China's leaders also displayed a determination to address these shortcomings.[59] More importantly, as the next section explores, China did not necessarily need to match developed economies' capacity for technolog-ical development or innovation to pose serious challenges to their economic or political interests. Assessing these implications requires first delving deeper into how and why countries compete over technology.

Invention in Service to the State: China's Approach to Science, Technology, and Innovation

In the mythology of Silicon Valley, few moments surpass January 22, 1984, in importance. On that day, as the L.A. Raiders squared off against the Washington Redskins in Superbowl XVII, Apple Computer, then led by Steve Jobs, aired its "1984" commercial. Named after George Orwell's dys-topian novel about a totalitarian future, the spot opens with a line of color-less figures marching in unison into a dark, cavernous hall where they sit watching a God-like figure on screen celebrate the "Information Purification Directives" which have freed the world from "the pests of any contradictory force." Suddenly, however, a woman in bright-red running shorts, previ-ously shown being pursued by helmeted guards, bursts in, hurling a sledge-hammer directly at the screen. As the downtrodden masses gasp, Big Brother disappears into a cloud of smoke, and a Star Wars–like message flashes onto the screen: "On January 24, Apple Computer will introduce Macintosh. And you'll see why 1984 won't be like '1984.'"[60]

The Mac was the world's first true mass-market personal computer, fea-turing a mouse and a graphical user interface that made it far easier to use than its command-entry predecessors. The genius of the 1984 commercial was in drawing a dramatic contrast between insurgent Apple, with its vi-sionary new product, and IBM, then the leader in computing but a veritable byword for establishment conformity. Apple, of course, went on to become one of the world's most successful and innovative companies, following the Mac with its equally revolutionary PowerBook laptop and iPhone mobile phone. The image captured in the 1984 ad stuck: Silicon Valley and its resident innovators were relentlessly contrarian, disruptive, and anti-conformist. They, not some corporate bureaucracy, had invented the future—and would keep doing so.[61]

There was also a deeper subtext to the 1984 commercial, and it had more to do with countries than companies. The year before the spot aired was one of the most momentous, and dangerous, in the entire Cold War period. In March, Ronald Reagan gave his famous "Evil Empire" speech in which he characterized the Soviet Union as a godless, totalitarian mortal enemy of the West. In September, Soviet forces shot down a civilian airliner, Korean Air Flight 007, killing everyone on board and seemingly vindicating Reagan's claims of Moscow's indifference to human life. The following month, an annual military exercise, code-named Able Archer, was upgraded to feature more senior US officials than in the past. Soviet leaders, already rattled by Reagan's speech, interpreted this change as a sign the exercise was in fact a cover to launch a nuclear first strike. Historian John Lewis Gaddis called it "probably the most dangerous moment since the Cuban missile crisis."[62] By the time Apple's 1984 commercial aired, the image of America as a nation of innovators and disruptors, rising up to challenge an authoritarian status quo, had started to become part of pop culture.

The image captured in Apple's 1984 ad, of a more individualistic and innovative free world arrayed against a more brutal yet brittle authoritarian one, captured an enduring reality when it comes to China. Beijing's approach to STI is a far more state-centered one than that which produced the Macintosh. Its objectives are more political than economic, its ideological drivers more authoritarian than liberal—and its record littered with more failures than successes. Still, stopping there would ignore a crucial feature of China's STI strategy: it is not necessarily intended to out-innovate the West, but rather to strengthen the pillars of state power, especially the armed forces, the Chinese Communist Party, and China's state-owned enterprises. Even if China never succeeds in matching the innovative capacity of developed economies, the fact that the fruits of its STI endeavors accrue disproportionately to the state nonetheless poses serious challenges for liberal-minded nations.

Countries and Competition over Technology

Understanding these challenges requires untangling the complicated concept of technological competition between countries. The first step is to differentiate between different types of technological development and inno-vation, especially the rare few that produce revolutionary breakthroughs and the more common variety that produce modest, incremental improvements. The former type is most often associated with technological competition be-tween countries, and not without reason.[63] New military technologies often have important commercial applications, and vice versa, so that a strong STI infrastructure can contribute to multiple elements of national power.[64] Where things get more complicated is that innovation does not need to be transformative to bolster a country's economic or geopolitical competitive-ness. By the same token, most technological advantages are quickly eroded as transformative innovations spread, are copied, and are improved upon. Far more important is creating economic, political, and institutional incentives favorable to economy-wide innovation.

Historical examples of countries developing technologies so transforma-tive that they confer a decisive, enduring advantage over others are rare. In the eighteenth century, British firms' embrace of the then-new technology of cotton-spinning helped England supplant the Netherlands as the world's preeminent commercial and trading nation, a position that eventually led to it acquiring the largest empire in history. However, conditions, including a wage differential that helped persuade English entrepreneurs to take a chance on cotton-spinning, had to be just right for this leapfrogging to occur.[65] In the late twentieth century, meanwhile, the United States developed a set of revolutionary weapons systems, including stealth technology and precision-guided missiles, that conferred a decisive advantage over potential rivals for several decades. But this was an anomaly. In the twenty-first century, a new crop of potentially transformative weapons, including autonomous weapons (covered in more detail in Chapter 7), sparked a heated global arms race, making it doubtful that any one nation could sustain an enduring advantage in military technology.[66]

In contrast, cases of incremental innovation driven by commercial com-petition are far more common. The Asian "tiger" economies of Taiwan, South Korea, and Singapore produced some of the highest growth rates in economic history, but, for the most part, did not deploy revolutionary tech-nologies to achieve them. Instead, their spectacular growth relied mostly on making more mundane, but equally valuable, improvements to existing manufacturing technologies. Many of these improvements built upon tech-nology that had been licensed, transferred, or otherwise acquired from for-eign competitors. Most of the innovation produced by Chinese firms in the

early twenty-first century followed this general pattern, and the final section of this chapter returns to China's potential advantages in technology
deployment.[67]

The historical prevalence of gradual and duplicate rather than breakthrough innovation belies another common misconception about technological competition, namely that it resembles a set-piece battle for supremacy
and leadership between countries and companies in emerging fields like AI
or robotics. To be sure, certain technologies do fit this description. The development of nuclear weapons and manned spaceflight both involved the
large-scale deployment of resources by nation-states, whose investment in
them was justified largely by military and geopolitical considerations.[68] In
the twenty-first century, quantum technologies feature similar economic and
geopolitical characteristics. Certain forms of quantum-based encryption, for
example, feature a theoretically hack-proof form of communication, potentially giving the first country to develop it a significant economic, political,
and military advantage.[69]

At first glance, China appeared to be ahead in the race to develop these
quantum communication applications. In the first decades of the twenty-first
century, Beijing began pouring money into the field, including $10 billion to
create a National Laboratory for Quantum Information Sciences. In 2016,
Chinese scientists launched the world's first quantum communications satellite, named Micius (墨子) after an ancient scientist-philosopher. A year
later, in 2017, the world's first long-distance quantum communication link
was opened between Beijing and Shanghai, and in 2020, a group of Chinese
scientists demonstrated a way to transmit useful volumes of quantum-
encrypted data between satellites and ground stations at distances of over
1,000 km.[70] The director of America's National Institute of Standards and
Technology was quoted as saying that although "it's a long journey to actually
get to quantum-based devices," it's also "very clear that we are in a race as a
nation, and we have China and the European Union dramatically investing
in this area."[71]

Yet despite the appearance of competition, it was less certain whether
China's apparent lead in making quantum communication practical was real,
or really mattered. Most analysts believed that the United States remained
ahead when it came to a broader range of quantum technologies—including
quantum computing, which was a focus of next-generation decryption research, and whose applications were likely of even greater significance
than quantum encryption itself.[72] And while development of quantum

technologies may in a very real sense be a competition between countries to get to the finish line first, in most cases technological competition does not resemble a single race or sprint. Instead, it looks, in the words of former US defense official Christine Fox, more like a track-and-field event, in which multiple contestants attempt to out-do one another in very different games.[73] Brute strength matters most in some of these competitions, speed and agility in others. What counts is how they fit together in a broader innovation ecosystem. And within these ecosystems, another crucial feature of technological development and innovation becomes readily apparent: it is rarely zero-sum.

Perhaps the best example of this feature is AI, though ironically it became the focus of greatest concern that the United States and other Western countries are falling behind China. As with other technologies, the crux of the concern had to do with the scale of investment in technological research and development. By some widely repeated but contested estimates, China's state committed some $150 billion into AI research for the 2020–2030 time period, far higher than comparable planned US government spending.[74]

To be sure, certain applications of AI did become a focus of competition, especially between the world's militaries. The People's Liberation Army began to aggressively explore the potential of AI to improve its capabilities and help defeat the United States should war occur.[75] The US Department of Defense's 2018 Artificial Intelligence strategy, meanwhile, referred to China's investment in AI technology as a threat that would produce "eroding cohesion among allies and partners, reduced access to markets that will contribute to a decline in our prosperity and standard of living, and growing challenges to societies that have been built upon individual freedoms."[76] As described further in Chapter 7, the integration of AI and autonomous weapons systems in violation of international norms posed a serious threat to the long-standing principle of nuclear deterrence that had kept the peace for over 75 years.

But while AI certainly has applications that fit the concept of technological competition, development of the technology itself is largely a positive- rather than zero-sum game. The development of AI algorithms and systems does not necessarily create winners and losers—everyone could win, at least in theory. Many leading AI developers, including tech giants like Amazon and Google, made many of their AI algorithms open source, meaning that developers almost anywhere could make use of the underlying code to develop new systems and platforms, which they were then expected to share with the global developer community.[77] In theory, at least, developers in

America could benefit from advances in China, or Cameroon for that matter, and vice versa. Because the nature of AI favored such open-source development, observers like former US defense official Christine Fox argued that it should be considered a "foundational technology" that shouldn't be "locked up by classification and commerce restrictions."[78]

China's massive investments in science and technology, especially areas like AI, created something close to panic among many Western policymakers. But the concept of countries competing to develop, own, and deploy the technologies of the future is of limited value. Just as important, despite major advances over the past few decades, China's science, technology, and innovation system faces serious challenges and systematic weaknesses that will take years to overcome. As the next section examines in detail, this means that for all its progress, China's technological capabilities remained behind those of the West into the 2020s and are likely to stay that way for some time. The most important reason is that they are so closely tied to the state.

China's State-Led Approach to Science, Technology, and Innovation

Despite its size and scale, the foundation of China's STI enterprise owes much to one man: Marshal Nie Rongzhen (聂荣臻). A hero of the Party's struggles against both the Japanese and the Nationalist government during the 1930s and 1940s, Nie was hand-picked by then-Premier Zhou Enlai to oversee defense production and mobilization during the Korean War. Chastened by the daunting challenge of combating America's industrial might amid the loss of Soviet technical assistance following the Sino-Soviet split in the mid-1950s, Nie honed a philosophy of technological self-reliance and subordination to state, and especially military, goals. At a seminal 1956 meeting, Nie laid out a vision for "putting the production of military goods first, linking the production of military and consumer goods, and preparing civilian industry to move quickly to a war footing."[79] The interlinking of civilian and military research objectives and institutions gave rise to what Western analysts would later term "military-civil fusion," a source of considerable tension between the United States and China, but one that, in Nie's mind, was born as much out of necessity as desirability.[80]

Nie's vision of science in service to the state was not entirely original: it largely echoed the Soviet approach to STI and was shared among many senior

Chinese leaders and officials of the period. Yet it was Nie, more than any other single individual, who advocated for what became a decisively state-led approach to science and technology. Along with the prioritization of military technologies, Nie championed "a centralized bureaucratic hierarchy, a task-led approach . . . and technological indigenization."[81] While each of these characteristics shaped China's approach to STI for decades, Nie's focus on self-reliance was perhaps the most prominent.

In the 1950s and 1960s, primarily under Nie's direction, China succeeded in developing several advanced technologies largely on its own, including the atomic and hydrogen bombs and orbital spaceflight—a constellation of achievements that gave rise to the phrase, "Two bombs, one satellite" (两弹一星), signifying a spirit of self-reliance in science and technology. Though nominally a reflection of China's indigenous technological capacity and determination, the spirit of self-reliance also reflected a deep sense of insecurity. As Richard Danzig and Lorand Laskai observed, "Technology plays a central role in China's mission to return to historical greatness. Chinese leaders have long viewed dependence on foreign technology as a straitjacket used to hold China down."[82] This sense of insecurity imbued China's approach to STI with both an orientation toward national security priorities and a strong brand of nationalism. Its "dominant philosophy," two leading scholars later wrote, was "an extreme version of techno-nationalism."[83]

The twin influences of self-reliance on one hand and nationalism on the other ensured that the state would control every important aspect of STI in the decades that followed. Nie's influence was reflected in two distinctive elements of this state-centric approach. The first was an orientation toward quantity over quality. From the beginning, Nie argued that the development of cutting-edge weaponry could not come at the expense of more basic, but equally important, war goods.[84] The second was a task-oriented approach to research and development in which the state identified scientific and technological priorities and then commissioned researchers to work on them. Nie later recalled engaging in a debate between advocates of this task-oriented approach and opponents who favored a more organic one, looking to academics and other experts to identify promising new areas of research and inquiry and pursue them with state support. Nie sided with the task-oriented view, establishing a top-down framework for STI that persisted into the twenty-first century.[85]

The experience of other countries suggests this was a mistake. State-centric STI systems have historically given rise to breathtaking inefficiency and dysfunction. In one remarkable example from the Soviet Union, the inspiration for much of Nie's approach, military leaders persuaded a state ministry to hoard key components for a high-performance computing project to prevent the project's sponsor, a rival state agency, from making progress—helping ensure that the Soviet Union produced nothing comparable to the Mac and leaving it far behind when personal computers began to dominate the workplace.[86]

Western market economies, too, fell prey to the perils of directing innovation from the perches of state power. In the 1960s, the French government decided that it needed to invest more resources in science and technology, lest it be left behind by the United States, Britain, Germany, and other countries. Rather than relying on market forces to guide such investment, however, France's state planners picked a few specific fields where "given their strategic importance, it seemed imperative for France not to let itself be outstripped."[87]

Several problems soon appeared with France's state-led approach. First, big businesses tended to be favored as recipients of public funds, rather than smaller, nimbler, and more innovative firms. Second, politics rather than scientific promise began directing public investment in technological development. Instead of technical merit, this political interference "led to the privileged treatment of particular research objectives that were considered especially important from a political point of view."[88] Third, major technology development programs became the scene of fierce bureaucratic infighting between government agencies who favored one technology and those favoring another.[89] The end result was that France missed out on many of the most important technological developments of the late twentieth century. Despite a major investment program focused on data-processing technology, for example, French firms too failed to capitalize on the personal computer revolution.[90]

The failure of France's state-led approach to technological development suggests that not only do governments tend to be unsuccessful at picking the technologies of the future, but their efforts to do so risk crowding out more innovative firms and entrepreneurs. In most cases, the resources that can be poured into technological development are limited: there are only so many scientists, laboratories, universities, and firms with the right expertise to work on large-scale programs. When governments deploy large amounts of public money to these programs, it inevitably draws this limited pool of talent like moths to a flame, diverting resources and attention from smaller firms and research groups that may be looking at riskier, more innovative, and ultimately more promising approaches to solving problems. In the case of France, the close involvement of the state in technological development effectively crowded out these smaller players. As one historian wrote, the ultimate legacy of France's approach "has been to divert very important financial and human resources from technology sectors that are purely civilian but of considerable industrial importance."[91]

Twenty-first-century China is very different from both the Soviet Union and mid-century France—its economic system and institutions are considerably more sophisticated, and in some ways less strictly controlled.[92] For instance, despite strong central direction, subnational governments were responsible for more than half of total Chinese R&D spending throughout the early twenty-first century. As in the Soviet Union, however, STI investment remained heavily concentrated in strategic industries identified by Beijing. In 2015, for example, the high-speed rail and transport sector, the state's highest infrastructure priority at the time, received over 25% of all public R&D spending, despite featuring mostly mature rather than emerging technologies. In the private sector, meanwhile, R&D spending was heavily concentrated in state-owned enterprises, which was estimated to account for at least a third of total private-sector investment. In general, state-owned enterprises were considerably less productive and innovative than privately held competitors, suggesting that this R&D allocation was highly inefficient.[93]

In keeping with this strong state direction, China's STI infrastructure became both centralized and focused on just a few elite universities and research centers in major cities.[94] Innovation policy was heavily bureaucratized, involving over 10 ministerial-level bodies, each of which produced neverending blizzards of policies, regulations, and plans, many of them mutually contradictory.[95] Moreover, whereas US research collaborations in critical fields like nanotechnology tended to involve large numbers of institutions, thereby tapping larger and more diverse talent networks, those in China were heavily concentrated, with Beijing alone receiving some 30% of China's total government R&D funding.[96] The bulk of advanced research was conducted at just 10 elite institutions.[97] Despite calls to mimic the West's less centralized approach to R&D, Beijing in fact bureaucratized it even further. In the late 2010s, China's National Natural Science Foundation (自然科学基金委), its most important civilian basic research funding body, was moved under the Ministry of Science and Technology (科技部), a much larger bureaucracy that traditionally funds large national research projects. This shift, several experts noted, threatened to squeeze out funding for smaller, riskier, and potentially more transformative research.[98]

Much like France's failed attempts to drive growth through state-directed research, China's approach risked backing the wrong technological horses. "China's continued effort to force commercial technology innovation through state planning," according to analyst Xiaomeng Lu, "resulted in a massive waste of resources and generated little result."[99] Instead, Chinese firms focused investment on heavily subsidized and protected industries, creating massive over-capacity, reducing competition, and producing few incentives to innovate.[100]

China's highly state-centric mode of STI may be inefficient, but there are even deeper reasons to believe a gap might persist between China and developed democracies in terms of innovation. In particular, as the next section details, corruption and censorship constrained China's potential to innovate and develop new technologies. Even with these additional constraints, however, China's state-centric approach to STI notched considerable achievements in applied research and technology deployment, with important implications for liberal-minded countries and companies.

The Secret Sauce: The Role of Informal Institutions, Norms, and Values in Innovation

Few technological developments caused as much alarm as the moment that Sputnik 1 entered orbit and became the world's first artificial satellite on October 4, 1957. In part because it was mostly heard, rather than seen—its most evident impact was to emit an ominous, high-pitched chirping signal that could be heard through any radio—Sputnik quickly became perceived as a kind of electronic, all-seeing eye in the sky, and a clear symbol of Soviet technological superiority. At first, the US government's official reaction was one of exasperation. At a White House Press Conference held just a few days after Sputnik entered orbit, President Eisenhower pleaded with skeptical journalists to understand that the Soviets had been first to launch a satellite not because America was technologically inferior, but because it refused to view space exploration as a "race with other nations." Instead, Eisenhower insisted, "We were doing it for science and not for security." Pressed by reporters about the satellite's "immense significance in surveillance,"

Eisenhower was dismissive, retorting that Sputnik amounted to "one small ball in the air."[101]

It quickly became clear, though, that the American public, and much of the rest of the world, saw things very differently. The US National Science Board issued a statement calling the launch "an impressive demonstration of the strong position of Russian science and education" and warning that it "challenges this nation's determination to strengthen its present scientific position."[102] A confidential assessment of international reaction to the launch concluded that it "underlines Soviet potential . . . to compete successfully in fields in which U.S. leadership has been taken for granted." In Mexico, newspaper editors stopped requesting access to technical information furnished by the US government, turning instead to Soviet sources. In Strasbourg, meanwhile, a meeting between America's closest European allies "severely criticized the U.S. for falling behind in the arms race."[103] A public opinion poll conducted right after Sputnik 1's launch found that 70% of Americans believed that "our schools have placed too little stress on science," and two-thirds agreed that "we Americans have been too smug and complacent about our national strength."[104]

In popular lore, this period of panic was followed by a heroic response: massive investment in research, development, and scientific education. "The Sputnik moment," the *Financial Times* later reported, "showered panic across the US and resulted in a subsequent surge in research spending."[105] In the year following the launch of Sputnik, the US Congress responded by passing the National Defense Education Act, which dramatically increased federal support for instruction in scientific subjects and created both the National Aeronautics and Space Administration and the Defense Advanced Research Project Agency. Despite Eisenhower's misgivings, it was one of the biggest bursts in federal government activity since the Second World War. It is a response that many commentators called to reprise in response to China's growing technological sophistication in the twenty-first century.[106]

America's response to the Sputnik challenge became mythologized as a textbook example of an enlightened policy response to technological threats from abroad. Yet many people at the time, including Eisenhower, viewed it as at best a distraction, and at worst an indefensible strain on already strapped budgets. In his first major speech on Sputnik, delivered from the Oval Office on November 7, 1957, Eisenhower attempted to frame growing calls for investment in science and technology as misguided. "Certainly, we need to feel a high sense of urgency," he conceded, "but this does not mean that we should mount our charger and try to ride off in all directions at once." Instead of a call to arms, Eisenhower proposed "selectivity in national expenditures of all kinds." Most of his proposals were downright dull, including the "pooling of scientific effort" with US allies—which Eisenhower was quick to note would entail "no cost."[107] In a second speech, while boasting that the federal government was "stepping up its basic research programs," he pointedly noted that "the biggest share of the job is in the hands of industry and private organizations."[108]

Eisenhower and his contemporaries clearly underestimated the long-term benefits of America's post-Sputnik public investments in science, technology, and innovation. These produced, among other things, the Silicon Valley of today, the world's most dynamic and important STI ecosystem.[109] But they were right that when it comes to bolstering technological competitiveness, money is not everything. It is a lesson that applies in spades to technological competition between China and developed democracies in the twenty-first century: the most important factor in maintaining technological leadership has more to do with values than with money. As Eisenhower himself put it, America's response to Sputnik should stand not "on the Communists' own terms—outmatching them in military power, general technological advance, and specialized education and research" but rather on "the vigor of our ideals."[110]

President Eisenhower's reaction to the Sputnik moment highlights the critical role that values, ideology, and institutions, including those surrounding the freedom of expression, play in fostering innovation. These basic features of politics, economics, and society are extremely difficult to change, and represent the biggest reason to believe that, even as it increasingly challenges the technological leadership of developed democracies, China might never entirely catch up. Yet the reverse is also true: if the US and other developed nations want to remain ahead, they need to protect their liberal values and institutions, which more than anything else underpin leadership in science, technology, and innovation.

Informal Institutions, Ideology, and Values: China's Prospects for Transformative Innovation

In his 1950s magnum opus, *Science and Civilization in China*, Joseph Needham sought to answer a historical mystery: Why did ancient China, which among other things developed gunpowder, the compass, and the printing press, become outstripped by the West in science and technology? His answer was that China failed to replicate the tradition of empiricism that emerged in Europe during the Enlightenment.[111] Needham's theory, though subsequently criticized, still echoes in a raging debate over whether China's institutions and ideology will ever allow it to close the innovation gap with the West.

In 2018, Liu Yadong (刘亚东), the editor of a leading science magazine, caused a nationwide stir when he lamented that Chinese society lacked a "scientific spirit," which prevented it from equaling the West's technological achievements.[112] The nationalistic *Global Times* (环球时报) newspaper unexpectedly amplified Liu's warning, writing that "a technology insider criticizing the exaggeration of China's technological achievements comes at just the right time."[113] Another *Global Times* article cited an estimate that "it will still take two generations' effort to eliminate the gap between China and the US in the science and technology sector."[114] And in 2019, the Chinese Communist Party's leading internal publication, 求实 (*Qiu Shi*, Seeking Truth) pointedly reprinted a speech in which Xi Jinping called China's lack of ability to innovate its "Achilles heel," signaling Beijing's continuing concern about China's ability to match the West's innovative potential.[115]

To foreign ears, the focus of this debate on fundamental features of Chinese society such as institutions, norms, and ideology might sound overly deterministic, if not over-wrought.[116] Research shows, however, that these underlying political, social, and cultural factors can in fact be just as critical for innovation as scientific and economic ones. This insight is central to a concept called the national innovation systems (NIS) framework.[117] Key features in this framework include regulatory regimes, capital and labor markets, and relationships between government, firms, and research institutions.[118] Because these features vary markedly across countries, so does innovation capacity. Drawing on the NIS framework, scholars propose that countries like the United States, which feature strong regulatory regimes, highly competitive firms, and efficient capital and labor markets, are more favorable to producing breakthrough innovations. Countries like China, in which elements of the state substitute for market forces in most aspects of the NIS, are better suited to the deployment of existing technologies rather than development of new ones. "Radical innovations," a comparative study of NIS in the United States, Japan, and China concluded, "are therefore less likely to emanate from China in the foreseeable future."[119]

Not everyone buys into the NIS concept, and one critique is that it places too strong an emphasis on formal institutional arrangements. Indeed, some research suggests that informal norms and values like trust and reciprocity might be at least as important in sustaining innovation as formal institutions.[120] Even by these alternative standards, though, China appears to be in a weak position, with several studies suggesting that crucial innovation processes are undermined by pervasive social mistrust, corruption, and an organizational culture that disincentivizes collaboration. A 2019 survey, for example, found that innovation in Chinese universities is "compromised by an atomistic understanding of learning, unwillingness to cooperate across institutions and sectors, top-down modes of control, and networks of corruption," including an allegedly widespread practice of admitting unqualified students for doctoral study in exchange for what are effectively bribes.[121] Moreover, though all countries exhibit forms of scientific dishonesty, China became a leading source of fraudulent research, in part because many Chinese universities awarded researchers handsome bonuses for publishing articles in international peer-reviewed journals. In July 2020, an independent researcher identified over 120 published articles credited to Chinese institutions that all appeared to use the same images as proof of experimental results, suggesting fraud.[122]

The biggest informal constraint on China's NIS, though, is the authoritarian control of information and expression.[123] Just as bureaucracy squeezes out innovation (detailed in the previous section), censorship tends to stifle new ideas. In a sure sign that China's rulers take the linkage between free expression and innovation seriously, Beijing in fact passed a law, the 1993 Scientific and Technological Progress Law, that explicitly guaranteed freedoms for researchers and inventors.[124] In 2016, Xi Jinping told scientists that they should "freely explore and test the bold hypotheses they are putting forward."[125] But security laws put in place in subsequent years discouraged, and in many cases prohibited, the sharing of research data (more on these restrictions in Chapter 6).[126] And while the close relationships between China's state, military, and private tech firms are often seen as a strength, several observers have noted they can also prevent useful debate and constrain the development of alternative approaches, likely to the detriment of technological development.[127]

While it is difficult to estimate the effect that censorship and secrecy have on research and innovation, anecdotal accounts suggest it is significant. In 2016, just as Xi was promoting free scientific inquiry, a Chinese scientist was anonymously quoted as saying "it is very difficult to achieve world-leading results or to be a frontrunner in global scientific research without unfettered access to the global internet."[128] A Stanford researcher with long experience working in China likewise observed that "the only thing that holds China back is that the nature of dissent and creativity are related. . . . Great entrepreneurs, great founders are dissidents."[129] Claims that China's authoritarianism undermines innovation are lent further credence by studies reporting that when surveyed about barriers to development of their fields, Chinese researchers in rapidly evolving fields like nanomedicine repeatedly cite censorship and restrictions on data-sharing.[130]

Despite its impact on basic research, onerous state control and supervision could be most grating, and most limiting, in the commercial sphere. In 2019, the Hangzhou (杭州) Municipal Government, which simultaneously claimed to be China's tech capital, announced it would embed 100 government officials in major tech companies like Alibaba—an unprecedented attempt to assert influence over private companies.[131] And in late 2020, reports surfaced that Xi Jinping himself had "personally scuttled" the planned Initial Public Offering of mobile-payment giant Ant Group, controlled by Jack Ma, China's best-known entrepreneur.

Ma's alleged offense was to have criticized Beijing for holding back financial innovation through onerous regulation. Though a common enough complaint among his executive peers in other countries, Ma's critique likely cost him billions.[132] Such political interference sharply reduced the incentive for other entrepreneurs to emulate the risk-taking that made Ma famous. As longtime McKinsey China expert Richard Foster noted, "China's growing commitment to research and development is not leading to entrepreneurship . . . the Chinese government has largely reserved the right to undertake risk to itself rather than delegate to independent individuals."[133]

China's early twenty-first-century NIS manifested significant, systemic deficiencies that compared unfavorably with those of more liberal societies. Since these challenges are so closely tied to fundamental norms, values, and institutions, they seem unlikely to be overcome any time soon. However, China does not necessarily need to develop a NIS that is better, or even more efficient, than its foreign competitors to succeed in gaining access to important technologies. China's strategy for STI places more emphasis on technology deployment than basic research per se, and this still threatens to bolster China's technological competitiveness at the expense of foreign countries and companies.

The Real Techno-Challenge: Countering China's Applied
Research and Deployment Advantage

Crucially, the NIS framework does not mean that countries like China are incapable of innovation. Instead, it predicts that certain institutional features of China's political, economic, and social system make it less likely to produce radically new technologies. But transformative innovation is not always the goal, and when it comes to applied research and technological deployment, China's NIS holds some important advantages.[134]

These advantages were highlighted with respect to AI by technologist and venture capitalist Kai-Fu Lee in a widely cited 2018 book, "AI Superpowers." Unlike more mundane inventions, Lee portrayed AI as a transformational technological advance on par with electricity. In much the same way that it took large-scale public investment to achieve widespread electrification, Lee argued that realizing AI's potential would require a powerful government to bear the risks of large-scale development and adoption.[135] To Lee, that meant China's top-down approach to technological development, while less efficient than that of countries like the United States, might nonetheless allow Beijing to effect "brute force transformations" and take "big bets on game-changing technologies" like AI.[136] Similar conclusions could be found in studies showing that China's state-dominated NIS demonstrated a remarkable ability to marshal technological resources in pursuit of national priorities like building high-speed rail.[137]

What is clear is that in certain technology fields, Beijing proved content to lead in deployment rather than basic research, helping Chinese firms grow market share even as they remained behind foreign competitors in cutting-edge R&D. Apart from AI, this was apparent in the field of robotics. Throughout the early twenty-first century, American companies and research institutions stood, by most accounts, in the forefront of basic robotics research, and US industries were far more heavily automated than their Chinese counterparts. As in many other technological sectors, though, Beijing put forward big plans to become a robotics superpower. Its Robot Industry Development Plan (RIDP), issued in the mid-2010s, aimed, among other things, to increase China's "robot density" to 100 robots for every 10,000 human workers, a goal it surpassed in 2018 by 40%, putting it within striking distance of the comparable American figure of 200 robots for every 10,000 human workers.[138] In absolute numbers, meanwhile, China put far more robots into service than any other country, boasting nearly 800,000 by 2019, as compared to the United States' roughly 300,000.[139]

At the same time, boosted by policy support from Beijing, Chinese robot suppliers began to steadily increase their market share at the expense of foreign competitors.[140] This position promised to help Chinese firms take advantage of growing demand for services robots, in addition to the industrial robots that had long dominated the sector. Chinese firms like JD and Alibaba, encouraged by the RIDP, became leaders in certain service robotic applications like automated restaurant equipment and even robotic coffee shop baristas.[141] In China, demand for these contactless services increased dramatically during the pandemic and looked set to continue to do so worldwide, potentially conferring on Chinese firms a significant long-term commercial advantage.[142]

The example of robotics indicates that even as countries like the United States seek to bolster their basic research capacity in response to the technological challenge from China, they cannot afford to neglect the application and deployment side of the technology development equation. As analysts Emily de la Bruyere and Nathan Picarsic point out, doing so creates the risk that Chinese firms might benefit from Western STI as much as foreign ones, either through technology transfer or more illicit channels.[143] But even the applied aspects of R&D are strongly influenced by informal institutions, norms, and values, like collaboration. In these areas, liberal societies retain significant advantages over China and need to continue to build on them.

Some of the most important such advantages are related to organizational culture. Several studies back the idea that societies that feature less hierarchical power structures and provide greater individual freedoms produce more patent applications on a per capita basis.[144] The best example of how social norms can bear on STI, though, is America's space race against the Soviet Union during the Cold War. The US space program formed flexible organizational relationships across different disciplines and government agencies, as well as between the public and private sectors. It also encouraged employees at both junior and senior levels to openly discuss and debate the causes of failure. The Soviet system, in contrast, relied on rigid bureaucratic hierarchies and went to great lengths to conceal failure, preventing lessons from being fully learned. These contrasting Soviet and American approaches to "systems culture" were instrumental in America's success in space exploration. In the end, it was not technology itself, but rather the organizational ability to direct "scores of thousands of minds in a close-knit, mutually enhancive combination of government, university, and private industry" that won the space race for the United States.[145]

The collaboration that played such an important role in America's space program remains a critical element of its competitive advantage in STI. Collaboration is especially important for translational research, a crucial step in commercializing and deploying new technology. A major problem with emerging technologies is that while they can be transformative, researchers, companies, and organizations often lack the internal resources and expertise to figure exactly how to use them. That is where translational research comes in, which has long been an integral part of STI in countries like the United States. US government agencies like the National Institutes of Health helped develop the original concept of translational research and remain some of its leading practitioners.[146]

The translational approach to research entails bringing people who know how to develop and use new technologies like AI together with those who have problems or challenges that AI can help solve, including doctors, librarians, and entrepreneurs. While collaboration and communication are important for research, they are equally valuable for large companies and organizations who may not necessarily understand how technologies like AI can help grow their businesses. In a study of how over 100 Chinese firms use big data, for example, researchers found that corporate leaders often lacked the ability to understand how techniques like big data could be used to improve decision-making.[147] Using translational research to bridge these gaps is essential to fostering innovation ecosystems.

Despite historic strengths in key areas like translational research, countries like the United States cannot afford to rest on their laurels. One approach to maintaining an edge in technological innovation is to create short-term fellowships of six months to a year, partly funded by governments and partly by companies, to give researchers and practitioners from a broad array of fields the chance to familiarize themselves with newer technologies like AI and synthetic biology. These fellowships can also give researchers in these emerging fields the chance to "embed" in organizations that might offer new use cases for their technological expertise. In both cases, the objective is to help identify new applications for new and emerging technologies.[148] These new collaborations between firms, governments, and research institutions can be hugely valuable within countries—but even more so between them. As President Eisenhower observed decades ago, sharing scientific knowledge is something that like-minded countries can do easily—and at little to no cost. Strengthening knowledge-sharing in important, but politically and militarily sensitive, technologies like AI should be a priority for like-minded democratic nations.

In the first few decades of the twenty-first century, the idea of technological competition between China and countries like the United States slowly gained popularity, but it could be misleading. For a few technologies that are complex, expensive, and difficult to develop, like nuclear weapons or some quantum devices, it does make sense to think in terms of competition—realistically, only national governments have the resources to develop these technologies and they have strong reasons to prevent other nations from acquiring them. For most technologies, though, like most AI algorithms, development and possession are not zero-sum. In many cases, it is in fact preferable for developers around the world to share underlying code, and further development benefits companies and users in all countries.

The real focus of technological competition between countries China, the United States, and other developed economies is on informal values, institutions, and organizational culture, rather than on the technology itself. Liberal societies look set to retain decisive advantages in each of these areas. Even so, China has significantly narrowed the gap in many technology areas, especially in deployment. Weaknesses in education systems and talent pipelines are a serious concern, a worry more fully addressed in Chapter 4.

Liberal-minded countries, companies, and organizations need to base their response to technological competition on long-standing norms and values and redouble investment in areas like translational research that can help power innovation into the future. There are a few fields, though, where China's growing technological prowess directly threatens these very institutions, norms, and values. As the next chapter details, these threats are especially evident in the digital domain.

6

Digital Dilemmas

Information Security, Data Privacy, and Digital Networks

One of twenty-first-century China's most profound influences is in the intangible realm of digital data, information, and communications. The early twenty-first century witnessed a transformation in the integration of digital data and information from a huge variety of sources, including a growing number of web-connected devices, into increasingly sophisticated communications networks. The scale and scope of this integration intensified concerns over information security and data privacy. As with so many other twenty-first-century transformations, China played a key role in each of these areas.[1] Thanks to its firms' investment in next-generation telecommunications equipment, China gained a significant advantage in developing key elements of the infrastructure that supports all this data collection. Meanwhile, thanks to the size of its population, relatively loose rules governing data collection, and generally lax privacy permissions, Chinese firms and its state accumulated vast troves of data. These domestic data riches were augmented by data collection from abroad, including through large-scale data hacks. Perhaps most concerning, China's state and its companies began to develop new ways to use digital data to keep tabs on individuals, even beyond China's borders. This creates a three-part digital dilemma for countries and companies around the world: how to balance information-sharing and security; prevent China from accumulating an insurmountable information advantage; and build secure digital communications networks. Beijing, too, faces digital dilemmas in the form of rising political pressure to protect data privacy. Resolving these dilemmas means finding better ways to secure information, on the one hand, and coordinate data management between the public and private sectors, on the other.

China's Next Act. Scott M. Moore, Oxford University Press. © Oxford University Press 2022.
DOI: 10.1093/oso/9780197603994.003.0007

Network Geopolitics: China, Huawei, and 5G

The tranquil Long Island village of West Sayville does not look like the kind of place that might start a war. But in the early twentieth century, it played host to a plot to dominate East Asia, and eventually much of the rest of the world. In what is now an open field just north of town, a German state-backed company called Telefunken built one of the world's most powerful radio transmitters, capable of receiving signals all the way from Berlin. This revolutionary technology, then known as wireless, had a crucial geopolitical benefit: it allowed Germany to communicate with its colonies in China and the South Pacific without relying on the British-controlled submarine cables that carried most of the world's electronic communications. Washington watched the station warily as the First World War raged across the Atlantic, and with good reason: the transmitter was frequently used to send secret messages to German agents and sympathizers in America.[2]

But the station's true star turn in history occurred in January 1917, when it relayed a message from Berlin to Mexico City. In return for declaring war on the United States, Mexico's president was told, Germany would help return the states of Texas, New Mexico, and Arizona to Mexican rule. Unfortunately for the Berlin-based plotters, the message was intercepted by British intelligence, and quickly handed over to the US government. Soon afterward, US President Wilson sent in Marines to seize the West Sayville transmitter, and the United States was at war with Germany.[3]

The story of Telefunken bears an eerie similarity to the case of China in the early twenty-first century and its leading telecom equipment provider, Huawei (华为). Like Germany in the late nineteenth century, China in the twenty-first began to aggressively build a new global communications network that promised to largely bypass the existing one dominated by rival powers. Like Telefunken, Huawei, with strong state backing, developed more advanced technology than its foreign competitors. Finally, as with Telefunken, it was not so much the technical equipment itself that was cause for concern as the data and information that flowed through it. While Huawei's efforts to build a new global communications network have not led to anything close to war, they have, like the West Sayville station, provoked increasing alarm throughout the West.

Concerns over China's role in digital communications networks date to at least the first decade of the twenty-first century. In 2007, a proposed acquisition of the American communications equipment provider Qualcomm by a set of investors that included Huawei as a minority stakeholder fell through because of concerns that the Chinese tech firm was too close to Beijing. In the aftermath, the US government began to look warily at Chinese foreign investment in the telecommunications sector, especially when it involved Huawei.[4] One consequence of China's rise in following decades was that as the influence and sophistication of firms like Huawei grew, the question of how to ensure the integrity of global communications networks began to be asked more often, and with greater urgency.

Exporting Authoritarian Network Control

The stakes of Chinese investment in sectors like telecommunications grew for two reasons. First, companies like Huawei became much more advanced, and in the opinion of many began to offer better technology, at lower prices, than their foreign competitors.[5] Huawei was moreover distinctive in offering an entire ecosystem of next-generation telecom equipment, which often allowed it to offer lower bids than its competitors to build complete networks.[6] Second, and even more important, Huawei effectively positioned itself as a leader in a suite of technologies known as "5G," for fifth-generation telecommunications; 5G technology dramatically increased the speed and volume of data that could be transmitted across wireless networks—a critical step toward deploying the Internet of Things, with millions of devices sharing and receiving information remotely, allowing consumers to turn off their curling iron from the car or have their espresso machine order more beans automatically.

The problem with Huawei's perceived leadership in 5G was that as more and more data became shared between more and more devices, from toasters to traffic lights, it became increasingly vulnerable to intrusion and disruption.[7] The nature of China's party-state led outside observers to fear that companies like Huawei would be unable to ignore orders from Beijing to tap the vast streams of 5G data without users' knowledge—or that, in the event of a military conflict, it could disrupt critical communications in countries like the United States. A provision in China's Intelligence Law obliging all Chinese citizens to aid in national security work was often cited as proof that Huawei and Beijing were effectively joined at the hip.[8] Eric Schmidt, former CEO of Google who was later appointed chair of the US National Security Commission on Artificial Intelligence, warned for example that "there's no question that information from Huawei routers has ultimately ended up in hands that appear to be the state."[9] US National Security Advisor Robert O'Brien likewise charged that "every medical record, every social media post, every email, every financial transaction . . . can be sucked up out of Huawei into massive servers in China."[10] Such fears were exacerbated by accounts like a 2017 article in the French newspaper *Le Monde*, alleging that for several years, data from the African Union's headquarters was secretly transmitted every night to servers in Shanghai—using Huawei equipment.[11]

In response to such concerns, telecommunications became a new arena for economic and geopolitical competition. Huawei slowly began to be squeezed out of many Western markets by a combination of political and regulatory pressure. In 2018, Facebook withdrew from a data-sharing partnership with Huawei amid pressure from the US Congress.[12] The US government also mounted a major pressure campaign to persuade other countries to enact similar curbs on the use of Huawei equipment. Several countries and foreign companies, including New Zealand, the Czech Republic, and major mobile carrier Vodafone, responded by introducing restrictions or outright bans on the use of Huawei 5G technology.[13]

Yet this response was far from universal. Because Chinese technology was usually cheaper than that of Western firms, it remained popular in the developing world. When Vodafone announced in 2019 that it would halt integration of Huawei equipment into 5G networks in Europe in response to security concerns, it also pointedly said it would keep using Huawei gear in markets like Africa and the Middle East.[14] Arguments that using Huawei equipment might leave countries and consumers vulnerable proved less than convincing in emerging markets like India. In New Delhi, security concerns took a back seat to Huawei's combination of advanced technology and low prices. In 2019, a senior Indian official roundly dismissed Huawei-related concerns by saying, "Huawei is today at the frontier on 5G. . . . All technologies have security concerns and vulnerabilities."[15]

As this statement shows, the biggest risks to the adoption of advanced Chinese telecommunications infrastructure apply not to developed democracies like the United States but to the many developing nations that giddily deployed Chinese technology. In these countries, which generally possess far less capacity than countries like the United Kingdom or Germany to protect their networks, Beijing threatens to bolster authoritarian approaches to information control and surveillance.

A chief source of such concerns is the inclusion of communications networks in China's overseas investment strategy, including the Belt and Road Initiative (BRI). First proposed in 2015, the "Digital Silk Road" (数字丝路) envisioned construction of fiber-optic cables and mobile data networks in Belt and Road countries to support the Internet of Things.[16] Huawei's "Energy Internet" (能源网络), for example, proposed to link smart meters installed on appliances to optimize electricity use across entire cities—but also possibly to surreptitiously share information on its inhabitants through their household devices. Similar technology found its way into BRI-linked projects like the Philippines' New Manila Bay City of Pearl. Other China-built systems like LOGINIK, a logistics platform developed by China's Ministry of Transportation (交通部), were adopted by several of the world's largest ports, including those of Bremen and Rotterdam. The potential reach of these networks highlights the possibility for China's state to disrupt, control, or spy on critical information. LOGINIK, for instance, might conceivably allow Beijing to collect militarily useful information on global ship movements.[17]

Even more alarming reports concerned Chinese-built communication networks in Africa and Latin America. In several of these countries, China-supplied communications technology became a tool for authoritarian-leaning governments to strengthen their ability to monitor and control their citizens.[18] In 2015, Tanzania awarded Huawei a US$182 million contract to build its landline and mobile networks. A few years later, a Tanzanian government official cited China's authoritarian cyber laws as a model for internet regulation, and in 2018, the government passed legislation requiring some internet users to register—seemingly emulating Beijing's mandatory licenses for internet users. Zimbabwe, meanwhile, granted Huawei a contract to deploy facial recognition technology, and a senior government official later confirmed that Chinese contacts had shared lessons on how "to ensure that the party exerts itself in terms of its supremacy over government."[19]

Such influence appeared to be widespread. A 2019 *Wall Street Journal* report found that engineers from Huawei helped authorities in Uganda hack encrypted messages sent by opposition politician Bobi Wine. A Ugandan official admitted with startling frankness that "the Huawei technicians worked for two days and helped us puncture through." The same investigation also found that Huawei employees had been embedded within a government agency in Zambia known as the Zambian Information and Communications

Technology Authority whose mission apparently included stifling online opposition to the government.[20] In Ecuador, meanwhile, a 2019 *New York Times* report revealed that images from Chinese-supplied surveillance cameras were being secretly fed to the country's intelligence service.[21] All of these incidents highlighted the lack of a serious foreign competitor to Huawei, and the potential danger it posed to free speech and expression beyond China's borders.

Tackling Telecom Dilemmas

The case of 5G underscores the need to rethink Western economic policy in response to China's rise. In many ways, Huawei's emergence as a global competitor signaled serious weaknesses in the industrial base of advanced economies. A senior UK official called Huawei's "dominance in 5G more a failure of Western industrial policy than anything else."[22] Indeed, Huawei's dominant market position emerged out of decades of deliberate industrial policy on Beijing's part. After being largely left out of third-generation communications network design, Huawei, with Beijing's backing, went on a patenting spree, claiming almost a quarter of total patents filed for fourth-generation technology. At the same time, the Ministry of Science and Technology (科技部) formed a working group with representatives of all major Chinese telecom operators, mobile device makers, universities, and research institutions, providing a platform for coordinated effort in 5G network design and development.[23]

Another crucial element of this approach is gaining influence in international communications standards-setting bodies. Beginning in first decade of the twenty-first century, Beijing made a determined push to expand its representation in bodies like the International Telecommunications Union (ITU) that set crucial standards for telecommunications networks worldwide and have enormous influence on which technologies win out. By the late 2010s, China could claim 10 out of about 60 representatives in ITU 5G working groups, in addition to the Union's secretary-general and its lead official for future technologies, who were both Chinese nationals. This influence directly benefited firms like Huawei: Chinese firms managed to get an industry working group to set a methodology known as polar coding as the standard for 5G over a US-backed alternative. Conveniently for Huawei, it owned most key polar coding patents.[24]

Of greatest concern, though, was the prospect that Beijing could use its influence in bodies like the ITU to codify authoritarian norms of data control like those described in the previous section.[25] These fears were bolstered by cases like one in which Chinese representatives to a UN cyberspace working group pushed to include "state sovereignty" as a basic principle for internet governance (more on the principle of cyber sovereignty later in this chapter).[26] Such influence risked allowing Beijing to set global telecommunications standards that could lock out foreign competitors and lock in developing countries to potentially vulnerable telecom networks.

Yet in responding to this risk, it is helpful to draw several distinctions. First of all, not all equipment sold by companies like Huawei is equally important for 5G networks. So-called core equipment, which acts as the backbone for these networks, presents far greater vulnerabilities than individual components like cell sites, which can be isolated if they are compromised. Some equipment types also feature a greater number of suppliers than others, making it easier to choose alternatives to Chinese firms. These distinctions are increasingly important for deciding when the risk of relying on Chinese telecommunications equipment can be tolerated, and when it may be too great.

In 2019, the head of Britain's communications security agency, the Government Communications Headquarters, outlined just such a risk-management approach to regulating Chinese investment in 5G, cautioning that "We have to understand the opportunities and threats from China's technological offer" and "decide which parts of this expansion can be embraced, which need risk management, and which will always need a sovereign, or allied, solution."[27] Following this approach necessitates new partnerships between government regulators, private telecom companies, and network providers—and requires much greater information-sharing between them than had previously been commonplace.[28]

What increasingly looks necessary to adopt this risk-management approach is a radical form of multilateral industrial policy—a Free World 5G Alliance built around three common lines of effort.[29] First, members should attach strict conditions, like permitting continuous inspection and emergency override capability, and obtaining regulatory approval for Chinese-backed investment in overseas networks. Second, members should establish a joint facility for assessing and monitoring network vulnerabilities and potential disruptions. Third, members should jointly capitalize an alternative to Huawei and other Chinese firms for supplying core 5G network infrastructure. This new entity could take the form of a public–private partnership involving government regulators and private telecom companies and network providers, as well as a blend of public and private finance. It might even resemble something like the International Finance Corporation, but should be specifically focused on strategic telecommunications infrastructure and other critical technologies.

This approach would depend on resolving thorny legal and policy questions and would almost certainly be much more expensive than opening Western networks to low-cost equipment providers like Huawei. It would also mark a departure from the long-standing aversion in some Western countries, especially the United States and the United Kingdom, to industrial policy. But twenty-first century communications networks are so central to commerce and everyday life that it would be dangerous to completely outsource their construction and operation. The risk of exposing foreign citizens to China-linked surveillance and service disruption is simply too great.[30]

At the same time, it could prove costly to develop different communications networks relying on different equipment and built to different standards. Apart from slowing information transfer and commerce, a balkanized set of 5G networks would likely make some systems mutually incompatible, and even mutually unintelligible. Chinese researchers have invested considerable effort in developing advanced encryption and employing blockchain to ensure the integrity of their own networks. If not developed according to international standards, these security features could effectively shut out foreign users, raising rather than lowering barriers to global communication.[31]

Without some level of cooperation to make next-generation networks interoperable, the torrents of data flowing through them are destined to run up against an age-old political obstacle: national borders. It would be both tragic, and painfully ironic, if the world's next-generation communications network were to end up leaving the world more isolated rather than integrated. That is why it is crucial to keep some areas of digital network development open to Chinese and other foreign investment and collaboration, even while other countries work together to establish a viable alternative to Beijing-operated 5G equipment. Yet at the same time, egregious examples of China-linked information theft cloud prospects for cooperation in the global information commons, and contribute to growing economic, geopolitical, and ideological competition over the world's digital data and information. The world is not likely to see a repeat of what happened at West Sayville, but China-linked information threats have started to appear much closer to home for many Western countries.

China and the Globalization of Digital Data Collection

As a doctoral student at Duke University, Liu Ruopeng (刘若鹏) initially seemed little different from hundreds of thousands of other Chinese students studying at American universities.[32] Unquestionably bright and ambitious, Liu gravitated to the work of David Smith, a Duke professor whose research had uncovered a stunning breakthrough. Certain materials, Smith and his team discovered, could function as a real-life cloaking device, shielding objects from some forms of radiation, like microwaves. This effectively made them invisible to radar—a property that quickly attracted the attention of the US military, which funded part of Smith's research. Though the work was not considered secret, its national security implications were obvious, and the United States was not the only country paying attention.

Yet no one seems to have thought much about any of this when the highly qualified Liu applied to work with Smith. As a graduate student, Smith had worked with an adviser he considered to be xenophobic, a failing he was determined not to emulate. Smith welcomed Liu and other foreign students into his lab. For a while, this openness seemed to pay off: Liu soon distinguished himself as a member of Smith's lab, as much with his entrepreneurial spirit as his academic talents. As Smith later recalled, Liu seemed "more of an organizer and manager than a scientist . . . he seemed to have an extraordinary ability to get others to do things."[33]

This proved to be a considerable understatement. Unbeknownst to Smith and his fellow researchers at Duke, Liu began secretly feeding the group's research to scientists in China. Liu soon persuaded Smith to host a group of Chinese researchers, including Liu's former advisor, at Duke, during which time they took photos of sensitive equipment designed by Smith's lab. Soon, Smith's team discovered that their work had been described, without proper attribution, in publications coauthored by Liu and his China-based mentor. Later, in 2008, the pair invited Smith to travel to China for what he thought was an all-expenses-paid conference. Soon, though, Smith found out that the trip had been funded through a Chinese state program that committed him to work directly to support research at Chinese universities. Eventually, fed up with false representations, Smith cut ties with Liu—but not before Liu received his doctorate in 2009.[34]

Despite becoming *persona non grata* in Smith's lab, Liu's time there turned out to be his golden goose: after returning to China, he started a company that eventually became worth some US$6 billion. Much of the funding reportedly came from Beijing, drawn to Liu's work on sensitive technologies like the cloaking device.[35] Liu certainly caught the eye of China's top leaders: President Xi Jinping visited Liu's company in 2012, and praised him for "returning to China to realize the Chinese dream."[36]

Liu's case helped make crystal-clear one of the most worrying implications of China's growing role in digital networks and data governance: a large-scale threat to the world's data and information. While citizens and companies of all nations constantly try to steal each other's data, what distinguishes China-linked data theft and appropriation is its scope, scale, and sophistication. Most of this theft and collection occurs in the digital domain. So much so, in fact, that intellectual property theft of the kind suffered by Smith became almost synonymous with China-based hacking and cybertheft. Throughout the early twenty-first century, many of the most complex and daring cyberattacks on foreign companies and governments, known as "advanced persistent threats," originated in China, most of which appeared to be acting at least loosely on Beijing's behalf.[37]

These threats moreover produced spectacular hauls of highly sensitive digital data from non-Chinese citizens and companies. Beijing's leading role in cybertheft was highlighted in spectacular fashion in 2016, when the US government revealed that tens of thousands of personnel records, including highly sensitive personal information, had been stolen by Chinese state-backed hackers.[38] In 2018, multiple Western countries identified China's main overseas intelligence service, the Ministry of State Security (MSS, 国安部), as the source of multi-year attacks against overseas internet service providers, yielding valuable access to key digital networks.[39] A year later, Reuters reported that MSS had been implicated in another hacking campaign, known as Cloud Hopper, which targeted sensitive digital data and intellectual property from several major Western firms. Victims included marquee companies like Ericsson, IBM, and Hewlett Packard.[40]

Less dramatic, yet ultimately no less consequential, than these covert campaigns were overt efforts to acquire valuable digital data and information from foreign companies, universities, and research institutions. This "non-traditional intelligence collection" in settings like academia was, for the most part, uncoordinated, and instead reflected certain Chinese government policies intended to foster innovation. Ambitious but vaguely defined targets placed intense pressure on individual university researchers, corporate research directors, and city officials to become more inventive—as fast as possible (more on these perverse incentives in Chapter 5). For ambitious but unethical go-getters, simply acquiring data, ideas, and intellectual property (IP) from abroad and bringing them back to China offered a shortcut to meeting these targets. Studies suggest that competition among Chinese local officials is a key driver of digital data theft, because it can boost productivity figures for local firms, in turn juicing annual performance figures for their jurisdictions.[41]

For foreign companies, the consequences were hugely harmful. A 2013 expert commission estimated that 50%–80% of IP violations suffered by American businesses were linked to China, many of which involved cybertheft.[42] Just a few years later, another commission, chaired by two former senior US intelligence officials, pegged the total loss of Chinese IP theft from US companies at $600 billion, which they called "the greatest transfer of wealth in history."[43] Most, if not all, foreign companies operating in China began to worry about losing their proprietary information and technology, especially in the digital domain. The US–China Business Council, for example, reported that IP enforcement "has consistently placed among the top handful of issues" cited by its members.[44] Even so, encouraging signs emerged that IP protections were improving within China—while eroding abroad, thanks to the growing role played by Chinese state-linked firms and entities in digital technology and networks around the globe.

How China-Linked Digital Information Theft Moved Abroad

Despite the scale of information theft linked to China, by the 2010s Beijing had good reason to crack down, especially as it tried to encourage innovation by Chinese firms. For one thing, widespread IP theft discouraged the foreign investment that China desperately needed to move up the economic value chain.[45] Second, while Chinese companies certainly did gain from digital data theft in the short run, it was not clear that the Chinese economy as a whole gained very much at all. Estimates of the value added by foreign technologies adopted by Chinese companies found they were overwhelmingly concentrated in low-skilled industries.[46] Moreover, a number of studies indicated that over-reliance on foreign technology transfer is harmful to Chinese companies because it discourages the independent innovation crucial to improving productivity—and profits—over the long run.[47]

At the same time, Chinese firms themselves found good reasons to lobby for stronger IP protections, especially in the digital domain. As they began to expand overseas and produce higher-value-added products at home, they began to need strong IP protections just as much as their foreign competitors (more on this shift in Chapter 1). Filings from both Chinese and foreign firms for patent and trademark protection skyrocketed after 2008 (see Figure 6.1). Beijing started to take these demands seriously, including by establishing specialized IP courts to help overcome pervasive local corruption; and sharply increasing financial penalties for IP infringement.[48] The number of IP criminal cases brought in Chinese courts, moreover, began to increase, suggesting tougher enforcement.[49] Perhaps most surprisingly, foreign firms operating in China began to win in court more often. According to

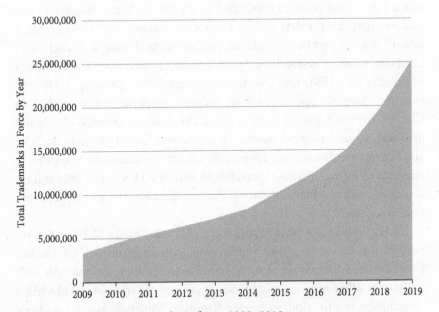

Figure 6.1. Chinese trademarks in force, 2009–2019.
Source: National Statistics Bureau of China 2019.

one estimate, foreign firms won approximately 80% of patent infringement suits by the late 2010s, up from some 70% in the period 2006–2011.[50]

Even the worst examples of IP appropriation from foreign firms, called "forced technology transfers," grew rare. A major 2018 study concluded that these transfers, which typically employ political pressure or semi-legal coercion to induce foreign companies to turn over IP to Chinese firms as a condition of entering the market, had become much less common than voluntary transfers.[51] A new Foreign Investment Law introduced in late 2019, moreover, formally banned forced technology transfers.[52]

But while the IP outlook for foreign firms began to brighten within China, foreign countries were increasingly targeted by Chinese actors looking for an information advantage abroad, especially in the digital domain. In the 2010s, about two-thirds of foreign economic espionage cases within the United States involved Chinese actors.[53] Moreover, cases like Liu's highlighted a growing "gray zone" in which Chinese actors attempt to gain an advantage in data collection—without necessarily breaking any laws.

Much of this gray-zone activity unfolded in Western universities and became an especially marked concern in the United States. In October 2018, the National Institutes of Health (NIH), a federal agency that funds much of the biomedical research conducted in the United States, issued an unusual warning that the data collected by its researchers was "under constant threat," in large part because of unauthorized data-sharing and disclosures involving Chinese researchers.[54] A few months later, the Federal Bureau of Investigation (FBI) sent a similarly unprecedented advisory to US universities charging that "foreign adversaries"—especially those linked to China—"exploit America's deeply held and vital culture of collaboration and openness on university campuses."[55] Within a year, investigations by the NIH and FBI reportedly uncovered some 200 cases of digital data theft by Chinese researchers, especially in the biotech field, at over 70 US universities and research institutions, including world-famous ones like the M. D. Anderson Cancer Center.[56]

The big problem for Washington, and for institutions like M. D. Anderson, though, was that none of this activity was necessarily illegal.[57] US law has long restricted the release of some sensitive technology and material with military or other security-related uses, including the transfer of knowledge or technical information, to foreign nationals. But there has always been an exception for "fundamental research," which covers most of the work performed in universities.

Moreover, though there is little doubt that gray-zone information theft is a problem, what is not clear is that the costs of open data and information-sharing outweigh the benefits.[58] One of the primary cases of university-based intellectual property theft cited by the FBI was valued at about $5,000—a trivial sum.[59] On the other hand, placing limitations on US–China research collaboration risks chilling all forms of international scientific exchange, with potentially disastrous effects for US-based research and development activity (more on the importance of this in Chapter 4). At least one study indicated that Chinese researchers became hesitant to share data with their international partners because of growing tensions,[60] and ethnically Chinese faculty perceived what appeared to be disproportionate scrutiny of their research activities as a form of discrimination.[61]

Even David Smith, the Duke professor whose research found its way to Liu's company without his knowledge, made clear he was opposed to restricting collaboration with Chinese students and researchers. "If we were to overreact," Smith warned, "I think it could be very damaging to our universities."[62]

In the late 2010s, the growing challenge of gray-zone information threats like that experienced by Smith forced the United States and other countries to reconsider the balance between information-sharing and digital information security, especially in basic research. Yet striking this balance was not an entirely new challenge, and previous attempts suggested that it was preferable to lean toward openness. During the Cold War, for example, when faced with a similar information security threat from Soviet-aligned countries, US government policy distinguished between so-called keystone technologies, which were subject to strict export controls, and others in which the benefits of free trade and research collaboration were judged to outweigh the risks.[63] In 2006, meanwhile, Washington established a body called the Deemed Export Advisory Committee to identify technologies and research that should be subject to export controls. One of the Committee's conclusions was that US national security would be harmed by unduly restricting collaborations with foreign partners.[64]

The challenge of preventing IP theft, especially from China-linked actors, while preserving the open exchange of digital information looks to be a defining challenge for many foreign universities, firms, and research institutions in the twenty-first century. But the increasing collection of individual consumer data outside China's borders threatens to become an even more vexing problem.

Digital Data Collection and Surveillance Outside China's Borders

By the late 2010s, Chinese consumer technology companies had become a force in many overseas markets, a phenomenon illustrated most dramatically by the rapid rise of the video-sharing social networking platform TikTok. In the first few months of 2019, the previously obscure Chinese-developed app surged ahead of foreign competitors like Instagram and Facebook Messenger to become the world's third-most-downloaded mobile phone app. Combining a user-friendly interface and proprietary AI algorithms to help videos go viral, TikTok managed, in the words of the *Wall Street Journal*, to create a kind of social media secret sauce, a "viral user-made video network that none of the other giants have managed to pull off."[65]

TikTok's parent company, Beijing-based ByteDance (字节跳动), became one of the world's most valuable start-ups, with a valuation of some US$75 billion. It was so successful that it reportedly expressed interest in buying American social media giant Twitter.[66] Soon after bursting onto the West's tech scene, though, TikTok became a target of the US government, which attempted to ban its use in the United States over fears that data gleaned from the app's millions of American users could be manipulated by Beijing. TikTok was later found to include a feature, concealed by an unusual layer of encryption not found in most similar consumer apps, that appeared to enable surreptitious data collection without the user's knowledge.[67]

Though perhaps the early twenty-first century's best-known Chinese-developed app, TikTok was only one of a growing number of consumer-facing apps that posed privacy concerns for users outside China. And while standards vary widely and unscrupulous developers exist in every corner of the globe, a large number of Chinese app developers appeared to play by a looser set of rules than their counterparts elsewhere.

In November 2018, Google accused two Chinese app developers, Cheetah Mobile (猎豹移动) and Kika Tech (北京新美互通科技), of using overbroad privacy permissions in widely downloaded apps as part of an advertising fraud scheme. Praneet Sharma, an executive at the fraud investigation firm that detected the practice, called the Chinese-developed apps "wildly over-permissioned" and warned that "they are logging everything." The practice, he added, was concerning because "from a privacy standpoint they are violating a lot of things."[68] Less than a year later, Google removed almost 50 apps developed by a Chinese firm called iHandy (汉迪移动) for presumably similar reasons—though the tech giant was coy about the rationale, it cited "deceptive or disruptive ads."[69]

Though individually attributable to corner-cutting on the part of unscrupulous app developers, when taken together these cases point to the growing ability of Chinese firms, and by extension potentially Beijing, to collect and store private data on foreign citizens abroad. A 2019 report prepared by the US–China Economic and Security Review Commission warned that Chinese entities were collecting large quantities of biomedical information on US residents through both overt research and covert means.[70] Later the same year, the US government used newly expanded authorities to force a Chinese firm to sell its majority stake in an American social network that aggregates healthcare data from users, primarily over worries this information could be used in attempts to recruit spies.[71] Only a few months after this first forced sale, the US government ordered a second Chinese company to sell its stake in the dating app Grindr over similar fears that its data could be used to compromise individuals holding security clearances.[72]

As these cases suggest, broader geopolitical tensions between the United States and China increasingly spilled into the digital domain, threatening not just individual privacy but also individual expression abroad. One such incident unfolded in the wake of large-scale anti-Beijing protests that wracked Hong Kong throughout most of 2019. In October, the official *People's Daily* (人民日报) newspaper, a leading mouthpiece for the Chinese Communist Party, singled out an app called HKmap.live that was widely used by Hong Kong protestors, calling it "toxic" to the territory's politics. Just a day later, Apple removed HKmap.live from its app store, effectively banning it for iPhone users. Apple, for its part, cited a policy preventing app developers from "capitalizing on sensitive events such as attempting to make money from serious ongoing conflicts." But this did little to quiet an ensuing firestorm of criticism from political leaders like Senator Josh Hawley of Missouri, who quickly asked by tweet, "Who's really running Apple? Tim Cook or Beijing?"[73]

Perhaps the clearest illustration of the degree to which Chinese data collection and management practices threatened free expression abroad came courtesy of the COVID-19 pandemic. Thanks to hundreds of millions of employees being told to work from home around the globe, the formerly little-used videocall platform Zoom experienced a 354% increase in customer numbers over a period of just a few months in early 2020.[74] In June of the same year, the accounts of several US-based activists were closed after they scheduled calls to commemorate the 1989 Tiananmen massacre, apparently at the behest of Chinese authorities. Zoom apologized and called the incident a mistake, but in December 2020 US federal prosecutors charged an executive at the company with passing sensitive information on American users to Chinese security services.[75]

In early 2021, meanwhile, an app called Clubhouse rapidly gained popularity as a platform for small-group discussion. Within China, it became a rare forum for relatively open debate. After just a few weeks, though, Beijing's censors blocked access to the app. More troubling still were reports that user audio data was transferred to servers within China, and signs that China's party state was prepared to use its data localization laws to identify individuals suspected of participating in subversive conversations.[76] "I came to Clubhouse to talk freely about things I care about," one Chinese user wrote, "but I guess this is something the Chinese Communist Party does not agree to."[77] According to some reports, moreover, content created and viewed solely within the United States was still censored on platforms like WeChat—a troubling extension of China's cyber censorship regime far beyond its borders.[78]

One consequence of Beijing's efforts to export authoritarian norms of digital data collection and management is that both China and foreign multinational tech firms face a growing set of ethical and policy dilemmas. While these dilemmas are readily apparent for foreign tech firms operating in China, like Apple, Chinese firms like ByteDance also find it hard to stay above the fray. As one of the company's employees confided, "We are stuck in between" the United States and China. "We are a Chinese company," the employee added, "and we do business overseas."

In response to this dilemma, ByteDance by all accounts tries to negotiate with Beijing rather than surrender wholesale to its whims, which would almost certainly endanger its access to markets like the United States. ByteDance reportedly hands over data to Chinese law enforcement entities when presented with a formal request to do so, and curries favor with Beijing by running public service announcements on its apps within China at no charge. But the firm also occasionally runs afoul of the authorities, including during a 2019 incident in which it was accused of promoting content that defamed a revolutionary hero.[79] During the Hong Kong protests in 2019–2020, moreover, ByteDance changed its content policies to allow more protest-related content to be shared on its apps, presenting a clear contrast with the Party's stance.[80] Other Chinese tech firms, including WeChat and

Alibaba, reportedly regularly contest data-sharing requests from Beijing, suggesting there is plenty of tension between them and the state.[81]

The continued shift to virtual work following the COVID-19 pandemic seems sure to pose many more of these digital censorship and security dilemmas for both Chinese and foreign tech firms. Though in many ways they draw a wedge between China and other nations, these changes also point to the emergence of shared interests in tackling digital privacy issues. The balancing act attempted by firms like ByteDance suggests that, in at least some limited areas like mobile app privacy permissions, Chinese and global standards might eventually converge. But on larger questions of digital and cyber policy, China and developed democracies look to be far apart given a decisive turn in Beijing toward an increasingly nationalistic form of digital protectionism in the mid-2010s.

China, Data Privacy, and Digital Protectionism

Few people played a bigger role in China's rise as a digital superpower than Li Yanhong (李彦宏). But in 1992, when Li applied to study computer science in New York State, that prospect seemed so remote that a skeptical professor asked him, "Do you have computers in China?" As it happened, Li's school had five computers—but they had to be shared between almost 2,000 students. Only pupils who showed a talent for mathematics were allowed to use them for any length of time, which made even the boxy Apple IIe seem "magical," as Li later recalled. Li, born to factory-worker parents in a north China coal town, had found his calling. "One day," he told himself, "I'll demonstrate that China has a really powerful computer industry."[82]

First, though, he proved himself in America's. After graduating from the State University of New York–Buffalo, Li patented an internet search algorithm and cut his teeth in the late 1990s internet economy scene, where he met Yahoo cofounder Jerry Yang. With Yang's encouragement and over US$10 million in funding from Silicon Valley venture capital firms, Li and his partner Eric Xu returned to China to found Baidu (百度), which went on to become China's most popular search engine. It also became the world's fourth most-visited website, with a valuation of some US$60 billion.[83]

Like his foreign CEO counterparts, who usually shy away from sensitive political issues, Li's views on political matters, like China's ever-tightening cyberspace regulations, were measured. "We always don't want anything regulated so we can do things freely," he conceded in an interview, "But I also recognize that's not practical and not even good for the country."[84] And despite Baidu's role in policing China's internet, Li could claim at least one genuine contribution to internet freedom: just after finishing his master's degree, Li created the software used for the first online version of *The Wall Street Journal*, a crucial contribution to putting a pillar of America's free press online.[85]

Li's seeming sense of balance and habit for careful phrasing failed him, though, when in 2018 he ignited a firestorm by stating, "In many cases, Chinese people are willing to trade privacy for convenience, safety and efficiency."[86] But it turned out that many Chinese netizens disagreed: Li's comments unleashed a fierce online debate over consumer data privacy protections, and whether those offered both by the state and companies like Baidu were strong enough. The scope of this debate showed something important about China in the digital age: that the desire for some measure of personal privacy is near-universal, and that Beijing, for all its formidable ability to control information, is not immune to the pressure. Paradoxically, though, just as China's privacy norms showed a few signs of converging with those of the West, Beijing began pursuing an aggressive brand of digital protectionism and data sovereignty that stood to leave everyone worse off.

China's Digital Treasure Trove and Evolving Norms on Privacy

This paradox had its roots in the fact that as the twenty-first century advanced, Chinese firms and the Chinese state accumulated a vast treasure trove of data—the fuel that powers its digital economy. Most artificial intelligence (AI) applications, for example, work by taking large quantities of data and parsing it in different ways, looking for patterns and commonalities that can be used to refine algorithms. The bigger and more diversified the data set, the more reliable and sophisticated these algorithms can become. In the early decades of the twenty-first century, Chinese firms and researchers built some of the biggest data sets in the world.

For the most part, this was simply a function of sheer scale: China's 800 million internet users dwarf those of any other country in number and generate vast amounts of data that are sucked up by firms like Baidu and e-commerce giant Alibaba (阿里巴巴).[87] Chinese consumers also became enthusiastic users of mobile payments through platforms like WeChat (微信). By the mid-2010s, roughly 50 times as many mobile transactions took place in China as in the United States, generating piles of valuable financial data.[88] All of this promises to give Chinese companies—and Beijing—a big leg up in the quantity and range of data they can use to develop better products, analyze social phenomena, and, of course, keep close tabs on individuals.

Just as important as the sheer quantity of data available to Chinese firms is its scope. Most developed-country tech companies rely primarily on collecting data generated by internet users within proprietary online and mobile applications like Facebook. Thanks to multi-functional platforms like WeChat, Chinese companies, in contrast, can gather data about a user's interactions with the physical as well as the digital world with relative ease. The ubiquity of e-commerce in China allows Chinese companies to aggregate large volumes of information about things like lunch order preferences alongside more routine data like social media contacts. The growing popularity of mobile-enabled bike and scooter rentals, meanwhile, adds detailed information on travel and commuting habits.[89]

All this data promises to give Chinese firms a more sophisticated and multidimensional portrait of consumer behavior than their foreign counterparts. Concerns grew that this rich data endowment might potentially put foreign firms at a significant disadvantage in understanding, and possibly shaping, consumer behavior through new techniques like AI-enabled marketing.[90] But it was within China that the consequences of uninhibited individual data collection generated the greatest controversy.

In contrast to many Western countries, where a long legal and political tradition upheld a certain right to privacy over personal information, China historically imposed few limitations on information-gathering, either by the state or by firms. Prior to 2018, when certain provisions of China's Cybersecurity Law took effect, Chinese citizens had no definitive legal right to privacy in the digital domain. Even then, the Law, though it did create a basic framework to protect individual data privacy, put forward only murky standards to guide implementation.[91] Draft data security measures proposed in late 2019, meanwhile, included only partial restrictions on bulk data collection.[92]

In part, the relative weakness of privacy protections reflected the fact that Chinese consumers historically expressed less concern than their Western peers over how much data companies collected about them. A 2015 survey, for example, found that while Germans and Americans were willing to pay to protect some consumer data from state and corporate snooping, Chinese consumers overwhelmingly reported being comfortable with trading their information for free access to websites and apps.[93] Subsequent studies largely echoed the conclusion that Chinese internet users have fewer privacy concerns than their Western counterparts—though at least one suggested, intriguingly, that Chinese users are simply concerned about different *kinds* of privacy risk, especially being singled out for criticism on social media platforms.[94] In any event, many Chinese consumers appear to accept trade-offs between personal data collection and the sheer convenience of platforms like WeChat: another survey revealed that at least 60% of mobile app users in China knew that data was being shared with third parties—but used the apps anyway.[95] Of course, China being China, these third parties are also very likely to include the state.

In the pre-internet age, Beijing maintained social order through a complex network of officials and informants, down to the block and street level.[96] Much of this control apparatus subsequently migrated online, as China's party-state began steadily building a sophisticated infrastructure to keep close digital watch on its citizens. This included detailed monitoring of nearly all internet activity and digital communication, as well as widespread blocking and censorship of material deemed objectionable.[97] Especially ominous developments included the recruitment of large numbers of paid internet users and development of special algorithms to manipulate online discourse, as well as stringent real-name registration requirements.[98] Surveillance and censorship were especially severe for groups, like the Muslim Uighur minority, seen as posing higher risk to state security and stability, and who consequently could expect little if any privacy in either the digital or physical world.[99]

Attempts to harness data for the purposes of social and political control reached its apogee in an Orwellian effort known as the Social Credit System (社会信用体系). The name can be misleading: instead of a single platform, the system is more like a framework to guide the efforts of state entities, financial institutions, and other organizations to collect and analyze data on individuals, and use it to penalize behavior deemed to be undesirable.[100] At least initially, most such sanctions were focused on bad habits like failing to pay bills on time or, in Shanghai, failing to properly sort household garbage.[101] Persistent offenders could be put on blacklists, which prevented them from gaining access to financial credit or riding public transportation.[102] But there was little doubt that the Social Credit System could also be used to monitor and coerce individual behavior.

Yet while efforts like the Social Credit System make it easy to tag Beijing as a digital Leviathan, other developments demonstrate that Chinese state control over the digital domain is not absolute, and even show some signs of weakening. Multiple surveys conducted in the mid- and late 2010s showed increasing levels of concern about digital data protection and privacy among Chinese consumers. A study published in 2015 revealed a "severe privacy trust crisis" among Chinese consumers,[103] and within a few years this crisis began to burst into public view. The year 2018 saw China's first major legal battle over privacy, when a consumer group sued Baidu over allegedly illegally listening in on phone calls. Because the consumer group involved was closely linked to the state, many observers viewed the suit as having tacit support from Beijing.[104]

Even so, a rampant, semi-legal market for personal information collected through platforms like Baidu and mobile payment apps continued to be a source of considerable grievance among consumers. In late 2018, the China Consumers Association (中国消费协会) published a detailed report alleging that many apps collected excessive amounts of information from users, in most cases without their knowledge.[105]

In the late 2010s, new regulatory measures were announced that appeared to represent a response to these public concerns. In 2019, Beijing announced that it would solicit opinions on draft regulations designed to prevent network operators from obtaining users' personal information without their consent. These measures emulated European Union regulations requiring tech companies to identify personal information and gain explicit consent to use it. Other provisions included a requirement that any content generated by AI be labeled "synthetic," and that the collection and use of personal information on minors be tightly restricted.[106] The government also began collecting reports of illicit data collection, which, according to one source, yielded over 5,000 complaints, primarily related to unnecessary information gathered through apps. In response, in July 2019 Beijing published a list of over two dozen apps, including the popular dating app TanTan (探探), which it charged had violated China's Cybersecurity Law by collecting excessive information.[107] The Personal Information Privacy Law, passed in 2021, introduced a raft of new regulations that, on paper at least, give Chinese citizens greater privacy protections than many of their peers abroad. Under the Law, employers, for example, are required to ensure that their employees' personal information is strictly protected.[108]

To be sure, responding to public privacy concerns was hardly Beijing's only motivation in strengthening digital data collection policies. The viral success of the AI-enabled deep fake video app Zao (造戏) in particular alarmed authorities, who feared it could be used to undermine the legitimacy of public figures and officials. *The Beijing News* (新京报) newspaper channeled these fears in a September 2019 editorial in which it warned that "artificial intelligence is not only a test for technological development, but a test for governance. . . . Right now it's very difficult to determine whether . . . collection of human facial data and authorization are malicious, but netizens' concerns are understandable."[109] In responding to these growing dilemmas, Beijing decided to take little to chance, turning toward a protectionist and even nationalistic cyber and data policy that heightened the sense of competition in the digital domain with countries like the United States.

Beijing's Turn toward Cyber Sovereignty and Digital Protectionism

Even as things began to look up when it came to individual privacy protections within China, Beijing also mounted an unprecedented effort to wall off its digital data from the outside world. Its cyber policy had long been restrictive, and throughout the early twenty-first century Beijing blocked access to a growing list of foreign websites and portals, including Google, Facebook, and Twitter.[110] But a Party policy document issued in 2013, soon after Xi Jinping took power, that has since become known as "Document No. 9," marked a turning point. After warning of the dangers of Western-style democracy, civil society, and journalism, the document's final section turned to taming cyberspace. Document No. 9 called for officials to "hold the cultural line" and to "to do one's duty to protect the homeland" as fervently online as in the real world.[111] So began Beijing's decisive turn toward data sovereignty and cyber nationalism under Xi.

As Xi's personal involvement in cyber policy suggested, China's leaders needed little convincing that internet and digital technologies would be central to the twenty-first-century economy. Beijing's "Internet Plus" (互联网 +) vision of integrating physical devices, next-generation networks, and data-management platforms presented a notably comprehensive and ambitious digital and cyber policy agenda. But in contrast to most of their Western counterparts, China's leaders were consumed by the desire to secure and control the endless streams of information surging across the world's networks. In part, this concern reflected a distinctive vulnerability: thanks to the prevalence of pirated software in China, which is more vulnerable to security flaws, Chinese firms experienced several devastating cyberattacks, including a widespread 2017 ransomware incident thought to be linked to North Korea. This fixation with security gave rise to a principle known as "cyber sovereignty" (网络主权)—essentially, that while information exchange and communication are to be welcomed, networks should be designed around national borders, and governments should retain the right to regulate information within and around their territory.[112]

For foreign companies, Beijing's increasingly protectionist approach to digital data collection and management was highly problematic. China's cyber policy put in place several unusually strict requirements on tech firms that effectively forbade the export or sharing of digital data outside China's borders. One, a provision known as "data localization," essentially banned the export of consumer and sensitive data outside of China. Vague provisions in the Cybersecurity Law, meanwhile, appeared to require both foreign and domestic tech firms to store copies of personally identifiable data within the country, where it could be inspected by Chinese law enforcement authorities, including presumably the security services. And while several countries, including Australia and Nigeria, had similar laws on the books, Beijing adopted an unusually broad interpretation of what it defined as information of national importance. This push toward cyber sovereignty meant that most any foreign tech firm operating in China was not only obliged to show its data to authorities on demand, but also faced significant limitations on how its own data could be used.[113] A Data Security Law that took effect in 2021 meanwhile appeared to tighten the screws of state control on both Chinese and foreign firms still further, by stipulating heavy penalties for failing to respond to requests from authorities for user information.[114]

Beijing's cyber sovereignty and digital protectionism policies became a source of growing concern for foreign firms. In a 2018 survey, 60% of US companies operating in China reported that internet regulations were detrimental to their businesses, and in several cases, it drove them to move their Asia-Pacific headquarters to places like Singapore.[115] These restrictions were especially stringent for certain forms of digital data, such as biomedical information, which Beijing believed were essential to its strategic economic ambitions (more on this in Chapter 7).[116]

China's growing cache of biomedical data underscored just how valuable population data can be—and why digital protectionism poses a significant economic threat to foreign firms in rapidly growing sectors like biotechnology.[117] In 2016, China's State Council issued a notice declaring biomedical data to be a "national strategic resource," and the government later established several dedicated centers to integrate data from China's national health insurance scheme (which covers 95% of the population), hospital records, and government vital statistics. The scale and scope of this data are truly staggering, which by some estimates cover some 600 million people—nearly twice the population of the entire United States. This aggregation was made possible by the almost total lack of restrictions on data-sharing between health providers, government, and other sources of biomedical data, all of which are generally viewed as state property.[118]

Yet while Beijing became a true believer in the value of collecting and aggregating biomedical data, it was highly reluctant to share it with foreign commercial or academic partners. In part, this reluctance reflected a history of unethical research projects, in which some medical data was collected from Chinese patients without their consent. More importantly, though, Beijing came to see the country's genetic data as a treasure trove that could lend its firms a significant competitive advantage in the life sciences industry. Beijing's efforts to encourage large-scale biomedical data aggregation in particular were based on the belief it could help Chinese firms become leaders in developing medical AI applications, often viewed as one of the biggest biotech growth areas in the 2020s.[119]

Restrictions put in place by Beijing made any use of genetic information outside China subject to approval by a special agency called the China Administration of Human Genetic Resources. Though not the only country to adopt similar restrictions, China's rules completely prohibited foreign access to Chinese genetic information without partnering with a Chinese institution. These sweeping rules provided for rejection of any foreign use of genetic information if it "may jeopardize national security, national interests or public security."[120] Just as important, Beijing strictly enforced these already stringent rules. In early 2018, it revoked licenses for two high-profile international biomedical data-sharing projects, one of which involved Oxford and Peking universities.[121] China's biomedical data vault became locked shut to foreign companies and researchers.

Such practices threaten to create a major competitive disadvantage for foreign firms in areas like biotechnology. The best way to respond to such digital protectionism is to build a multinational partnership between the United States and like-minded countries that combines strong individual privacy protections with an emphasis on aggregating very large data sets of anonymized information which can be used by companies and researchers. Apart from matching the sheer scale of China-sourced data sets, a multinational data collection and sharing initiative has the advantage of capturing greater population diversity than can be reflected in a single national data set. And when it comes to data, diversity is just as important as overall quantity. As Nand Mulchandani, chief technology officer of the Pentagon's Joint Artificial Intelligence Center points out, "Diversity of data is better than even a huge dataset from within a single country such as China."[122]

Even so, making such a partnership a reality means addressing thorny questions over the role of the government and private companies in sharing and aggregating individual data. The United States, the European Union, and other jurisdictions differed markedly in these respects, and any multilateral framework needs to forge common standards on digital data protection and privacy.[123] Another critical consideration in cross-national data sharing is data quality. Data gathered about things like how many steps you walk in a day or how well done you like your morning bagel has to be structured and coded in such a way as to be easily readable by software programs and algorithms. Multilateral data-sharing partnerships accordingly need to follow common structures and protocols (more on the related issue of data and algorithmic integrity in Chapter 7). Fortunately, precedents exist for large-scale, international data collection and analysis efforts. The Human Genome Project, which involved a massive multinational effort to gather, protect, and share sensitive and enormously valuable genetic information, could serve as a model.[124]

China's rapidly growing role in the digital world has created a set of digital dilemmas for foreign countries, companies, and organizations, particularly those in developed democracies. While the IP risks and cyber threats posed by Chinese actors became well known in the early decades of the twenty-first century, what was less apparent was that IP risks for foreign firms began to shrink within China's borders. Outside China, though, the risks to foreigners' proprietary information and individual privacy continued to grow as Chinese actors sought to hoover up digital information beyond China's borders. Despite its own growing vulnerability to cyber-attacks,

China looks unlikely to be able to agree with other countries on enforceable international rules to prevent them.[125] At the same time, China's state has sought to hoard its growing stash of digital data, potentially giving its firms a distinct competitive advantage over foreign rivals. Finally, and most alarmingly, Beijing seems intent on parlaying its dominance of the telecoms sector to set the rules for digital networks—and provide greater scope for authoritarian control.

Across all these areas, China has increasingly sought to export its approach to censorship and surveillance in the digital domain. This means that foreign countries, companies, and organizations need to rethink how digital data and information are collected, stored, and transmitted. For the United States, policies governing individual data collection and sharing are clearly due for an upgrade.[126] More stringent data privacy laws might, for example, force China-based firms to disclose to American users if they are being surveilled in response to requests from Beijing.[127] As human rights advocate Sophie Richardson argues, "For most people around the world, U.S. techno-capitalism and Chinese techno-authoritarianism are not good choices. If it wants to lead, the U.S. has to strengthen its own digital privacy norms."[128] This imperative presents fertile ground for cooperation with American's European allies, who in many ways lead the world in digital and privacy policy.

At the same time, it is clear that developed democracies need to build new institutional partnerships between public- and private-sector entities and rethink the role of government in safeguarding and transmitting data through 5G and other digital networks. This is a necessity we return to in the Conclusion. The next chapter, though, turns to even more cutting-edge challenges and opportunities in emerging technology areas like synthetic biology and fully autonomous systems.

7

The Need for Norms

Why the World Must Work with China to Regulate Emerging Technologies

Despite their seemingly fierce technological competition, China, the United States, and other major countries have good reason to work together to regulate emerging technologies that threaten to become a matter of life and death, not just for individuals but whole countries, and possibly for the entire planet. The best-known such challenges in the early twenty-first century are the use of artificial intelligence to make vehicles and weapons systems fully autonomous, potentially freeing them of human control and raising the prospect of Terminator-like future battlefields. At the same time, advancements in the life sciences utterly transformed what it meant to be human—or a member of any other species, for that matter. Most of these developments show great promise to improve the human condition. But others threaten to unleash virtually unimaginable danger, including the prospect that nuclear deterrence, a principle that has helped keep the peace despite the spread of nuclear weapons, might be undermined. A different threat is posed by the fact that many emerging technologies are highly democratic. Gene editing is perhaps the best example. In many cases, all that is needed to make transformational advances is a lab, a few tools, and a little knowledge of biology. This ease makes it in all countries' interest, including China's, to create a new set of rules, norms, and institutions to help humanity navigate a brave new world of genetic engineering, fully autonomous systems, and other emerging technologies.

Brave New Worlds of Biotechnology

In late 2018, a Chinese physicist-turned-geneticist named He Jiankui (贺建奎) took the stage at an international summit on genetics research in Hong Kong. His work centered on the relatively new science of gene editing, using

China's Next Act. Scott M. Moore, Oxford University Press. © Oxford University Press 2022.
DOI: 10.1093/oso/9780197603994.003.0008

a tool called CRISPR to alter the genes of mammal embryos.[1] The rumor swirling among scientists gathered at the summit was that He planned to begin work on human embryos, building on the work of other researchers at Sun Yat-Sen University, where he held a faculty position. Even by the frenzied standards of Hong Kong, the atmosphere was electric as hundreds of the world's top genetics researchers crowded excitedly into a cavernous conference room. But for all the anticipation, nothing could have prepared them for what came next.

Dr. He walked confidently across the stage and stepped to the podium. After a lengthy preamble in which he admitted his university had not known about his research, He began toggling through his slides. Ten minutes of dense biochemistry later, a single, pale-green phrase flashed across the screen: "First established pregnancy." The collective gasp was audible. Instead of merely announcing plans to edit human genomes, He revealed the existence of humankind's first-ever gene-edited babies, Lulu and Nana, who had both entered the world a few months before.

Just like that, in a Hong Kong conference hall, a completely new era began for humanity—the first time anyone had artificially edited human genes that were then carried into the world.[2] Probably more than anyone before him, He had played God, tinkering with the very basis of life itself and launching the world head first into the previously sci-fi age of genetic engineering.

Equally as significant as He's work, though, was the country and context in which it occurred. Historically, developed democracies, and especially the United States, have been the epicenter of research in the life sciences. But thanks to heavy state investment of the kind described in Chapter 5, by the 2010s Chinese firms and research institutions stood at the forefront of biomedical and biotechnology development. At the same time, the use of new techniques, like the gene editing tool CRISPR, dramatically lowered barriers to making transformational advances in biotechnology.

The upshot of these shifts is that breakthroughs in the life sciences began to occur outside the ethical and regulatory framework that guided such research in the United States—leading to shocks like the He Jiankui incident. Though the scandal was hardly representative of China's biotechnology researchers or the sector at large, it underscored that the implications of China's rise extended to emerging technologies, and with it serious ethical as well as economic and security concerns. As with other technologies, gene editing became subject to conflicting and competing norms and values.

China's Biotech Boom

"The twentieth century was the Age of Physics," wrote *Wall Street Journal* columnist Walter Russell Mead in April 2020, as the COVID-19 pandemic raged across the world, but "the 21st century looks now to be an Age of Biology, where the capacity to unleash gene-engineered plagues . . . can provide countries with a strategic advantage."[3,4] Mead's characterization was both simplified and over-dramatic, given that biotechnology promised to produce at least as many benefits as hazards for humanity. But at its core was an important insight: by the early twenty-first century it was clear that biotechnology and biomedical research would be the source of the most important scientific advancements, as well as technological and ethical risks. For most of the postwar period, the United States was the dominant player in these increasingly frontier fields.[5] In the first part of the twenty-first century, the United States alone produced nearly half of all biotechnology patents filed worldwide.[6] China's scientific and research establishment, in contrast, focused more on the physical than the life sciences.[7]

In the early decades of the twenty-first century, though, China became a leading player in the life sciences, biotechnology, and biomedical research thanks to ambitious goals set by Beijing, coupled with massive state-led investment. The 13th Fifth Year Plan (2016–2020) called for the biotechnology sector to account for more than 4% of China's total GDP, almost double its share of the US economy.[8] And while only one of a host of areas in which Beijing aspired for China to challenge developed countries in scientific research and development, biotechnology enjoyed a special emphasis. In an article written in *Qiushi* (求实), the Chinese Communist Party's preeminent ideological journal, amidst the COVID-19 pandemic in September 2020, Xi Jinping himself called for China to "master" biotechnology and mount a "society-wide effort" to achieve breakthroughs in the field.[9]

Policy changes added to the perception that Beijing sought to challenge the United States' dominant position in biotechnology. Whereas China's previous biotechnology policies emphasized international exchange and cooperation and support for relatively mature biotechnology subsectors like genetic crop modification, new guidance issued as part of the 13th Five Year Plan called for developing globally competitive companies and hefty investment in cutting-edge fields.[10] In line with a long-standing desire to promote indigenous innovation, the plan also explicitly refocused policy goals from "quantity accumulation" toward "qualitative transformations."[11] Specifically, these policies outlined a vision to "form a group of new internationally-competitive biotechnology enterprises and biotech economy clusters."[12] China's biotechnology policy also featured elements of protectionism seemingly intended to disadvantage foreign firms: drug approval policies, for example, provided for fast-track review of drugs developed by Chinese companies, while foreign ones were subject to a considerably longer, more arduous process.[13]

China's firms and subnational governments enthusiastically answered Beijing's call to make big bets on biotechnology. Estimates suggest that by the late 2010s, central, provincial, and local governments were investing over US$100 billion in the life sciences annually.[14] Chinese venture capital and private equity investment in the life sciences, meanwhile, totaled some US$45 billion just from 2015 to 2017. These figures could be deceptive: annual research and development (R&D) expenditures by Chinese pharmaceutical firms, often counted as part of the biotechnology industry, grew rapidly but remained low by developed-country standards. Though annual R&D spending among these firms rose steadily from some 39 billion RMB in 2014 (US$5.5 billion) to over 53 billion RMB (US$7.5 billion) by 2017, Swiss drugmaker Roche spent some US$11 billion in 2018 alone (see Figure 7.1).[15]

Even so, Beijing's aspiration to compete with the United States in biotechnology were apparent in areas like talent recruitment. Of some 7,000 recruits under the Thousand Talents Plan since 2008, more than 1,400 specialized in the life sciences, including several non-Chinese foreigners.[16] These moves certainly caught the eye of American policymakers, who viewed them as signs that Beijing intended to mount a full-spectrum challenge to US leadership in the biotechnology sector. One told a US Senate committee, for example, that China "intends to own the biorevolution ... and they are building the infrastructure, the talent pipeline, the regulatory system, and the financial system they need to do that."[17]

Thanks in part to these moves by Beijing, the United States' absolute advantage in biotechnology began to erode throughout the early twenty-first century. Its share of life science patents declined from 57% of the world's total in 1981 to just over half in 2011, while its share of patents deemed to be "highly valuable" decreased from 73% to 59% over the same period. As in other scientific fields, it seemed likely that China would eventually replace the United States as the largest single producer of life sciences research.[18]

In a sign of things to come, in July 2019 a Chinese-led consortium of researchers released the results of the Ruminant Genome Project, an

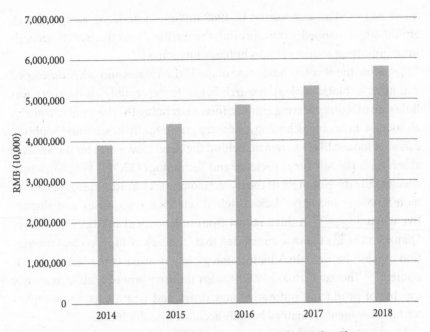

Figure 7.1. Annual research and development expenditures by Chinese pharmaceutical firms, 2014–2017.

Source: National Statistics Bureau of China 2019.

outgrowth of the Human Genome Project that had been led primarily by US-based researchers and institutions. Though less high-profile than its human-focused predecessor, the Ruminant Genome Project promised to help scientists better understand a whole class of animals ranging from cows to gazelles. A leading American geneticist, Harris Lewin, called the results of the project a sign that "we're starting to fall behind . . . the Ruminant Genome Project is a really good example of the Chinese, who have always been good collaborators, now taking the lead."[19]

Along with producing increasingly advanced research, China also produced several leading global biotechnology firms. By the late 2010s, Shenzhen-based BGI (华大) boasted one of the world's largest DNA sequencing capacities and became seen as a Chinese national champion in the field of genomics.[20] Notably, 5 of the 10 largest biotechnology firm Initial Public Offerings in 2019, the last year before the COVID-19 pandemic, were issued by China-based firms. One of these, the drugmaker Hansoh (豪森 药业), whose portfolio included treatments for diabetes and neurological diseases, raised an astonishing US$980 million in its Hong Kong offering, almost single-handedly transforming the territory into the world's second-most important source of biotechnology financing.[21]

Yet while the absolute advantage of the United States and other developed countries in biotechnology research began to perceptibly erode, there was little sign of it disappearing entirely. Instead, echoing the theme of Chapter 5, although China's biotechnology industry grew rapidly in scale and sophistication, it looked likely to remain behind the developed world for the foreseeable future. The Ministry of Science and Technology (MOST, 科技部), which oversees the development of the biotechnology sector, admitted that China's biotechnology industry "lacks original scientific discoveries and disruptive technologies."[22] A 2018 report from independent market consultancy Qianzhan (前瞻) likewise concluded that "the lack of independent innovation capabilities of China's biotechnology sector restricts the sector's development."[23] Though China's biotechnology industry proved itself increasingly capable of producing innovative new drugs and treatments, these unflattering assessments remained broadly accurate into the 2020s.

Moreover, despite the rapid growth of China's biotechnology market, financing for commercialization was limited. The pre-commercial state of many biotechnologies and their high-risk, capital-intensive nature restricted the availability of financing for small- and medium-sized biotech enterprises in China's state-dominated financial landscape.[24] These financing barriers helped ensure that China's biotechnology industry remained some distance from being truly globally competitive. Even MOST conceded that the industry's international "market competitiveness is not strong."[25] Cross-border investment flows and collaboration, especially with the United States, remained critical sources of financing, talent, and cutting-edge technology into the 2020s. These trends made biotechnology an arena of co-production and joint commercialization as well as competition among the United States, China, and other countries.

To foreign firms, the main attraction of investing in China's biotechnology sector was the sheer size of its market, especially for biologically inspired drugs and medical treatments. By 2019, China accounted for one in four cancer cases diagnosed worldwide.[26] Its population of over-60-year-olds, meanwhile, reached 200 million in 2020, creating explosive growth in demand for medical care. China's pharmaceutical market was expected to grow from US$123 billion in 2017 to up to US$175 billion by 2022.[27] Total health-care spending reached upwards of US$1 trillion annually, making China the world's second-most important market for virtually everything related to biotechnology.[28] The rewards for foreign firms entering this market could be breathtaking, despite having to comply with onerous regulations, such as having to heavily discount drugs to qualify for coverage under China's national health insurance scheme. American pharmaceutical giant Merck's revenue in China, for example, grew 84% over the course of just one year, thanks mainly to sales of a human papillomavirus (HPV) vaccine.[29] Unsurprisingly, many foreign biotechnology firms decided they could not afford to ignore the Chinese market.

As in other areas where China's market potential seemed irresistible to foreign firms, there was a dark side to this commercial bonanza. And as in so many other areas explored in this book, eye-popping numbers concealed deep normative challenges. While Beijing, and its provincial and municipal governments, began to give countries like the United States a run for its money in biotechnology development, they proved less assiduous in implementing ethical and regulatory frameworks to guide biomedical research. This became a growing cause for economic and security, as well as ethical, concern. Biotechnology specialist Jamie Metzl, for example, argued that China's combination of scientific and technological capacity and expertise with comparatively loose regulations and ethical standards in biomedical research had the potential to give it a "strategic advantage" in the sector.[30] As in other fields, biotechnology and bioethics became an arena of competition between China and other nations, especially the United States.

Bioethical Blunders and Bypasses

A sadly common feature of the history of biomedical research, in the United States, China, and elsewhere, is that advances in technology are often accompanied by abuses, especially of minority and marginalized populations.[31] Some of these abuses reflected deliberate exploitation of disadvantaged populations, others carelessness and a failure to follow established procedures. Unfortunately, the rapid pace of advancement in biotechnology and biomedical science and the complexity of research safety protocols meant that lapses could occur even in countries where, as in the United States, stringent regulatory review and legal accountability mechanisms were in place.[32] The rapid growth and development of China's biotechnology and biomedical research sectors, though, made it the focus of concerns that science was advancing more rapidly than safety measures—with worrying implications for patients, minority populations, and the durability of ethical frameworks to guide pathbreaking research.

In some ways, it is unfair to single out China as a focus of bioethical breaches. Chinese regulations governing biomedical research are not markedly different from those followed elsewhere. Rules introduced in 2007 by the then-Ministry of Health (卫生部), for example, required all clinical research involving humans to abide by two core principles of biomedical research in the United States and elsewhere: that trials be reviewed by independent Institutional Review Boards, and that researchers obtain "informed consent" from all participants, meaning that human subjects must be properly informed of any risks involved in the research, and explicitly consent to taking part. Moreover, as in most developed countries, China's administrative rules banned human gene editing for the purpose of reproduction.[33] Yet as China's biotechnology and biomedical sectors grew, even isolated breaches of established principles and protocols took on outsized implications, especially as economic, geopolitical, and ideological competition with the United States grew more acute.

Legal and ethical abuses by China's biomedical sector became a focus of foreign attention in the 1990s, when a series of Western human rights organizations accused Chinese authorities of tolerating, and in some cases enabling, forced organ donation from prisoners, many of them adherents of the banned Falun Gong (法轮功) religious group.[34] Though strenuously denied by Chinese officials, these allegations forged a perception both in China and abroad that medicine and biotechnology were sectors rife with abuse. This perception was bolstered by several tragic incidents throughout the early twenty-first century, most notably a 2016 case in which a young student died after agreeing to be part of a high-risk experimental treatment that proved to be fraudulent and based on false advertising. The resulting outcry, known as the Wei Zexi incident (魏则西事件), spawned attempts to strengthen oversight of clinical trials.[35]

As concern for abuse in biomedical research grew, Chinese researchers became enthusiastic participants in international bioethics dialogues. In 2016, a group of leading Chinese biomedical researchers took part in efforts sponsored by the US National Academy of Sciences to develop detailed guidelines on human gene editing, which included "maintaining high ethical standards."[36] But while such standards and regulations were generally treated as binding in the United States, in China they were frequently ignored—including by Dr. He, who not only violated China's ban on editing genes for reproductive purposes, but also raised fundamental questions surrounding the ethics of gene editing.

Despite the growing attention placed on bioethics within China, several developments in the late 2010s made clear that the practices of at least a few leading Chinese life science researchers differed markedly from their overseas counterparts. In 2018, Chinese researchers achieved a significant milestone by producing the world's first primate clones. They hailed the development as one that would advance biomedical research by producing two genetically identical test subjects, helping better assess the effect of medical treatments. But the risks of the cloning procedure—only a handful of monkeys survived out of dozens of attempts—raised significant objections on animal welfare and research ethics grounds. A leading British scientist deemed the research a "very inefficient and hazardous procedure."[37] The director of one of the laboratories involved in the research replied with startling candor: "Ethics," he explained, "should not be a reason that hinders scientific development."[38] The study's principal investigator, meanwhile, responded to a separate concern that the technique might eventually be used to clone human beings by dismissively stating that "I would think society and the general public and governments will not allow extension of this method from nonhuman primates to humans."[39]

The subsequent track record of biomedical research in China, though, provided little comfort that such prohibitions would be followed, even when they were in place. In 2019, Chinese researchers recorded another mind-bending milestone when they implanted human genes associated with intelligence into monkey embryos. Sure enough, the monkeys performed better on memory tests. Foreign bioethicists blasted the research, warning that these transgenic modifications could lead to a whole new set of moral hazards. Because transgenic organisms are neither fully human nor fully monkey, bioethicists argued, they could fall outside existing legal, ethical, and regulatory frameworks, leaving them vulnerable to exploitation and abuse.[40]

Even in less cutting-edge research areas, China's bioethical rules and practices proved to be full of holes. Regulations governing biomedical research were both confusing and lacked legal force.[41] He Jiankui reportedly dismissed them as "guidelines," not laws.[42] Fierce competition between researchers, institutions, and local governments, meanwhile, led at least a few scientists to cut ethical and regulatory corners to be the first to publish groundbreaking results. For several years before Dr. He's announcement, several Chinese researchers had been edging closer to gene editing in human germline cells—while still abiding by the general prohibition on implanting edited genomes in the womb. The desire to leap ahead of these rival researchers reportedly contributed to Dr. He's decision to smash through that ethical barrier and become "the first to carry out germline genome editing."[43]

But bioethical corner-cutting clearly went beyond individual ambition. Oversight of biomedical research was placed largely with provincial governments like Guangdong, a hub of China's life sciences industry and the site of Dr. He's research.[44] News reports indicated that the Guangdong provincial government and Shenzhen, the municipality in which Dr. He worked, encouraged and funded He's research in an effort to help local biomedical research stay ahead of rivals based in other cities.[45] These perverse incentive structures placed intense pressure on individual researchers like Dr. He to take unnecessary risks to help local officials meet performance metrics tied to boosting basic scientific research and innovation (more on the effects of these metrics in Chapter 5).[46]

Ironically, though, loose bioethical regulations proved to be one of the biggest constraints on the development of China's biotechnology sector. Relatively weak research protocols could make clinical trials cheaper and easier to conduct in China than in the United States. In mid-2018, when US researchers were just beginning to seek approval for clinical trials to use CRISPR for cancer treatment, at least eight such trials were already underway in China.[47] A doctor involved in one such trial remarked that, given that CRISPR was invented in the United States, "China shouldn't have been the first one" to begin clinical trials. "But" he conceded, "there are fewer restrictions."[48]

In biomedical research, though, being first is not always a good thing. Several cases emerged in which Chinese researchers, prioritizing speed over compliance, lost track of experimental subjects due to improper record-keeping, thereby making it impossible to track patient outcomes. The result was that the research sometimes stalled, and promising medial and commercial applications went unidentified.[49] The implications for patients could also be profound. In the case of He Jiankui, shoddy use of gene editing had several unintended consequences, including "completely novel mutations," about which a leading foreign scientist warned, "we have absolutely no understanding."[50]

Such bioethical lapses were not just a concern for Chinese patients, but also implicated foreign companies in serious human rights violations—yet another sign of how the consequences of China's rise spread far beyond its borders. A 2019 *New York Times* report indicated that Chinese authorities had assembled a vast trove of genetic data on Chinese citizens without their consent, specifically targeting the Uighur minority group. Perhaps even more disturbing, the report alleged, US companies and researchers provided the know-how to make this bio-sampling effort possible.[51] Such activity threatened to embroil leading Western biomedical research institutions in potential human rights violations. Another *Times* report found that several Chinese scientists implicated in the collection of DNA data from Uighurs to feed into facial recognition software—a technique known as DNA phenotyping—held affiliations and had received funding from prestigious European bodies like the Max Plank Institute.[52]

A seemingly even more serious threat to other nations emerged from signs that Beijing was backing increasingly exotic bioweapons research. At least one Chinese military text broached the concept of "specific ethnic genetic attacks,"[53] though the specifics of this unsettling approach were unclear. In December 2020, one of Clapper's successors as director of National Intelligence, John Ratcliffe, claimed in an editorial that "U.S. intelligence shows that China has even conducted human testing on members of the People's Liberation Army in hope of developing soldiers with biologically enhanced capabilities. There are no ethical boundaries to Beijing's pursuit of power."[54] These alarming capabilities needed to be viewed with nuance: the technology behind them was almost entirely speculative. Moreover, there was little evidence that China was pursuing bioweapons capabilities with any more enthusiasm than other major military powers, including the United States.[55] Nonetheless, these accounts contributed to the idea that biotechnology, too, was becoming an arena of Sino-American competition. And as with so many other issues in China's relationship with the world, the perception as much as the reality of economic, geopolitical, and ideological competition colored prospects for cooperation in biotechnology.

Other developments within China unfortunately enhanced this perception. Aspects of aspects of life science research in China began to carry an uncomfortably militaristic, nationalistic, and protectionist tone (more on the growth of Chinese nationalism in Chapter 1). As early as the 2003 SARS crisis, the well-known Chinese nationalist writer Wang Xiaodong (王小东) began discussing the "possibility of genetic weapons," which he baselessly alleged were already being deployed against China by the United States.[56] As described in Chapter 6, moreover, China adopted an exceptionally strict set of prohibitions on gathering and sharing biomedical data, at least in part because Beijing viewed it as a national strategic resource and source of competitive advantage in biotechnology. Xi's 2020 article in Qiushi calling for increased investment in biotechnology struck an often-aggressive tone, calling the sector a "national treasure" that must be "seized with our own hand."[57]

Echoing one of the core themes of this book, these potentially nefarious uses of technology, overlaid with divergent norms, values, and ideology, complicated meaningful cooperation between China and other countries over biotechnology as the twenty-first century deepened. But unlike many other technologies, biotechnology was both highly democratic and exceptionally difficult, even for powerful states like China, to effectively control. That meant that even though Beijing appeared in some respects to use biotechnology to bolster its repression at home and belligerence abroad, it also had good reasons to work with other countries to prevent tools like CRISPR from falling into the wrong hands.

Exotic Weaponization Worries

In January 2016, then-US Director of National Intelligence James Clapper appeared before Congress to present an annual briefing on threats to the United States. The world's newspaper pages gave him plenty of material. Just a few weeks earlier, North Korea had tested a nuclear device, and Russia had begun deploying cruise missiles that violated a crucial arms-control agreement. But to the surprise of many, Clapper devoted a good chunk of his time and space in an accompanying report to describing a much more exotic threat: biomedical research, including the kind that He Jiankui would soon initiate in China. Specifically, the report warned that "research in genome editing conducted by countries with different regulatory or ethical standards than those of Western countries probably increases the risk of the creation of potentially harmful biological agents or products."[58] Clapper's warning came almost two years before He Jiankui's announcement, but it proved eerily prescient in a world in which the human genome could be modified just as easily in Shanghai or Syria as in San Francisco.

The ethical concerns surrounding advanced technologies like gene editing were clearly profound, but only part of the problem. The risk these technologies could be weaponized rose steadily. Just as cheap and easy-to-use gene-editing techniques like CRISPR made it much simpler for the He Jiankuis of the world to skirt ethical restrictions, they also made it terrifyingly straightforward for both countries and terrorist groups to develop fearsome biological weapons. Research on developing genetically engineered bioweapons began decades before the invention of CRISPR in the early twenty-first century. But CRISPR dramatically increased the ease with which rouge states or scientists—whether He Jiankui waving aside restrictions on human embryo modification or a terrorist trying to make diseases more potent—could make use of gene editing techniques.[59]

To be sure, the vast majority of biotechnology research, both in China and elsewhere, carried little risk and promised substantial rewards in the form of new treatments for diseases and many other benefits. But from the perspective of economic and geopolitical competition, the threat of bioweapons development carried outsized importance. By lowering the bar to entry for biomedical research, CRISPR enhanced the risk that countries, terrorists, and non-state actors might gain the ability to make biological agents more dangerous, and even more lethal. It also made the accidental release of harmful viruses or other biological agents more likely. The very specter of these scenarios gave countries like China a very good reason to work together with other countries to develop a new set of rules to guide and restrain the development of potentially new and exotic weapons—even while competing in the realm of biotechnology. As one of Dr. He's colleagues proclaimed in the aftermath of his revelations, "Once the gate of gene editing is wide open, the human race will be finished."[60]

The Pandora's Box of Genetic Engineering and Synthetic Biology

Nation-states have long sought to harness biology for the cause of warfare and military advantage. The former Soviet Union was especially keen on developing biological weapons and built a vast infrastructure to design and build them. Along the way, Soviet scientists tried to modify diseases like anthrax to make them more lethal. Fortunately, this research never made it out of the lab (at least, as far as anyone knows). In large part this was because researching, designing, and producing weapons proved to be a complex, difficult, and expensive affair. Most bioweapons proved to be too unpredictable to be militarily useful. It was hard to predict how they would spread, and they were indiscriminate, acting with just as much potency against allies as adversaries.[61] In the early twenty-first century, though, advances in synthetic biology threatened at least in theory to solve each of these problems, providing a cheap and easy way to modify pathogens to make them more lethal—and possibly to resurrect others that had long laid dormant.[62]

Research in the first decade of the twenty-first century showed that this kind of biohacking could be alarmingly straightforward. In 2002, scientists at the State University of New York managed to recreate the polio virus, which had been eliminated in the United States decades earlier, from scratch. They did so by reconstructing the virus's deoxyribonucleic acid (DNA), an approach known as synthetic biology. It took the researchers three years, but they proved that this form of do-it-yourself biology could recreate harmful viruses. They used DNA ordered by mail and synthesized it using publicly accessible online databases. A decade or so later, another group of researchers took an even more disconcerting step by synthesizing a close relative of the smallpox virus. Smallpox was one of the world's deadliest diseases, and the first to be eradicated, save for a few samples kept for research purposes. The work carried out by a group at the University of Alberta, though, showed it was entirely possible to reconstruct the smallpox virus. It was not even particularly difficult: it took the team about 18 months, $200,000, and some DNA fragments purchased online.[63]

Such research is exceedingly difficult for countries and governments to regulate. An international organization, the International Gene Synthesis Consortium, was formed in 2009 in part to screen online DNA orders and try to stop individuals from using genetic material for nefarious purposes. Most of the world's major DNA synthesis firms joined the Consortium, but membership was entirely voluntary.[64] Moreover, even this minimal regulatory framework was full of holes: guidelines called only for screening orders involving large chunks of DNA, but new techniques meant that even smaller sequences could potentially be weaponized. The rise of DNA printing techniques, meanwhile, threatened to make even these patchy attempts at controlling access to genetic material almost obsolete.[65] Perhaps most worrying of all, DNA templates were featured on a global black market, including within China.[66]

As terrifying as the threat of synthetic bioweapons is, biohazards are more likely to emerge from accidental or sloppy, rather than deliberately malicious, research. The growth of biomedical and biotechnology research around the world heightened the need to prevent research on viruses, genetic material, and micro-organisms from accidentally wreaking havoc outside the laboratory, a field known as biosafety. Both the United States and China possessed strong post-pandemic reasons to fear biosafety breaches by the other. Before the COVID-19 pandemic, the US government supported work to make highly transmissible viruses like bird flu spread even more easily, an approach known as "gain of function" research. The purpose was strictly to better understand how these viruses infected new hosts, but it understandably made many scientists, both in China and elsewhere, very nervous, especially given that bird flu had killed millions of Chinese citizens in recent decades.[67] Developing norms to govern gain of function research became a frequently cited priority for US–China dialogue.[68]

The importance of biosafety, and the related field of biosecurity, was further highlighted by debates over the origins of the COVID-19 pandemic. After the COVID-19 virus spread to Europe and the Americas in the spring of 2020, theories emerged that its origin was artificial rather than natural. A Chinese viral research institute located in Wuhan became the focus of allegations that it had developed, and then accidentally released, the SARS-CoV-2 virus.[69] Though the evidence for this claim was circumstantial, scientists roundly warned that the prospect of a future accidental release, either in Wuhan, New Delhi, or elsewhere, was frighteningly plausible, highlighting the need to invest in international efforts to regulate how dangerous pathogens are handled, including for research purposes.[70] According to a World Health Organization report, in 2018, there were some 54 laboratory facilities classified as "BSL-4," meaning they were equipped to handle highly transmissible pathogens, in countries from Argentina to Côte d'Ivoire.[71] A robust international biosafety regime would have to apply common standards to all such facilities, in both China and elsewhere, to prevent the accidental release of viruses of other biological agents.

Fortunately, developments following the He Jiankui incident showed that China's leaders viewed developing and implementing a new set of norms relating to biotechnology, biomedical research, and biosafety to be firmly in China's interest. Though Dr. He's work was pathbreaking, the episode turned out to be a disaster for Chinese science. The use of CRISPR to alter human genomes was almost universally condemned by the international genetics research community, causing acute embarrassment to Chinese researchers and officials. China's science ministry declared it was "resolutely opposed" to the use of gene editing for human embryos. Chinese researchers, meanwhile, quickly made clear to policymakers their belief that weak ethical standards undermined scientific research and innovation. As one leading life science researcher commented, "We must change the impression that people can always sneak through regulations in China. Only then can the country's stem-cell research and regenerative medicine be fully recognized in the world."[72]

Beijing soon heeded these calls by backing measures to tighten oversight of biomedical research. In February 2019, the Chinese government announced that "high risk" biomedical research would be overseen by the State Council, China's equivalent of the Cabinet—a sign of how seriously Beijing took the implications of the He Jiankui scandal.[73] In a further sign of this seriousness, in August 2019, the Chinese Communist Party announced the creation of a new committee to advise top leaders on research ethics.[74] A draft law introduced later the same year even included human genes and embryos on a list of "personality rights," opening the door to treating gene editing as a fundamental violation of individual rights. Though it was unclear how this provision would be implemented, on paper it gave Chinese citizens far greater bioethical protections than their counterparts in most other countries.[75]

Even more promising were signs of self-organization among Chinese researchers. A few days after the new research ethics committee was established, meanwhile, several leading Chinese research institutes, including the Chinese Academy of Sciences (中国科学院) and the Chinese Society for Cell Biology, announced publication of a common set of standards to guide research using human embryonic stem cells. This was the first such effort organized by individual research institutes rather than the government, and a striking sign that Chinese researchers themselves were taking bioethical issues seriously.[76] Bai Chunli (白春礼), the president of the Chinese Academy of Sciences and a member of the National People's Congress, gave this effort a further boost when he gave an unusual speech before the Congress's 2019 session, calling for Chinese researchers to join the United States in adopting a bioethics framework as an essential part of developing its biomedical research capacity. "The United States is not only the leading country in biomedical research," Bai noted approvingly, "but also the first country to develop biosafety regulations and legislation."[77]

Thanks in part to Bai's advocacy, China's Biosecurity Law was approved in October 2020, less than a year from its first reading—an unusually fast pace, implying it was a high priority for China's leaders. As with the law on personality rights, it was unclear how the Biosecurity Law would be implemented, but it followed what were, on paper, many best practices, like a risk-based regulatory system to guide biotechnology research; countermeasures against growing microbial resistance; and protocols for management of laboratory pathogens. The law also established a controlled substance regime whereby certain biological items would require registration and approval for purchase or import, and generally barred individuals from possessing controlled biological materials, including biotoxins, microbes, and most plants and animals. Notably, it also strengthened penalties for noncompliance. Illegal biotechnology research, for example, could be punished by fines up to 10 million RMB (US$1.5 million) and prison sentences of up to 10 years.[78]

Such regulation represented a promising investment in biosafety and biosecurity, and potentially even a model for other countries, including the United States. But given that biomedical research continued to advance much more quickly than laws or regulations, it is clear that self-regulation among scientists remains the best bet for keeping Pandora's box closed when it comes to dangerous advances in areas like genetic engineering synthetic biology. And while far from guaranteed, there are signs that developing new norms in these emerging technological fields might even bring China and other countries closer together with respect to certain ethical standards and values.

Building Ethical Bridges between China and Other Nations

Biology was not the only field notching mind-bending breakthroughs in the early decades of the twenty-first century. Many of the most exciting, and problematic, techno-ethical conundrums of the age in fact sit at the intersection of two emerging technologies, biotechnology and artificial intelligence (AI). As detailed in Chapter 5, AI in many ways became Exhibit A for technological competition between China and major powers like the United States. Yet, like biotechnology, AI also became laden with concern for its ethical and ideological as well as economic and military implications. US Congressman Will Hurd, for example, proclaimed in 2019 that the United States needed to maintain leadership in AI to ensure that the technology reflected the values of "Western liberal democracies, not China."[79] But despite the seeming divide between countries like the United States and China on technologies like

AI, there are signs that Beijing is willing to build a bridge to other countries on certain principles.

In mid-2018, an unusual article appeared in a Chinese journal called *Contemporary International Relations* (现代国际关系), a sort of Chinese version of *Foreign Affairs*. Though authored by two scholars at China's National University of Defense Technology, the article read more like a philosophical treatise than a war plan. The emerging competition between China, the United States, and other countries over AI amounted, the article explained, to a "Pandora's box" that could well lead to the end of the world. As a "responsible great power," the article went on to argue, China had a fundamental duty to contribute to developing an international AI arms control framework.[80] At the same time, other reports emerged citing widespread concern among Chinese military planners at the risk of war between AI-controlled drones, which they feared might increase the likelihood of war between countries like the United States and China.[81]

These accounts were hardly representative of Beijing's thinking and sat uneasily alongside moves that appeared clearly aimed at attaining both military and technological dominance in AI.[82] Moreover, some observers were quick to cast doubt on the motives for what looked like olive branches on the ethics of emerging technologies: they could simply be a distraction or a ruse to maintain access to overseas research in areas where Chinese firms and institutions remained behind.[83] But even if outreach on emerging technologies is less than sincere, it nonetheless points to an important reality: the ethical questions surrounding the use of AI, as well as biotechnology, pose genuine dilemmas for China's technologists and policymakers as much as their counterparts in other countries. That reality opens a narrow path to further dialogue on some of the great techno-moral questions of tomorrow.

Part of the reason these overtures were so promising was that many of them came not from Beijing itself, but from groups only loosely linked to the state. In 2018, the China Association for Artificial Intelligence (中国人工智能学会) set up an ethics committee chaired by Chen Xiaoping (陈小平), a robotics professor who became well-known for building a stunningly lifelike android known as the "Robot Goddess."[84] Under Chen's direction, the committee invited comments from experts in sociology and law in addition to technology, and developed recommendations to address privacy issues in the use of AI, especially in sensitive fields like healthcare. "We can take preventive measures to avoid going in a certain direction," Chen observed in an interview, "or take measures to control the risks."[85]

Of course, controlling such risk is easier said than done. Yet the importance placed by Chen and his colleagues on ethical risks in AI implementation was strikingly similar in both tone and substance to statements by the US government, suggesting the possibility of further dialogue on AI ethics. The US Department of Defense's (DOD) own AI Strategy, issued in 2018, for example, devoted a surprising amount of attention to ethics. The Strategy pledged to "consult with leaders from across academic, private industry, and the international community to advance AI ethics and safety in the military context" and to "seek opportunities to use AI to reduce unintentional harm and collateral damage."[86] Just as importantly, the strategy appeared to extend an olive branch to China and other leading AI powers in the form of a dialogue on AI ethics. The document proposed to work with these powers in "advocating for a global set of military AI guidelines."[87]

It would doubtless be difficult and politically challenging to reach agreement on such guidelines. But given the stakes involved, it would be equally irresponsible to allow these offers from both sides of the Pacific to go unanswered. Nowhere is this more apparent than in the evolving relationship between AI and the most destructive technology of all—nuclear weapons. By the 2020s, major powers were on the cusp of integrating AI into nuclear command and control systems—potentially freeing nuclear weapons from direct human control and raising the specter of a horrifying "Space Odyssey" scenario, but one that could hold the entire planet hostage instead of just a few spaceship crew members. The promise of AI to help detect nuclear ballistic missile submarines at sea likewise threatens to profoundly destabilize the tenuous nuclear peace the world has enjoyed since 1945. Most nuclear powers rely on submarines to provide an ultimate insurance policy: if attacked by a rival nuclear power, they can unleash massive retaliation from undetectable undersea platforms. But if AI were to make supposedly invisible submarines prone to detection and tracking, the whole mad logic of nuclear deterrence might collapse, tempting countries to strike first.[88]

These terrifying scenarios make it clear that the world will have to invest just as much effort in regulating emerging technologies as it has in preventing the spread of nuclear weapons. Though very different technologies, AI and synthetic biology bear one important similarity to nuclear energy in that they hold both enormous promise and peril for humanity. As Bill Gates observed, these emerging technologies are distinguished by being "both promising and dangerous."[89] Unlike nuclear weapons, though, these new technologies are relatively cheap and easy to deploy, and it is far from straightforward how countries might meaningfully and effectively draw lines around their development.

For that very reason, while the US, Chinese, and other governments are critical to regulating emerging technologies, efforts to regulate emerging technologies cannot be limited to nation-states. They will also have to include individual researchers, institutions, companies, and organizations like the International Gene Synthesis Consortium. Rather ironically, when it comes to the risks posed by emerging technologies, China's fast-growing role means that Beijing, like other governments, will have to face the limits of its ability to solve the problem on its own.

The Pressing Need for a New Era of Norm-Creation

It is a sad fact of history that new technologies often lead to new forms of bloodshed. One of the biggest such leaps came in the mid-nineteenth century, when advancements like the repeating rifle introduced a whole new level of carnage into modern warfare. Witnessing the aftermath of a battle between the French and Austrian armies in 1859, a Swiss businessman provided one of the first descriptions of what later became known as total war, a life-or-death contest between armed forces backed by the might of industrialized states. It was, Henry Dunant recalled, "sheer butchery; a struggle between savage beasts, maddened with blood and fury. Even the wounded fight to the last gasp."[90]

Unlike most nightmares, though, those recorded by Dunant turned out to have a hopeful ending. Shaken by what he had seen, Dunant proposed that trained medical personnel be allowed to give aid to the wounded of both sides of a conflict and be protected from attack while doing so. In 1863, a group that later became known as the International Committee of the Red Cross was formed to put Dunant's proposal into action. The group convened a meeting in Geneva that included medical professionals, nongovernmental societies, and diplomats from 16 countries. Their efforts eventually led to the Geneva Conventions, the world's first international agreements designed to protect people and outline a code of conduct for nations during wartime.[91]

A century later, during the Cold War, the international community devised a whole new set of norms and institutions to restrain the use of the most terrifying weapons technology ever devised, the nuclear bomb. For four decades, the United States, the Soviet Union, and their allies aimed tens of thousands of nuclear bombs, missiles, artillery shells, and torpedoes at one another. Fortunately, none were ever fired in anger. But it was not simply good fortune that prevented planetary catastrophe. From the dawn of the atomic age, the scientists and researchers who worked to turn the uranium chain reaction into usable weapons devoted themselves with equal enthusiasm to ensuring that they would never be used—echoing the efforts of Dunant and his counterparts a century before.

Albert Einstein is often remembered for authoring a famous letter to then-President Franklin Roosevelt that helped launch the Manhattan Project, eventually producing the world's first atomic bomb. But he devoted equal effort to warning that unless steps were taken to control nuclear weapons, the "annihilation of life on earth has been brought within the range of technical possibilities." Einstein and many of his counterparts remained champions of nuclear arms control throughout their lives, doing much to inspire the creation of institutions like the International Atomic Energy Agency that sought to ensure nuclear power was devoted to constructive rather than destructive ends.[92]

As the twenty-first century deepened, the need for a new era of norm-building became apparent that would equal the one Dunant had helped usher in during the nineteenth century, and Einstein in the twentieth. Just as the technology of these previous centuries has been used for destructive ends, there is every reason to believe the emerging technologies of the twenty-first century, especially artificial intelligence and synthetic biology, will be weaponized. The development of transformational, and potentially destructive, technologies like gene editing and artificial intelligence calls for a new era of norm-creation to equal the path-breaking Geneva Conventions and emulate the technological safeguards developed to combat nuclear proliferation. And while national governments are essential to these discussions, just like in the case of the body that eventually became the Red Cross, individuals and nongovernmental organizations will have to play a leading role in helping humanity avert new techno-catastrophes in the twenty-first century.

Standard-Setting for a New Age

The biggest reason non-state actors are so important in twenty-first century norm-setting is a practical one: it proved increasingly difficult for institutional bureaucracies, whether in Beijing or Berlin, to keep up with the pace of technological change. China's rapidly growing role in fields like synthetic biology quickly outstripped many of the frameworks, like export control regimes, that states had put in place to deal with threats like the proliferation of weapons of mass destruction. One such export control regime, known as the Australia Group, emerged in response to the Iran-Iraq War to restrict materials that could aid chemical and biological weapons programs. Its membership, though, failed to keep pace with the world's expanding biotechnology sector. By 2020, the Australia Group had grown to include most industrialized countries, but not emerging biotechnology powers like China, Israel, or Singapore.[93]

Developments in synthetic biology, meanwhile, undermined key features of multilateral export regimes like the Australia Group. While in theory the group can simply be expanded to include countries like China, it became increasingly challenging to apply export controls to cheap, easily obtained items like DNA synthesizers. An even more fundamental problem is the fact that for many emerging technologies, the most important input is not raw materials or equipment but rather people and the know-how they possess. For both legal and practical reasons, it is much harder to restrict the spread of people and knowledge than physical things and objects, a topic Chapter 4 covers in detail.[94] As in many of the issues covered in this book, the intangible aspects of synthetic biology are the ones that matter most.

There is an even deeper reason that states find it difficult to effectively regulate emerging technologies. When it comes to gene editing or artificial intelligence, it is inevitably difficult to forsee how technology will evolve—yet in the future, it may become clear its development should have been steered in one direction or another. This paradox, known as the "Collingridge dilemma," has always vexed governmental attempts to regulate new technologies. Given this dilemma, it is important that attempts to create rules and regulations around new technologies be based on extensive consultation between researchers, companies, nongovernmental organizations, and ordinary citizens to try to reach a consensus on what concerns a new technology might generate.

This approach, known as anticipatory governance, involves collecting as much information from as many sources as possible to assess and mitigate potential risks involved in the development of new technologies. The process may lead governments to set firm limits on how far a technology can progress—for example, by prohibiting gene editing of viable human embryos—or to tightly regulate the development of technologies that may pose security risks, such as bioengineered viruses. Critically, anticipatory governance requires extensive public engagement, something that was sorely lacking in countries like China that have a strong tradition of authoritarian and technocratic government.[95] Yet the Collingridge dilemma still applies to China's state and Chinese firms just as strongly as American or European ones. In an era when the actions of individual researchers in China, Brazil, or elsewhere could have humanity-wide repercussions, debates that have previously taken place mostly within countries will quite clearly have to become global.

Despite its reluctance to permit wide-ranging debates over norms and values at home, Beijing for its part proved to be an enthusiastic participant in international standard-setting—at least when it could make the rules. While China was keen to engage in multilateral standard-setting where it could shape the rules to its benefit, it was less willing to commit to prevailing, largely Western-designed, standards.[96] As noted in Chapter 6, China became an engaged participant in multilateral telecommunications standard-setting bodies in the first decade of the twenty-first century—involvement that proved highly beneficial to firms like Huawei. Beijing's strategy involved holding pre-meetings with industry groups, sending large delegations to aggressively lobby countries that benefited from its aid and commercial largesse to back China's positions.[97]

There was also some evidence that Beijing's willingness to engage in international standard-setting is a function of the competitive position of its firms: where they stood to gain from continued access to foreign technology and researchers, cooperation was more likely.[98] As with other shared global challenges, these tendencies make it unlikely that Beijing, Brussels, and Washington will entirely see eye-to-eye when it came to regulating emerging technologies like synthetic biology. Below the nation-state level, though, the picture looks considerably brighter, and Beijing's coordinated approach even offers a useful model to make non-state dialogue more effective.

The Importance of Dialogue below the Nation-State Level

Despite widespread tension at the intergovernmental level, there is enormous potential for non-state actors in the United States, China, and other countries to drive dialogue on technological ethics and standard setting. Such discussions often revealed that the concerns of the other side were misplaced. A series of US–China technology dialogues, for example, revealed that the Chinese side was fixated on the perceived threat from what turned out to be a long-defunct Pentagon-backed program that never advanced beyond the concept stage, and was regarded by American participants as a technological dead-end.[99] A roundtable discussion convened in July 2020 at the University of Pennsylvania, meanwhile, recorded universal belief in the potential of reaching a shared understanding between Chinese and Western researchers on certain bioethical standards, especially research involving human subjects.[100] The promise of sub-state dialogue is also suggested by a rich history of efforts, led mostly by scientists rather than by politicians or diplomats, to contain the risks involved in path-breaking life science research.

In the 1960s, American scientists grew increasingly concerned that progress in genetics research could cause dangerous viruses to be unwittingly introduced into human populations. This concern led to a 1973 conference in Asilomar, California, sponsored by the US National Science Foundation, the National Cancer Institute, and several other US-based organizations. These initial meetings produced a set of safety precautions to be followed by all researchers dealing with certain viruses. But further developments in using recombinant DNA created additional concerns related to combining different types of genetic material. In 1974, accordingly, plans were made to hold a second Asilomar conference to strengthen ethical and safety guidelines for genetics research. Tellingly, by this point, international collaboration was so widespread in the field of genetics that the organizers' first order of business was to discuss the participation of researchers from abroad. In the end, roughly one-third of the participants were from abroad, including Japan.[101]

This second Asilomar conference, held in 1975, was groundbreaking, and helped to formulate what has become known as the "precautionary principle," namely that when research involves many unknowns, work should proceed slowly and cautiously, with safeguards and protocols that weigh known and anticipated risks against expected benefits.[102] It is a principle that remains highly relevant to help the world deal with challenges like gene editing and artificial intelligence. But at the same time, the world has clearly changed quite a bit since 1975. What is needed is a new Asilomar conference, with a much broader set of participation—especially from China.

Such a dialogue will face significant hurdles: even generally like-minded European countries differ considerably from the United States in the practice of bioethics. These countries also vary widely in the extent to which issues like the legacy of eugenics and the morality of stem cell research played a significant role—in the United States they were central, but in China much less so.[103] Nonetheless, an Asilomar 2.0 will be an important first step to addressing emerging questions like how to treat transgenic organisms under international law.[104] Moreover, an emphasis on collective action among researchers could make a next-generation Asilomar process more effective than inter-governmental negotiations over biotechnology. The reality of many emerging biotechnologies is that responsible use ultimately depends on individual scientists and researchers. The chair of a World Health Organization committee established to set international guidelines for the use of CRISPR, for example, took pains to emphasize the responsibility of individual researchers, admonishing scientists worldwide that "it is irresponsible for anyone to proceed with human germline genome editing."[105]

Another issue ripe for nongovernmental dialogue and standard setting is data integrity and reliability. One of the biggest challenges for technology like AI is its ability to determine whether the data it receives can be trusted. Deliberate falsification of data used for AI applications could be deadly if, for example, someone convinces an autonomous vehicles' AI that a "Stop" sign in fact means "Speed up." Because such falsified data could come from anywhere, international collaboration is essential to establishing the provenance and pedigree of data used to train AI and other systems. One way to address shared concerns over data integrity is to conduct joint, multi-party algorithm testing. By conducting AI algorithm tests according to commonly agreed international protocols and making the results freely available, individual companies and research groups could build confidence in emerging technologies in much the same way countries have historically built diplomatic trust with one another.[106]

One barrier to relying more heavily on these kinds of multi-stakeholder, public–private dialogue is that, unlike in diplomatic negotiations, it can be difficult to determine whether participants speak for themselves or for their respective national governments. In nongovernmental dialogues, often referred to as "Track 1.5" or "Track II" discussions, US and other Western participants often find themselves representing individual views or those of their organizations, while Chinese participants frequently coordinate in advance to present a single, coherent perspective. As a result, aided by the shift to virtual meetings during the COVID-19 pandemic, some American

nongovernmental organizations began coordinating in advance of participating in Track 1.5 and Track II dialogues with Chinese counterparts. This
kind of coordination among non-state participants in multilateral dialogues
helped American participants present a united front and made the dialogues
themselves more effective.[107]

This coherence is important, because it makes governments on all sides
more likely to pay attention to the outcome of Track 1.5 and Track II dialogues.
For all their importance, the ultimate aim of these dialogues is to prod national governments to develop binding rules to prevent individuals from wit-
tingly or unwittingly creating the next super virus; from opening the door
to reckless human genetic modification; or from building killer robots. To
provide hope of doing so, Washington, Beijing, and other governments will
have to work together to update existing international agreements, including
the cumbersomely named Convention on the Prohibition of Development,
Production, and Stockpiling of Biological and Toxin Weapons, in light of
CRISPR and other rapidly evolving technologies.[108] An effort of similar scale
and ambition is likely needed to replicate elements of the world's nuclear
nonproliferation infrastructure, like the Cooperative Threat Reduction program and the Nuclear Suppliers Group, to better secure potentially harmful
biological agents and address the threat of AI to destabilize nuclear deterrence postures.[109]

Encouragingly, there is at least one shining example of China working
with other countries to prevent the proliferation of dangerous technologies.
The field of nuclear security, which focuses on preventing nuclear material
from being used to make illicit weapons, has long been a bright spot in US–
China bilateral cooperation—so much so, in fact, that it became perhaps the
single best example of the two countries working together in response to a
shared global challenge. While, as detailed in Chapters 2 and 3, US–China
cooperation produced some successes in the fields of public health and climate protection, both became intensely politicized. Nuclear security cooperation, though, largely avoided this fate. Following a high-profile Nuclear
Security Summit convened by the Obama administration in 2010, the United
States and China launched a series of "under-the-radar" initiatives to secure
potentially dangerous, Chinese-supplied nuclear material in third countries
such as Ghana and Nigeria.[110] During this same period, and in stark contrast to its behavior in other areas, Beijing became notably transparent about
its nuclear security policies, and ensured that it conformed to the highest

international standards.[111] It is not clear that this example can be replicated in other areas, but it does provide a compelling example of cooperation to prevent the spread of potentially harmful technologies.

As the He Jiankui incident demonstrates, the twenty-first century demands a new era of norm-building in response to emerging technologies, just as the Geneva Conventions created a new set of rules to deal with destructive new forms of warfare in the nineteenth century, and the Asilomar Conference helped anticipate growing risks from biomedical research in the twentieth. This time, though, it is apparent that countries like China will need to play a much bigger role in these discussions than they had in the past. Several aspects of emerging technologies demand further dialogue between governments, companies, researchers, and other players in the United States, China, and other countries. Technological capabilities emerging on the horizon, like human genetic modification, present questions whose answers have implications for the entire planet, and so need to be made together. Forging common principles and standards will clearly be difficult, not just between China and more liberal-minded countries, but also between the United States and European nations. This new era of norm-setting will inevitably look much different than the previous one, marked by conferences in Geneva and California. But it is just as crucial for the world to get right—and to get started before technological realities outstrip regulatory frameworks even further.

A major implication of China's rise is that transformational technologies are being developed and deployed outside of existing, largely Western-dominated ethical and regulatory frameworks. In many cases, these frameworks as applied in China and other developing countries echo those of their counterparts in the United States, but nonetheless reflect very different cultural values, and political and economic realities. Contending with these practical and normative differences is an important consequence of China's rise for foreign governments, businesses, and civil society organizations. At the same time, there is enormous potential in launching new discussions and dialogues on standards, rules, and norms to guide the use of technologies like gene editing and artificial intelligence. This process should entail cooperation on issues where the United States, China, and other countries can agree—like better protections for human subjects in research—as well as those where differences are big enough that the world will probably have to settle for some level of loose coordination.

When it comes to regulating emerging technologies, there are no easy answers. But one thing is certain: no country, or government, can address them alone. In the next, concluding chapter, we turn to how people, companies, and organizations, as well as governments, can seize the potential created by the rise of China while also addressing its associated challenges.

Conclusion

How China's Next Act Shapes the Future

The main message of this book is that China's role in the world is increasingly defined by the need for it to address ecological and technological challenges that are shared across countries—but that responses to these common challenges are hampered by growing differences in basic values. Decarbonization, data privacy, and other issues that not so long ago were low priority for China's decision-makers have suddenly rocketed to the top of the list. Yet as they have wrestled to respond to these newer issues and challenges, China's leaders have relied on problematic older impulses, including authoritarianism, protectionism, and nationalism. Even as the need to combat climate change and develop advanced technology has become a significant influence on Beijing's, economic, social, and foreign policy, the contrast between liberal and illiberal solutions to shared ecological and technological challenges has become sharper, and the stakes of choosing one or the other higher.

The risk is that China's rise will drive divergence in the values, norms, and standards the world desperately needs to navigate these shared challenges in the decades ahead. If liberal societies fail to lead the way in providing global public goods and regulating emerging technologies, the illiberal values Beijing increasingly relies on are more likely to hold sway. That in turn could make the world less free, less open, and less tolerant, as well as ecologically impoverished and technologically vulnerable. If a single takeaway emerges from the preceding chapters, it is that the need to act collectively in response to shared challenges cannot be separated from the need to contest liberal and illiberal values. The choice between cooperating over public goods and emerging technologies, and competing for economic, geopolitical, and ideological advantage, is a false one. When it comes to China, companies and countries must do both. If they do, China's rise may still be disruptive, but it need not be destructive, either for the planet or for liberal values.

China's Next Act. Scott M. Moore, Oxford University Press. © Oxford University Press 2022.
DOI: 10.1093/oso/9780197603994.003.0009

Several other common themes emerge from re-envisioning China's rise in terms of its role in providing global public goods and regulating emerging technologies.

First, though the most visible symbols of China's rise are things, including growing fleets of fighter jets and Belt and Road megaprojects, intangible assets, resources, and institutions are becoming the focal points of economic and geopolitical competition. Chapters 5–7 emphasize that as technology, its applications, and its consequences have become a bigger part of China's relationship with the world, human capital, data, and organizational culture have become more important sources of competitive advantage. To compete effectively with China in the twenty-first century, liberal-minded countries and companies should invest in intangible assets, infrastructure, and institutions, especially norm- and standard-setting processes; data sharing and management; and human capital, including education systems, immigration reform, and social inclusion.

Second, non-state and sub-state actors are becoming more important within China as well as in other countries. Chinese firms, industry associations, and local governments increasingly stand at the forefront of pushing for public goods and developing and deploying new technologies. Though subject to control, co-option, and repression by the state, these players are becoming more powerful for several reasons. In some areas, like environmental protection, nongovernmental organizations have genuine influence with China's leaders, as described in Chapter 3. In others, like the case of artificial intelligence detailed in Chapter 5, technology is evolving so quickly that even Beijing cannot keep up. In fields such as bioethics, meanwhile, universities and research institutions offer a comparatively neutral platform for discussing highly contentious and politicized issues, as detailed in Chapter 7. Moreover, and most importantly, the growing number of non-state and sub-state actors have increasingly diverse interests—not all of them aligned with those of the Chinese Communist Party. The ability of nongovernmental and non-state actors to help provide public goods and regulate emerging technologies, both in China and around the world, will become more essential to averting climate, biodiversity, and other catastrophes in the twenty-first century.[1]

Third, the risks and harms associated with China's rise are becoming thoroughly globalized. The impact of Beijing's problematic policies and actions is increasingly felt less in China itself and more in other countries. Chapter 3 points out that China's environmental policies have substantially reduced pollution at home while contributing to increased environmental degradation abroad. Chapter 6, meanwhile, observes that intellectual property and data privacy protections have improved within China even as China-linked actors have accelerated digital censorship, surveillance, and data theft abroad. On a related note, as Chapter 4 highlights, the geographic focus of competition between China, foreign countries, and companies is shifting from developed markets like the United States and Germany to developing ones like Zambia and India. These developing nations will increasingly inform the world's wider response to China's rise in the decades ahead.

Fourth, and counterintuitively, liberal-minded countries should invest more effort in cooperating with China on emerging technologies and more in competing when it comes to climate change and public health. Beijing faces growing domestic and international pressure to strengthen provisions for consumer data privacy, biosafety, and biosecurity, opening a narrow window to pursue dialogue on common standards in these areas. On the other hand, many global public goods, from climate protection to scientific exchange, have become intensely politicized and marked not only by geopolitical competition but also by authoritarian, protectionist, and nationalistic impulses. Though worrisome, there is a silver lining: under the right circumstances, competition with other powers can provide a powerful justification for governments to invest in global health, education, and other areas. Addressing shared challenges by competing as well as cooperating will be difficult and, in some ways, suboptimal. But it is nonetheless essential.

Finally, and on a closely related note, the stakes of cooperating with Chinese counterparts have changed for liberal-minded countries, companies, and other organizations. Beijing's deepening repression at home, belligerence abroad, and lingering protectionism have created economic, political, and moral costs to cooperation that, though not entirely new, must be weighed more carefully than in the past. That does not mean cooperation cannot or should not take place. But it does mean that the relative costs and benefits of competition, cooperation, and everything in between must be reevaluated, especially when it comes to navigating shared ecological and technological risks in the decades ahead.

Rethinking the Balance of Competition and Cooperation with China

For decades, debates over how to respond to China's rise could be roughly characterized in terms of hawks versus doves, namely those who favored more aggressive and antagonistic measures versus those who argued for a less confrontational or nuanced approach. In the third decade of the twenty-first century, though, this debate appeared to be settled in the hawks' favor. Something close to consensus emerged in the advanced industrial democracies, including the United States, Japan, Australia, and much of Europe, that China's rise posed a significant threat. Debate turned to where and how—not whether—to counter China's growing economic, military, and geopolitical power. In the United States, this debate extended to unwinding the economy's interdependence with China, an approach known as decoupling. In the rest of the world, though, the question was mostly how to blunt Beijing's military and geopolitical might while still welcoming its trade and investment.

Re-envisioning China's rise in terms of shared ecological and technological challenges shows that neither side of this debate has it quite right. Aspects of China's rise present serious threats to democracy, free trade and free enterprise, and a generally open and tolerant world. Some of these threats require a vigorous response. But decoupling is deeply misguided, even if it were possible—which it is not.[2] This reality creates a new imperative not just for foreign governments, but companies and nongovernmental organizations as well: they must mobilize both to preserve liberal values and to engage their Chinese counterparts on matters of shared concern. The fundamentally shared challenges and opportunities of the twenty-first century demand that we re-envision China's rise in different terms: not whether it is hopeful or harmful, for it is clearly both, but instead how to provide global public goods and regulate emerging technologies by competing as well as cooperating.

This book suggests a new way of thinking about when and how to do so. The preceding chapters are full of reasons that we cannot count on international cooperation in response to shared challenges. Among them are the tendency for public goods and new technologies to become politicized and employed for geopolitical ends; the fact that all nation-states are having trouble keeping pace with fast-changing developments in areas like gene editing and data privacy; and the dangerous influence of authoritarian, protectionist, and nationalistic values across countries, and especially on Beijing.

But just as important, this book also shows when and how liberal-minded countries, companies, and other organizations can most effectively engage their Chinese counterparts.

Engagement in the form of diplomacy, marketing agreements, or other interactions is likely to be most effective, and most likely to advance liberal values, when one of three conditions applies: if liberal-minded countries, companies, and other organizations can present a unified stance; if China needs talent, investment, or technology from abroad; or if governments on all sides manage to prevent issues from becoming heavily politicized. The first of these conditions, presenting a unified stance, is especially important when it comes to the principles that determine how emerging technologies are regulated, as discussed in Chapter 6. It is no coincidence that several of the areas where cooperation is most promising are those where Beijing has been subject to sustained and widespread criticism from the international community. The acute embarrassment suffered by Chinese biomedical researchers in the aftermath of the He Jiankui incident, for example, created intense pressure to strengthen Western-style human subjects protections. Concerted international pressure, including from liberal-minded governments, civil society groups, and multinational companies, can be effective in nudging Beijing away from illiberal policies. Such advocacy is most likely to succeed when it also appeals to key constituencies within China. Bolstering bioethics provisions responded both to international pressure and the interests of China's scientific community.

Yet maintaining a united front to promote liberal values is much easier said than done. Climate change and data localization are becoming important issues in China's relationship with countries like India and Indonesia, as well as with the United States and Germany. Countering China's influence in these contentious, values-laden areas will require difficult negotiations between these diverse societies.[3] In areas like data governance, it may prove impossible to craft a single set of global norms and standards. But in others, especially biosafety and biosecurity, prospects are brighter. These areas should be prioritized in cooperation among likeminded countries.

Despite deep political and ethical differences, liberal-minded countries and companies must also expand dialogue with their Chinese counterparts on emerging technologies. The biggest risks posed by artificial intelligence, genetic engineering, and other disruptive technologies are fundamentally shared between countries, including newer, deadlier forms of terrorism. Moreover, though Beijing's willingness to adopt internationally agreed rules of the road will vary depending on the issues involved, smart strategy can exploit differences between China's state, its firms, and sub-state entities. The incentives for Beijing to participate in international standard- and norm-setting processes are likely to be greatest in biotechnology and other cutting-edge fields where China generally remains dependent on other countries for financing, technology, and talent. They should use this leverage to the full.

At the same time, there is no substitute for cooperation with China. As each chapter has emphasized, almost no global challenge can be properly addressed without it. In the process of examining how competition shapes both public goods and emerging technologies, this book identifies several promising areas for greater cooperation, notably including biodiversity conservation, cited in Chapter 2; scientific collaboration and academic exchange, discussed in Chapter 4; and biosafety, biosecurity, and nuclear security, all described in Chapter 7. Another lesson from these chapters bears emphasis: whether in solar panel manufacture or 5G development, competition is more complex and expensive than cooperation.

These chapters in turn suggest two main lessons for how to bolster cooperation with China on a few matters of crucial common concern. First, for governments, "ring fencing" certain especially critical areas as much as possible from politicization should be a priority. The case of US–China nuclear security cooperation cited in Chapter 7 has been highly effective both in securing dangerous nuclear material and in pushing Beijing to adopt international norms and standards.[4] This strategy is most likely to be effective where, as with nuclear security, the issues are highly technical and specialized, and the number of critical actors relatively few. Ring fencing is unlikely to be effective in areas like climate change.

Second, non-state actors must carry more of the weight of cooperation in response to shared challenges. To be sure, private firms and nongovernmental organizations are not a replacement for states and governments. This is especially true in China, where their independence is sharply curtailed. Yet, though hardly immune to tensions between Washington, Beijing, and other capitals, the non-state sector and subnational levels of government are better equipped to navigate politically sensitive issue areas. And as their role in areas from climate to data science has expanded, so too has their number: the universe of important non-state actors includes universities, laboratories, and industry associations, alongside nongovernmental organizations and multinational corporations. Subnational governments, moreover, play an important role in issues like technology innovation and human capital development. These non-state actors have an especially critical role to play in re-envisioning China's rise.

Implications for China, Foreign Countries, and Companies

This different way of seeing China's rise has a twofold implication for understanding China itself. First, environmental, health, and technological risks will continue to stress China's existing one-party political system.[5] Beijing will be increasingly pressed to meet growing demands for ecological sustainability, data privacy, and other priorities that sit uneasily alongside the Chinese Communist Party's authoritarian, protectionist, and nationalistic impulses. The contentious, values-laden questions involved in responding to climate change and regulating emerging technologies will moreover be difficult to answer in the constrained public sphere enforced by China's party-state. The pluralization of Chinese society, and the proliferation of actors and interests that comes with it, sharpens this challenge, as it is increasingly difficult to reconcile their competing preferences and demands. While there is often assumed to be little daylight between Beijing, Chinese firms, and the non-state sector, in fact there is frequent tension.

Second, Beijing's other illiberal impulses, namely economic protectionism and an aggressive brand of nationalism, cloud China's future and that of the world at large. Conflicting nationalisms are a Pandora's box as China's rise advances. Distinct identities are building in Hong Kong and Taiwan despite the Party's efforts to contain them, heightening the risk of conflict. Moreover, Chinese jingoism may be on a collision course with the raw nationalism common in many other developing countries as China's economic and geopolitical footprint expands abroad.[6] At home, meanwhile, Beijing faces continuing tension and dissent over the need to reform and liberalize its economy and the impulse to maintain the state control and autarkic policies that have shaped its development strategy since the days of Mao. For foreign governments, the combined effect of authoritarianism, protectionism, and aggressive nationalism is likely to make Beijing a difficult and often unappealing, yet still essential, partner.[7]

For these reasons, relations between China and developed democracies are likely to be defined by economic and geopolitical competition for the foreseeable future. For foreign countries and companies, competing effectively with China means investing in intangible assets, resources, and institutions. Critically important priorities include reforming education systems; promoting social inclusion (both addressed in Chapter 4); and strengthening data governance frameworks (Chapter 6). Liberal societies must also prioritize norm- and standard-setting processes both at home and abroad, a priority that features strongly in Chapters 5 and 7. Chapter 5 also points to the need to rethink relations between the state and private sector, including in the use of industrial policy.

Governments must also learn to work with non-state and sub-state actors more effectively, including in the provision of public goods. While in China close coordination between state, corporate, and sub-state entities is common, it is less typical in the West. This must change. Central governments should establish dedicated offices, like the proposed US State Department Office of Subnational Diplomacy, to coordinate more extensively and effectively with the private sector, civil society, and sub-state actors.[8] At the same time, governments and multilateral bodies must become friendlier to the input provided by non-state actors. They should normalize and regularize the processes that lead to stakeholder-driven regulation in areas like biosafety.[9]

Multinational companies, industry associations, and other non-state actors should seize the moment to help shape relations between China and the rest of the world. They too should embrace better coordination, both with each other and with governments, in international norm- and standard-setting processes. They must also invest in greater China-specific expertise. The best approach is to incorporate exposure to China as a regular part of organizational talent-development plans, including travel to the region and exposure to China watchers with a wide range of expertise, including technology and sustainability issues as well as economic and political ones. China specialists, for their part, must shake the tendency to focus intently on the world's most populous nation, and develop greater global and cross-functional knowledge to better understand China in a wider context. Organizations will also need to embed China-related issues across functional teams and units. One example is the US Central Intelligence Agency's "China Mission Center," created in October 2021 to handle China-related issues that cut across the Agency's other organizational units and priorities.[10]

Universities and research institutions have an especially important role to play in developing non-state and sub-state ties with China. They should embrace the potential to host and facilitate "Track II" dialogues between former government, business, nonprofit, and other leaders that tackle tough normative, ideological, and ethical questions. In addition, as proposed in Chapter 4, they can play a critical role in enhancing human capital by better integrating the large numbers of Chinese students and scholars that populate many campuses across the globe. At the same time, universities must equip themselves to handle threats to academic freedom, improper information collection, and other China-linked challenges highlighted in Chapter 4.

For companies, meanwhile, this new way of looking at China's rise holds three main lessons. First, sustainability is an increasingly high priority for China, both politically and economically. Awareness of and pressure from political leaders, influencers, and individual consumers is likely to grow, forcing companies to pay more attention to their environmental footprint, both in their direct China operations and in their global supply chains. For the time being, foreign firms typically have more capacity to implement sustainability solutions than their Chinese competitors. This is an important competitive advantage, both in China and in other emerging markets. When Pepsi decided in 2019 to fork out nearly US$2 billion to buy South Africa's Pioneer Foods, it also agreed to expand a sustainable farming program.[11] Investment in this kind of corporate social responsibility is an increasingly important edge for liberal-minded companies—and for liberal-minded countries.

Second, across sectors and industries, the intersection of multiple emerging technologies holds the greatest potential for growth and disruption. The integration of artificial intelligence (AI) and autonomous systems and of AI and biotechnology, both described in Chapter 7, is rich in potential scientific and commercial applications. But all these intersections are fraught with ethical issues and questions, especially when it comes to their potential to help Beijing advance illiberal values.

The dual nature of emerging technologies, full of promise and peril in equal measure, foreshadows a third key lesson: every company operating internationally needs a China policy centered on its core values. This includes Chinese multinational firms: as the example of ByteDance cited in Chapter 6 suggests, the challenge of reconciling Chinese and foreign data protection and privacy practices involves constant negotiation with authorities on both sides. Companies need to think carefully about how to engage with governments on increasingly politicized sustainability and technology issues.

Finally, this book poses several questions that deserve more attention from researchers. Other public goods which space has not permitted me to address, including financial system stability, deserve much more attention from China specialists.[12] Another priority for further research and analysis is how newer technologies change the ability of countries and non-state actors to provide public goods. As described in Chapter 2, virtual physician-to-physician networks may offer a cheaper and more politically feasible alternative to intergovernmental diplomacy to strengthen epidemiological data-sharing with China. Likewise, ahead of a controversial visit to China in early 2021, US climate envoy John Kerry referred to the potential of AI-enabled remote sensing, which he suggested could help monitor and verify China's greenhouse gas emissions, even if Beijing refuses to provide data to international authorities.[13] Such technologies offer new ways for governments, or non-state actors, to provide public goods even in the context of economic, geopolitical, and ideological competition which, for better or worse, marks China's relationship with the world in the decades ahead.

Yet even as competition with China looks to be a defining feature of politics, economics, and policy for the foreseeable future, we must also remember that contemporary China is a diverse and fast-changing society. It would be a grave mistake to assume that China's course for the twenty-first century is set. China's challenges, be they dealing with climate change or wrestling with the implications of automation, are increasingly similar to those of the United States and other developed countries. Liberal-minded countries and companies must adapt to an era of pervasive economic, geopolitical, and ideological competition—but must also be willing and able to engage cooperatively when the right opportunities present themselves.

China's next act poses deep and vexing challenges for the rest of the world, and especially for liberal values. But even as they face a contentious future together, no nation or society, either in China, the West, or elsewhere, can afford to give up on any another. In a future shaped by climate change, pandemics, and technology, all countries ultimately need China to succeed—and vice versa.

Notes

Introduction

1. Bill Clinton, "President Clinton's Beijing University Speech, 1998 | US-China Institute," USC US-China Institute, June 29, 1998, https://china.usc.edu/president-clintons-beijing-university-speech-1998.

2. Described and quoted by Michael Laris, "Beijing U. Students Grill U.S. President," *Washington Post*, June 29, 1998, https://www.washingtonpost.com/archive/politics/1998/06/29/beijing-u-students-grill-us-president/3f340e1e-06ed-4ead-ab02-e9664 9a01e5c/.

3. The concept of public goods in general, and global ones in particular, is complex. The distinction between pure public goods and private goods with externalities is especially murky. In practice, many things are public goods under some circumstances and private ones in others. See Inge Kaul, Pedro Conceicao, Katell Le Goulven, and Ronald Mendoza, eds., *Providing Global Public Goods: Managing Globalization* (Cary, NC: Oxford University Press, 2003).

4. If readers need any convincing of the need to combat climate change and prevent future pandemics, see Intergovernmental Panel on Climate Change, "Sixth Assessment Report: IPCC," accessed October 11, 2021, https://www.ipcc.ch/assessment-report/ar6/; and United Nations, "Reduce Risk to Avert 'Era of Pandemics,' Experts Warn in New Report," accessed October 11, 2021, https://news.un.org/en/story/2020/10/1076392.

5. World Bank, "China Overview," accessed June 18, 2019, http://www.worldbank.org/en/country/china/overview; International Monetary Fund, "World Economic Outlook (April 2019): GDP Per Capita, Current Prices," accessed June 18, 2019, https://www.imf.org/en/Publications/WEO/Issues/2019/03/28/world-economic-outlook-april-2019.

6. Figures cited by Arthur Kroeber, *China's Economic Transformation: A Threat to the Liberal Global Order?* (Atlanta, GA: Carter Center, 2018).

7. See Danny Quah, "The Global Economy's Shifting Centre of Gravity," *Global Policy* 2, no. 1 (January 2011): 3–9. https://onlinelibrary.wiley.com/doi/abs/10.1111/j.1758-5899.2010.00066.x..

8. Cited by James T. Areddy, "China Sheds Millionaires as Slowdown Shaves Fortunes," *Wall Street Journal,*, July 9, 2019, https://www.wsj.com/articles/china-sheds-milli onaires-as-slowdown-shaves-fortunes-11562644802.

9. Stockholm International Peace Research Institute, "World Military Expenditure Grows to $1.8 Trillion in 2018," accessed June 18, 2019, https://www.sipri.org/media/press-release/2019/world-military-expenditure-grows-18-trillion-2018.

10. Bonnie Bley, "World Diplomacy Stocktake: A Shifting of the Ranks," accessed December 29, 2019, https://www.lowyinstitute.org/the-interpreter/world-diplomacy-stocktake-shifting-ranks.

11. Statistics and plot summary cited by Muqing M. Zhang, "What Western Media Got Wrong about China's Blockbuster 'The Wandering Earth,'" accessed June 24, 2019, https://www.vice.com/en_us/article/j577z3/the-wandering-earth-what-western-media-got-wrong-about-chinas-sci-fi-blockbuster.

12. This point is made by Kroeber 2018.

13. These points are made extensively with respect to China by Yanzhong Huang, *Toxic Politics: China's Environmental Health Crisis and Its Challenge to the Chinese State* (Cambridge, UK: Cambridge University Press, 2020).

14. Ulrich Beck, *Risk Society: Towards a New Modernity* (London: SAGE Publications, 1992), 81.

15. Similar points are made by Damien Ma and William Adams, *In Line behind a Billion People* (Upper Saddle River, NJ: FT Press, 2013).

16. Quoted by Stephanie Nebehay, "U.N. Says It Has Credible Reports That China Holds Million Uighurs in Secret Camps," *Reuters*, August 10, 2018, https://www.reuters.com/article/us-china-rights-un-idUSKBN1KV1SU.

17. Quoted by Humeyra Pamuk and David Brunnstrom, "New U.S. Secretary of State Favors Cooperation with China Despite Genocide of Uighurs," *Reuters*, January 27, 2021, https://www.reuters.com/article/us-usa-china-blinken-idUSKBN29W2RC.

18. I am grateful to Sara Plana, University of Pennsylvania, for this point.

19. This definition and characterization of the role of ideology in China based on Franz Schurmann, *Ideology and Organization in Communist China* (Berkeley: University of California Press, 1968), 19.

20. Both are key elements of Xi Jinping's "new era." See Xinhuashe [Xinhua News Agency]. "习近平：新时代的领路人 [Xi Jinping: The New Era's Leading Man]," accessed February 3, 2021, http://www.gov.cn/zhuanti/2017-11/17/content_5240304.htm. I am also indebted to Scott Kennedy, Center for Strategic and International Studies, for emphasizing this point.

21. I am grateful to Kyle Haddad-Fonda for pushing me to emphasize this point.

22. "The West," is a problematic construct that can obscure and elide the ethnic, cultural, and normative heterogeneity of countries like Canada or the United Kingdom. Nonetheless, it is a useful shorthand to distinguish older developed democracies in Europe, North America, and Oceania from newer ones like South Korea and Taiwan.

23. This message is echoed by Ryan Hass, *Stronger: Adapting America's China Strategy in an Age of Competitive Interdependence* (New Haven, CT: Yale University Press, 2021).

24. This definition loosely echoes the academic literature on game theory and collective action.

25. Many of these interviews are cited anonymously to protect the confidentiality of informants.

26. Hass 2021 calls attention to the importance of Sino-American cooperation on global challenges, and several books pay special attention to climate change, including Barbara Finamore, *Will China Save the Planet?* (Cambridge, UK: Polity Press, 2018).

Kai-fu Lee presents a compelling, if at times simplified, account of how AI is altering ties with the United States and other nations; see Kai-Fu Lee, *AI Superpowers: China, Silicon Valley, and the New World Order* (Boston, MA: Houghton Mifflin Harcourt, 2018). Perhaps the book that comes closest to this one is Ma and Adams 2013, which among other things draws attention to environmental, ideational, and public goods issues in the context of scarcity. It does not, however, focus as much on either the global dimension or on technology issues.

27. See Hass 2021 and Kevin Rudd, "Short of War," *Foreign Affairs*, March 8, 2021, https://www.foreignaffairs.com/articles/united-states/2021-02-05/kevin-rudd-usa-chinese-confrontation-short-of-war.

Chapter 1

1. To be sure, criticism of China's growth-led development model had been consistent since its inception in 1978 and accelerated following China's accession to the World Trade Organization in the early 2000s. See Jude Blanchette, *China's New Red Guards: The Return of Radicalism and the Rebirth of Mao Zedong* (Oxford: Oxford University Press, 2019).

2. This incident is described by Stephanie Ho, "World Bank Call for Chinese Reforms Elicits Rare Protest," *Voice of America*, February 27, 2012, https://www.voanews.com/east-asia/world-bank-call-chinese-reforms-elicits-rare-protest.

3. Described in Malcolm Moore, "We Should Not Worship Mao as a God, Says China's President," *The Telegraph*, 2013. https://www.telegraph.co.uk/news/worldnews/asia/china/10538324/We-should-not-worship-Mao-as-a-god-says-Chinas-president.html.

4. A Starbucks operated within the Forbidden City from 2000 to 2007. At the time of writing, one remained within sight of Mao's mausoleum just south of Zhengyangmen.

5. The tolerance for, and even veneration of, contradiction in Chinese Maoist thought is described by Franz Schurmann, *Ideology and Organization in Communist China* (Berkeley: University of California Press, 1968).

6. This is not to minimize the ideological debates that continued after Reform and Opening and were especially marked after Tiananmen. See Blanchette 2019, 40–45.

7. See Schurmann 1968, especially 27–28.

8. See Ezra F. Vogel, *Deng Xiaoping and the Transformation of China* (Cambridge, MA: Belknap Press of Harvard University Press, 2011), 391.

9. See Vogel 2011, 400; and Fusheng Xie, An Li, and Zhongjin Li, "Can the Socialist Market Economy in China Adhere to Socialism?" *Review of Radical Political Economics* 45, no. 4 (December 2013): 440–448.

10. See English translation of the speech hosted by China Internet Information Center, "Jiang Zemin's Speech at the Meeting Celebrating the 80th Anniversary of the Founding of the Communist Party of China," accessed June 21, 2019, http://www.china.org.cn/e-speech/a.htm.

11. Quoted by Blanchette 2019, 59–60.

12. Blanchette 2019, 102.

13. See E. Perry Link, "Charter 08, One Year On," *Wall Street Journal*, December 2009, https://www.wsj.com/articles/SB10001424052748703558004574582773035958350.

14. Kerry Brown, *Friends and Enemies: The Past, Present, and Future of the Communist Party of China* (New York: Anthem Press, 2009), 7. Brown's primary objective is to explain how China has managed this feat and emphasizes the extraordinary organizational abilities of the Chinese Communist Party.

15. See Jinping Xi, "President Xi's Speech to Davos in Full," World Economic Forum, 2017, https://www.weforum.org/agenda/2017/01/full-text-of-xi-jinping-keynote-at-the-world-economic-forum/.

16. Quoted by Yanzhong Huang, *Toxic Politics: China's Environmental Health Crisis and Its Challenge to the Chinese State* (Cambridge, UK: Cambridge University Press, 2020), 125.

17. Multiple personal communications to the author during a research trip to China, January 2020.

18. See Blanchette 2019, 140.

19. Chinese translation obtained from Rogier Creemers, *Communiqué on the Current State of the Ideological Sphere (Document no. 9)*, China Copyright and Media, 2013.

20. Eleanor Albert, "The State of Religion in China," *Council on Foreign Relations*, last modified September 2020, https://www.cfr.org/backgrounder/religion-china. Note that Chinese Buddhism is distinct from Tibetan Buddhism, not least in that the spiritual leader of the latter, the Dalai Lama, is a noted antagonist of China's party-state.

21. See Ian Johnson, *The Souls of China: The Return of Religion after Mao* (New York: Pantheon Books, 2017).

22. Jiwei Ci, *Moral China in the Age of Reform* (New York: Cambridge University Press, 2014), 1.

23. Evan Osnos, "A Billion Stories," *The New Yorker*, 2013, https://www.newyorker.com/news/evan-osnos/a-billion-stories.

24. World Bank, "Exports of Goods and Services (Current US$)," accessed June 28, 2019, https://data.worldbank.org/indicator/NE.EXP.GNFS.CD?locations=CN.

25. Cited by Tyler Cowen, "China's Economy May Be No. 1, but It Is Still Poor," *Bloomberg Opinion*, December 22, 2019, https://www.bloomberg.com/opinion/articles/2019-12-22/u-s-china-comparisons-should-look-at-wealth-not-just-gdp.

26. Data from Max Roser, "Economic Growth," *Our World in Data*, 2013, https://ourworldindata.org/economic-growth.

27. Derek Scissors, "China's Economic 'Miracle' in Context," *American Enterprise Institute*, 2019, https://www.aei.org/publication/chinas-economic-miracle-in-context/.

28. Scissors 2019.

29. Zhuo Chen, Zhiguo He, and Chun Liu, "The Financing of Local Government in the People's Republic of China: Stimulus Loan Wanes and Shadow Banking Waxes," ADBI Working Papers 800, Asian Development Bank Institute, 2018. A growing share of China's total government debt (over 20% in 2017) remains held by local governments, who over the past few years have resorted to borrowing to plug a growing gap between

tax revenues, which are largely controlled by the central government, and expenses, most of which are local government responsibilities.

30. See W. Raphael Lam and Jingsen Wan, "China's Local Government Bond Market," Working Paper No. 18/219, International Monetary Fund, 2018, 4–7.

31. Chen, He, and Liu 2018.

32. Quoted by Ryan Woo, "China Local Governments' Hidden Debt could Total $5.8 Trillion: S&P," *Reuters*, 2018, https://www.reuters.com/article/us-china-economy-debt-idUSKCN1MQ0JH.

33. Douglas Fuller, "China's Political Economy: Prospects for Technological Innovation-Based Growth," in *China's Innovation Challenge: Overcoming the Middle-Income Trap*, ed. Arie Lewin, Martin Kenney, and Johann Murmann (New York: Cambridge University Press, 2016), 126–133.

34. See Nicholas Eberstadt, "China's Demographic Outlook to 2040 and its Implications," *American Enterprise Institute*, 2019, https://www.aei.org/wp-content/uploads/2019/01/China%E2%80%99s-Demographic-Outlook.pdf.

35. Cited by Fuller 2016, 131.

36. Figures cited by Scissors 2019.

37. Kristin Shi-Kupfer and Max Zenglein, "Focus Topic: Youth Unemployment in China," Mercator Institute for China Studies, accessed July 19, 2019, https://www.merics.org/en/merics-trackers/economic-indicators-q2-2019.

38. See Yi-Ling Liu, "China's AI Dreams Aren't for Everyone," *Foreign Policy*, 2019. https://foreignpolicy.com/2019/08/13/china-artificial-intelligence-dreams-arent-for-everyone-data-privacy-economic-inequality/.

39. Cited by Brent Orrell, "Automation, Jobs, and Productivity: New Insights on the Future of Robotics," *American Enterprise Institute*, July 12, 2019, http://www.aei.org/publication/automation-jobs-productivity/.

40. Scott Rozelle and Natalie Hell, *Invisible China* (Chicago, IL: University of Chicago Press, 2020).

41. Inequality data from Central Intelligence Agency, "World Factbook: China," *The World Factbook*, last modified June 26, 2019, https://www.cia.gov/library/publications/the-world-factbook/geos/ch.html.

42. Johnson 2019.

43. Central Intelligence Agency 2019.

44. See Wayne Morrison, *China's Economic Rise: History, Trends, Challenges, and Implications for the United States* (Washington, DC: Congressional Research Service, 2019).

45. Cited by Fuller 2016, 125.

46. Michael Pettis, "The Problems with China's 'Dual Circulation' Economic Model," *Financial Times*, August 25, 2020, https://www.proquest.com/trade-journals/problems-with-china-s-dual-circulation-economic/docview/2476349885/se-2?accountid=14707. Quotation from author interview with macroeconomic strategist.

47. See Greg Larson, Norman Loyaza, and Michael Woolcock, *The Middle-Income Trap: Myth or Reality?* (Kuala Lumpur: The World Bank, 2016). and Linda Glawe and Helmut Wagner, "The People's Republic of China in the Middle-Income Trap?" ADBI Working Paper 749, 2017, https://www.econstor.eu/handle/10419/179205.

48. See Scissors 2019.

49. See Martin Wolf, "Xi Jinping's China Seeks to Be Rich and Communist," *Financial Times*, last modified April 9, 2019, https://www.ft.com/content/671a8fdc-57ca-11e9-91f9-b6515a54c5b1.

50. He Liu, "3 Critical Battles China Is Preparing to Fight," accessed December 28, 2020, https://www.weforum.org/agenda/2018/01/pursue-high-quality-development-work-together-for-global-economic-prosperity-and-stability/.

51. Described by Ross Chainey, "The Biggest Stories from Davos 2018," accessed December 28, 2020, https://www.weforum.org/agenda/2018/01/davos-2018-biggest-stories/.

52. There is a considerable literature on China's "fragmented authoritarianism," including as it pertains to decentralization. See Andrew Mertha, "'Fragmented Authoritarianism 2.0': Political Pluralization in the Chinese Policy Process," *The China Quarterly* 200 (2009): 995–1012.

53. On the system itself, see Maria Eden, "State Capacity and Local Agent Control in China: CCP Cadre Management from a Township Perspective," *The China Quarterly* 173 (2003): 35–52; and Thomas Heberer and René Trappel, "Evaluation Processes, Local Cadres' Behaviour and Local Development Processes," *Journal of Contemporary China* 22, no. 84 (2013): 1048–1066.

54. These kinds of perverse incentives are described in Scott Moore, "Hydropolitics and Inter-Jurisdictional Relationships in China: The Pursuit of Localized Preferences in a Centralized System," *The China Quarterly* 219 (2014): 760–780.

55. See Freedom House's annual report; "Freedom in the World 2019: China," Freedom House, accessed June 22, 2019, https://freedomhouse.org/country/china/freedom-world/2019.

56. See research cited by Maria Repnikova, "How Chinese Authorities and Individuals Use the Internet," Hoover Institution, last modified October 29, 2018, https://www.hoover.org/research/how-chinese-authorities-and-individuals-use-internet. The Party also seeks to shape as well as solicit and understand public opinion.

57. On consultative authoritarianism, see Oscar Almén, "Participatory Innovations under Authoritarianism: Accountability and Responsiveness in Hangzhou's Social Assessment of Government Performance," *Journal of Contemporary China* 27, no. 110 (2018): 165–179.

58. Jennifer Pan, Gary King, and Margaret E. Roberts. "How Censorship in China Allows Government Criticism but Silences Collective Expression," *American Political Science Review* 107, no. 2 (2013): 326–343. The same principle generally holds true for other forms of speech and expression, but again restrictions have generally increased considerably since Xi took power.

59. On this logic and history, see Weihsuan Lin, "Religion as an Object of State Power: The People's Republic of China and Its Domestic Religious Geopolitics after 1978," *Political Geography* 67 (2018): 1–11.

60. See, for example, Sarah Cook and Truong Mai. "China Media Bulletin: 2019 Internet Freedom Trends, Shutterstock Censorship, Huawei 'Safe Cities' (November 2019)," accessed May 3, 2021, https://freedomhouse.org/report/china-media-bulletin/2020/china-media-bulletin-2019-internet-freedom-trends-shutterstock.

61. There are plenty of caveats to this broad trend, and the party-state reserves the right to use its power arbitrarily and without prejudice to the law. See Taisu Zhang, "Maybe the Law Does Actually Matter to Xi Jinping," *ChinaFile*, March 1, 2018, http://www.chinafile.com/reporting-opinion/viewpoint/maybe-law-does-actually-matter-xi-jinping.

62. "习近平：新时代的领路人 [Xi Jinping: The New Era's Leading Man]," Xinhuashe [Xinhua News Agency], 2017.

63. This assertion is based on multiple personal communications with civic, NGO, and political leaders during a research trip in January 2020.

64. This characterization based on personal interaction with a leading economist of China, October 18, 2021.

65. See Yasheng Huang, *Capitalism with Chinese Characteristics: Entrepreneurship and the State* (New York: Cambridge University Press, 2008).

66. See Wenfang Tang and Benjamin Darr, "Chinese Nationalism and Its Political and Social Origins," *Journal of Contemporary China* 21, no. 77 (2012): 811–826.

67. See Jessica Chen Weiss, "Introduction," in Weiss, *Powerful Patriots* (New York: Oxford University Press, 2014), who makes the point that the Party faces a persistent dilemma between attempting to harness nationalist sentiment and prevent it from subverting regime preferences and priorities.

68. Wenfang Tang and Benjamin Darr, "Chinese Nationalism and Its Political and Social Origins," *Journal of Contemporary China* 21, no. 77 (2012): 811–826, doi:10.1080/10670564.2012.684965, found that Chinese were the most nationalistic of 35 populations surveyed. However, other studies found no increase in nationalistic sentiment or few meaningful differences between China and other countries on measures of nationalism. On the muddled link between nationalism and Chinese foreign policy, see Alastair Iain Johnston, "Is Chinese Nationalism Rising? Evidence from Beijing," *International Security* 41, no. 3 (2017): 7–43, https://doi.org/10.1162/ISEC_a_00265. On cross-national comparisons of nationalist sentiment, see Florian Bieber, "Is Nationalism on the Rise? Assessing Global Trends," *Ethnopolitics* 17, no. 5 (2018): 519–540, https://doi.org/10.1080/17449057.2018.1532633.

69. For a thoughtful exploration of nationalism, identity, and the role of education in contemporary China, see Zheng Wang, *Never Forget National Humiliation* (New York: Columbia University Press, 2012).

70. See Suisheng Zhao, "A State-Led Nationalism: The Patriotic Education Campaign in Post-Tiananmen China," *Communist and Post-Communist Studies* 31, no. 3 (1998): 287–302, especially on the role patriotic education played in fostering popular nationalism, and James Reilly, "Remember History, Not Hatred: Collective Remembrance of China's War of Resistance to Japan," *Modern Asian Studies* 45, no. 2 (March 1, 2011): 463–490.

71. Guangqiu Xu, "Anti-Western Nationalism in China, 1989–99," *World Affairs* 163, no. 4 (2001): 151–162; William A. Callahan, "History, Identity, and Security: Producing and Consuming Nationalism in China," *Critical Asian Studies* 38, no. 2 (2006): 179–208.

72. Quoted by Matthew Carney, "President Xi's Hyper-Nationalism Has People Believing in His China Dream," October 14, 2017, https://www.abc.net.au/news/2017-10-15/president-xi-and-his-china-dream/9048966.

73. On the role the concept of national humiliation has played in nationalistic sentiment, and especially nationalistic propaganda, see Callahan 2006.

74. Both incidents cited in Scott Moore, "Nuclear Conflict in the 21st Century: Reviewing the Chinese Nuclear Threat | NTI," *Nuclear Threat Initiative*, 2006, https://www.nti.org/analysis/articles/reviewing-chinese-nuclear-threat/.

75. Weiss 2014. There is a vibrant literature on how extensively popular nationalism shapes Chinese foreign policy, and considerable debate as to the extent. Most researchers agree, however, that the overall trend has been toward increasing influence.

76. Suisheng Zhao, "Foreign Policy Implications of Chinese Nationalism Revisited: The Strident Turn," *Journal of Contemporary China* 22, no. 82 (2013): 535–553, doi:10.1080/10670564.2013.766379, for instance, argues that after about 2008 Chinese nationalism, and Chinese foreign policy, exhibited a "strident turn." Elizabeth Economy, *The Third Revolution: Xi Jinping and the New Chinese State* (New York: Oxford University Press, 2018), emphasizes the influence of the 2008 financial crisis on Chinese foreign policy. To be sure, the appeal of anti-Western nationalism held some appeal throughout Asia, not just China. See Guangqiu Xu, "Anti-Western Nationalism in China, 1989–99," *World Affairs* 163, no. 4 (2001): 151–162.

77. I thank Ken Lieberthal for this observation.

78. See Suisheng Zhao, "Xi Jinping's Maoist Revival," *Journal of Democracy* 27, no. 3 (2016): 83–97, doi:10.1353/jod.2016.0051; and Economy 2018.

79. Perhaps the best account of the historical dynamics of these disputes can be found in Fravel 2008. However, there were several signs that growing nationalism contributed to a more aggressive stance on these issues, and in 2020 an armed clash occurred between Chinese and Indian troops along their shared Himalayan border.

80. Quoted by Drew Hinshaw, Sha Hua, and Laurence Norman, "Pushback on Xi's Vision for China Spreads beyond U.S," *Wall Street Journal*, December 28, 2020, https://www.wsj.com/articles/pushback-xi-china-europe-germany-beyond-u-s-11609176287.

81. See Alexandra Ma, "China's New, Hardline 'Wolf Warrior' Diplomacy Is Supposed to Cement its Dominance—but It's Also Uniting Its Rivals Abroad and Dividing People at Home," *Business Insider*, July 27, 2020, https://www.businessinsider.com/china-wolf-warrior-diplomacy-backfires-uniting-rivals-dividing-at-home-2020-6.

82. Quoted by Thomas Grove, "A Spy Case Exposes China's Power Play in Central Asia," *Wall Street Journal*, July 10, 2019, https://www.wsj.com/articles/a-spy-case-exposes-chinas-power-play-in-central-asia-11562756782.

83. On the strength of this prioritization, see M. T. Fravel, *Strong Borders, Secure Nation: Cooperation and Conflict in China's Territorial Disputes* (Princeton, NJ: Princeton University Press, 2008).

84. Data cited by Chun H. Wong and Jeremy Page, "For China's Xi, the Hong Kong Crisis Is Personal," *Wall Street Journal*, September 27, 2019, https://www.wsj.com/articles/for-chinas-xi-the-hong-kong-crisis-is-personal-11569613304?mod=hp_lead_pos8.

85. See Edith Lederer, "Nearly 40 Nations Criticize China's Human Rights Policies," October 6, 2020, https://apnews.com/article/virus-outbreak-race-and-ethnicity-tibet-hong-kong-united-states-a69609b46705f97bdec509e009577cb5.

86. Polling can be deceptive, and identity does not automatically indicate support for Taiwan independence. Nonetheless, these broad trends hold. See Kat Devlin and Christine Huang, "How People in Taiwan View Mainland China and the U.S," *Pew Research*, May 12, 2020, https://www.pewresearch.org/global/2020/05/12/in-taiwan-views-of-mainland-china-mostly-negative/.

87. On this alignment, see Hardina Ohlendorf, "The Taiwan Dilemma in Chinese Nationalism: Taiwan Studies in the People's Republic of China," *Asian Survey 54*, no. 3 (2014): 471–491.

88. Quoted by Helen Davidson, "China Could Invade Taiwan in Next Six Years, Top US Admiral Warns," March 9, 2021, http://www.theguardian.com/world/2021/mar/10/china-could-invade-taiwan-in-next-six-years-top-us-admiral-warns.

89. Nikkei Asia, "Japan, U.S. Defense Chiefs Affirm Cooperation over Taiwan Emergency," March 21, 2021, https://asia.nikkei.com/Politics/International-relations/US-China-tensions/Japan-U.S.-defense-chiefs-affirm-cooperation-over-Taiwan-emergency. It remained unclear how durable this partnership would hold in the event of actual conflict.

90. This visit is recounted in Chen Li, "The Origin and Early Development of Chinese Connections at the University of Pennsylvania Law School," *Asian Journal of Legal Education 7*, no. 2 (2020): 195–215.

91. Cited in "Remarks of Ambassador Wu Ting Fang," *The Outlook* 64, no. 9 (1900): 470–471.

92. Wu was very much concerned by the Chinese Exclusion Act, a fact highlighted by Li 2020.

93. World Bank 2019.

94. See Alexander Simoes and Cesar Hidalgo, "OEC—China (CHN) Exports, Imports, and Trade Partners: The Economic Complexity Observatory: An Analytical Tool for Understanding the Dynamics of Economic Development," Workshops at the Twenty-Fifth AAAI Conference on Artificial Intelligence, accessed June 28, 2019, https://atlas.media.mit.edu/en/profile/country/chn/.

95. See Joao Amador and Sonia Cabra, *Networks of Value-Added Trade* (Frankfurt-am-Main: European Central Bank, 2016).

96. See Isabella Cingolani, Pietro Panzarasa, and Lucia Tajoli, "Countries' Positions in the International Global Value Networks: Centrality and Economic Performance," *Applied Network Science* 2, no. 21 (2017), https://doi.org/10.1007/s41109-017-0041-4.

97. Mary Amiti and Caroline Freund, "China's Export Boom," *Finance and Development | F&D* 44, no. 3 (2007), 38–41.

98. "Trade in Value Added: China: Organization for Economic Co-operation and Development," Organization for Economic Co-operation and Development, December 2018, https://www.oecd.org/industry/ind/TIVA-2018-China.pdf.

99. "How Trade Works—OECD," Organization for Economic Co-operation and Development, 2019, https://www.oecd.org/trade/understanding-the-global-trading-system/how-trade-works/.

100. Greg Linden, Jason Dedrick, and Kenneth L. Kraemer, "We Estimate China Only Makes $8.46 from an iPhone—and That's Why Trump's Trade War Is Futile," *The Conversation*, July 6, 2018, http://theconversation.com/we-estimate-china-only-makes-8-46-from-an-iphone-and-thats-why-trumps-trade-war-is-futile-99258.

101. Lam and Wang 2018.

102. This figure was cited by Kevin Yao, "China Says Diversifying FX Reserves, Warns Report on U.S. Bonds May . . . ," *Reuters*, January 10, 2018, https://www.reuters.com/article/us-china-usa-debt-idUSKBN1F00CC.

103. See Kevin Yao, "China Says Diversifying FX Reserves, Warns Report on U.S. Bonds May . . . ," *Reuters*, January 11, 2018, https://www.reuters.com/article/us-china-usa-debt-idUSKBN1F00CC.

104. Nicholas Lardy, "The Fundamentals of Growth in China," in *China's Economic Transformation: Lessons, Impact, and the Path Ahead* (Washington, DC: Peterson Institute for International Economics, 2015), 4–6.

105. See National Bureau of Statistics (China), "National Economic Performance Maintained within an Appropriate Range in 2018 with Main Development Goals Achieved," National Bureau of Statistics of China, January 2019, http://www.stats.gov.cn/english/PressRelease/201901/t20190121_1645832.html.

106. Central Intelligence Agency 2019.

107. See Pettis 2020.

108. Morgan Stanley, "What Will China Be Like in 10 Years?," February 15, 2017, https://www.morganstanley.com/ideas/china-economic-market-transformation-bluepaper.

109. Nathaniel Taplin, "China's Inward Tilt Could Cripple It," *Wall Street Journal*, June 26, 2019, https://www.wsj.com/articles/chinas-inward-tilt-could-cripple-it-11561543149.

110. See Shangwubu [Ministry of Commerce], "Zhongguo Qiye 'Zouchuqiu' Fazhan Zhanlue [the 'Going Out' Development Strategy of Chinese Firms]," Shangwu lishi [History of Commerce], accessed June 30, 2019, https://history.mofcom.gov.cn/?newchina=%E4%B8%AD%E5%9B%BD%E4%BC%81%E4%B8%9A%E8%B5%B0%E5%87%BA%E5%8E%BB%E5%8F%91%E5%B1%95%E6%88%98%E7%95%A5.

111. Center for Strategic and International Studies, "Is China a Global Leader in Research and Development?" ChinaPower Project, accessed February 10, 2019, https://chinapower.csis.org/china-research-and-development-rnd/.

112. These figures and examples cited by David Cogman, Paul Gao, and Nick Leung, "Making Sense of Chinese Outbound M&A," *McKinsey*, July 3, 2017, https://www.mckinsey.com/business-functions/strategy-and-corporate-finance/our-insights/making-sense-of-chinese-outbound-m-and-a.

113. These figures and examples cited by Cogman, Gao, and Leung 2017.

114. These figures and examples cited by Cogman, Gao, and Leung 2017.

115. Cited by Catherine Bosley, "Chinese Ambassador Says ChemChina's Syngenta Purchase Was a Mistake," *Bloomberg Businessweek*, accessed June 29, 2019, https://

www.bloomberg.com/news/articles/2019-06-29/chinese-ambassador-says-chemchina-s-syngenta-purchase-a-mistake.

116. See Niharika Mandhana, "Manufacturers Want to Quit China for Vietnam: They're Finding It Impossible," *Wall Street Journal*, August 21, 2019, https://www.wsj.com/articles/for-manufacturers-in-china-breaking-up-is-hard-to-do-11566397989.

117. Cited by ActionForex, "40% US Manufacturers Moving Out of China on Trade War, Only 6% Back to US," May 22, 2019, https://www.actionforex.com/live-comments/200511-40-us-manufacturers-moving-out-of-china-on-trade-war-only-6-back-to-us/.

118. Lauly Li and Ting-Fang Cheng, "Apple Weighs 15%–30% Capacity Shift Out of China Amid Trade War," *Nikkei Asian Review*, June 19, 2019, https://asia.nikkei.com/Economy/Trade-war/Apple-weighs-15-30-capacity-shift-out-of-China-amid-trade-war.

119. Debby Wu and Mark Bergen, "Google Is Moving More Hardware Production Out of China," *Bloomberg*, last modified June 12, 2019, https://www.bloomberg.com/news/articles/2019-06-11/google-is-quickening-a-shift-of-hardware-production-from-china.

120. Cited by Orange Wang, "US Investment in China Slumps, as Beijing Warns of Global Recession," *South China Morning Post*, June 13, 2019, https://www.scmp.com/economy/china-economy/article/3014407/trade-war-could-cause-global-recession-beijing-official-warns.

121. Li and Cheng 2019.

122. Cited by ActionForex 2019.

123. Center for Strategic and International Studies 2019.

124. On financial services, see Thomas Hale, Tom Mitchell, and Hudson Lockett, "Beijing and Wall Street Deepen Ties Despite Geopolitical Rivalry," *Financial Times*, October 26, 2020, https://www.ft.com/content/8cf19144-b493-4a3e-9308-183bbcc6e76e.

125. Nisha Gopalan, "China's Big, Splashy Shopping Sprees Are So 2016," *Bloomberg Businessweek*, June 10, 2019, https://www.bloomberg.com/opinion/articles/2019-06-10/china-m-a-isn-t-dead-but-limited-to-belt-and-road-foreign-brands.

126. Cited by Yao 2018.

127. Issaku Harada, "ASEAN Becomes China's Top Trade Partner as Supply Chain Evolves," *Nikkei Asia*, July 15, 2020, https://asia.nikkei.com/Politics/International-relations/ASEAN-becomes-China-s-top-trade-partner-as-supply-chain-evolves. In the case of the EU, much of the shift reflected the UK's departure from the Union.

128. See Chad Brown, "Trump's Phase One Trade Deal with China and the US Election," Peterson Institute for International Economics, October 27, 2020, https://www.piie.com/blogs/trade-and-investment-policy-watch/trumps-phase-one-trade-deal-china-and-us-election.

129. See Pettis 2020.

130. See Pei Li and Brenda Goh, "No Place Like Home: Chinese Firms Stung by Trade War Build Up Domestic Brands," *Reuters*, September 5, 2019, https://www.reuters.com/article/us-usa-trade-china-manufacturers-idINKCN1VQ2W4.

131. Quoted by Dong Lye and Rebecca Spalding, "Trade Tensions Have a Chinese Giant Rethinking U.S. Deals," *Bloomberg*, May 30, 2019, https://www.bloomberg.com/news/articles/2019-05-30/trade-tensions-mean-china-s-fosun-is-rethinking-u-s-deal.

132. Alexandra Wexler, "Pepsi Expands in Africa with $1.7 Billion Deal," *Wall Street Journal*, July 19, 2019, https://www.wsj.com/articles/pepsi-expands-in-africa-with-1-7-billion-deal-11563530797.

133. Quoted by *Fortune* Editors, "Inside the Trade War's Tech Battle That Neither China nor the U.S. Can Afford to Lose," *Fortune*, November 7, 2019, https://fortune.com/2019/11/07/trade-war-tech-china-us/.

134. Stephen K. Bannon, "We're in an Economic War with China: It's Futile to Compromise," *Washington Post*, May 6, 2019, https://www.washingtonpost.com/opinions/steve-bannon-were-in-an-economic-war-with-china-its-futile-to-compromise/2019/05/06/0055af36-7014-11e9-9eb4-0828f5389013_story.html.

135. "EU–China: A Strategic Outlook," European Commission, 2019, 5.

136. See Richard Wike et al., "Views of China Divided Internationally," Pew Research Center's Global Attitudes Project, October 1, 2018, https://www.pewresearch.org/global/2018/10/01/international-publics-divided-on-china/.

137. See "China," Gallup, accessed June 19, 2019, https://news.gallup.com/poll/1627/China.aspx.

138. See Gallup 2019.

139. See Jeremy Diamond, "Trump: 'We Can't Continue to Allow China to Rape Our Country,'" *CNN Politics*, May 2, 2019, https://www.cnn.com/2016/05/01/politics/donald-trump-china-rape/index.html.

140. See Gallup 2019.

141. Laura Silver, Kat Devlin, and Christine Huang, "Unfavorable Views of China Reach Historic Highs in Many Countries," Pew Research Center's Global Attitudes Project, October 6, 2020, https://www.pewresearch.org/global/2020/10/06/unfavorable-views-of-china-reach-historic-highs-in-many-countries/.

Chapter 2

1. I am indebted to Joan Kaufman of Schwarzman Scholars for pointing out to me that per Chinese health guidelines, all undiagnosed pneumonias are classified as "atypical."

2. Hong Kong's emergency number is 999. These details from Jeremy Laurance, "An Uncommon Cold," *The Independent*, 2003, http://www.independent.co.uk/news/science/an-uncommon-cold-113445.html.

3. Cited by Laurance 2003. After the SARS epidemic ebbed, the Metropole changed its name—it's now the Metropark Kowloon Hotel—and eliminated Room 911. Room numbers now go from 909 to 913.

4. "WHO | Update 95—SARS: Chronology of a Serial Killer," World Health Organization, 2003, https://www.who.int/csr/don/2003_07_04/en/. The classification of SARS as a pandemic is debatable, but it is frequently referred to as such. See Yongshi Yang, Fujun Peng, Runsheng Wang, Kai Guan, Taijiao Jiang, Guogang Xu, Jinlyu Sun, and Christopher Chang, "The Deadly Coronaviruses: The 2003 SARS Pandemic and the 2020 Novel Coronavirus Epidemic in China," *Journal of Autoimmunity* 109 (2020): 102434. doi:https://doi.org/10.1016/j.jaut.2020.102434. https://www.sciencedirect.com/science/article/pii/S0896841120300470.

5. Clifford Krauss, "Toronto Mayor Calls for Understanding from Businesses and Consumers," *New York Times*, April 25, 2003, https://www.nytimes.com/2003/04/25/world/sars-epidemic-canada-toronto-mayor-calls-for-understanding-businesses-consumers.html.

6. Gaby Hinsliff, Mark Townsend, and John Aglionby, "The Day the World Caught a Cold," *The Observer*, April 26, 2003, https://www.theguardian.com/world/2003/apr/27/sars.johnaglionby.

7. "WHO | SARS Outbreak Contained Worldwide," World Health Organization, July 5, 2003, https://www.who.int/mediacentre/news/releases/2003/pr56/en/.

8. The world experienced three serious outbreaks involving a new coronavirus in the first two decades of the twenty-first century, the third being MERS. See Yang et al. 2020.

9. John M. Barry, "The Site of Origin of the 1918 Influenza Pandemic and Its Public Health Implications," *Journal of Translational Medicine* 2, no. 1 (2004): 3.

10. I thank Joan Kaufman for emphasizing this point.

11. Peter Daszak, "Anatomy of a Pandemic," *Lancet* 380, no. 9857 (2012): 1883–1884; Zeke Emanuel and Scott Moore, "Analysis | Economics, Not Politics, Helps Explain Why Coronavirus and Other Diseases Started in China," *Washington Post*, May 1, 2020, https://www.washingtonpost.com/politics/2020/05/01/economics-not-politics-helps-explain-why-coronavirus-other-diseases-started-china/.

12. See "Here Are the 20 Busiest Ports on the Planet," *World Economic Forum*, February 5, 2019, https://www.weforum.org/agenda/2019/02/visualizing-the-world-s-busiest-ports/.; and "ACI Reveals Top 20 Airports for Passenger Traffic, Cargo, and Aircraft Movements," Airports Council International, May 19, 2020, https://aci.aero/news/2020/05/19/aci-reveals-top-20-airports-for-passenger-traffic-cargo-and-aircraft-movements/.

13. Emanuel and Moore 2020.

14. Joan A. Kaufman. "China's Heath Care System and Avian Influenza Preparedness," *The Journal of Infectious Diseases* 197 (2008): S7–S13, accessed April 29, 2021, http://www.jstor.org/stable/30086986.

15. See Elaine Yau, "China Enraged by 'Sick Man of Asia' Headline, but Its Origin May Surprise Many," *South China Morning Post*, February 27, 2020, https://www.scmp.com/lifestyle/article/3052434/china-enraged-sick-man-asia-headline-its-origin-may-surprise-many.

16. See Yau 2020.

17. Kaci Kennedy McDade and Wenhui Mao, "Making Sense of Estimates of Health Aid from China," *BMJ Global Health* 5, no. 2 (2020): 2.

18. Titiporn Tuangratananon et al., "China: Leapfrogging to Become a Leader in Global Health?," *Journal of Global Health* 9, no. 1 (2019): 010312.

19. Matthew Brown, Tim Mackey, and Bryan Liang, "Global Health Diplomacy and Management Mechanisms of US-China Public Health Collaborations in China: Lessons for Emerging Markets," *Journal of Commercial Biotechnology* 18, no. 4 (2012): 44–50.

20. Bridie Andrews and Mary Brown Bullock, eds. *Medical Transitions in Twentieth-Century China* (Bloomington: Indiana University Press, 2014). Accessed April 29, 2021. ProQuest Ebook Central, 293. I thank Joan Kaufman for drawing my attention to this history.

21. Mary Bullock, *An American Transplant: The Rockefeller Foundation and Peking Union Medical College* (Berkeley: University of California Press, 1980), https://books.google.com/books?id=oCqUfPwUw94C, 8.

22. Jeoffrey Gordon, "The Organization and Financing of Health Services," in *China Medicine as We Saw It*, ed. Joseph R. Quinn (Bethesda, MD: US Dept. of Health, Education, and Welfare, Public Health Service, National Institutes of Health, 1974), 63–94.

23. "Cooperation in Health: Report of Secretary Califano's Visit to the People's Republic of China, 1979," Department of Health, Education, and Welfare Office of International Health, 1980, 6.

24. The point about establishing credibility and this quotation are from Katherine Mason, *Infectious Change* (Stanford, CA: Stanford University Press, 2020), 12.

25. Deborah Seligsohn, "The Rise and Fall of the US-China Health Relationship," *Asian Perspective* 45, no. 1 (2021): 203–224. https://muse.jhu.edu/article/771320/pdf.

26. I am indebted to Joan Kaufman for drawing attention to this importance. See also Seligsohn 2021.

27. Brown, Mackey, and Liang 2012, 46.

28. US Congressional-Executive Commission on China, "China's Mounting HIV/AIDS Crisis: How Should the United States Respond?: Roundtable before the Congressional-Executive Commission on China," 108th Cong., 1st sess., 2004.

29. Seligsohn 2021, 206.

30. US Congressional-Executive Commission on China 2004, 19; 23–24.

31. US Congressional-Executive Commission on China 2004, 4–5.

32. Brown, Mackey, and Liang 2012, 46.

33. Seligsohn 2021, 203.

34. Zhongguowang [China Network], "[中国网]解读中美医疗卫生领域合作新成果 [China Net: Understanding the New Results of Sino-American Cooperation in the Field of Medicine and Health]," China Centers for Disease Control and Prevention, accessed October 19, 2020, http://www.chinacdc.cn/mtbd_8067/201510/t20151008_120881.html.

35. According to Mike Pompeo, "enormous evidence" supported this theory, despite subsequently walking back the claim. See Aruna Viswanatha and Alex Leary, "Pompeo

Says There Is Evidence Coronavirus Came from Wuhan Lab," *Wall Street Journal*, May 3, 2020, https://www.wsj.com/articles/pompeo-says-there-is-evidence-coronavirus-came-from-wuhan-lab-11588544574.

36. This section is drawn largely from the author's personal experience of events during the COVID-19 pandemic; the initial cover-up of the COVID-19 outbreak is described by Seligsohn 2021. On the politicization of COVID-19, see Yanzhong Huang, *Toxic Politics: China's Environmental Health Crisis and Its Challenge to the Chinese State* (Cambridge, UK: Cambridge University Press, 2020).

37. Yanzhong Huang, "The SARS Epidemic and Its Aftermath in China: A Political Perspective," in *Learning from SARS: Preparing for the Next Disease Outbreak: Workshop Summary*, ed. S. Knobler, A. Mahmoud, and S. Lemon (Washington, DC: National Academies Press, 2004, 91–136).

38. Huang 2004.

39. Mary Augusta Brazelton, *Mass Vaccination* (Ithaca, NY: Cornell University Press, 2019), 12.

40. Mason 2020, 8.

41. Brazelton 2019, 2.

42. Brazelton 2019, 5.

43. US Congressional-Executive Commission on China, "Dangerous Secrets: SARS and China's Healthcare System: Roundtable before the Congressional-Executive Commission on China," 108th Cong., 1st sess., 2003, 13.

44. Gordon 1974, 72.

45. Cited by Gordon 1974, 70.

46. Gordon 1974, 74.

47. Brazelton 2019, 162–163.

48. Brazelton 2019, 146–155. Reference to every Chinese province sending medical teams thanks to Joan Kaufman.

49. Brazelton 2019, 155–156.

50. Brazelton 2019, 165.

51. Kerry Dumbaugh and Wayne Morrison, "CRS Report for Congress: SARS, Avian Flu, and Other Challenges for China's Political, Social, and Economic Transformation," Washington, DC: Congressional Research Service, 2004, 10.

52. Mason 2020, 9.

53. US Congressional-Executive Commission on China 2003, 9–22.

54. US Congressional-Executive Commission on China 2004, 22.

55. Joan Kaufman. "Policy Case Study: Public Health," in *Politics in China: An Introduction*, ed. William A. Joseph, 1–30 (New York: Oxford University Press, 2018), 7.

56. Cited by Dumbaugh and Morrison 2004, 10.

57. Gordon 1974, 78.

58. Quoted by Mason 2020, 25.

59. Dumbaugh and Morrison 2004, 5.

60. US Congressional-Executive Commission on China 2003, 19.

61. Kaufman 2018, 14.

62. US Congressional-Executive Commission on China 2003, 23.

63. US Congressional-Executive Commission on China 2003, 24.

64. US Congressional-Executive Commission on China 2003, 6.

65. US Congressional-Executive Commission on China 2003, 6.

66. Huang 2020, 30–32.

67. See Xi Li et al., "Quality of Primary Health Care in China: Challenges and Recommendations," *The Lancet* 395, no. 10239 (2020): 1802–1812.

68. Brown, Mackey, and Liang 2012.

69. See Jing-Bao Nie et al., "The Crisis of Patient-Physician Trust and Bioethics: Lessons and Inspirations from China," *Developing World Bioethics* 18, no. 1 (2017): 56–64; Lijie Wang, and Chengshang Yang, "Corruption or Professional Dignity: An Ethical Examination of the Phenomenon of 'Red Envelopes' (Monetary Gifts) in Medical Practice in China," *Developing World Bioethics* 18, no. 1 (2018): 37.

70. US Congressional-Executive Commission on China 2003, 24.

71. This scene described by "1955 Polio Vaccine Trial Announcement," University of Michigan School of Public Health, accessed October 8, 2019, https://sph.umich.edu/polio/.

72. Recounted in Renilde Loeckx, *Cold War Triangle: How Scientists in East and West Tamed HIV* (Leuven: Leuven University Press, 2017), 25.

73. Peter J. Hoetz, "Russian–United States Vaccine Science Diplomacy: Preserving the Legacy," *PLOS Neglected Tropical Diseases* 11, no. 5 (May 25, 2017): e0005320. doi:10.1371/journal.pntd.0005320. https://journals.plos.org/plosntds/article?id=10.1371/journal.pntd.0005320.

74. Dóra Vargha, *Polio across the Iron Curtain: Hungary's Cold War with an Epidemic* (New York: Cambridge University Press, 2018), 147.

75. Edward A. Raymond, "US-USSR Cooperation in Medicine and Health on JSTOR," *The Russian Review* 32, no. 3 (1973): 232–233.

76. National Museum of American History, "Two Vaccines: Salk and Sabin." Smithsonian Institution, 2005, https://amhistory.si.edu/polio/virusvaccine/vacraces2.htm.

77. Loeckx 2017, 41–42.

78. The story of Holy's collaboration with De Clercq and others is chronicled by Loeckx 2017.

79. "U.S.-China Dialogue on Global Health Background Report," Georgetown University Initiative on U.S.-China Dialogue on Global Issues, May 3, 2017, https://uschinadialogue.georgetown.edu/publications/u-s-china-dialogue-on-global-health-background-report.

80. Georgetown University Initiative for U.S.-China Dialogue 2017.

81. Yanzhong Huang, "China's Healthcare Sector and U.S.-China Health Cooperation," *Council on Foreign Relations*, April 27, 2016.

82. Zhongguowang 2020.

83. Seligsohn 2021, 211.

84. Zhongguo Xinwen Wang [China News Network], "国家卫健委回应美卫生部长访台：美方行径严重损害中美卫生健康合作 [National Health Commission Responds to U.S. Health Secretary's Taiwan Visit: The U.S. Side has Seriously Harmed Sino-American Health Cooperation]," *China News*, August 12, 2020, https://www.chinanews.com/gn/2020/08-12/9263128.shtml.

85. Katrina Manson and David Pilling, "US Warns over Chinese 'Spying' on African Disease Control Centre," *The Financial Times*, February 6, 2020, https://www.ft.com/content/cef96328-475a-11ea-aeb3-955839e06441.

86. Jevans Nyabiage. "After US Retreat, China Breaks Ground on Africa CDC Headquarters Project," accessed April 29, 2021, https://www.scmp.com/news/china/diplomacy/article/3114052/after-us-retreat-china-breaks-ground-africa-cdc-headquarters.

87. This chronology taken from Dumbaugh and Morrison 2004; BBC News, "武汉肺炎：人和事 中国萨斯留下的时代记忆 [Wuhan Pneumonia: People and Events in China's Record of SARS]," *BBC News Zhongwen*, January 21, 2020, https://www.bbc.com/zhongwen/simp/chinese-news-51195689.

88. This chronology taken from Dumbaugh and Morrison 2004; BBC News 2020.

89. US Congressional-Executive Commission on China 2003, 6.

90. Seligsohn 2021, 209.

91. US Congressional-Executive Commission on China 2004, 31.

92. Mason 2020, 11.

93. US Congressional-Executive Commission on China 2003.

94. I thank Joan Kaufman for emphasizing this point.

95. See Javier Hernandez, "Two Members of W.H.O. Team on Trail of Virus Are Denied Entry to China," *New York Times*, January 13, 2021, https://www.nytimes.com/2021/01/13/world/asia/china-who-wuhan-covid.html.

96. Described by David Cyranoski, "Bat Cave Solves Mystery of Deadly SARS Virus—and Suggests New Outbreak Could Occur," *Nature* 552 (2017): 15.

97. Dumbaugh and Morrison 2004.

98. This phenomenon is described by Shuangyi Sun et al., "China Empowers Internet Hospital to Fight against COVID-19," *The Journal of Infection* 81, no. 1 (2020): e67–e68.

99. During COVID-19, informal, transnational physician communications helped spread awareness of effective treatments. Author's personal communications with University of Pennsylvania physicians.

100. Yun Liu et al., "Multilevel Analysis of International Scientific Collaboration Network in the Influenza Virus Vaccine Field: 2006–2013," *Sustainability* 10, no. 1032 (2018): 3–19.

101. Chao Deng, "China Seeks to Use Access to Covid-19 Vaccines for Diplomacy," *Wall Street Journal*, August 17, 2020, https://www.wsj.com/articles/china-seeks-to-use-access-to-covid-19-vaccines-for-diplomacy-11597690215.

102. I am indebted to Richard Danzig for this observation.

103. US Congressional-Executive Commission on China 2003, 5–9.

104. This point is made by Scott Moore, "In Biotech, the Industry of the Future, the U.S. Is Way Ahead of China," accessed April 6, 2021, https://www.lawfareblog.com/biotech-industry-future-us-way-ahead-china.

105. Africa Centers for Disease Control, *The Rockefeller Foundation Announces Grant to Expand Access to COVID-19 Testing and Tracing in Africa*, Africa CDC, 2021. https://africacdc.org/news-item/the-rockefeller-foundation-announces-grant-to-expand-access-to-covid-19-testing-and-tracing-in-africa/.

Chapter 3

1. On China's participation in pre-2009 climate negotiations and the National Climate Change Plan, see Barbara Finamore, *Will China Save the Planet?* (Cambridge, UK: Polity Press, 2018).

2. The importance of the MVR issues is described by John Lee, "How China Stiffed the World in Copenhagen," *Foreign Policy*, December 19, 2009, https://foreignpolicy.com/2009/12/21/how-china-stiffed-the-world-in-copenhagen/.

3. There is some ambiguity on this point, as many of the final negotiations took place at high levels with little public record. This characterization based on Mark Lynas, "How Do I Know China Wrecked the Copenhagen Deal? I Was in the Room," *The Guardian*, December 22, 2009, https://www.theguardian.com/environment/2009/dec/22/cop enhagen-climate-change-mark-lyna. On the ambiguity, see Bjorn Conrad, "China in Copenhagen: Reconciling the 'Beijing Climate Revolution' and the 'Copenhagen Climate Obstinacy,'" *The China Quarterly* 210 (2012): 435–455.

4. Lynas 2009.

5. The seminal theory of the veto player is George Tsebelis, *Veto Players: How Political Institutions Work* (Princeton, NJ: Princeton University Press, 2002).

6. Darrell West and Christian Lansang, "Global Manufacturing Scorecard: How the US Compares to 18 Other Nations," *Brookings*, July 10, 2018, https://www.brookings.edu/research/global-manufacturing-scorecard-how-the-us-compares-to-18-other-nations/.

7. See Boqiang Lin and Kui Liu, "How Efficient Is China's Heavy Industry? A Perspective of Input–Output Analysis," *Emerging Markets Finance and Trade* 52, no. 11 (2016): 2546–2564.

8. Debra Tan, Feng Hu, and Inna Lazareva, "8 Facts on China's Wastewater," *China Water Risk*, March 12, 2014, http://www.chinawaterrisk.org/resources/analysis-revi ews/8-facts-on-china-wastewater/.

9. See Lin and Liu 2016.

10. Jintai Lin et al., "China's International Trade and Air Pollution in the United States," *Proceedings of the National Academy of Sciences* 111, no. 5 (2014): 1736–1741.

11. Hannah Ritchie and Max Roser, "CO$_2$ and Greenhouse Gas Emissions," *Our World in Data*, 2020, https://ourworldindata.org/co2/country/china.

12. Xu Tian et al., "Evolution of China's Water Footprint and Virtual Water Trade: A Global Trade Assessment," *Environment International* 121 (2018): 178–188.

13. Perhaps the best account of this crisis comes from Yanzhong Huang, *Toxic Politics: China's Environmental Health Crisis and Its Challenge to the Chinese State* (Cambridge, UK: Cambridge University Press, 2020); a major concern is food safety stemming from the accumulation of heavy metals in soil.

14. On soil contamination, see Tiankui Li et al., "Soil Pollution Management in China: A Brief Introduction," *Sustainability* 11, no. 3 (2019): 1–15; on e-waste see Huang 2020, 49.

15. Yale Center for Environmental Law and Policy, "Environmental Performance Index," accessed May 14, 2021, https://epi.yale.edu/epi-country-report/CHN. See also World

Bank Group, "Promoting Innovation in China: Lessons from International Good Practice," *Finance, Competitiveness and Innovation Insight*, World Bank, 2020, https:// openknowledge.worldbank.org/handle/10986/33680.

16. Scott Moore, "Legitimacy, Development and Sustainability: Understanding Water Policy and Politics in Contemporary China," *The China Quarterly* 237 (2019): 153–173.

17. Some support for such a claim is offered in Finamore 2018.

18. Cheryl Katz, "Piling Up: How China's Ban on Importing Waste has Stalled Global Recycling," Yale School of the Environment, March 7, 2019, https://e360.yale. edu/features/piling-up-how-chinas-ban-on-importing-waste-has-stalled-global-recycling.

19. Hannah Ritchie and Max Roser, "Plastic Pollution," *Our World in Data*, September 2018, https://ourworldindata.org/plastic-pollution.

20. Katz 2019.

21. Bo Li, "2 Ways for China to Play a Bigger Role in Protecting Global Forests," World Resources Institute, April 17, 2018, https://www.wri.org/blog/2018/04/2-ways-china-play-bigger-role-protecting-global-forests.

22. Tian et al. 2018.

23. Scott Moore, "Why China's Belt and Road Is Off Track," Foreign Policy Research Institute, December 13, 2018, https://www.fpri.org/article/2018/12/why-chinas-belt-and-road-is-off-track/.

24. Elena F. Tracy et al., "China's New Eurasian Ambitions: The Environmental Risks of the Silk Road Economic Belt," *Eurasian Geography and Economics* 58, no. 1 (2017): 56–88; Divya Narainet al., "Best-Practice Biodiversity Safeguards for Belt and Road Initiative's Financiers," *Nature Sustainability* 3, no. 8 (2020): 650–657.

25. See Souzanna Stephens and Matthew Southerland, "China's Role in Wildlife Trafficking and the Chinese Government's Response," Washington, DC: U.S.–China Economic and Security Review Commission, December 6, 2018, 4.

26. Cited by Farah Master, "As China Pushes Traditional Medicine Globally, Illegal Wildlife Trade Flourishes," *Reuters*, March 28, 2019, https://www.reuters.com/arti cle/us-china-tcm/as-china-pushes-traditional-medicine-globally-illegal-wildlife-trade-flourishes-idUSKCN1R90D5?il=0.

27. Cited by Master 2019.

28. Michael Fabinyi et al., "Aquatic Product Consumption Patterns and Perceptions among the Chinese Middle Class," *Regional Studies in Marine Science* 7 (2016): 1–9.

29. See Scott Moore, "Fishing Boat Diplomacy," *Foreign Affairs*, September 14, 2016, https://www.foreignaffairs.com/articles/china/2016-09-14/fishing-boat-diplomacy.

30. Tabitha Grace Mallory, "China's Distant Water Fishing Industry: Evolving Policies and Implications," *Marine Policy* 38 (2013): 99–108; Douglas McCauley, "This Is How China Can Be a Friend to Ocean Conservation," World Economic Forum, June 25, 2019, https://www.weforum.org/agenda/2019/06/oceans-china-conservation/.

31. Mark Godfrey, "New Data Indicates Big Jump in China Distant-Water Catch," accessed April 27, 2021, https://www.seafoodsource.com/news/supply-trade/new-data-indicates-big-jump-in-china-distant-water-catch.

32. For discussion of the role that public diplomacy plays in China's climate policy, see Scott Moore, "Strategic Imperative? Reading China's Climate Policy in Terms of Core Interests," *Global Change, Peace & Security* 23, no. 2 (2011): 147–157.

33. See The White House, "U.S.-China Joint Presidential Statement on Climate Change," WhiteHouse.gov, September 25, 2015, https://obamawhitehouse.archives.gov/the-press-office/2015/09/25/us-china-joint-presidential-statement-climate-change.

34. International Renewable Energy Agency, "Avoided Emissions Calculator," International Renewable Energy Agency, 2018, https://www.irena.org/climatecha nge/Avoided-Emissions-Calculator.

35. See UN Environment Programme, "Emissions Gap Report 2019," Nairobi: United Nations Environment Programme, 2019.

36. Yuanyuan Liang, Biying Yu, and Wang Lu, "Costs and Benefits of Renewable Energy Development in China's Power Industry," *Renewable Energy* 131 (2019): 700–712.

37. "Avoided Emissions Calculator," International Renewable Energy Agency, accessed March 20, 2019, https://www.irena.org/climatechange/Avoided-Emissions-Cal culator.

38. Kavita Surana and Laura Diaz Anadon, "Public Policy and Financial Resource Mobilization for Wind Energy in Developing Countries: A Comparison of Approaches and Outcomes in China and India," *Global Environmental Change* 35 (2015): 340–359.

39. See David Stanway, "China CO_2 Emissions to Peak in 2022, Ahead of Schedule: Government Researcher," *Reuters*, September 5, 2019, https://www.reuters. com/article/us-china-carbon-idUSKCN1VQ1K0.

40. See Scott Moore, "Why China's New Climate Commitments Matter for U.S. National Security," *Lawfare*, October 13, 2020, https://www.lawfareblog.com/why-chinas-new-climate-commitments-matter-us-national-security.

41. See Yanzhong Huang, *Toxic Politics: China's Environmental Health Crisis and Its Challenge to the Chinese State* (New York: Cambridge University Press, 2020).

42. David Stanway and Cate Cadell, "President Xi Says China Will Start Cutting Coal Consumption from 2026," accessed April 28, 2021, https://www.reuters.com/world/china/chinas-xi-says-china-will-phase-down-coal-consumption-over-2026-2030-2021-04-22/.

43. Huang 2020.

44. Figures cited by Faseeh Mangi and Dan Murtaugh, "China Seen Slowing Spending on Belt and Road Energy Projects," *Bloomberg*, March 12, 2018, https://www.bloomberg. com/news/articles/2018-03-12/china-seen-slowing-spending-on-belt-and-road-ene rgy-projects.

45. On Xi's announcement, see Vincent Ni and Helen Sullivan, "Big Line in the Sand?: China Promises No New Coal-Fired Power Projects Abroad," *The Guardian*, September 21, 2021, https://www.theguardian.com/world/2021/sep/22/china-clim ate-no-new-coal-fired-power-projects-abroad-xi-jinping.

46. US Department of State, *The Chinese Communist Party: Threatening Global Peace and Security*, 2020, https://2017-2021.state.gov/the-chinese-communist-party-threaten ing-global-peace-and-security/.

47. "Opening Ceremony Draws 2 Billion Global Viewers," The Nielsen Company, August 14, 2008, https://www.nielsen.com/us/en/insights/article/2008/beijing-opening-ceremonys-global-tv-audience-hit-2-billion.

48. Scott Moore, "Hydropolitics and Inter-Jurisdictional Relationships in China: The Pursuit of Localized Preferences in a Centralized System," The China Quarterly 219 (2014a): 760–780.

49. Cited by James Pomfret, "Velvet Glove Trumps Iron Fist in South China Land Riot," Reuters, September 29, 2011, https://in.reuters.com/article/idININdia-5960972 0110929.

50. Andrew Jacobs, "Chinese Village of Wukan Locked in Rebellion against Authorities," New York Times, December 14, 2011, https://www.nytimes.com/2011/12/15/world/asia/chinese-village-locked-in-rebellion-against-authorities.html.

51. In 2016, the popularly elected leader, Liu Zulan, was arrested on bribery charges, seemingly ending Wukan's democratic experiment.

52. "Chinese Official Denies Reports of Deaths at Haimen Protest," Reuters, December 21, 2011, https://www.reuters.com/article/china-protest-plant-idUSL3E7NL0KR2 0111221.

53. Described by Yu Xin, "污染项目暂停抗议仍未停　什邡周边民众加入声援 [Protests against Polluting Project Suspended as People Around Shifang Join in Support]," Radio Free Asia, July 3, 2012, https://www.rfa.org/mandarin/yataibaodao/syl-07032012104711.html.

54. Cited by Pinghui Zhuang, "Thousands Protest in Central China over Waste Incineration Plant," South China Morning Post, July 5, 2019, https://www.scmp.com/news/china/society/article/3017386/thousands-protest-central-china-over-waste-incineration-plant.

55. Hwa-Jen Liu, Leverage of the Weak: Labor and Environmental Movements in Taiwan and South Korea (Minneapolis: University of Minnesota Press, 2015), 4.

56. H. Christoph Steinhardt and Fengshi Wu, "In the Name of the Public: Environmental Protest and the Changing Landscape of Popular Contention in China," The China Journal 75 (2016): 62.

57. Cited by Huang 2020, 66.

58. Shui-Tan Tang and Ching-Ping Tang, "Democratization and the Environment: Entrepreneurial Politics and Interest Representation in Taiwan on JSTOR," The China Quarterly 158 (1999): 352.

59. See Wen-Chin Wu, Yu-Tzung Chang, and Hsin-Hsin Pan, "Does China's Middle Class Prefer (Liberal) Democracy?" Democratization 24, no. 2 (2017): 347–366.

60. Scott Moore, "Pollution without Revolution," Foreign Affairs, June 10, 2014, https://www.foreignaffairs.com/articles/china/2014-06-10/pollution-without-revolution.

61. Quoted by Stanway 2019.

62. Quoted by Matthew Carney, "President Xi's Hyper-Nationalism Has People Believing in His China Dream," ABC News, October 14, 2017, https://www.abc.net.au/news/2017-10-15/president-xi-and-his-china-dream/9048966.

63. See John S. Dryzek et al., Green States and Social Movements: Environmentalism in the United States, United Kingdom, Germany, and Norway (Oxford: Oxford University Press, 2003).

64. Angela G. Mertig and Riley E. Dunlap, "Environmentalism, New Social Movements, and the New Class: A Cross-National Investigation," *Rural Sociology* 66, no. 1 (2001): 114.

65. The literature on environmentalism and socioeconomic status is a bit more complex, and suggests that environmental concern increases with income, making the contradiction with Marxism potentially less glaring. A good description of this debate is provided by Raphael J. Nawrotzki and Fred C. Pampel, "Cohort Change and the Diffusion of Environmental Concern: A Cross-National Analysis," *Population and Environment* 35, no. 1 (2013): 1–25.

66. Moore 2018.

67. For a description of this Target Responsibility System, see Xiaoliang Liet al., "Authoritarian Environmentalism and Environmental Policy Implementation in China," *Resources, Conservation and Recycling* 145 (2019): 87.

68. For a good description of the limitations of this model, see Elizabeth Economy, "Environmental Governance in China: State Control to Crisis Management," *Daedalus* 143, no. 2 (2014): 184–197.

69. This point is made by Yifei Li and Judith Shapiro, *China Goes Green: Coercive Authoritarianism for a Troubled Planet* (Cambridge, UK: Polity Press, 2020).

70. See, for example, the report of the Fifth Tibet Work Conference, Renminwang [People's Daily], "时隔五年再次召开西藏工作座谈会 习近平给出治藏新方略 [After Five Years, the Tibet Work Forum Was Held Again, Xi Jinping Gave a New Strategy for Governing Tibet]," *Zhongguo gongchandang xinxiwang* [*Chinese Communist Party News Network*], August 31, 2020, http://cpc.people.com.cn/n1/2020/0830/c164113-31841720.html.

71. Li and Shapiro 2020, 24.

72. Guangqin Li et al., "Environmental Non-Governmental Organizations and Urban Environmental Governance: Evidence from China," *Journal of Environmental Management* 206 (2018): 1296.

73. Xueyong Zhan and Shui-yan Tang. "Political Opportunities, Resource Constraints and Policy Advocacy of Environmental NGOs in China," *Public Administration* 91, no. 2 (2013): 381–399. doi:10.1111/j.1467-9299.2011.02011.x. https://doi-org.proxy.library.upenn.edu/10.1111/j.1467-9299.2011.02011.x.; on environmental GONGOs, see Jonathan Schwartz, "Environmental NGOs in China: Roles and Limits," *Pacific Affairs* 77 (2004): 28–49.

74. Bruce Gilley, "Authoritarian Environmentalism and China's Response to Climate Change," *Environmental Politics* 21, no. 2 (2012): 287–307.; Matthew Gaudreau and Huhua Cao, "Political Constraints on Adaptive Governance: Environmental NGO Networks in Nanjing, China," *The Journal of Environment & Development* 24, no. 4 (2015): 418–444; Li et al. 2018.

75. Elizabeth Economy, *The River Runs Black: The Environmental Challenge to China's Future (A Council on Foreign Relations Book)* (Ithaca, NY: Cornell University Press, 2010), and Joanna Lewis, *Green Innovation in China's Wind Power Industry and the Global Transition to a Low-Carbon Economy* (New York: Columbia University Press, 2012), provide a good description of this international influence.

76. This is described by Anna L. Ahlers and Yongdong Shen, "Breathe Easy? Local Nuances of Authoritarian Environmentalism in China's Battle against Air Pollution," *The China Quarterly* 234 (2018): 299–319.

77. On the scale of restructuring and upgrading and implications for emissions, see Finamore 2018.

78. Michael Greenstone and Patrick Schwarz, "Air Quality Life Index Update: Is China Winning Its War on Pollution?," Chicago: University of Chicago, 2018; Jing Li, "China Softens 'Iron Fist' Pollution Fight," *Dialogo Chino*, March 15, 2019, https://dialogoch ino.net/24851-china-softens-iron-fist-pollution-fight/.

79. The campaign model is described in Elizabeth Economy, "Environmental Governance in China: State Control to Crisis Management," *Daedalus* 143, no. 2 (2014): 184–197. http://www.jstor.org.proxy.library.upenn.edu/stable/43297326 and Li and Shapiro 2020.

80. Sarah Eaton and Genia Kostka, "Authoritarian Environmentalism Undermined? Local Leaders' Time Horizons and Environmental Policy Implementation in China," *The China Quarterly* 218 (2014): 359–380; Kevin Lo, "How Authoritarian Is the Environmental Governance of China?" *Environmental Science & Policy* 54 (2015): 152–159.; Genia Kostka, "Command without Control: The Case of China's Environmental Target System," *Regulation & Governance* 10, no. 1 (2016): 58–74

81. See Economy 2014 and Moore 2014.

82. See Finamore 2018, 24.

83. Moore 2011.

84. Cited by Finamore 2018, 30.

85. Qinghui Song, "生态文明 [Ecological Civilization]," *Baidu*, January 9, 2018, https://baike.baidu.com/item/%E7%94%9F%E6%80%81%E6%96%87%E6%98%8E; Jinping Xi, "Shenke Renshi Xinshidai Wo Guo Yingdui Qihoubianhua Lishi Shiming—Cong 'Dili Fenjin De Wunian' Daxing Chengjiu Zhan Jiedu Shijiu Da Baozhi [Sincerely Recognizing China's Historic Mission to Address Climate Change]," Guojia yingdui qihoubianhua zhanlue yanjiu he guoji hezuo zhongxin [National Center for Climate Change Strategy and Cooperation], August 22, 2018, http://www.ncsc.org.cn/yjcg/fxgc/201804/P020180920510043936945.pdf.

86. On the relationship to Marxism, see Li and Shapiro 2020, 6–7.

87. Scott Moore, "Even China Is Tackling Climate Change, While US Takes a Back Seat," *The Hill*, October 16, 2017, https://thehill.com/opinion/energy-environment/355 693-even-china-is-tackling-climate-change-while-the-us-takes-a-back.

88. Jieyi Lu, "Comparing U.S. and Chinese Electric Vehicle Policies," Environmental and Energy Study Institute, February 28, 2018, https://www.eesi.org/articles/view/comparing-u.s.-and-chinese-electric-vehicle-policies.

89. Michael J. Coren, "Nine Countries Say They'll Ban Internal Combustion Engines. So Far, It's just Words," *Quartz*, August 7, 2018, https://qz.com/1341155/nine-countries-say-they-will-ban-internal-combustion-engines-none-have-a-law-to-do-so/.

90. Keith Zhai and Yoko Kubota. "China to Restrict Tesla Use by Military and State Employees," *Wall Street Journal*, March 19, 2021. https://www.wsj.com/articles/china-to-restrict-tesla-usage-by-military-and-state-personnel-11616155643.

91. Xinhuanet, "特稿：人类命运同体理念之光照亮世界前行之路——写在中国人民抗日战争暨世界反法西斯战争胜利75周年之际（ [Feature: The Light of the Idea of a Community with a Shared Future for Mankind Illuminates the Way Forward for the World-Written on the Occasion of the 75th Anniversary of the Victory of the Chinese People's War of Resistance against Japanese Aggression and the World Anti-Fascist War (Short Version)]," *Xinhua*, September 2, 2020, http://www.xinhuanet.com/2020-09/02/c_1126441176.htm.

92. See, for example, Wang Yi's visit to France in August 2020, described in Xiao Shan, "中官方透露王毅向马克龙转达习近平口信 "中欧是伙伴不是竞争对手" [Chinese Officials Revealed That Wang Yi Conveyed Xi Jinping's Message to Macron, "China and Europe Are Partners, Not Competitors"]," *Radio France International*, August 29, 2020, https://www.rfi.fr/cn/%E4%B8%AD%E5%9B%BD/20200829-%E4%B8%AD%E5%AE%98%E6%96%B9%E9%80%8F%E9%9C%B2%E7%8E%8B%E6%AF%85%E5%90%91%E9%A9%AC%E5%85%8B%E9%BE%99%E8%BD%AC%E8%BE%BE%E4%B9%A0%E8%BF%91%E5%B9%B3%-E5%8F%A3%E4%BF%A1-%E4%B8%AD%E6%AC%A7%E6%98%AF%E4%BC%99%E4%BC%B4%E4%B8%8D%E6%98%AF%E7%AB%9E%E4%BA%89%E5%AF%B9%E6%89%8B.

93. Xinhua, "Shouhu 'Yidai Yilu' Shang De Lushui Qingshan [Protecting the Water and Mountains Along the 'One Belt One Road']," *Xinhua Net*, August 22, 2018, http://www.xinhuanet.com/politics/2018-08/22/c_1123307413.htm.

94. Moore 2018.

95. Quoted by Reuters, "A Hospital and Clean Water: China on the Charm Offensive in Sri Lanka," *New York Times*, November 20, 2019, https://www.nytimes.com/reuters/2019/11/20/world/asia/19reuters-sri-lanka-politics-china.html.

96. Shah M. Baloch, "Protests in Pakistan Erupt against China's Belt and Road Plan," *The Guardian*, August 20, 2021, http://www.theguardian.com/environment/2021/aug/20/water-protests-in-pakistan-erupt-against-chinas-belt-and-road-plan.

97. Huang 2020, 81.

98. Huang 2020, 80–82.

99. Scott Moore, "The China Climate Challenge," *The Diplomat*, September 1, 2020, https://thediplomat.com/2020/09/the-china-climate-challenge/.

100. This description of Engelsberger is drawn from Aaron Wiener, "Made in the Shade," *Foreign Policy*, July 9, 2012, https://foreignpolicy.com/2012/07/09/made-in-the-shade/., and Michael Aklin and Johannes Urpelainen, *Renewables: The Politics of a Global Energy Transition* (Cambridge, MA: MIT Press, 2018).

101. This description of Engelsberger is drawn from Wiener 2012 and Aklin and Urpelainen 2018.

102. The cost of solar power has fallen faster and to a greater extent than any other major energy generation technology, with correspondingly rapid growth in installed capacity. See Amro M. Elshurafa et al., "Estimating the Learning Curve of Solar PV Balance-of-system for over 20 Countries: Implications and Policy Recommendations," *Journal of Cleaner Production* 196 (2018): 122–134.

103. See Aleh Cherp et al., "Comparing Electricity Transitions: A Historical Analysis of Nuclear, Wind and Solar Power in Germany and Japan," *Energy Policy* 101 (2017): 612–628.

104. Aklin and Urpelainen 2018, 150.

105. Elshurafa et al. 2018.

106. Cited by Ellen Thalman and Benjamin Wehrman, "What German Households Pay for Power," *Clean Energy Wire*, January 24, 2020, https://www.cleanenergywire.org/factsheets/what-german-households-pay-power.

107. Cherp et al. 2017; Aklin and Urpelainen 2018.

108. On the competitive dimension, see Merethe Dotterud Leiren and Inken Reimer, "Historical Institutionalist Perspective on the Shift from Feed-in Tariffs Towards Auctioning in German Renewable Energy Policy," *Energy Research & Social Science* 43 (2018): 33–40.

109. See Cherp et al. 2017.

110. These measures are an inherent part of China's energy policy, but they also provide a template for "leap-frogging" high-carbon technologies. See Lewis 2012.

111. See Xi Lu et al., "Gasification of Coal and Biomass as a Net Carbon-Negative Power Source for Environment-Friendly Electricity Generation in China," *Proceedings of the National Academy of Sciences* 116 (2019): 8206–8213.

112. Kelly Simms Gallagher, *Key Opportunities for U.S.–China Cooperation on Coal and CCS* (Washington, DC: Brookings Institution; International Energy Agency, 2009); "5 Keys to Unlock CCS Investment," International Energy Agency, 2017; "CCUS in Industry & Transformation," International Energy Agency, 2019, https://www.iea.org/tcep/industry/ccs/.

113. This suggestion has been made perhaps most convincingly by John Helveston and Jonas Nahm, "China's Key Role in Scaling Low-Carbon Energy Technologies," *Science* 366, no. 6467 (2019): 794–796.

114. Arnaud De la Tour, Matthieu Glachant, and Yann Meniere, "Innovation and International Technology Transfer: The Case of the Chinese Photovoltaic Industry," *Energy Policy* 39 (2011): 764.

115. See Diane Cardwell, "China's Feud with West on Solar Leads to Tax," *New York Times*, July 18, 2013, https://www.nytimes.com/2013/07/19/business/energy-environment/chinas-feud-with-West-on-solar-leads-to-tax.html.

116. Office of the US Trade Representative, "President Trump Approves Relief for U.S. Washing Machine and Solar Cell Manufacturers," *USTR Press Office*, January 22, 2018, https://ustr.gov/about-us/policy-offices/press-office/press-releases/2018/january/president-trump-approves-relief-us.

117. Surana and Anadon 2015; Dan Prud'homme et al., "'Forced Technology Transfer' Policies: Workings in China and Strategic Implications," *Technological Forecasting & Social Change* 134 (2018): 150–168.

118. Frauke Urban, Yu Wang, and Sam Geall, "Prospects, Politics, and Practices of Solar Energy Innovation in China," *The Journal of Environment & Development* 27 (March 1, 2018): 74–98. doi:10.1177/1070496517749877. https://doi.org/10.1177/1070496517749877.

119. See Tom Mitchell, Demetri Sevastopulo, and Sun Yu, "China Targets Rare Earth Export Curbs to Hobble US Defence Industry," *Financial Times*, February 16, 2021, https://www.ft.com/content/d3ed83f4-19bc-4d16-b510-415749c032c1.

120. On the concentration of polysilicon production, see Jennifer Dlouhy, "How China Beat Three U.S. Presidents to Dominate the Solar Industry," *Bloomberg*, June 4, 2021, https://www.bloomberg.com/news/articles/2021-06-04/solar-jobs-2021-how-china-beat-u-s-to-become-world-s-solar-champion.

121. Cited by Scott Moore, "Why China's New Climate Commitments Matter for U.S. National Security," *Lawfare*, October 13, 2020, https://www.lawfareblog.com/why-chinas-new-climate-commitments-matter-us-national-security, using data from US Energy Information Agency.

122. John Kerry and Ro Khanna, "Don't Let China Win the Green Race," *New York Times*, December 9, 2019, https://www.nytimes.com/2019/12/09/opinion/china-renewable-energy.html.

123. Janka Oertel, Jennifer Tollmann, and Byford Tsang, "Climate Superpowers: How the EU and China Can Compete and Cooperate for a Green Future," European Council on Foreign Relations, December 3, 2020, https://ecfr.eu/publication/climate-superpowers-how-the-eu-and-china-can-compete-and-cooperate-for-a-green-future/.

124. World Bank 2020, 13.

125. See Edmund Downie, "Sparks Fly over Ultra-High Voltage Power Lines," *China Dialogue*, January 29, 2018, https://www.chinadialogue.net/article/show/single/en/10376-Sparks-fly-over-ultra-high-voltage-power-lines.

126. John Parnell, "New Chinese Solar Plant Undercuts Cost of Coal Power," *Forbes*, December 30, 2018, https://www.forbes.com/sites/johnparnell/2018/12/30/new-chinese-solar-plant-undercuts-cost-of-coal-power/.

127. "Overview—Mission Innovation," Mission Innovation, accessed March 22, 2019, http://mission-innovation.net/about-mi/overview/.

128. See Scott Moore, "The New Geopolitics of Climate Change," *The Diplomat*, December 1, 2020, https://thediplomat.com/2020/12/the-new-geopolitics-of-climate-change/.

129. Scott Moore, "The China Climate Challenge," *The Diplomat*, September 18, 2020, https://thediplomat.com/2020/09/the-china-climate-challenge/.

130. See Brian Eyler, Courtney Weatherby, and Regan Kwan, "New Evidence: How China Turned Off the Tap on the Mekong River," Stimson Center, April 13, 2020, https://www.stimson.org/2020/new-evidence-how-china-turned-off-the-mekong-tap/.

131. Narain et al. 2020 report that of 65 BRI financiers, only 17 require biodiversity impact measures.

132. This characterization based on multiple author interactions with US, Chinese, and European officials throughout early 2021.

133. Urban 2018.

134. See Office of the Spokesperson, "China Joins the Global Alliance for Clean Cookstoves," US Department of State, May 3, 2012, https://2009-2017.state.gov/r/pa/prs/ps/2012/05/189275.htm.

135. See Ellen Gilmer and Michael Standaert, "Coronavirus Prompts China to Change Environment Law on Wildlife," *Bloomberg Law*, February 27, 2020, https://news.bloomberglaw.com/environment-and-energy/coronavirus-prompts-china-to-change-environment-law-on-wildlife.

136. Elizabeth Fitt, "China Issues New Sustainability Rules for Its Notorious Fishing Fleet," *Mongabay Environmental News*, August 14, 2020, https://news.mongabay.com/2020/08/china-issues-new-sustainability-rules-for-its-notorious-fishing-fleet/.

137. Kylie Knott, "Jackie Chan, Yao Ming Back Ad Campaign against Illegal Wildlife Trade," *South China Morning Post*, March 14, 2018, https://www.scmp.com/lifestyle/article/2137101/jackie-chan-yao-ming-back-ad-campaign-against-illegal-wildlife-trade.

138. Fabinyi et al. 2016.

139. Peter Tait et al., "Emerging Versus Developed Economy Consumer Willingness to Pay for Environmentally Sustainable Food Production: A Choice Experiment Approach Comparing Indian, Chinese and United Kingdom Lamb Consumers," *Journal of Cleaner Production* 124 (2016): 65–72.

140. Zhuo La, Mesfin Mekonnen, and Arjen Hoekstra, "Consumptive Water Footprint and Virtual Water Trade Scenarios for China—with a Focus on Crop Production, Consumption and Trade," *Environment International* 94 (2016): 211–223.

141. See Jonathan Woetzel, "Three Things China Can Do to Fight Climate Change," McKinsey & Company, September 1, 2020, https://www.mckinsey.com/business-functions/sustainability/our-insights/sustainability-blog/three-things-china-can-do-to-fight-climate-change.

Chapter 4

1. Jennifer Harbaugh, "Biography of Wernher Von Braun," NASA, February 18, 2016, http://www.nasa.gov/centers/marshall/history/vonbraun/bio.html.

2. "Qian Xuesen," Caltech Department of Aerospace, accessed April 11, 2019, http://galcit.caltech.edu/about/qian. On the connection to von Braun, see Michael Wines, "Qian Xuesen, Father of China's Space Program, Dies at 98," *New York Times*, November 3, 2009, https://www.nytimes.com/2009/11/04/world/asia/04qian.html.

3. Caltech Department of Aerospace 2019.

4. Cited by Yelong Han, "An Untold Story: American Policy Toward Chinese Students in the United States, 1949–1955," *The Journal of American-East Asian Relations* 2, no. 1 (1993): 80.

5. Han 1993, 94.

6. Quoted by Zouyue Wang, "Transnational Science during the Cold War the Case of Chinese/American Scientists," *Isis* 101 (2010): 373.

7. Han 1993, 90.

8. Han 1993, 90.

9. Wang 2010.

10. Han 1993.

11. Han 1993.

12. Wang 2010, 373.

13. Cited by Yingyi Ma, *Ambitious and Anxious: How Chinese College Students Succeed and Struggle in American Higher Education* (New York: Columbia University Press, 2020), 53.

14. Quoted in Xiaojuan Zhou, "The Influences of the American Boxer Indemnity Reparations Remissions on Chinese Higher Education," *Educational Administration: Theses, Dissertations, and Student Research* 189 (2014): 20–21.

15. Quoted in Zhou 2014, 20–21.

16. Zhou 2014, 51–56.

17. Han 1993.

18. "2017 Sees Increase in Number of Chinese Students Studying Abroad and Returning after Overseas Studies," Ministry of Education of the People's Republic of China, April 3, 2018, http://en.moe.gov.cn/News/Top_News/201804/t20180404_332354.html.

19. Ministry of Education of the People's Republic of China, 2018.

20. Tea Leaf Nation, "The Most Chinese Schools in America," *Foreign Policy*, January 4, 2016, https://foreignpolicy.com/2016/01/04/the-most-chinese-schools-in-america-rankings-data-education-china-u/.

21. Judy Chu and Pramila Jayapal, "Restoring Fairness for Chinese International Students," National Association of Foreign Student Advisers, October 2020, https://www.nafsa.org/policy-and-advocacy/what-we-stand-for/dear-colleague-letter-restoring-fairness-chinese-international-students.

22. Daniel Goodkind, "The Chinese Diaspora: Historical Legacies and Contemporary Trends," United States Census Bureau, August 2019, https://www.census.gov/content/dam/Census/library/working-papers/2019/demo/Chinese_Diaspora.pdf.

23. "CASS Report: Number of Overseas Chinese Up to 35 Mln," Embassy of the People's Republic of China in the United States of America, 2007, http://www.china-embassy.org/eng/qwgz/t297510.htm.

24. Goodkind 2019, 13.

25. "China's Overseas Workforce Rises in the First Three Quarters," *Xinhua*, November 3, 2019, http://www.xinhuanet.com/english/2019-11/03/c_138525814.htm.

26. Cited by Goodkind 2019, 10.

27. See Joseph Stiglitz, "Knowledge as a Public Good," in *Global Public Goods: International Cooperation in the 21st Century*, ed. Inge Kaul, Isabelle Grunberg, and Marc Stern (New York: Oxford University Press, 1999).

28. See Loveday Morris, "Their Coronavirus Vaccine Candidate Has Made Them Billionaires. This Modest German Turkish Couple Doesn't Own a Car," *Washington Post*, November 12, 2020, https://www.washingtonpost.com/world/europe/coornavirus-vaccine-biontech-pfizer/2020/11/12/37acb78c-2467-11eb-9c4a-0dc6242c4814_story.html.

29. On how Chinese migrants embody transnational human capital, see David Zweig, Chen Changgui, and Stanley Rosen, "Globalization and Transitional Human

Capital: Overseas and Returnee Scholars to China," *The China Quarterly* 179 (2004): 735–757. See also Jarim Kim, "Public Relations and Public Diplomacy in Cultural and Educational Exchange Programs: A Coorientational Approach to the Humphrey Program," *Public Relations Review* 42, no. 1 (2016): 135–145.

30. K. M. Bourne, "The Shanghai Municipal Police: Chinese Uniform Branch," *The Police Journal* 2, no. 1 (1929): 30.

31. Quoted in "Chinese Police Removed after Row in Zambia," *British Broadcasting Company*, December 19, 2017, https://www.bbc.com/news/world-africa-42413330.

32. Though there were several anti-Chinese pogroms in the twentieth century, several scholars argue that an outbreak of violence in 1965–1966 can properly be termed a genocide against Indonesian Chinese communities. See Jess Melvin, "Why Not Genocide? Anti-Chinese Violence in Aceh, 1965–1966," *Journal of Current Southeast Asian Affairs* 32, no. 3 (2013): 63–91.

33. Described in Heidi Østbø Haugen and Jørgen Carling, "On the Edge of the Chinese Diaspora: The Surge of Baihuo Business in an African City," *Ethnic and Racial Studies* 28, no. 4 (2005): 639–662.

34. Haugen and Carling 2005.

35. See Jonathan Sullivan and Jing Cheng, "Contextualising Chinese Migration to Africa," *Journal of Asian and African Studies* 53, no. 8 (2018): 1173–1187.

36. Quoted by Huifeng He, "Chinese Manufacturers Keep Silent on Trade War, Fearing Retaliation," *South China Morning Post*, May 16, 2019, https://www.scmp.com/economy/china-economy/article/3010530/chinese-companies-moving-vietnam-keep-quiet-trade-war-avoid.

37. On the history of these concerns, and especially the Wen Ho Lee case, see Richard P. Suttmeier. "State, Self-Organization, and Identity in the Building of Sino-U.S. Cooperation in Science and Technology," *Asian Perspective* 32, no. 1 (2008): 5–31.

38. Patricia Zengerle and Matt Spetalnick, "Exclusive: Fearing Espionage, U.S. Weighs Tighter Rules on Chinese," *Reuters*, November 29, 2018, https://www.reuters.com/article/us-usa-china-students-exclusive-idUSKCN1NY1HE.

39. US Government Accountability Office, *Long-Range Emerging Threats Facing the United States as Identified by Federal Agencies* (Washington, DC: US Government Printing Office, 2018); Benjamin Wermund, "Chinese-Funded Institutes on U.S. College Campuses Condemned in Senate Report," *Politico*, February 27, 2019, https://www.politico.com/story/2019/02/27/china-college-confucius-institutes-1221768.

40. Ma 2020.

41. US Government Accountability Office 2019; Wermund 2019.

42. For an account of these often-false suspicions, see Peter Waldman, "The U.S. Is Purging Chinese Cancer Researchers from Top Institutions," *Bloomberg Businessweek*, June 13, 2019, https://www.bloomberg.com/news/features/2019-06-13/the-u-s-is-purging-chinese-americans-from-top-cancer-research.

43. See Eric Fish, "Chinese Students Overseas Face Depression and Disillusionment," *South China Morning Post*, February 3, 2018, https://www.scmp.com/magazines/post-magazine/long-reads/article/2131738/how-chinese-overseas-students-are-learning-harsh.

44. This incident described by Simon Denyer and Congcong Zhang, "A Chinese Student Praised the 'Fresh Air of Free Speech' at a U.S. College. Then Came the Backlash," *Washington Post*, May 23, 2017, https://www.washingtonpost.com/news/worldvi ews/wp/2017/05/23/a-chinese-student-praised-the-fresh-air-of-free-speech-at-a-u-s-college-then-came-the-backlash/.

45. Described by Gerry Shih and Emily Rauhala, "Angry over Campus Speech by Uighur Activist, Chinese Students in Canada Contact Their Consulate, Film Presentation," *Washington Post*, February 14, 2019, https://www.washingtonpost.com/world/ angry-over-campus-speech-by-uighur-activist-students-in-canada-contact-chin ese-consulate-film-presentation/2019/02/14/a442fbe4-306d-11e9-ac6c-14eea99 d5e24_story.html.

46. Center on Religion and Chinese Society, "Purdue Survey of Chinese Students in the United States: A General Report," Purdue University, November 15, 2016.

47. Fish 2018.

48. Center on Religion and Chinese Society 2016. The statement regarding COVID-19 is based on the author's personal experience in supporting Chinese students at the University of Pennsylvania.

49. Ma 2020.

50. Ma 2020, 228.

51. Yingjie Fan et al., "How Discrimination Increases Chinese Overseas Students' Support for Authoritarian Rule," 21st Century China Center Research Paper No. 2020-05, June 30, 2020.

52. Quoted by Patrick Tucker, "Chinese Students Are Key to US National Security, Eric Schmidt Says," *Defense One*, June 17, 2020, https://www.defenseone.com/technol ogy/2020/06/chinese-students-are-key-us-national-security-eric-schmidt-says/ 166212/.

53. Ma 2020, 228.

54. Jeffrey Mervis, "Bipartisan Bill Would Create Forum for Discussing How to Counter U.S. Academic Espionage," *Science | AAAS*, May 30, 2019, https://www.sciencemag. org/news/2019/05/bipartisan-bill-would-create-forum-discussing-how-counter-us-academic-espionage.

55. Quoted in Shannon Ellis, "Biotech Booms in China," *Nature* 553 (2018): S19–S22.

56. Quoted in Ellis 2018.

57. Joseph Needham, *Science and Civilisation in China*. Volume 1: *Introductory Orientations* (Cambridge, UK: Cambridge University Press, 1954).

58. Caroline S. Wagner and Loet Leydesdorff, "Network Structure, Self-Organization, and the Growth of International Collaboration in Science," *Research Policy* 34, no. 10 (2005): 1608–1618. doi:https://doi.org/10.1016/j.respol.2005.08.002. https://www. sciencedirect.com/science/article/pii/S0048733305001745.

59. Leonardo Costa Ribeiro, Marcia Siqueira Rapini, Leandro Alves Silva, and Eduardo Motta Albuquerque, "Growth Patterns of the Network of International Collaboration in Science," *Scientometrics* 114 (2018): 159–179. https://link.springer.com/article/ 10.1007/s11192-017-2573-x.

60. Ricky Leung, "Networks as Sponges: International Collaboration for Developing Nanomedicine in China," *Research Policy* 42 (2013): 212.

61. This discussion is not to elide the fact that ethnic and national identity plays an important role in the collaboration of international scientific networks. In the world of science, the world is not "flat." For a compelling discussion of the role of ethnic and national identity in US–China science networks, see Suttmeier 2008.

62. Caroline S. Wagner, Travis A. Whetsell, and Loet Leydesdorff, "Growth of International Collaboration in Science: Revisiting Six Specialties," *Scientometrics* 110, no. 3 (2017): 1633–1652. doi:10.1007/s11192-016-2230-9. https://doi.org/10.1007/s11192-016-2230-9, 1634.

63. F. Barjak and S. Robinson, "International Collaboration, Mobility and Team Diversity in the Life Sciences: Impact on Research Performance," *Social Geography* 3, no. 1 (2008): 30. However, the paper's model suggests that the optimum level of citizenship diversity for maximizing publication output is moderate rather than high.

64. Giuseppe Scellato, Chiara Franzoni, and Paula Stephan, "A Mobility Boost for Research," *Science* 356, no. 6339 (2017): 694.

65. David Tyfield, Yongguan Zhu, and Jinghua Cao, "The Importance of the 'International Collaboration Dividend': The Case of China," *Science and Public Policy* 36, no. 9 (2009): 723–735.

66. Rune Dahl Fitjar and Franz Huber, "Global Pipelines for Innovation: Insights from the Case of Norway," *Journal of Economic Geography* 15 (2015): 561–583.

67. Holger Graf and Martin Kalthaus, "International Research Networks: Determinants of Country Embeddedness," *Research Policy, Elsevier* 47, no. 7 (2018): 1198.

68. Sebastian Pfotenhauer et al., "Architecting Complex International Science, Technology and Innovation Partnerships (CISTIPs): A Study of Four Global MIT Collaborations," *Technological Forecasting and Social Change* 104 (2016): 38–56.

69. Jiawen Wang and Qiuyu Ren, "China Is Top Producer of AI Papers, but Researchers Are 'Isolated,'" *Caixin Global*, January 17, 2019, https://www.caixinglobal.com/2019-01-17/china-is-top-producer-of-ai-papers-but-researchers-are-isolated-101371163.html.

70. Tufool Alnuaimi, Jasjit Singh, and Gerard George, "Not with My Own: Long-Term Effects of Cross-Country Collaboration on Subsidiary Innovation in Emerging Economies Versus Advanced Economies," *Journal of Economic Geography* 12 (2012): 956.

71. Fitjar and Huber 2015, 562. See also Alicia Rodriguez, Maria Jesus Nieto, and Luis Santamaria, "International Collaboration and Innovation in Professional and Technological Knowledge-Intensive Services," *Industry and Innovation* 25, no. 4 (2018): 408–431.

72. Li Tang and Philip Shapira, "China-US Scientific Collaboration in Nanotechnology: Patterns and Dynamics," *Scientometrics* 88 (2011): 2.

73. From 1997 to 2013, China's share of US international collaboration papers increased from 35% to 47.8%. See Richard B. Freeman and Wei Huang, *China's "Great Leap Forward" in Science and Engineering* (San Diego, CA: National Bureau of Economic Research, 2015). doi:10.3386/w21081. https://www.nber.org/papers/w21081.165.

74. Tang and Shapria 2011, 6.

75. Jenny J. Lee and John P. Haupt, "Winners and Losers in US-China Scientific Research Collaborations," *Higher Education* 80, no. 1 (2020): 57–74. doi:10.1007/s10734-019-00464-7. https://doi.org/10.1007/s10734-019-00464-7.

76. Jenny J. Lee and John P. Haupt, "Scientific Collaboration on COVID-19 Amidst Geopolitical Tensions between the US and China," *The Journal of Higher Education* 92, no. 2 (2021): 303–329. doi:10.1080/00221546.2020.1827924. https://doi.org/10.1080/00221546.2020.1827924.

77. An extensive literature explores the role that different types of scientists play in building collaborative networks. For a useful discussion in the context of China, see Suttmeier 2008.

78. Leonardo Costa Ribeiro, Marcia Siqueira Rapini, Leandro Alves Silva, and Eduardo Motta Albuquerque, "Growth Patterns of the Network of International Collaboration in Science," *Scientometrics* 114 (2018): 159–179. https://link.springer.com/article/10.1007/s11192-017-2573-x.

79. Marcio L. Rodrigues, Leonardo Nimrichter, and Radames Cordero, "The Benefits of Scientific Mobility and International Collaboration," *FEMS Microbiology Letters* 363 (2016): 1–5.

80. Rodrigues, Nimrichter, and Cordero 2016.

81. Scellato, Franzoni, and Stephan 2017, 694.

82. Richard Freeman, "Migration of Ideas: China and U.S.," *Science* 356, no. 6339 (2017): 696.

83. Giulio Cimini, Andrea Zaccaria, and Andrea Gabrielli, "Investigating the Interplay between Fundamentals of National Research Systems: Performance, Investments and International Collaborations," *Journal of Informetrics* 10, no. 1 (2016): 205.

84. See Stefan Hennemann, Diego Rybski, and Ingo Liefner, "The Myth of Global Science Collaboration: Collaboration Patterns in Epistemic Communities," *Journal of Informetrics* 6 (2012): 218; Pardeep Sud and Mike Thelwall, "Not All International Collaboration Is Beneficial: The Mendeley Readership and Citation Impact of Biochemical Research Collaboration," *Journal of the Association for Information Science & Technology* 67, no. 8 (2016): 1854.

85. Freeman and Huang 2015, 161.

86. Elizabeth Redden, "Foreign Students and Graduate STEM Enrollment | Inside Higher Ed," *Inside Higher Ed*, October 11, 2017, https://www.insidehighered.com/quicktakes/2017/10/11/foreign-students-and-graduate-stem-enrollment

87. Freeman and Huang 2015, 161.

88. Freeman and Huang 2015, 161.

89. Quoted by Tucker 2020.

90. Freeman and Huang 2015.

91. Cited by Celia Chen, "Trade War Sees US Losing Chinese Students to UK, Canada and Australia," *South China Morning Post*, May 28, 2019, https://www.scmp.com/tech/policy/article/3011956/trade-war-turning-chinese-students-us-many-opting-uk-canada-and.

92. Teresa Watanabe and Don Lee, "Trump Is Cracking Down on China. Now UC Campuses Are Paying the Price," *Los Angeles Times*, July 22, 2019, https://www.lati mes.com/california/story/2019-07-21/uc-china-trump-trade-visa.

93. Zengerle and Spetalnick 2018.

94. Cited and quoted by Jordan Schneider, "How Bad US Immigration Policy Helps China Get Ahead," *ChinaTalk*, July 8, 2020, https://chinatalk.substack.com/p/how-bad-us-immigration-policy-helps.

95. Alexandra Yoon-Hendricks, "Visa Restrictions for Chinese Students Alarm Academia," *New York Times*, August 7, 2018, https://www.nytimes.com/2018/07/25/us/politics/visa-restrictions-chinese-students.html.

96. Jeff Tollefson, "Chinese American Scientists Uneasy amid Crackdown on Foreign Influence," *Nature* 570, no. 7759 (2019): 13–14.

97. Quoted by Watanabe and Lee 2019.

98. Jane Perlez, "Citing Spying Fears, F.B.I. Curbs Visits to U.S. by Chinese Scholars," *New York Times*, April 15, 2019, https://www.nytimes.com/2019/04/14/world/asia/china-academics-fbi-visa-bans.html

99. Beijing had been concerned about the "brain drain" associated with so many students studying overseas since at least the early 1990s, and for decades pursued policies intended to harness the human capital of these overseas migrants. In the twenty-first century, though, the focus appeared to shift more toward luring highly talented students home while keeping others at home in the first place. On the history of these policies, see David Zweig, Chung Siu Fung, and Donglin Han, "Redefining the Brain Drain: China's 'Diaspora Option,'" *Science, Technology and Society* 13, no. 1 (2008): 1–33.

100. Personal communication with University of Pennsylvania visa official.

101. Cited by Goodkind 2019, 16.

102. Sidney Leng, "China 'Fooling Itself' in Thinking It Leads on Science and Tech," *South China Morning Post*, June 26, 2018, https://www.scmp.com/news/china/soci ety/article/2152617/china-must-stop-fooling-itself-it-world-leader-science-and;.

103. Quoted in Daniel Golden, *Spy Schools: How the CIA, FBI, and Foreign Intelligence Secretly Exploit America's Universities* (New York: Henry Holt, 2017), 18.

104. Cited by Kate O'Keefe and Aruna Viswanatha, "How China Targets Scientists via Global Network of Recruiting Stations," *Wall Street Journal*, August 20, 2020, https://www.wsj.com/articles/how-china-targets-scientists-via-global-network-of-recruiting-stations-11597915803.

105. On the modest effects of at least the early versions of talent programs, see Huiyao Wang and David Zweig, "Can China Bring Back the Best? The Communist Party Organizes China's Search for Talent," *The China Quarterly* no. 215 (2013): 590–615. http://www.jstor.org/stable/23510804.

106. In June 2019, the US government announced a ban on US Department of Energy scientists and researchers participating in talent programs. See Timothy Puko and Kate O'Keeffe, "U.S. Targets Efforts by China, Others to Recruit Government Scientists," *Wall Street Journal*, June 10, 2019, https://www.wsj.com/articles/ene

rgy-department-bans-personnel-from-foreign-talent-recruitment-programs-1156
0182546.

107. Insert quoted in Donnelle Eller, "Chinese-Backed Newspaper Insert Tries to
Undermine Iowa Farm Support for Trump, Trade War," *Des Moines Register*,
September 26, 2018, https://www.desmoinesregister.com/story/money/agricult
ure/2018/09/24/china-daily-watch-advertisement-tries-sway-iowa-farm-support-
trump-trade-war-tariffs/1412954002/.

108. Scott Paul, "Americans Know Blatant Propaganda When They See It," *Des Moines
Register*, September 28, 2018, https://www.desmoinesregister.com/story/opinion/
columnists/2018/09/28/china-advertisement-des-moines-register-newspaper-
trade-tariffs/1444579002/.

109. This story reported by Simon Montlake, "For Chinese High-Schoolers, There's
Value to Living and Learning in Iowa," *Christian Science Monitor*, October 4, 2018,
https://www.csmonitor.com/EqualEd/2018/1004/For-Chinese-high-schoolers-
there-s-value-to-living-and-learning-in-Iowa.

110. Kenneth Rapoza, "China-Like Wages Now Part of U.S. Employment Boom," *Forbes*,
August 4, 2017, https://www.forbes.com/sites/kenrapoza/2017/08/04/china-like-
wages-now-part-of-u-s-employment-boom/..

111. Avraham Ebenstein, Ann Harrison, and Margaret S. McMillan, *Why Are American
Workers Getting Poorer? China, Trade and Offshoring* (Cambridge: National Bureau
of Economic Research, 2015).

112. Freeman and Huang 2015, 170.

113. Quoted by PR Newswire, "Population Size and Immigration Policy Could Define
the Outcome of US-China Tech Race, Says Ctrip Executive Chairman James Liang,"
Yahoo Finance, August 22, 2019, https://finance.yahoo.com/news/population-size-
immigration-policy-could-043500584.html.

114. Asa Fitch, "U.S. Slows Hiring of Chinese Nationals by Chip Makers," *Wall Street
Journal*, May 21, 2019, https://www.wsj.com/articles/u-s-slows-hiring-of-chinese-
nationals-by-chip-makers-11558431000.

115. Jennifer Hunt, "Immigrant Patents Boost Growth," *Science* 356, no. 6339 (2017): 697.

116. Hunt 2017, 697.

117. Anonymous WeChat positing featured by Jordan Schneider, "How Bad US
Immigration Policy Helps China Get Ahead," accessed December 22, 2020, https://
chinatalk.substack.com/p/how-bad-us-immigration-policy-helps.

118. Michael Roach, Henry Sauermann, and John Skrentny, "U.S. Immigration Policies
and the STEM Entrepreneurial Workforce," National Bureau of Economic Research,
April 27, 2018, https://conference.nber.org/conf_papers/f102080/f102080.pdf.

119. Caglar Ozden, "Moving for Prosperity: Global Migration and Labor Markets,"
World Bank, June 15, 2018, 238, http://www.worldbank.org/en/research/publicat
ion/moving-for-prosperity.

120. See Darrell M. West, "Assessing Trump's Artificial Intelligence Executive Order,"
Brookings, February 12, 2019, https://www.brookings.edu/blog/techtank/2019/02/
12/assessing-trumps-artificial-intelligence-executive-order/.

121. Oren Etzioni, "What Trump's Executive Order on AI Is Missing," *Wired*, February 13, 2019, https://www.wired.com/story/what-trumps-executive-order-on-ai-is-missing/.

122. "Artificial Intelligence | Data USA," *Data USA*, 2016, https://datausa.io/profile/cip/artificial-intelligence.

123. See survey of submissions to one highly-competitive AI conference in 2018 conducted by Joy D. Ma, "The AI Race Is Wide Open, if America Remains Open," *MacroPolo*, April 15, 2019, https://macropolo.org/us-china-ai-race-talent/.

124. Etzioni 2019.

125. "Final Report," National Security Commission on Artificial Intelligence, March 2021, https://www.nscai.gov/wp-content/uploads/2021/03/Full-Report-Digital-1.pdf.

126. Elissa Strome, "Annual Report of the CIFAR Pan-Canadian Artificial Intelligence Strategy," Canadian Institute for Advanced Research, 2019, 4, https://cifar.ca/wp-content/uploads/2020/04/ai_annualreport2019_web.pdf.

127. US Department of Defense, "Summary of the 2018 Departments of Defense Artificial Intelligence Strategy," *Department of Defense*, January 2018, https://media.defense.gov/2019/Feb/12/2002088963/-1/-1/1/SUMMARY-OF-DOD-AI-STRATEGY.PDF.

128. See Partnership on AI, "Visa Laws, Policies, and Practices: Recommendations for Accelerating the Mobility of Global AI/ML Talent," September 2019, https://www.partnershiponai.org/visa-laws-policies-and-practices-recommendations-for-accelerating-the-mobility-of-global-ai-ml-talent/.

129. Sangyoon Yi and Jinho Choi, "The Organization of Scientific Knowledge: The Structural Characteristics of Keyword Networks," *Scientometrics* 90, no. 3 (2012): 1015–1026, https://akjournals.com/view/journals/11192/90/3/article-p1015.xml, 27.

130. Igor Linkov, Sankar Basu, Cathleen Fisher, Nancy Jackson, Adam C. Jones, Maija M. Kuklja, and Benjamin D. Trump, "Diplomacy for Science: Strategies to Promote International Collaboration," *Environment Systems and Decisions* 36, no. 4 (2016): 331–334, https://doi.org/10.1007/s10669-016-9614-5.

131. Han Zhang, "Leave China, Study in America, Find Jesus," *Foreign Policy*, February 11, 2016, https://foreignpolicy.com/2016/02/11/leave-china-study-in-america-find-jesus-chinese-christian-converts-at-american-universities/.

132. Helen Spencer-Oatey, Daniel Dauber, Jing, and Lifei Wang, "Chinese Students' Social Integration into the University Community: Hearing the Students' Voices," *Higher Education* 74, no. 5 (November 2017): 739–756.

133. This point is made by Ma 2020.

134. Ki-Seok Kwon et al., "Has Globalization Strengthened South Korea's National Research System? National and International Dynamics of the Triple Helix of Scientific Co-Authorship Relationships in South Korea," *Scientometrics* 90 (2012): 174.

135. Yun Liu et al., "Multilevel Analysis of International Scientific Collaboration Network in the Influenza Virus Vaccine Field: 2006–2013," *Sustainability* 10, no. 1032 (2018): 8.

136. Marion Frenz and Grazia Ietto-Gillies, "The Impact on Innovation Performance of Different Sources of Knowledge: Evidence from the UK Community Innovation Survey," *Research Policy* 38 (2009): 1132–1133.

137. Fitjar and Huber 2015, 563.

138. For a summary of these trends, see Jacques Bughin and Jonathan Woetzel, "Global Trends: Navigating a World of Disruption | McKinsey," *McKinsey Global Institute*, January 22, 2019, https://www.mckinsey.com/featured-insights/innovation-and-growth/navigating-a-world-of-disruption.

139. These shortcomings were referenced by a variety of officials and organizations in the 2018–2020 period, including by the National Security Commission on Artificial Intelligence and in multiple interviews conducted by the author.

140. Bughin and Woetzel 2019.

141. Barbara Schulte, "Innovation and Control: Universities, the Knowledge Economy and the Authoritarian State in China," *Nordic Journal of Studies in Educational Policy* 5, no. 1 (2019): 34.

142. Ma 2020, 108.

143. See, for example, Weiguo Pang and Jonathan A. Plucker, "Recent Transformations in China's Economic, Social, and Education Policies for Promoting Innovation and Creativity," *The Journal of Creative Behavior* 46, no. 4 (2012): 247–273.

144. Cited in Wayne Cascio and John Boudreau, "The Search for Global Competence: From International HR to Talent Management," *The Search for Global Competence: From International HR to Talent Management* 51, no. 1 (2016): 111–112.

Chapter 5

1. These details were compiled from James Fincannon, "Six Flags on the Moon: What Is Their Current Condition?" *Apollo Lunar Surface Journal*, April 21, 2012, https://www.hq.nasa.gov/alsj/ApolloFlags-Condition.html, and Sebastian Kettley, "Moon Landing Shock: Buzz Aldrin Planted a Swiss Flag before Unfurling the American Banner," *Express.co.uk*, July 24, 2019, https://www.express.co.uk/news/science/1156343/Moon-landing-Buzz-Aldrin-Swiss-flag-Apollo-11-American-US-flag-space-NASA-news.

2. Xinhuawang, "国家航天局公布嫦娥五号月表国旗展示照片 [National Space Agency Releases Photo of Chang'e 5 Displaying the National Flag]," *Xinhua*, December 4, 2020, 国家航天局公布嫦娥五号月表国旗展示照片.

3. Steven Lee Myers and Zoe Mou, "'New Chapter' in Space Exploration as China Reaches Far Side of the Moon," *New York Times*, January 2, 2019, https://www.nytimes.com/2019/01/02/world/asia/china-change-4-moon.html.

4. Dustin Volz and Warren P. Strobel, "China and Russia, Aligned More Closely, Seen as Chief Security Threat to U.S.," *Wall Street Journal*, January 29, 2019, https://www.wsj.com/articles/allies-seeking-more-independence-from-u-s-intelligence-leaders-warn-11548773031.

5. Peoples 2008, 61.

6. Columba Peoples, "Sputnik and 'Skill Thinking' Revisited: Technological Determinism in American Responses to the Soviet Missile Threat," *Cold War History* 8, no. 1 (2008): 55–75.

7. Kai-Fu Lee, "Why China Can Do AI More Quickly and Effectively than the US," *Wired*, October 23, 2018, https://www.wired.com/story/why-china-can-do-ai-more-quickly-and-effectively-than-the-us/.

8. "国务院关于印发《中国制造2025》的通知　[Notice of the State Council on Printing and Distributing "Made in China 2025" (Guo Fa [2015] no. 28)]," Guowuyuan [State Council], May 8, 2015, http://www.gov.cn/zhengce/content/2015-05/19/content_9784.htm.

9. Xiang Li, ""中国制造2025"：从网红到敏感词 | 专题 [Made in China 2025: From Patriotic Buzzword to Taboo]," *Radio Free Asia*, July 30, 2018, https://www.rfa.org/mandarin/duomeiti/tebiejiemu/zt-07302018165745.html.

10. See Arie Lewin, Martin Kenney, and Johann Peter Murmann, "China's Innovation Challenge: An Introduction," in *China's Innovation Challenge: Overcoming the Middle-Income Trap*, ed. Arie Lewin, Martin Kenney, and Johann Peter Murmann (New York: Cambridge University Press, 2016), 1–33.

11. Quoted by Lewin, Kenney, and Murmann 2016, 8.

12. Xinhuawang [Xinhua Net] 2020.

13. Robert D. Atkinson and Caleb Foote, "Is China Catching Up to the United States in Innovation?," Information Technology & Innovation Foundation, April 8, 2019, 4.

14. Office of the US Trade Representative, "President Trump Approves Relief for U.S. Washing Machine and Solar Cell Manufacturers," USTR Press Office, January 22, 2018, /about-us/policy-offices/press-office/press-releases/2018/january/president-trump-approves-relief-us.

15. "EU-China: A Strategic Outlook," European Commission, 2019.

16. A good overview of China's scientific and technological development in the 1970s and 1980s can be found in Denis Fred Simon and Merle Goldman, eds., *Science and Technology in Post-Mao China* (London: Harvard University Asia Center, 1989).

17. Compilation and Translation Bureau, and Central Committee of the Communist Party of China, "The 13th Five-Year Plan for Economic and Social Development of the People's Republic of China," Central Compilation & Translation Press, 2016.

18. China Power Team, "Is China a Global Leader in Research and Development?" China Power, January 31, 2018, https://chinapower.csis.org/china-research-and-development-rnd/

19. CSIS 2018.

20. World Bank, "Research and Development Expenditure (% of GDP)," World Bank Data, 2019, https://data.worldbank.org/indicator/gb.xpd.rsdv.gd.zs.

21. "Promoting Innovation in China," Washington, DC: World Bank, 2020.

22. Aihua Chen, Donald Patton, and Martin Kenney, "University Technology Transfer in China: A Literature Review and Taxonomy," *The Journal of Technology Transfer* 41, no. 5 (2016): 891–929.

23. Richard B. Freeman and Wei Huang, "China's 'Great Leap Forward' in Science and Engineering," San Diego, CA: National Bureau of Economic Research, 2015, 155, https://www.nber.org/papers/w21081.

24. National Science Board, "Science and Engineering Indicators 2018," National Science Foundation, 2018, https://nsf.gov/statistics/2018/nsb20181/.

25. Lewin, Kenney, and Murmann 2016.

26. See Cong Cao, "Progress and Challenges for Science and Technology in China," *East Asia Forum*, December 27, 2019, https://www.eastasiaforum.org/2019/12/27/progress-and-challenges-for-science-and-technology-in-china/.

27. I am indebted to a paper written by Ria Jain for the Spring 2021 class "China and the World in the 21st Century" at the University of Pennsylvania for these points, citing sources including Fuller 2020 (see next citation).

28. Douglas B. Fuller, "Cutting Off Our Nose to Spite Our Face: US Policy towards China in Key Semiconductor Industry Inputs, Capital Equipment and Electronic Design Automation Tools," JHU APL Two Worlds Working Paper Series, August 12, 2020.

29. See "Final Report," National Security Commission on Artificial Intelligence, March 2021, https://www.nscai.gov/wp-content/uploads/2021/03/Full-Report-Digital-1.pdf.

30. Richard Danzig and Lorand Laskai, "Symbiosis and Strife: Where Is the Sino–American Relationship Bound?" An Introduction to the APL Series "Measure Twice, Cut Once: Assessing Some China–US Technology Connections," The Johns Hopkins University Applied Physics Laboratory, 2020.

31. Reuters Staff, "China Semiconductor Trade Association Establishes Work Group with U.S. Counterpart." *Reuters*, March 11, 2021, https://www.reuters.com/article/us-china-semicons-us-idUSKBN2B315T.

32. Guowuyuan 2015.

33. National Science Board 2018.

34. Hepeng Jia, "China's Citations Catching Up," *Nature Index*, November 30, 2017, https://www.natureindex.com/news-blog/chinas-citations-catching-up.

35. Xiaoli Tang and Jian Du, "The Performance of China's Biomedical Innovation: A Scientometric Analysis," *Science China Life Sciences*, 2016: 1074–1082.

36. Barbara Schulte, "Innovation and Control: Universities, the Knowledge Economy and the Authoritarian State in China," *Nordic Journal of Studies in Educational Policy* 5, no. 1 (2019): 30–42.

37. Ricky Leung, "Networks as Sponges: International Collaboration for Developing Nanomedicine in China," *Research Policy* 42 (2013): 212.

38. Jiawen Wang and Qiuyu Ren, "China Is Top Producer of AI Papers, but Researchers Are 'Isolated,'" *Caixin Global*, January 17, 2019, https://www.caixinglobal.com/2019-01-17/china-is-top-producer-of-ai-papers-but-researchers-are-isolated-101371163.html.

39. Wang and Ren 2019.

40. China Institute for Science and Technology Policy, "China AI Development Report 2018," Beijing, China: Tsinghua University, 2018.

41. Wang and Ren 2019.

42. Gregory Allen, "Understanding China's AI Strategy," Washington, DC: Center for a New American Security, 2019, https://www.cnas.org/publications/reports/unders tanding-chinas-ai-strategy.

43. Quoted by Luiza Savage and Nancy Scola, "'We Are Being Outspent. We Are Being Outpaced': Is America Ceding the Future of AI to China?" *Politico*, July 18, 2019, https://www.politico.com/story/2019/07/18/global-translations-ai-china-1598442.

44. World Intellectual Property Organization, "Global Innovation Index 2019: India Makes Major Gains as Switzerland, Sweden, U.S., Netherlands, U.K. Top Ranking; Trade Protectionism Poses Risks for Future Innovation," Global Innovation Index 2019, July 24, 2019, https://www.wipo.int/pressroom/en/articles/2019/article_0 008.html.

45. World Bank 2020, 5.

46. This point made by Derek Scissors, "China's Economic 'Miracle' in Context," American Enterprise Institute, August 26, 2019, https://www.aei.org/publication/chi nas-economic-miracle-in-context/.

47. Figures cited by Georgina Lee, "China's Share of Hi-Tech Unicorns Tiny Compared to US Start-Ups," *South China Morning Post*, March 26, 2019, https://www.scmp.com/ business/companies/article/3003248/china-no-match-us-unicorns-ai-big-data-and-robotics-it-continues.

48. Yingkai Tang and Kevin H. Zhang, "Absorptive Capacity and Benefits from FDI: Evidence from Chinese Manufactured Exports," *International Review of Economics & Finance* 42 (2016): 423–429.

49. Hua Liu and Ying Zhou, "On a Synergistic Operating Mechanism for China's Intellectual Property Public Policy System: A Study of China's Technology Transfer Policy System," *Social Sciences in China* 34 no. 1 (2013): 184–186.

50. Albert G. Z. Hu, Peng Zhang, and Lijing Zhao, "China as Number One? Evidence from China's most Recent Patenting Surge," *Journal of Development Economics* 124 (2017): 110.

51. Hu, Zhang, and Zhao 2017, 107.

52. Hu, Zhang, and Zhao 2017, 116.

53. World Bank 2020, 13–14.

54. I am indebted to a paper written by Alicia Lu for the Spring 2021 class "China and the World in the 21st Century" at the University of Pennsylvania for these points, citing sources including Lewin, Kenney, and Murmann 2016 (see citation below).

55. World Bank Open Data, "World Bank Open Data," World Bank Data, 2021, https:// data.worldbank.org/.

56. Paul Miesing, Mingfeng Tang, and Mingfang Li, "University Technology Transfer in China: How Effective Are National Centers?," in *Academic Entrepreneurship: Creating an Entrepreneurial Ecosystem*, ed. A. C. Corbett, J. A. Katz, and D. S. Siegel (Bingley, UK: Emerald Group, 2014), 115–136.

57. Chen, Patton, and Kenney 2016, 920.

58. Cited in Kai-Fu Lee, *AI Superpowers: China, Silicon Valley, and the New World Order* (Boston, MA: Houghton Mifflin Harcourt, 2018).

59. This was especially evident in the 14th Five Year Plan, first unveiled in 2021. See Damien Ma, "No GDP Target? Analyzing China Just Got Harder but More Interesting," March 22, 2021, https://macropolo.org/the-post-gdp-target-paradigm-analyzing-china/..

60. The commercial can be viewed on YouTube, Robert Cole, "Apple 1984 Super Bowl Commercial Introducing Macintosh Computer (HD)," June 25, 2010, Video, 1:03, https://youtu.be/2zfqw8nhUwA.

61. This trope, and its significance with respect to technological competition with China, is highlighted by Kaiser Kuo, "Fear of a Red Tech Planet—Why the U.S. Is Suddenly Afraid of Chinese Innovation," October 13, 2020, https://supchina.com/2020/10/13/fear-of-a-red-tech-planet-why-the-u-s-is-suddenly-afraid-of-chinese-innovation/.

62. This quotation and sequence of events from John Lewis Gaddis, *The Cold War: A New History* (New York: Penguin Press, 2005), 267–268.

63. Brendan Thomas-Noone, "Is China Set to Dominate over America in Quantum Computing and Artificial Intelligence?" The Center for the National Interest, July 17, 2018, https://nationalinterest.org/blog/buzz/china-set-dominate-over-america-quantum-computing-and-artificial-intelligence-25976.

64. Lewin, Kenney, and Murmann 2016.

65. Elise Brezis, Paul Krugman, and Daniel Tsiddon, "Leapfrogging in International Competition: A Theory of Cycles in National Technological Leadership," *American Economic Review* 83 (1993): 1211–1219.

66. See US Government Accountability Office, "Long-Range Emerging Threats Facing the United States as Identified by Federal Agencies," Washington, DC: US Government Printing Office, 2018.

67. Jan Fagerberg, Martin Srholec, and Mark Knell, "The Competitiveness of Nations: Why Some Countries Prosper While Others Fall Behind," *World Development* 35, no. 10 (2007): 1595–1620.

68. Pierre Papon, "The State and Technological Competition in France or Colbertism in the 20th Century," *Research Policy, Elsevier* 4, no. 3 (1975): 214–244.

69. See Yuen Yiu, "Is China the Leader in Quantum Communications?," *Inside Science*, January 19, 2018, https://www.insidescience.org/news/china-leader-quantum-communications; and Eleni Diamanti, "A Step Closer to Secure Global Communication," *Nature* 582, no. 7813 (2020): 494–495.

70. Juan Yin et al., "Entanglement-Based Secure Quantum Cryptography over 1,120 Kilometers," *Nature* 582, no. 7813 (2020): 501–505.

71. Yiu 2018.

72. Personal communication with Max Mintz, University of Pennsylvania.

73. Christine Fox, "An Entwined AI Future: Resistance Is Futile," Johns Hopkins University Applied Physics Laboratory, 2020.

74. Darrell M. West, "Assessing Trump's Artificial Intelligence Executive Order," *Brookings*, February 12, 2019, https://www.brookings.edu/blog/techtank/2019/02/12/assessing-trumps-artificial-intelligence-executive-order/.

75. Elsa Kania, "Learning without Fighting: New Developments in PLA Artificial Intelligence War-Gaming," *Jamestown China Brief* 19, no. 7 (2019).

76. "Summary of the 2018 Departments of Defense Artificial Intelligence Strategy," US Department of Defense, 2018, 5, http://parlinfo.aph.gov.au/parlInfo/search/display/display.w3p;query=library/jrnart/6506004.

77. Patrick Shafto, "Why Big Tech Companies Are Open-Sourcing their AI Systems," *The Conversation*, February 22, 2016, http://theconversation.com/why-big-tech-compan ies-are-open-sourcing-their-ai-systems-54437.

78. Christine Fox, "An Entwined AI Future: Resistance is Futile," Johns Hopkins Applied Physics Laboratory, 2020, https://www.jhuapl.edu/assessing-us-china-technology-connections/publications, 1.

79. This history is described in Dang dai Zhongguo cong shu bian; [Editorial bureau of the Modern China Collection], "Nie Rongzhen zhuan," Dang dai Zhongguo chu ban she: Xin hua shu dian jing xiao, 1994. Quotation from page 532.

80. The concept of military-civil fusion has come in for significant criticism for being easily oversimplified and mythologized. See Elsa B. Kania and Lorand Laskai, "Myths and Realities of China's Military-Civil Fusion Strategy," Center for a New American Security, January 28, 2021, https://www.cnas.org/publications/reports/myths-and-realities-of-chinas-military-civil-fusion-strategy.

81. Tang and Zhang 2016.

82. Danzig and Laskai 2020, 5.

83. Yu Zhou and Xielin Liu, "Evolution of Chinese State Policies on Innovation," in *China as an Innovation Nation*, ed. Yu Zhou, William Lazonick, and Yifei Sun (Oxford: Oxford University Press, 2016), 5.

84. Dangdai Zhongguo cong shu bijianbu 1994, 531–532.

85. Zhou and Liu 2016.

86. H. Ichikawa, "Strela-1, the First Soviet Computer: Political Success and Technological Failure," *IEEE Annals of the History of Computing* 28, no. 3 (2006): 18–31

87. Papon 1975, 217.

88. Papon 1975, 219.

89. Papon 1975, 217.

90. Papon 1975, 237.

91. Papon 1975, 230.

92. Lewis Siegelbaum, "Sputnik Goes to Brussels: The Exhibition of a Soviet Technological Wonder," *Journal of Contemporary History* 47, no. 1 (2012): 120–136.

93. World Bank 2020, 6–10.

94. Hua and Ying 2013, 187.

95. Hua and Ying 2013.

96. Li Tang and Philip Shapira, "China-US Scientific Collaboration in Nanotechnology: Patterns and Dynamics," *Scientometrics* 88 (2011): 9.

97. Li 2018.

98. Dennis Normille, "Surging R&D Spending in China Narrows Gap with United States," *Science | AAAS*, October 10, 2018, https://www.sciencemag.org/news/2018/10/surging-rd-spending-china-narrows-gap-united-states.

99. Quoted by Panos Mourdoukoutas, "China Is Closing the Innovation Gap with America," *Forbes*, January 22, 2019, https://www.forbes.com/sites/panosmourdo ukoutas/2019/01/22/china-is-closing-the-innovation-gap-with-america-bad-news-for-us-china-trade-war/.

100. This point is made by Jacky Wong and Nathaniel Taplin, "Will China's Tech Titans be Heavyweights or Overweights?," *Wall Street Journal*, June 5, 2019, https://www. wsj.com/articles/will-chinas-tech-titans-be-heavyweights-or-overweights-1155 9728804. When firms are excessively protected in domestic markets, they have few incentives to become globally competitive.

101. The White House. "Official White House Transcript of President Eisenhower's Press and Radio Conference #123," https://www.eisenhowerlibrary.gov/sites/defa ult/files/research/online-documents/sputnik/10-9-57.pdf; The White House, "Minutes of Cabinet Meeting," Eisenhower Library, December 2, 1957, https:// www.eisenhowerlibrary.gov/sites/default/files/research/online-documents/sput nik/12-2-57.pdf.

102. US National Science Board, "Statement Prepared by the National Science Board Regarding the Russian Satellite," accessed December 14, 2020, https://www.eisenh owerlibrary.gov/sites/default/files/research/online-documents/sputnik/10-1957-statement.pdf.

103. White House Office of the Staff Research Group, "Reaction to the Soviet Satellite: A Preliminary Evaluation," accessed December 14, 2020, https://www.eisenhowerlibr ary.gov/sites/default/files/research/online-documents/sputnik/reaction.pdf.

104. O. M. Gale, "Memorandum for Mr. McElroy," accessed December 14, 2020, https:// www.eisenhowerlibrary.gov/sites/default/files/research/online-documents/sput nik/4-14-58.pdf, 1.

105. John Thornhill, "From Sputnik to Brexit: The Case for Public Research Spending," December 23, 2019, https://www.ft.com/content/868fe300-2563-11ea-9a4f-963f0 ec7e134.

106. See David Ignatius, "Opinion | China's Application of AI should be a Sputnik Moment for the U.S. but Will It Be?," *Washington Post*, November 6, 2018, https:// www.washingtonpost.com/opinions/chinas-application-of-ai-should-be-a-sput nik-moment-for-the-us-but-will-it-be/2018/11/06/69132de4-e204-11e8-b759-3d88a5ce9e19_story.html.

107. Dwight Eisenhower, "Text of the Address by the President," accessed December 14, 2020, https://www.eisenhowerlibrary.gov/sites/default/files/research/online-documents/sputnik/11-7-57.pdf.

108. Dwight Eisenhower, "Text of the Address on 'Our Future Security,'" accessed December 14, 2020, https://www.eisenhowerlibrary.gov/sites/default/files/resea rch/online-documents/sputnik/11-13-57.pdf..

109. See Thornhill 2019.

110. Eisenhower, "Text of the Address on 'Our Future Security.'"

111. Joseph Needham, *Science and Civilization in China*, Vol. 2 (Cambridge, UK: Cambridge University Press; first edition, 1956), 579.

112. Trym Aleksander Eiterjord, "Liu Yadong, Mr. Science, and China's Shaky Modernity," *The Diplomat*, August 31, 2018, https://thediplomat.com/2018/09/liu-yadong-mr-science-and-chinas-shaky-modernity/.

113. "Stay Calm on Tech Gap between China, West," *Global Times*, June 24, 2018, http://www.globaltimes.cn/content/1108210.shtml.

114. "Chinese Editor Extols Western Tech, Splits Opinion," *Global Times*, June 24, 2018, http://www.globaltimes.cn/content/1108210.shtml.

115. Ben Blanchard, "Lack of Innovation Is 'Achilles Heel' for China's Economy, Xi Says," *Reuters*, May 16, 2019, https://www.reuters.com/article/us-china-politics-xi-idUSKCN1SM08G.

116. The question of China's relative technological and economic development relative to the West prior to the Industrial Revolution has been the subject of many articles. Justin Lin, for example, argued influentially that the size of China's population gave it the advantage in premodern technological development but fell behind as progress shifted more to experimentation and empirical observation, in which the West's post-Enlightenment principles gave it the advantage. See Justin Yifu Lin, "The Needham Puzzle," *Economic Development and Cultural Change* 43, no. 2 (1995): 276.

117. See Richard Nelson and Nathan Rosenberg, "Technical Innovation and National Systems," in *National Innovation Systems: A Comparative Analysis*, ed. Richard Nelson (New York: Oxford University Press, 1993), 3–29.

118. See Cornelia Storz and Sebastian Schäfer, *Institutional Diversity and Innovation: Continuing and Emerging Patterns in Japan and China* (London: Routledge, 2011).

119. Storz and Schafer 2011, 114–115.

120. Storz and Schafer 2011, 101–104.

121. Schulte 2019, 33.

122. Cited by Eva Xiao, "WSJ News Exclusive | Red Flags Raised over Chinese Research Published in Global Journals," *Wall Street Journal*, July 5, 2020, https://www.wsj.com/articles/chinese-research-papers-raise-doubts-fueling-global-questions-about-scientific-integrity-11593939600.

123. This relationship can nonetheless be complex; authoritarian countries are not necessarily less likely to encourage internet access, for example. See Javier Corrales and Frank Westhoff, "Information Technology Adoption and Political Regimes," *International Studies Quarterly* 50, no. 4 (2006): 911–933, and Sebastian Stier, "Internet Diffusion and Regime Type: Temporal Patterns in Technology Adoption," *Telecommunications Policy* 41, no. 1 (2017): 25–34.

124. Chen, Patton, and Kenney 2016, 896.

125. Hannah Beech, "China's Great Firewall Is Harming Innovation, Say Scholars," *Time*, June 2, 2016, http://time.com/4354665/china-great-firewall-innovation-online-censorship/.

126. Lester Ross, "China's New Research Rules Will Shackle Xi's Innovation Drive," *Nikkei Asian Review*, July 3, 2018, https://asia.nikkei.com/Opinion/China-s-new-research-rules-will-shackle-Xi-s-innovation-drive.

127. Elsa Kania, "China's Strategic Ambiguity and Shifting Approach to Lethal Autonomous Weapons Systems," *Lawfare*, April 17, 2018, https://www.lawfareblog.com/chinas-strategic-ambiguity-and-shifting-approach-lethal-autonomous-weapons-systems.

128. Beech 2016.

129. Quoted in Zen Soo and Iris Deng, "Chinese-Style, State-Led Innovation Does Work—Just Ask Silicon Valley," *South China Morning Post*, June 15, 2019, https://www.scmp.com/tech/start-ups/article/3014541/does-top-down-state-led-innovation-work-just-ask-silicon-valley.

130. Leung 2013, 215.

131. Chloe Taylor, "China to Place Government Officials Inside 100 Private Companies, Including Alibaba," *CNBC*, September 23, 2019, https://www.cnbc.com/2019/09/23/china-to-place-government-officials-in-100-companies-including-alibaba.html.

132. Jing Yang and Lingling Wei, "China's President Xi Jinping Personally Scuttled Jack Ma's Ant IPO," *Wall Street Journal*, November 12, 2020, https://www.wsj.com/articles/china-president-xi-jinping-halted-jack-ma-ant-ipo-11605203556.

133. Richard Foster, "China's Real Economic Problem. (Hint: It Has Nothing to Do with the Trade War)," *Fortune*, August 6, 2019, https://fortune.com/2019/08/06/causes-us-china-trade-war/.

134. Emily de la Bruyere and Nathan Picarsic, "Beijing's Innovation Strategy: Threat-Informed Acquisition for an Era of Great Power Competition," Naval Postgraduate School, April 28, 2020, 3.

135. Lee 2018, 2–3.

136. Lee 2018, 103.

137. Tang and Zhang 2016, 5.

138. Eugene Demaitre, "Robotics R&D Driven by Government Funding Worldwide, Says IFR Report," *The Robot Report*, June 8, 2020, https://www.businesswire.com/news/home/20200608005203/en.

139. Cited by Alexandre Tanzi, "China Far Outpaces America in Bringing Robots to Factories," *Bloomberg*, September 24, 2020, https://www.bloomberg.com/news/articles/2020-09-24/china-far-outpaces-america-in-bringing-robots-to-factories.

140. "Robot Investment Reaches Record 16.5 Billion USD—IFR Presents World Robotics," International Federation of Robotics, September 18, 2019, https://ifr.org/ifr-press-releases/news/robot-investment-reaches-record-16.5-billion-usd.

141. "Asia Pacific Service Robots Market | Growth, Trends, Forecasts (2020–2025)," Mordor Intelligence, 2020, https://www.mordorintelligence.com/industry-reports/asia-pacific-service-robots-market-industry.

142. Mai Tao, "Service Robotics Market Grows by 33 Percent in China," *Robotics & Automation News*, September 23, 2020, https://roboticsandautomationnews.com/2020/09/23/service-robotics-market-grows-by-33-percent-in-china/36663/.

143. Their critique is in fact a pithier and more provocative one: "The United States responds by investing more in basic R&D. Beijing siphons that R&D." See de la Bruyere and Picarsic 2020, 5.

144. Youngsun Jang, Youngjoo Ko, and So Young Kim, "Cultural Correlates of National Innovative Capacity: A Cross-National Analysis of National Culture and Innovation Rates," *Journal of Open Innovation: Technology, Market, and Complexity* 2, no. 23 (2016): https://doi.org/10.1186/s40852-016-0048-6.

145. Andrew Erickson, "Revisiting the U.S.–Soviet Space Race: Comparing Two Systems in Their Competition to Land a Man on the Moon," *Acta Astronautica* 148 (2018): 377.

146. Declan Butler, "Translational Research: Crossing the Valley of Death," *Nature* 453 (2008): 840–842.

147. Saqib Shamim et al., "Role of Big Data Management in Enhancing Big Data Decision-Making Capability and Quality among Chinese Firms: A Dynamic Capabilities View," *Information & Management* 56, no. 6 (2018): 103–135, find, for example, that in a study of over 100 Chinese firms most firms have tried to use big data but aren't able to do so effectively because of internal barriers to knowing what to do with the data.

148. This was one of several recommendations made by a group of faculty and staff from the University of Pennsylvania to the National Security Commission on Artificial Intelligence. See "Penn Input to National Security Commission on Artificial Intelligence," Penn Global and Perry World House, February 10, 2020, https://global.upenn.edu/perryworldhouse/news/penn-input-national-security-commission-artificial-intelligence.

Chapter 6

1. Information is a general term that encompasses data, usually defined more narrowly as a set of electrical signals. Digital data, the focus of this chapter, focuses more narrowly still as data expressed in binary form—the basis of most computing and modern telecommunications networks. The issues addressed in this chapter all concern aspects of digital data and information, namely how it is collected, transmitted, stored, and secured. I thank Aynne Kokas for underscoring the importance of these distinctions.

2. This fascinating case is described in Heidi Tworek, "How Not to Build a World Wireless Network: German-British Rivalry and Visions of Global Communications in the Early Twentieth Century," *History and Technology* 32, no. 2 (2016): 178–200, and Liz Finnegan, "Revisiting Telefunken" November 8, 2018, https://www.suffolkcountynews.net/suffolkcountynews/suffolkcountynews/stories/revisiting-telefunken-during,5101.

3. Tworek 2016; Finnegan 2018.

4. Theodore Moran, "Foreign Acquisitions and National Security: What Are Genuine Threats? What Are Implausible Worries?," in *Regulation of Foreign Investment: Challenges to International Harmonization*, ed. Drabek Zdenek and Petros Mavroidis (Singapore: World Scientific, 2013), 371–394.

5. See Stu Woo, "Major Mobile Carrier Halts Huawei Purchases Amid Security Concerns," *Wall Street Journal*, January 25, 2019, https://www.wsj.com/articles/major-mobile-carrier-halts-huawei-purchases-amid-security-concerns-11548418611.

6. Michael Shoebridge, "Chinese Cyber Espionage and the National Security Risks Huawei Poses to 5G Networks," Ottawa, ON: Macdonald–Laurier Institute, 2018.

7. This point has been made by Emily de la Bruyere and Nathan Picarsic, "Worldwide Web: Why China Is Taking over the Internet of Things," *Octavian Report* 5, no. 2 (Spring 2019), https://octavianreport.com/article/why-china-is-taking-over-the-internet-of-things/.

8. Nigel Inkster, "The Huawei Affair and China's Technology Ambitions," *Survival* 61, no. 1 (January 2, 2019): 105–111.

9. Quoted by Ryan Browne, "Former Google CEO Eric Schmidt Says There's 'No Question' Huawei Routed Data to Beijing," June 18, 2020, https://www.cnbc.com/2020/06/18/ex-google-ceo-eric-schmidt-no-question-huawei-routed-data-to-china.html.

10. Quoted by Franco Ordonez, "China Wants Your Personal Information, Trump's National Security Adviser Warns," December 10, 2019, https://www.npr.org/2019/12/10/786381649/trumps-national-security-adviser-warns-china-wants-your-personal-information.

11. Cited by Shoebridge 2018.

12. David Shepardson, "Facebook Confirms Data Sharing with Chinese Companies," *Reuters*, June 6, 2018, https://www.reuters.com/article/us-facebook-privacy-congress-idUSKCN1J11TY.

13. See Woo 2019a and Stu Woo and Dan Strumpf, "Battle in Barcelona: U.S.–Huawei Fight to Take Center Stage at Trade Show," February 22, 2019, https://www.wsj.com/articles/battle-in-barcelona-huawei-flexes-as-u-s-officials-head-to-trade-show-11550831400.

14. Woo 2019a.

15. Quoted in Newley Purnell, Rajesh Roy, and Dustin Volz, "U.S. Campaign against Huawi Runs Aground in an Exploding Tech Market," *Wall Street Journal*, February 21, 2019, https://www.wsj.com/articles/india-a-pivotal-internet-market-isnt-buying-u-s-campaign-against-huawei-11550762080.

16. See Keshav Kelkar, "From Silk Threads to Fiber Optics: The Rise of China's Digital Silk Road," Observer Research Foundation, August 8, 2018, https://www.orfonline.org/expert-speak/43102-from-silk-threads-to-fiber-optics-the-rise-of-chinas-digital-silk-road/.

17. Quoted by Ryan Heath, "China's Tech Authoritarianism Too Big to Contain," *Politico*, November 20, 2020, https://www.politico.com/news/2020/11/20/chinas-tech-authoritarianism-438646.

18. I am grateful to Robert O'Brien for emphasizing this point.

19. Emily de la Bruyere and Nathan Picarsic, "Beijing's Innovation Strategy: Threat-Informed Acquisition for an Era of Great Power Competition," Naval Postgraduate School, April 28, 2020, 3.

20. Heath 2020.

21. Paul Mozur, Jonah M. Kessel, and Melissa Chan, "Made in China, Exported to the World: The Surveillance State," *New York Times*, April 26, 2019, https://www.nyti mes.com/2019/04/24/technology/ecuador-surveillance-cameras-police-governm ent.html.

22. Personal communication with UK Ambassador to China.

23. Paul Triolo, "The Telecommunications Industry in US–China Context Evolving Toward Near-Complete Bifurcation," The Johns Hopkins University Applied Physics Laboratory, 2020.

24. Doug Brake, "Economic Competitiveness and National Security Dynamics in the Race for 5G between the United States and China (August 2018)," TPRC 46: The 46th Research Conference on Communication, Information and Internet Policy, 2018.

25. Inkster 2019.

26. Cited by Melanie Hart and Blaine Johnson, "Mapping China's Global Governance Ambitions," Center for American Progress, February 28, 2019, https://www.ameri canprogress.org/issues/security/reports/2019/02/28/466768/mapping-chinas-glo bal-governance-ambitions/.

27. "GCHQ: Chinese Tech 'Threats' Must Be Understood," *BBC News*, February 25, 2019, https://www.bbc.com/news/business-47352079.

28. This was suggested by Brake 2018.

29. Many of these proposals are echoed by Melanie Hart and Jordan Link, "There Is a Solution to the Huawei Challenge," Center for American Progress, October 14, 2020, https://www.americanprogress.org/issues/security/reports/2020/10/14/491476/ solution-huawei-challenge/.

30. This proposal bears some similarities to initiatives like the Clean Network, but differs in proposing a significant industrial policy element.

31. Xinsheng Ji et al., "Overview of 5G Security Technology," *Science China Information Sciences* 61, no. 8 (August, 2018): 1–25.

32. The story of Smith and Liu was first publicly described in Daniel Golden, *Spy Schools: How the CIA, FBI, and Foreign Intelligence Secretly Exploit America's Universities* (New York: Henry Holt, 2017).

33. Golden 2017, 12.

34. Golden 2017.

35. Ana Swanson and Keith Bradsher, "White House Considers Restricting Chinese Researchers over Espionage Fears," *New York Times*, December 10, 2018, https://www. nytimes.com/2018/04/30/us/politics/trump-china-researchers-espionage.html.

36. Golden 2017, 29.

37. Nir Kshetri, "Cybercrime and Cyber-Security Issues Associated with China: Some Economic and Institutional Considerations," *Electronic Commerce Research* 13, no. 1 (March, 2013): 41–69.

38. David E. Sanger et al., "Marriott Data Breach Is Traced to Chinese Hackers as U.S. Readies Crackdown on Beijing," *New York Times*, December 12, 2018, https://www. nytimes.com/2018/12/11/us/politics/trump-china-trade.html.

39. "Canada and Allies Identify China as Responsible for Cyber-Compromise," Communications Security Establishment (Canada), 2018, https://cse-cst.gc.ca/en/ media/media-2018-12-20; and Government Communications Security Bureau (New

Zealand), "Cyber Campaign Attributed to China," 2018, https://www.gcsb.govt.nz/news/cyber-campaign-attributed-to-china/.

40. Jack Stubbs, Joseph Menn, and Christopher Bing, "Exclusive: China Hacked Eight Major Computer Services Firms in . . . ," June 26, 2019, https://www.reuters.com/article/us-china-cyber-cloudhopper-companies-exc-idUSKCN1TR1D4.

41. Competition between Chinese researchers for funding and publication rankings has been linked to pervasive academic misconduct. For example, a survey cited by Qing-Jiao Liao et al., "Perceptions of Chinese Biomedical Researchers Towards Academic Misconduct: A Comparison between 2015 and 2010," *Science and Engineering Ethics* 24, no. 2 (April 2018): 629–645, indicated that Chinese researchers believe up to 40% of academic papers are associated with some form of misconduct, such as unattributed data collection. For the Chamber of Commerce report, see Bob Davis and Lingling Wei, "China's Plan for Tech Dominance Is Advancing, Business Groups Say," *Wall Street Journal*, January 22, 2019, https://www.wsj.com/articles/u-s-business-groups-weigh-in-on-chinas-technology-push-11548153001.

42. Golden 2017, 16.

43. Dennis C. Blair and Keith Alexander, "Opinion | China's Intellectual Property Theft Must Stop," *New York Times*, January 20, 2018, https://www.nytimes.com/2017/08/15/opinion/china-us-intellectual-property-trump.html.

44. "Best Practices: Intellectual Property Protection in China," US-China Business Council, 2015, https://www.uschina.org/reports/best-practices-intellectual-property-protection-china.

45. Lawrence Fredendall, Peter Letmathe, and Nadine Uebe-Emden, "Supply Chain Management Practices and Intellectual Property Protection in China: Perceptions of Mittelstand Managers," *International Journal of Operations & Production Management* 36, no. 2 (2016): 149.

46. Dan Prud'homme et al., "'Forced Technology Transfer' Policies: Workings in China and Strategic Implications," *Technological Forecasting & Social Change* 134 (2018): 153.

47. Y. U. Li, Peipei Mao, and Yanming Zhang, "Empirical Research on the Different Innovation Engine between China and US Manufacturing using an Improved Method," *Applied Economics* 48, no. 6 (2016): 471–482; Prud'homme et al. 2018, 150.

48. William Weightman, "China's Progress on Intellectual Property Rights (Yes, Really)," *The Diplomat*, January 20, 2018, https://thediplomat.com/2018/01/chinas-progress-on-intellectual-property-rights-yes-really/.

49. Yingyu Bao, "Statistics and Characteristics Analysis of China's Intellectual Property Crimes," *MATEC Web of Conferences* 228 (2018): 05013, https://www.matec-conferences.org/articles/matecconf/pdf/2018/87/matecconf_cas2018_05013.pdf.

50. Weightman 2018.

51. Prud'homme et al. 2018.

52. Anna Fifield and David Lynch, "China Pushes through Changes to Foreign Investment Law as U.S. Trade Talks Start," *Washington Post*, January 30, 2019, https://www.washingtonpost.com/world/asia_pacific/china-pushes-through-changes-to-foreign-investment-law-as-us-trade-talks-start/2019/01/30/70cd4c4c-23c0-11e9-b5b4-1d18dfb7b084_story.html.

53. Golden 2017, 17.
54. Llanarte 2018; Sara Reardon, "NIH Considers Restrictions to Counter Foreign Influence in Research," *Nature Publishing Group*, December 13, 2018, http://www.nature.com/articles/d41586-018-07775-2.
55. "China: The Risk to Academia," Federal Bureau of Investigation, 2019, https://www.fbi.gov/file-repository/china-risk-to-academia-2019.pdf/view.
56. Genia Kolata, "Scientists with Links to China May Be Stealing Biomedical Research, U.S. Says," *New York Times*, November 4, 2019, https://www.nytimes.com/2019/11/04/health/china-nih-scientists.html?action=click&module=Top%20Stories&pgtype=Homepage.
57. FBI 2018.
58. See, for example Elsa Kania, "Technological Entanglement," Australian Strategic Policy Institute, June 28, 2018, https://www.aspi.org.au/report/technological-entanglement, who warns of the dangers of "entanglement."
59. FBI 2018.
60. Ricky Leung, "Networks as Sponges: International Collaboration for Developing Nanomedicine in China," *Research Policy* 42 (2013): 216.
61. Personal communication with University of Pennsylvania administrators, 2019.
62. Swanson and Bradsher 2018.
63. "Panel on the Impact of National Security Controls on International Technology Transfer. Balancing the National Interest: U.S. National Security Export Controls and Global Economic Competition," Washington, DC: National Academy Press, 1987.
64. See Robert Shaw, "Export Controls and the Life Sciences: Controversy or Opportunity? Innovations in the Life Sciences' Approach to Export Control Suggest There Are Ways to Disrupt Biological Weapons Development by Rogue States and Terrorist Groups without Impeding Research," *EMBO Reports* 17, no. 4 (April 2016): 474–480.
65. Cited by Georgia Wells, Yang Jie, and Yoko Kubota, "TikTok's Videos Are Goofy. Its Strategy to Dominate Social Media Is Serious," *Wall Street Journal*, June 29, 2019, https://www.wsj.com/articles/tiktoks-videos-are-goofy-its-strategy-to-dominate-social-media-is-serious-11561780861.
66. Cited by Wells, Yang, and Kubota 2019.
67. Kevin Poulsen and Robert McMillan, "WSJ News Exclusive | TikTok Tracked User Data using Tactic Banned by Google," *Wall Street Journal*, August 11, 2020, https://www.wsj.com/articles/tiktok-tracked-user-data-using-tactic-banned-by-google-11597176738.
68. Quoted by Craig Silverman, "These Hugely Popular Android Apps Have Been Committing Ad Fraud Behind Users' Backs," *Buzzfeed News*, November 26, 2018, https://www.buzzfeednews.com/article/craigsilverman/android-apps-cheetah-mobile-kika-kochava-ad-fraud.
69. Quoted by Craig Silverman, "Google Removed Dozens of Android Apps from a Major Chinese Developer Due to "Deceptive or Disruptive Ads," *Buzzfeed News*, September 26, 2019, https://www.buzzfeednews.com/article/craigsilverman/sweet-camera-play-store-removed-ihandy.

70. Mark Kazmierczak et al., *China's Biotechnology Development: The Role of US and Other Foreign Engagement* (Takoma Park, MD; New York: Gryphon Scientific, LLC, and Rhodium Group, LLC, 2019).

71. Rebecca Robbins, Matthew Herper, and Damian Garde, "U.S. Forces Health Firm PatientsLikeMe to Ditch Owner over China Concerns," *Stat News*, April 4, 2019, https://www.statnews.com/2019/04/04/u-s-forces-health-company-to-ditch-chin ese-investor-in-sign-of-heightened-concern-over-foreign-influence/.

72. Georgia Wells and Kate O'Keeffe, "U.S. Orders Chinese Firm to Sell Dating App Grindr over Blackmail Risk," *Wall Street Journal*, March 27, 2019, https://www.wsj. com/articles/u-s-orders-chinese-company-to-sell-grindr-app-11553717942.

73. Quoted by Tripp Mickle, Jeff Horwitz, and Yoko Kubota, "Apple, Google Pull Hong Kong Protest Apps amid China Uproar," *Wall Street Journal*, October 10, 2019, https://www.wsj.com/articles/apple-pulls-hong-kong-cop-tracking-map-app-after-china-uproar-11570681464.

74. Cited by Rishi Iyengar, "Zoom's Revenue Soars 169% as People Flock to Service during Pandemic," *CNN*, June 2, 2020, https://www.cnn.com/2020/06/02/tech/zoom-earnings-coronavirus/index.html.

75. Drew Harwell and Ellen Nakashima, "Federal Prosecutors Accuse Zoom Executive of Working with Chinese Government to Surveil Users and Suppress Video Calls," *Washington Post*, December 18, 2020, https://www.washingtonpost.com/technology/2020/12/18/zoom-helped-china-surveillance/.

76. Josh Rogin, "Opinion | How Clubhouse (Briefly) Exposed China's Fear Society," *Washington Post*, February 9, 2021, https://www.washingtonpost.com/opinions/2021/02/09/clubhouse-briefly-gave-chinese-citizens-free-speech-now-make-that-permanent/; audio data issue cited by Jonathan Greig, "Security Concerns Arise over Popular Clubhouse App after Ties to China-Based Company Revealed," *Tech Republic*, February 25, 2021, https://www.techrepublic.com/article/security-concerns-arise-over-popular-clubhouse-app-after-ties-to-china-based-company-revealed/.

77. Quoted by Rogin 2020.

78. See Jeanne Whalen, "Chinese Censorship Invades the U.S. via WeChat," *Washington Post*, January 7, 2021, https://www.washingtonpost.com/technology/2021/01/07/wec hat-censorship-china-us-ban/.

79. Quoted by Raymond Zhong, "TikTok's Chief Is on a Mission to Prove It's Not a Menace," *New York Times*, November 18, 2019, https://www.nytimes.com/2019/11/18/technology/tiktok-alex-zhu-interview.html?action=click&module=News&pgt ype=Homepage.

80. Quoted by Georgia Wells, Yoko Kubota, and Kate O'Keeffe, "WSJ News Exclusive | TikTok Looking at Ways to Shake Off its Ties to China," *Wall Street Journal*, November 18, 2019, https://www.wsj.com/articles/tiktok-looking-at-ways-to-shake-off-its-ties-to-china-11574073001.

81. See Samm Sacks, "Data Security and U.S.-China Tech Entanglement," *Lawfare Blog*, April 2, 2020, https://www.lawfareblog.com/data-security-and-us-china-tech-entan glement.

82. All quotations are from Charlie Campbell, "Meet the Man Who Created Baidu, the Google of China," *Time*, January 18, 2018, http://time.com/5107485/baidus-robin-li-helping-china-win-21st-century/.

83. This portrait of Li is from Campbell 2018 (quotations) and "Bloomberg Billionaires Index—Robin Li," *Bloomberg*, 2018, https://www.bloomberg.com/billionaires/profiles/li-yanhong/.

84. Campbell 2018.

85. Nat Berman, "10 Things You Didn't Know about Baidu Founder Robin Li," *Money Inc.*, 2017, https://moneyinc.com/10-things-didnt-know-baidu-founder-robin-li/.

86. Qing Ma, "李彦宏：中国人多数情况下愿意用隐私换便利，获用户许可后可收集数据 [Li Yanhong: In Most Cases Chinese People Are Willing to Trade Privacy for Convenience]," *BJ News*, March 26, 2018, http://www.bjnews.com.cn/finance/2018/03/26/480626.html.

87. See "China May Match or Beat America in AI," *The Economist*, July 15, 2017, https://www.economist.com/business/2017/07/15/china-may-match-or-beat-america-in-ai#:~:text=In%20October%202016%20the%20White,accrue%20to%20China%2C%20it%20reckons.

88. Kevin Carter, "China Leads in Mobile Payments," *Seeking Alpha*, April 12, 2018, https://seekingalpha.com/article/4162586-china-leads-mobile-payments.

89. Kai-Fu Lee, "Why China Can Do AI More Quickly and Effectively than the US," *Wired*, October 23, 2018, https://www.wired.com/story/why-china-can-do-ai-more-quickly-and-effectively-than-the-us/.

90. Lee 2018.

91. Yanfang Wu et al., "A Comparative Study of Online Privacy Regulations in the U.S. and China," *Telecommunications Policy* 35, no. 7 (2011): 603–616; Samm Sacks, "New China Data Privacy Standard Looks More Far-Reaching than GDPR," The Center for Strategic Studies, January 29, 2018, https://www.csis.org/analysis/new-china-data-privacy-standard-looks-more-far-reaching-gdpr.

92. Specifically, the draft measures include no requirement for transparency, as does the European Union's General Data Privacy Regulation (GDPR). See Olivia Z. Zhan and Daniel Csigirinszkij, "China's Draft Data Security Measures and How They Compare to the GDPR," *The National Law Review*, June 24, 2019, https://www.natlawreview.com/article/china-s-draft-data-security-measures-and-how-they-compare-to-gdpr.

93. Timothy Morey, Theodore Forbath, and Allison Schoop, "Customer Data: Designing for Transparency and Trust," *Harvard Business Review* 93, no. 5 (May 2015): 96–105.

94. See Xuequn Wang and Zilong Liu, "Online Engagement in Social Media: A Cross-Cultural Comparison." *Computers in Human Behavior* 97 (2019): 137–150. doi:https://doi.org/10.1016/j.chb.2019.03.014. https://www.sciencedirect.com/science/article/pii/S0747563219301062; and Yao Li, Eugenia Ha Rim Rho, and Alfred Kobsa, "Cultural Differences in the Effects of Contextual Factors and Privacy Concerns on Users' Privacy Decision on Social Networking Sites." *Behaviour & Information Technology* (2020): 1–23. doi:10.1080/0144929X.2020.1831608.

95. *The Economist*, "In China, Consumers Are Becoming More Anxious about Data Privacy," January 25, 2018, accessed February 17, 2019, https://proxy.library.upenn. edu:3518/china/2018/01/25/in-china-consumers-are-becoming-more-anxious-about-data-privacy.

96. This system built in turn on the *baojia* mutual responsibility structure, which dated to imperial times.

97. Hauke Gierow, *Cyber Security in China: Internet Security, Protectionism and Competitiveness: New Challenges to Western Businesses* (Berlin: Mercator Institute for China Studies, 2017).

98. Max Parasol, "The Impact of China's 2016 Cyber Security Law on Foreign Technology Firms, and on China's Big Data and Smart City Dreams," *Computer Law and Security Report* 34, no. 1 (2018): 67–98. doi:10.1016/j.clsr.2017.05.022.

99. Rogier Creemers, "Cyber China: Upgrading Propaganda, Public Opinion Work and Social Management for the Twenty-First Century," *Journal of Contemporary China* 26, no. 103 (2017): 85–100.

100. I am indebted to Aynne Kokas for emphasizing the devolved nature of the Social Credit System.

101. Author personal communication (K. H.), March 2021.

102. Yongxi Chen and Anne S. Y. Cheung, "The Transparent Self under Big Data Profiling: Privacy and Chinese Legislation on the Social Credit System," *Journal of Comparative Law* 12, no. 2 (2017): 356–378; Jamie Horsley, "China's Orwellian Social Credit Score Isn't Real," *Foreign Policy*, November 16, 2018, https://foreignpol icy.com/2018/11/16/chinas-orwellian-social-credit-score-isnt-real/.

103. Zhong Wang and Qian Yu, "Privacy Trust Crisis of Personal Data in China in the Era of Big Data: The Survey and Countermeasures," *Computer Law & Security Review* 31, no. 6 (2015): 782–792.

104. *The Economist* 2018.

105. Sarah Dai, "China's Mobile Apps Collect Too Much Data, Says Consumer Body," *South China Morning Post*, December 1, 2018, https://www.scmp.com/tech/apps-social/article/2175884/chinas-mobile-apps-collect-too-much-data-says-consu mer-body.

106. "China Moves to Curb Online Privacy Breaches," Mercator Institute for China Studies, June 6, 2019, https://www.merics.org/en/newsletter/china-update-102 019#the-european-view; Carol Sun and Jenny Chen, "China's Draft Cybersecurity Measures Suggest Increased Focus on Data Security," *The National Law Review*, August 28, 2019, https://www.natlawreview.com/article/china-s-draft-cybersecur ity-measures-suggest-increased-focus-data-security.

107. Katharin Tai, "Chinese Interagency Group Calls Out Apps for Illegally Collecting User Data," *New America*, July 29, 2019, https://www.newamerica.org/cybersecur ity-initiative/digichina/blog/chinese-interagency-group-calls-out-apps-illegally-collecting-user-data/.

108. See Morgan Lewis, "Personal Information Protection Law: China's GDPR Is Coming," August 24, 2021, https://www.jdsupra.com/legalnews/personal-informat ion-protection-law-4689872/.

109. Quoted by Evelyn Shao and Grace Cheng, "Growing Backlash in China Against A.I. and Facial Recognition," *CNBC*, September 5, 2019, https://www.cnbc.com/2019/09/06/ai-worries-about-the-dangers-of-facial-recognition-growing-in-china.html.

110. See Kaiser Kuo, "Fear of a Red Tech Planet—Why the U.S. Is Suddenly Afraid of Chinese Innovation," October 13, 2020, https://supchina.com/2020/10/13/fear-of-a-red-tech-planet-why-the-u-s-is-suddenly-afraid-of-chinese-innovation/.

111. Chinese translation obtained from Rogier Creemers, "Communiqué on the Current State of the Ideological Sphere (Document no. 9)," China Copyright and Media, April 22, 2013, https://chinacopyrightandmedia.wordpress.com/2013/04/22/communique-on-the-current-state-of-the-ideological-sphere-document-no-9/.

112. Parasol 2018.

113. Yuxi Wei, "Chinese Data Localization Law: Comprehensive but Ambiguous," The Henry M. Jackson School of International Studies: University of Washington, February 7, 2018, https://jsis.washington.edu/news/chinese-data-localization-law-comprehensive-ambiguous/.

114. Hunton Andrews Kurth, "China Issues the Second Version of the Draft of Data Security Law," *The National Law Review*, 2021, https://www.natlawreview.com/article/china-issues-second-version-draft-data-security-law; and Aynne Kokas, "China's 2021 Data Security Law: Grand Data Strategy with Looming Implementation Challenges," December 1, 2021, https://www.prcleader.org/kokas.

115. Gierow 2017.

116. Yongqi Chen and Lingqiao Song, "China: Concurring Regulation of Cross-Border Genomic Data Sharing for Statist Control and Individual Protection," *Human Genomics* 137, no. 8 (2018): 605–615.

117. For details on plans to develop and use biomedical data at large scales, see Zhen Wang, Zefeng Wang, and Yixue Li, "Strategic Planning for National Biomedical Big Data Infrastructure in China," *Quantitative Biology* 5, no. 3 (2017): 272–275.

118. Luxia Zhang et al., "Big Data and Medical Research in China," *British Medical Journal* 360 (2018): 1–3.

119. Yihu Wang, "2018 年生物技术产业发展趋势分析；生物科技产业布局初步形成；技术突破将推动产业进一步变革 [2018 Biotechnology Industry Development Trend Analysis; Bioscience Industry Initial Structure and Layout; Technological Breakthroughs Will Promote Reform of the Sector]," Qianzhan, October 15, 2018, https://www.qianzhan.com/analyst/detail/220/181015-b1ceb838.html.

120. Chen and Song 2018, 607.

121. Chen and Song 2018.

122. Quoted by Heath 2020.

123. I am grateful to Robert O'Brien for emphasizing this point.

124. "An Overview of the Human Genome Project," National Human Genome Research Institute, 2016, https://www.genome.gov/12011238/an-overview-of-the-human-genome-project/.

125. Author interviews with current and former US government officials.

126. I am indebted to Abigail Coplin and fellow members of a working group convened under the auspices of the US-China Futures Project organized by Young Leaders in Foreign Policy with funding from Schmidt Futures for this observation.

127. This point is made by Whalen 2021.

128. Author interview, April 2021. Fellow human rights advocate Maya Wang made the same argument; see Maya Wang, "China's Techno-Authoritarianism has Gone Global," *Foreign Affairs*, April 8, 2021, https://www.foreignaffairs.com/articles/china/2021-04-08/chinas-techno-authoritarianism-has-gone-global.

Chapter 7

1. CRISPR stands for "clustered regularly interspaced short palindromic repeats." Which is why everyone just calls it CRISPR!

2. This story is recounted by Robin Lovell-Badge, "CRISPR Babies: A View from the Centre of the Storm," *Development* 146 (2019): 1–5.

3. This section is adapted from Scott Moore, "China's Biotech Boom Could Transform Lives—or Destroy Them," accessed May 23, 2021, https://foreignpolicy.com/2019/11/08/cloning-crispr-he-jiankui-china-biotech-boom-could-transform-lives-destroy-them/, and Scott Moore, "China's Role in the Global Biotechnology Sector and Implications for US Policy," *Brookings Institution*, April 2020, https://www.brookings.edu/research/chinas-role-in-the-global-biotechnology-sector-and-implications-for-us-policy/. Used with permission from Brookings Institution Press.

4. Walter Russell Mead, "The Century of Bioweapons," *Wall Street Journal*, April 27, 2020, https://www.wsj.com/articles/the-century-of-bioweapons-11588025901.

5. See Declan Butler, "Translational Research: Crossing the Valley of Death," *Nature* 453 (2008): 840–842.

6. See, for example, Joe Kennedy, "How to Ensure That America's Life-Sciences Sector Remains Globally Competitive," Washington, DC: Information Technology and Innovation Foundation, March 26, 2018, https://itif.org/publications/2018/03/26/how-ensure-americas-life-sciences-sector-remains-globally-competitive.

7. See Li Tang and Philip Shapira, "China-US Scientific Collaboration in Nanotechnology: Patterns and Dynamics," *Scientometrics* 88 (2011): 1–16.

8. Moore 2019.

9. Quoted by Xiao Shan, "习近平促生物科技要自己掌握 用举国体制突破技术 [Xi Jinping: Biotechnology Must Urgently Be Mastered and a Society-Wide Effort Used to Achieve Breakthroughs]," *RFI*, September 16, 2020, https://www.rfi.fr/cn/中国/20200916-习近平促生物科技要自己掌握-用举国体制突破技术.

10. See Runjian Zhou, "中国采取五项措施推动生物技术研究和产业化发展 [China Adopts Five Measures to Promote Biotechnology Research and Industrial Development]," *Xinhua News Agency*, June 26, 2011, http://www.gov.cn/jrzg/2011-06/26/content_1893192.htm.

11. See Zhe Hu, "科技部：2020年我国生物技术产业GDP比重将超4% [Ministry of Science and Technology: Biotechnology Sector Will Account for More than 4% of GDP by 2020]," *Xinhua*, April 28, 2017, accessed May 23, 2021, http://www.gov.cn/xinwen/2017-04/28/content_5189628.htm.

12. See PRC State Council, "Circular of the State Council on Issuing the National 13th Five-Year Plan for the Development of Strategic Emerging Industries," Official website of the Central People's Government of the People's Republic of China, November 29, 2016, https://cset.georgetown.edu/wp-content/uploads/Circular-of-the-State-Council-on-Issuing-the-National-13th-Five-Year-Plan-for-the-Development-of-Strategic-Emerging-Industries.pdf.

13. Mark Kazmierczak et al., *China's Biotechnology Development: The Role of US and Other Foreign Engagement* (Takoma Park, MD; New York: Gryphon Scientific, LLC; and Rhodium Group, LLC, 2019).

14. See Shannon Ellis, "Biotech Booms in China," *Nature* 553 (2018): S19.

15. See "China Statistical Yearbook," National Statistics Bureau of China, 2019, http://www.stats.gov.cn/tjsj/ndsj/2019/indexeh.htm., especially Tables 20-6 and 20-9.

16. Ellis 2018.

17. Quoted by Claudia Adrien, "Chinese Biotechnology Dominates U.S. Senate Hearing on Biological Threats," *Homeland Preparedness News*, November 21, 2019, https://homelandprepnews.com/countermeasures/40093-chinese-biotechnology-dominates-u-s-senate-hearing-on-biological-threats/.

18. Hamilton Moses, David H. M. Matheson, Sarah Cairns-Smith, Benjamin P. George, Chase Palisch, and E. Ray Dorsey. "The Anatomy of Medical Research: US and International Comparisons," *Journal of the American Medical Association* 313, no. 2 (January 13, 2015): 174–189. doi:10.1001/jama.2014.15939. https://jamanetwork.com/journals/jama/fullarticle/2089358.

19. Megan Molteni, "Deer DNA Starts Spilling Its Weird, Cancer-Fighting Secrets," *Wired*, June 20, 2019, https://www.wired.com/story/wildebeest-okapi-giraffe-ibex-come-peruse-their-genomes/.

20. Hamilton Moses et al., "The Anatomy of Medical Research: US and International Comparisons," *Journal of the American Medical Association* 313, no. 2 (2015): 174–189, and author interview with Jamie Metzl, March 2021.

21. Dina Spencer, "Hansoh IPO Raises $1 Billion on Hong Kong Exchange," *Pharma Boardroom*, June 11, 2019, accessed April 7, 2021, https://pharmaboardroom.com/articles/hansoh-ipo-raises-1-billion-on-hong-kong-exchange/; and Dina Spencer, "Hong Kong Now the World's Second Largest Funding Hub for Biotech," *Pharma Boardroom*, June 6, 2019, accessed April 7, 2021, https://pharmaboardroom.com/articles/hong-kong-now-the-worlds-second-largest-funding-hub-for-biotech/.

22. See Hu 2017.

23. Yihu Wang, "2018年生物技术产业发展趋势分析；生物科技产业布局初步形成；技术突破将推动产业进一步变革 [2018 Biotechnology Industry Development Trend Analysis; Bioscience Industry Initial Structure and Layout; Technological Breakthroughs Will Promote Reform of the Sector]," *Qianzhan*, October 16, 2018, https://www.qianzhan.com/analyst/detail/220/181015-b1ceb838.html.

24. Wang 2018.

25. See Hu 2017.

26. Cited by Kate Lamb, "The Next Google in Biotech: Will It Be Chinese?," *WeForum*, July 1, 2019, https://www.weforum.org/agenda/2019/07/biotech-ethics-next-google-will-be-chinese-amnc19/.

27. Cited by Alex Keown, "Exponential Pharma Growth Expected in China by 2022," *BioSpace*, April 20, 2018, https://www.biospace.com/article/exponential-pharma-growth-expected-in-china-by-2022/.

28. Greg Scott, *Overall Factors Driving China Life Science Investment*, ChinaBio Group. Presentation delivered to the China Institute, June 2, 2021 .

29. Jacky Wong, "China's Drug Market Is Opening Up," *Wall Street Journal*, November 11, 2019, https://www.wsj.com/articles/chinas-drug-market-is-opening-up-1157 3468202.

30. Author interview with Jamie Metzl, 2021.

31. This section adapted from Moore 2019.

32. I thank Abigail Coplin for pushing me to emphasize this point.

33. See Die Zhang and Riedar Lie, "Ethical Issues in Human Germline Gene Editing: A Perspective from China," *Monash Bioethics Review* 36, no. 1–4 (December 2018): 23–35.

34. For an authoritative source who takes these claims very seriously, see Wendy Rogers, "Bioethics and Activism: A Natural Fit?," *Bioethics* 33 no. 8 (February 2019): 881–889.

35. Cited by Zhang and Lie 2018.

36. Quoted by Jane Qiu, "Stem-Cell Research and Regenerative Medicine in China," *National Science Review* 3, no. 2 (2016): 257–261.

37. Helen Briggs, "First Monkey Clones Created in the Lab," *BBC*, January 24, 2018, https://www.bbc.com/news/health-42809445.

38. Siqi Cao and Shasha Chen, "Great Potential for China to Lead Biomedical Research as US Enters Bottleneck," *Global Times*, July 23, 2018, http://www.globaltimes.cn/content/1112003.shtml.

39. Dennis Normille, "These Monkey Twins Are the First Primate Clones Made by the Method That Developed Dolly," *Science Magazine*, January 24, 2018, https://www.sciencemag.org/news/2018/01/these-monkey-twins-are-first-primate-clones-made-method-developed-dolly.

40. Antonio Regalado, "Chinese Scientists Have Put Human Brain Genes in Monkeys—and Yes, They May Be Smarter," *Technology Review*, April 10, 2019, https://www.technologyreview.com/s/613277/chinese-scientists-have-put-human-brain-genes-in-monkeysand-yes-they-may-be-smarter/.

41. Douglas Sipp and Duanqing Pei, "Bioethics in China: No Wild East," *Nature News* 534, no. 7608 (2016): 465.

42. Described by Lovell-Badge 2019, 3.

43. Lovell-Badge 2019, 3.

44. Zhang and Lie 2018.

45. See analysts quoted by Jane Qiu, "Chinese Government Funding May Have Been Used for 'CRISPR Babies' Project, Documents Suggest," *Stat News*, February 25, 2019,

https://www.statnews.com/2019/02/25/crispr-babies-study-china-government-funding/.

46. Similar points have been made extensively by Abigail Coplin, Vassar College. See https://www.vassar.edu/faculty/acoplin/.

47. Cited by Yangyang Cheng, "China Will Always Be Bad at Bioethics," *Foreign Policy*, April 13, 2018, https://foreignpolicy.com/2018/04/13/china-will-always-be-bad-at-bioethics/.

48. Preetika Rana, Amy Dockser Marcus, and Wenxin Fan, "China, Unhampered by Rules, Races Ahead in Gene-Editing Trials," *Wall Street Journal*, January 21, 2018, https://www.wsj.com/articles/china-unhampered-by-rules-races-ahead-in-gene-editing-trials-1516562360.

49. Author interview with University of Pennsylvania researcher, March 2019.

50. Lovell-Badge 2019, 3.

51. Sui-Lee Wee, "China Uses DNA to Track Its People, with the Help of American Expertise," *New York Times*, February 21, 2019, https://www.nytimes.com/2019/02/21/business/china-xinjiang-uighur-dna-thermo-fisher.html.

52. Quoted by Sui-Lee Wee and Paul Mozur, "China Uses DNA to Map Faces, with Help from the West," *New York Times*, December 3, 2019, https://www.nytimes.com/2019/12/03/business/china-dna-uighurs-xinjiang.html?action=click&module=Top%20Stories&pgtype=Homepage.

53. Cited by Elsa Kania and Wilson Vorndick, "Weaponizing Biotech: How China's Military Is Preparing for a 'New Domain of Warfare,'" *Defense One*, August 14, 2019, https://www.defenseone.com/ideas/2019/08/chinas-military-pursuing-biotech/159167/.

54. John Ratcliffe, "Opinion | China Is National Security Threat No. 1," *Wall Street Journal*, December 3, 2020, https://www.wsj.com/articles/china-is-national-security-threat-no-1-11607019599.

55. I thank Abigail Coplin for pushing me to emphasize this point.

56. Quoted by Jude Blanchette, *China's New Red Guards: The Return of Radicalism and the Rebirth of Mao Zedong* (Oxford: Oxford University Press 2019), 91.

57. Quoted by Shan 2020. Another reading of the remark would be "must be mastered by ourselves."

58. Antonio Regalado, "Top U.S. Intelligence Official Calls Gene Editing a WMD Threat," *Technology Review*, February 9, 2016, https://www.technologyreview.com/s/600774/top-us-intelligence-official-calls-gene-editing-a-wmd-threat/.

59. See Daniel Gerstein, "How Genetic Editing Became a National Security Threat," *Bulletin of the Atomic Scientists*, April 25, 2016, https://thebulletin.org/2016/04/how-genetic-editing-became-a-national-security-threat/.

60. David Grossman, "Chinese Government Officially Charges CRISPR Baby Scientist," *Popular Mechanics*, January 22, 2019, https://www.popularmechanics.com/science/health/a25991256/chinese-government-officially-charges-crispr-baby-scientist/.

61. See Jan van Aken and Edward Hammond, "Genetic Engineering and Biological Weapons: New Technologies, Desires and Threats from Biological Research," *EMBO Rep.* 4, no. S1 (2003): S57–S60.

62. This remains a theoretical possibility but one that looks increasingly plausible, if not in the foreseeable future. See Peter Apps, "Commentary: The Next Super Weapon Could Be Biological," *Reuters*, April 21, 2017, https://www.reuters.com/article/us-bio logical-weaons-commentary-idUSKBN17L1SZ.

63. Ryan S. Noyce, Seth Lederman, and David H. Evans, "Construction of an Infectious Horsepox Virus Vaccine from Chemically Synthesized DNA Fragments," *Plos One* 13, no. 1 (2018): e0188453.; David Kushner, "Synthetic Biology Could Bring a Pox on Us All," *Wired*, March 25, 2019, https://www.wired.com/story/synthetic-biology-vaccines-viruses-horsepox/.

64. "International Gene Synthesis Consortium," 2017, https://genesynthesisconsort ium.org/.

65. Nell Greenfield-Boyce, "As Made-to-Order DNA Gets Cheaper, Keeping It Out of the Wrong Hands Gets Harder," *NPR*, September 24, 2019, https://www.npr.org/sections/health-shots/2019/09/24/762834987/as-made-to-order-dna-gets-cheaper-keeping-it-out-of-the-wrong-hands-gets-harder.

66. Kushner 2019.

67. Marc Lipsitch and Tom Inglesby, "Opinion | The U.S. Is Funding Dangerous Experiments It Doesn't Want You to Know About," *Washington Post*, February 27, 2019, https://www.washingtonpost.com/opinions/the-us-is-funding-dangerous-experiments-it-doesnt-want-you-to-know-about/2019/02/27/5f60e934-38ae-11e9-a2cd-307b06d0257b_story.html.

68. Author interview with former US government official, 2021.

69. Mark Mazzetti et al., "U.S. Asks Spies to Trace Virus to Wuhan Lab," *New York Times*, May 1, 2020, https://www.nytimes.com/2020/04/30/us/politics/trump-administrat ion-intelligence-coronavirus-china.html?auth=login-email&login=email.

70. See John Ruwitch, "Calls for an Open Investigation into the Possibility COVID-19 Leaked from a Lab," *NPR*, March 31 2021, https://www.npr.org/2021/03/31/983157441/calls-for-an-open-investigation-into-the-possibility-covid-19-lea ked-from-a-lab.

71. "WHO Consultative Meeting on High/Maximum Containment (Biosafety Level 4) Laboratories Networking," World Health Organization, December 13–15, 2018.

72. Qiu 2016, 261.

73. Associated Press, "China Unveils New Rules on Biotech after Gene-Editing Scandal," *Stat News*, February 27, 2019, https://www.statnews.com/2019/02/27/china-unveils-new-rules-on-biotech-after-gene-editing-scandal/.

74. Hepeng Jia, "China Approves Ethics Advisory Group after CRISPR-Babies Scandal," *Nature Publishing Group*, August 8, 2019, http://www.nature.com/articles/d41 586-019-02362-5.

75. David Cyranoski, "China Set to Introduce Gene-Editing Regulation Following CRISPR-Baby Furore," *Nature*, May 20, 2019.

76. "China Introduces Product Standard for Human Embryonic Stem Cells," *Xinhua*, February 26, 2019, http://www.xinhuanet.com/english/2019-02/26/c_137852 641.htm.

77. "人大代表白春礼：基因编辑技术研发不能因噎废食_立法   [Renowed Representative Bai Chunli: Gene Editing Technology Research and Development Cannot Be Degraded]," Sohu, March 11, 2019, www.sohu.com/a/300363453_123753.

78. Ting Xiao, Horace Lam, and William Fisher, "Guest Blog: China Signs Off on First PRC Biosecurity Law: What This Means for Israeli Companies in China?" *DLA Piper*, November 18, 2020, https://www.lexology.com/library/detail.aspx?g=accc3647-7163-4a2e-b53d-bbd873645b7d.

79. Quoted in James Vincent, "China Is Worried an AI Arms Race Could Lead to Accidental War," *The Verge*, February 6, 2019, https://www.theverge.com/2019/2/6/18213476/china-us-ai-arms-race-artificial-intelligence-automated-warfare-military-conflict.

80. Article cited and quoted by Lyle J. Goldstein, "China's Olive Branch to Save the World from AI Weapons," The Center for the National Interest, February 1, 2019, https://nationalinterest.org/feature/chinas-olive-branch-save-world-ai-weapons-42972.

81. Vincent 2019.

82. Many of these are cited in the final report of the "2021 Final Report: National Security Commission on Artificial Intelligence," National Security Commission on Artificial Intelligence, 2021, https://www.nscai.gov/2021-final-report/.

83. I am indebted to Michael Rawding for this observation.

84. Pheobe Zhang, "China's Top AI Scientist Drives Development of Ethical Guidelines," *South China Morning Post*, January 10, 2019, https://www.scmp.com/news/china/science/article/2181573/chinas-top-ai-scientist-drives-development-ethical-guidelines.

85. Zhang 2019.

86. "Summary of the 2018 Departments of Defense Artificial Intelligence Strategy," US Department of Defense, 2018, 5, http://parlinfo.aph.gov.au/parlInfo/search/display/display.w3p;query=library/jrnart/6506004.

87. US Department of Defense 2018, 15.

88. These points based on interview with former US government official, March 2021.

89. Kelsey Piper, "Bill Gates: AI Is Like 'Nuclear Weapons and Nuclear Energy' in Danger and Promise," *Vox*, March 20, 2019, https://www.vox.com/future-perfect/2019/3/20/18274350/bill-gates-stanford-ai-like-nuclear-weapons.

90. Henry Dunant, *A Memory of Solferino*, 2nd ed. (Geneva, Switzerland: International Committee of the Red Cross, 1959), 19.

91. "The Geneva Conventions of 1949 and their Additional Protocols," International Committee of the Red Cross, April 2011, https://www.redcross.org/content/dam/redcross/atg/PDF_s/International_Services/International_Humanitarian_Law/IHL_SummaryGenevaConv.pdf.

92. Albert Einstein, "Arms Can Bring No Security," *Bulletin of the Atomic Scientists* 6, no. 3 (March 1950), https://thebulletin.org/premium/2020-12/1950-what-the-scientists-are-saying-about-the-h-bomb/.

93. Robert Shaw, "Export Controls and the Life Sciences: Controversy or Opportunity? Innovations in the Life Sciences' Approach to Export Control Suggest There Are Ways to Disrupt Biological Weapons Development by Rogue States and Terrorist Groups without Impeding Research," *EMBO Reports* 17, no. 4 (April 2016): 474–480.

94. Shaw 2016.

95. Christopher Thomas Scott and Cynthia Selin, "What to Expect When Expecting CRISPR Baby Number Four," *The American Journal of Bioethics* 19, no. 3 (2019): 7–9.

96. See Roderic Wye, "China Paves Its Way in New Areas of International Law," *Chatham House*, March 31, 2017, https://www.chathamhouse.org/expert/comm ent/china-paves-its-way-new-areas-international-law.

97. Christine Fox, "An Entwined AI Future: Resistance Is Futile," Johns Hopkins University Applied Physics Laboratory, 2020, 8.

98. This characterization based on interviews with US private sector representatives.

99. Author interview with former US government official, March 2021.

100. Some of these conclusions are described in Mahlet Mesfin and Scott Moore, "Why the Nobel Prize Shows the US and China Need to Work Together on Gene Editing," *The Hill*, October 18, 2020, https://thehill.com/opinion/international/521579-why-the-nobel-prize-shows-the-us-and-china-need-to-work-together-on.

101. Donald Fredrickson, "Asilomar and Recombinant DNA: The End of the Beginning," in *Biomedical Politics*, ed. Kathi Hanna (Washington, DC: National Academy Press, 1991), 258–298.

102. Paul Berg et al., "Summary Statement of the Asilomar Conference on Recombinant DNA Molecules," *Proceedings of the National Academy of Sciences* 72, no. 6 (1975): 1981–1984.

103. I am indebted to Abigail Coplin for this observation.

104. Bart Kolodziejczyk and John Malone, "How Would International Agreements on Genetically Engineered Organisms Apply to Humans?," *Brookings*, December 12, 2018, https://www.brookings.edu/blog/techtank/2018/12/18/how-would-intern ational-agreements-on-genetically-engineered-organisms-apply-to-humans/.

105. Sharon Begley, "WHO Advisers Call for Registry of Studies on Human Genome Editing," *Stat News*, March 19, 2019, https://www.statnews.com/2019/03/19/who-advisers-call-for-registry-of-human-genome-editing/.

106. Fox 2020, 8–10.

107. This statement based on author interviews with US Track 1.5 and Track II participants, March 2021.

108. This has been suggested by Claire M. Fraser and Malcolm R. Dando, "Genomics and Future Biological Weapons: The Need for Preventive Action by the Biomedical Community," *Nature Genetics* 29, no. 3 (2001): 253–256.

109. Similar suggestions have been made by Margaret E. Kosal, "Emerging Life Sciences and Possible Threats to International Security," *Orbis* 64, no. 4 (2020): 599–614.

110. See Miles Pomper and Ferenc Dalnoki-Veress, "The Little Known Success Story of U.S.-China Nuclear Security Cooperation," accessed April 7, 2021, https://www.nti.org/analysis/articles/little-known-success-story-us-china-nuclear-security-coop eration/.

111. Sara Z. Kutchesfahani, "And the Prize for Global Nuclear Security Goes to . . . China," *Bulletin of Atomic Scientists*, December 6, 2019, https://thebulletin.org/2019/12/and-the-prize-for-global-nuclear-security-goes-to-china/.

Conclusion

1. This point is also made in Inge Kaul, Pedro Conceicao, Katell Le Goulven, and Ronald Mendoza, eds., *Providing Global Public Goods: Managing Globalization*. (Cary, NC: Oxford University Press, 2003).

2. On this reality, see Richard Danzig and Lorand Laskai, "Symbiosis and Strife: Where Is the Sino–American Relationship Bound? An Introduction to the APL Series 'Measure Twice, Cut Once: Assessing Some China–US Technology Connections,'" The Johns Hopkins University Applied Physics Laboratory, 2020.

3. I am grateful to Robert O'Brien for emphasizing this point.

4. There are few research or analysis pieces on this subject, and it appears never to have been the subject of detailed academic study.

5. This argument is also made by Yanzhong Huang, *Toxic Politics: China's Environmental Health Crisis and Its Challenge to the Chinese State* (Cambridge, UK: Cambridge University Press, 2020).

6. Many measures of nationalist sentiment are highest in lower- and middle-income countries. See Florian Bieber, "Is Nationalism on the Rise? Assessing Global Trends," *Ethnopolitics* 17, no. 5 (2018): 519–540. https://doi.org/10.1080/17449 057.2018.1532633.

7. These points are made by Jessica Chen Weiss, "Introduction," in Weiss, *Powerful Patriots* (New York: Oxford University Press, 2014). https://oxford.universitypress scholarship.com/10.1093/acprof:oso/9780199387557.001.0001/acprof-9780199387 557-chapter-1.

8. Cited in Caroline Chang, Scott Moore, and Ali Wyne, "Federalism in the Time of Coronavirus: A Comparative US Advantage," *The Diplomat*, accessed February 11, 2021, https://thediplomat.com/2020/05/federalism-in-the-time-of-coronavirus-a-comparative-us-advantage/.

9. I thank Jamie Metzl for this point.

10. See Quint Forgey and Daniel Lippman, "CIA Launches New China-Focused Unit," *Politico*, accessed October 8, 2021, https://www.politico.com/news/2021/10/07/cia-china-focused-unit-515548.

11. See Alexandra Wexler, "Pepsi Expands in Africa with $1.7 Billion Deal," *Wall Street Journal*, accessed July 19, 2019, https://www.wsj.com/articles/pepsi-expands-in-afr ica-with-1-7-billion-deal-11563530797.

12. This priority was cited by Kevin Rudd, "Short of War," *Foreign Affairs*, March 8, 2021, https://www.foreignaffairs.com/articles/united-states/2021-02-05/kevin-rudd-usa-chinese-confrontation-short-of-war.

13. Timothy Puko, "John Kerry Says U.S. Will Hold China to Account on Climate Pledges," *Wall Street Journal*, accessed April 13, 2021, https://www.wsj.com/articles/kerry-says-u-s-will-hold-beijing-to-account-on-climate-pledges-11618338675.

Index

For the benefit of digital users, indexed terms that span two pages (e.g., 52–53) may, on occasion, appear on only one of those pages.

Tables and figures are indicated by *t* and *f* following the page number